United Press Invades India

United Press Invades India

✦

Memoirs of a Foreign Correspondent, 1944–1952

John Hlavacek

Hlucky Books

Omaha, Nebraska

© 2006, 2009 John M. Hlavacek. All rights reserved. No part of this book may be used or reproduced by any means, graphic, electronic or mechanical, including photocopying, recording, taping or by any information storage retrieval system without the written permission of the publisher, except in the case of brief quotations embodied in critical articles and reviews.

Hlucky Books is an imprint of Concierge Publishing, Omaha, Nebraska

Books are available through Baker & Taylor or www.HluckyBooks.com

Hlucky Books
c/o Concierge Publishing
13518 L. Street
Omaha, NE 68137
(402) 884-5995

ISBN13: 978-0-9819034-6-0
ISBN10: 0-9819034-6-0
Library of Congress Control Number: 2009930476

Printed in the United States of America

10 9 8 7 6 5 4 3 2 1

Contents

FOREWORD... xi

CHAPTER 1 NEW YORK................................ 1
(October to December 1944)

CHAPTER 2 CALCUTTA AND BOMBAY 9
(January to August 1945)

CHAPTER 3 BOMBAY AFTER THE WAR ENDED 18
(Fall of 1945)

CHAPTER 4 ACTING MANAGER FOR INDIA 24
(October 1945 to March 1946)

CHAPTER 5 THE FAMOUS PHOTOGRAPH 41
(March to July 1946)

CHAPTER 6 RIOTING IN CALCUTTA AND BOMBAY 47
(July to August 1946)

CHAPTER 7 BOMBAY AFTER THE RIOTS 56
(September to December 1946)

CHAPTER 8 THE SWAMI STORY 59
(January to March 1947)

CHAPTER 9 MADRAS AND COLOMBO 69
(April 1947)

CHAPTER 10 NEW DELHI 73
(May to July 1947)

| CHAPTER 11 | HOME LEAVE AND AFTERWARD | 82 |

(August to December 1947)

| CHAPTER 12 | HYDERABAD | 92 |

(January to June 1948)

| CHAPTER 13 | BOMBAY MANAGER FOR INDIA | 106 |

(July to September 1948)

| CHAPTER 14 | MARIE'S VISIT TO INDIA | 110 |

(October 1948 to May 1949)

| CHAPTER 15 | AFGHANISTAN | 121 |

(November to December 1948)

| CHAPTER 16 | BOMBAY TO COLOMBO BY AUTOMOBILE | 137 |

(May to June 1949)

| CHAPTER 17 | KLM PLANE CRASH | 216 |

(July 1949)

| CHAPTER 18 | COLOMBO CONFERENCE | 218 |

(January 1950)

| CHAPTER 19 | A SPRING AND SUMMER OF TRAVELS | 228 |

(1950)

CHAPTER 20	GOLF	240
CHAPTER 21	BASEBALL	244
CHAPTER 22	NEPAL P.O.W.	260

(November 1950)

| CHAPTER 23 | HOME LEAVE AROUND THE WORLD | 276 |

(July to November 1951)

| CHAPTER 24 | BACK TO WORK AFTER HOME LEAVE | 286 |

(December 1951 to January 1952)

Chapter 25 BOWLES IN KATHMANDU 295
(February 1952)

Chapter 26 MRS. ROOSEVELT'S VISIT 303
(1952)

Chapter 27 THE COURTSHIP OF PEGGE 315
(December 1951 to October 1952)

Manager for India
Stewart Hensley

Manager for China
Walter Rundle

All *news-wise*
All *oriented to the Orient*

Far Eastern Manager Miles W. Vaughn

Both experienced and expert are the correspondents covering the quickening Indo-Burman and Chinese war fronts for the United Press. A few of them are pictured here.

They have, on an average, been reporting news for some 13 years, and for nine of them have worked throughout the Far East, from Singapore to Tientsin, from Hong Kong to Kandy.

As a consequence this U. P. corps knows thoroughly not only how to get news but understands thoroughly the special viewpoints and the conditions which underlie the news in the region.

The dispatches from these correspondents, all news-wise, all oriented to the Orient, show plainly the benefit of their double fitness. They form an essential, and every day more extensive, part of "the world's best coverage of the world's biggest news."

U. P. Correspondent Albert Ravenholt (above) gets from Maj. Gen. Claire Chennault an explanation of air tactics against the Japs.

Outside an army headquarters, John Hlavacek, U. P. war reporter in India, types a dispatch.

The commander-in-chief at Kweilin, Gen. Wei Yun-Sung, gives an interview to George Wang, of United Press.

...UNITED PRESS

FOREWORD

This book began as an ego trip.

Originally I was going to title it *India B.P.* (Before Pegge), because I had lived in India for seven years as a gay (what word can you substitute for *gay* now that the homosexual tribe has co-opted the word?) bachelor before we were married in October of 1952.

Another title, since discarded, was *What If?* If one of the many young women I dated had risked marrying a glamorous (ha ha), balding, underpaid newspaperman, where would I be now?

I arrived in India in February of 1945, expecting to go into China. Fate intervened. My new boss of United Press, Miles "Peg" Vaughn, asked me to delay my trip to China to help open a news bureau in the city of Bombay.

I was a very junior reporter for United Press, and I regularly sent letters home about my job and where I lived. Originally I thought that they would make good reading only for my children and grandchildren as to what Father/Grandfather did during the war.

As the years went by and I remained in India, I continued writing home, usually once a week—every Sunday or Monday. My mother saved all the letters, and I also kept copies of what I had written. They recorded my days of playing golf, baseball, swimming, etc., and of my travels within India and to the neighboring countries of Pakistan, Ceylon, Nepal, Afghanistan, and Burma—including days and weeks of partying—drinking, dancing, and eating. In re-reading them, I discovered I had created a (personal) history of the rise of the United Press news service in Southeast Asia.

During my seven years before Pegge, United Press grew from a hotel room in Bombay with an antennae on our balcony receiving news from London by Morse Code in 1945 to opening news bureaus in the Indian cities of Bombay, Delhi, and Calcutta by 1952. During those years United Press also opened a news bureau in Karachi, Pakistan, and sold news to newspapers in Colombo, Ceylon, another British Colonial country that became independent after the war. In addition to serving newspapers, United Press also numbered All India Radio, Radio Pakistan, Radio Ceylon, and Radio Afghanistan among its clients.

And for me, who began as an assistant manager in the bureau in Bombay and went on to eventually become the General Manager for United Press with responsibility for the sale of news and news coverage in Afghanistan, Pakistan, India, Ceylon, and Burma, it was an exhilarating experience.

My letters also reflect a portion of the history of the Indian subcontinent. I was able to witness the transformation of British colonies into the free countries of India, Pakistan, Ceylon, and Burma—along with the political, economic, and cultural changes brought about by the years after World War II. In my job I was able to travel extensively from Afghanistan to Ceylon and from Karachi to Rangoon. And on my "home leaves" I was able to visit Europe and the Far East after checking into the UP headquarters in New York. My father once remarked, shaking his head, "They pay you to do that!"

I was only one of a large group of hard-driving, underpaid reporters who slaved for United Press. Jim Michaels, a colleague from our time in India, and a person who has helped refresh my memory for this opus, sent me the following e-mail about the first time we met.

> I recall you flew in looking for me. I was very green in those days, September of 1946. Had never worked on any newspaper except for a short stint on the *Harvard Crimson.* Peg Vaughn hired me in Bangkok in the early summer of 1945 on the recommendation of my boss in the OWI and because I was cheap labor and on the spot. My OWI boss was the late Teg Grondahl, a Swede from Red Wing, Minn. He had been a Unipresser in SF prewar and earlier a kid reporter in China in the mid-1930's. Teg told "Peg" he had a smart eager kid, Jim Michaels, "Mike" as I was then generally known. Peg hired me on the spot, in Bangkok, after the Japanese surrender. I was thrilled. I was to be a real newspaperman and a genuine foreign correspondent, glamorous—ha ha—and no more Buffalo. When I took the job, Teg told me UP would be the best training I would ever get but added if I stayed more than three years as a UP wage slave he would never speak to me again. He warned me I would generally be over my head, outnumbered two or three to one by AP, and would either learn fast or sink.
>
> When he took me on, Peg explained UP wanted to stockpile reporters in Asia against the outbreak of the expected civil war in China. At the same time he also hired three other guys who had served during the war as AFS (American Field Service) ambulance drivers—Bob Clurman and Hugh Crumpler and Stanley Rich, all cheap, all green, three of us from Harvard and one from Princeton. $35 a week—and watch those expenses.

To keep us busy in the meantime he sent me to Calcutta, Rich to Bangkok, Crumpler to Korea, and Clurman to India (later to Singapore). Some of us complained about getting by on that munificent stipend. Peg actually suggested we might be able to qualify for some kind of food stamps!

Now, a brief history: the United Press began (believe it or not) in 1907—almost 100 years ago. Before United Press, news sources were controlled by governments and foreign news agencies based in their respective countries. These news agencies established monopoly arrangements and divided up the news territories among the so-called Allied News Agencies. Examples: The French agency, Havas, was allotted South America and had an exclusive right among the Allied Agencies to sell news of all the world to the newspapers of that continent. Reuters, the British news agency, took the Far East and in China and Japan had the exclusive right to sell its news of the rest of the world.

In addition, these Allied Agencies, which included all the important European press associations and Rengo of Japan, exchanged news among themselves and covered their respective countries for each other. The news of France, Germany, or Italy, for example, originated with a French, German, or Italian news agency—a circumstance that did not lend itself to dispassionate, impartial news reporting.

The United Press never joined this alliance. The United Press was founded to oppose the news monopoly and immediately set out to demonstrate the worth of the contrary theory of operation—that is, that a news organization wholly independent of any other could cover the news of all the world with its own correspondents and profitably sell that news to all who wanted it, in every part of the world.

The United Press proceeded to invade the precincts of the Allied Agencies and their associates, selling a news product that was entirely its own and frankly boasted of its freedom from any taint or bias that government influence or subsidy might impose on others.

From the beginning the United Press was welcomed by the newspapers of other countries, both for its excellence and because it could guarantee freedom from any official viewpoint. In South America the United Press became the principal source of foreign news. In the Far East, until the outbreak of World War II, United Press clientele grew along with rapidly improving transmission facilities. On the continent of Europe, the United Press was serving a total of 151 newspapers when the war began in 1939.

Such was the situation in India when I arrived in 1945. Reuters had been the sole supplier of foreign news to Indian newspapers. Our United Press office—based in a hotel room—would provide Indian newspapers with their first access to an independent source of foreign news.

ACKNOWLEDGMENTS

Although the bulk of information in this memoir came from my letters written more than 60 years ago, the book could not have been published without the help of many friends and colleagues.

Janet Tilden, my editor, an alumna of Carleton College, worked closely with me as she had done with my earlier books which were self-published by iUniverse: *Diapers on a Dateline, Alias Pegge Parker,* and *Letters Home.* Janet worked overtime to be sure I got this manuscript "to the church (publisher) on time."

Max Desfor, a Pultizer-Prize-winning photographer, allowed me to publish his famous photo of Mahatma Gandhi with Jawaharlal Nehru and shared his memories of the times we spent together covering stories in India.

James "Jim" Michaels, a United Press colleague, granted permission to publish his award-winning stories on the assassination of Mahatma Gandhi and shared his memories of the Hindu-Muslim disturbances that we covered together.

Marie (Hlavacek) Holbrooke, my sister, sent me copies of the letters she had written to family and friends during the seven months she spent with me in India.

Rex Daugherty, a neighbor, came to the rescue when I needed help with my computer and also helped print photos from old negatives.

Vern Greunke, a friend whom I interviewed in Vietnam, helped me arrange my letters and clippings for this and previous memoirs.

1

NEW YORK

◆

(October to December 1944)

"We will be looking for you about midday of October 6th, 1944 and will find some place where you can stay until you find the sort of quarters you want. Perhaps you can arrange to bunk in with some of the fellows here after you have got acquainted."

This was the two-sentence letter I received from my new Far Eastern Manager, Miles "Peg" Vaughn, before reporting for duty at United Press headquarters in New York. There was a P.S. in Peg's handwriting: "Joe James Custer says he can put you up in his apartment near the office."

I was 26 and had been a United Press war correspondent in China for less than a year. In September 1944 I had returned to my parents' home in LaGrange, Illinois, to recuperate from a serious bout of dysentery. My parents had not seen me since I had left for China in 1939 to teach English at the Carleton (College) in China middle school in North China. After two years of teaching, I had spent a year working for the International Relief Committee. When the Japanese bombed Pearl Harbor, I worked for another year and a half with the American Military Attaché's office in Chungking as a civilian code clerk. In February of 1944, the Far Eastern Manager of the United Press had been an overnight guest at the house I shared with five other Americans. In the morning, after a long night of dinner and drinking, I asked the Far Eastern Manager, "Mr. Morris, what does it take to be a United Press correspondent?" He asked, "What have you done?" My answer: "I taught English, and I speak Chinese." "You're hired!" he said. Thus, with absolutely no background in journalism, two weeks later I became a war correspondent for United Press in Chungking.

While I was still in LaGrange, I received the following note about my draft status dated September 18, 1944: "Dear John, MWM [Miles Vaughn] asked me to get in touch with your draft board to ask for a deferment. I'll need the following information for the Form 42A affidavit: local board, address, your order number, date joined up, birthday. Regards, Irving Peck."

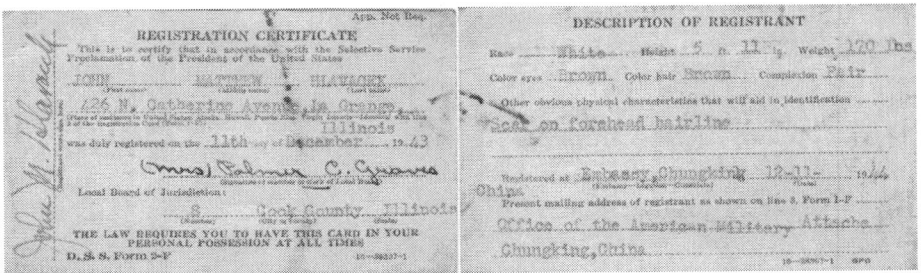

*My draft card was issued in LaGrange, Illinois on December 11, 1943.
I was 1-A, subject to be called at any moment.*

In October 1944, the United Press cable rewrite desk in New York was a horseshoe with the editor at the base and three rewrite editors on either side. The rewrite desk received cables and telegrams from all over the world. The editors would take the few sentences in the cable—words cost money—and develop those words into headline stories. At that time, New York City had seven daily newspapers, and each newspaper would put out several editions each evening. In rewriting, editors typed on "books" consisting of layers of thin yellow sheets of paper so there would be seven copies of the stories to be relayed on the teletype lines to newspapers and radio stations that subscribed to the United Press news service.

Because the newspapers were putting out several editions, the cable desk would send out new leads on the stories for each edition. After sending out the new leads, the regulars on the desk would repair to Sellman's Bar across the street for a drink, then return and write another lead. There were times when the last "leads" of the night were rather blurry. Most of my fellow writers were also smokers, and there was usually a pall of smoke over the cable desk.

I was assigned a slot on the night cable rewrite desk when I reported for work at the United Press offices on the twelfth floor of the New York Daily News building at 42nd Street and Third Avenue in Manhattan.

Although I had managed to learn some basic rules during six months of traveling throughout China with the Chinese armies and the American Fourteenth Air Force, I was still a very junior cub reporter when I reported for duty that October. I had been fortunate to bunk in with a United Press reporter, Joe J. Custer, for the first few weeks.

In a letter to family members in La Grange dated October 13, 1944, I wrote,

> I think I told you about going to the anniversary dinner at the Waldorf" [a dinner commemorating the thirty-third anniversary of the founding of the Republic of China] "but in case I didn't, here goes again.
>
> I was out shopping for a suit which I am now wearing when a call came to the store asking me if I wanted to go. So I went home, got on my best bib and tucker and went along with Miles Vaughn, the new Far Eastern manager, and Joe Jones, one of the Vice-Presidents of UP. I sat at the press table, met a few of my friends from Chungking and had a swell time. Before the end of the show (i.e., the speeches), I ducked out with a beautiful young lady who works for United China Relief and went to a CBS show which was being put on by United China Relief. Then, as I was in uniform, we could go to an officers' club to dance, which we did. Had a swell time.
>
> Still here on the cable desk and still very green. Looks as though I may be making some more speeches but nothing definite yet.
>
> Still living in the apartment with the UP man but looking around for something for myself. However, they are scarcer than hen's teeth, and there is not much hope yet.

4   United Press Invades India

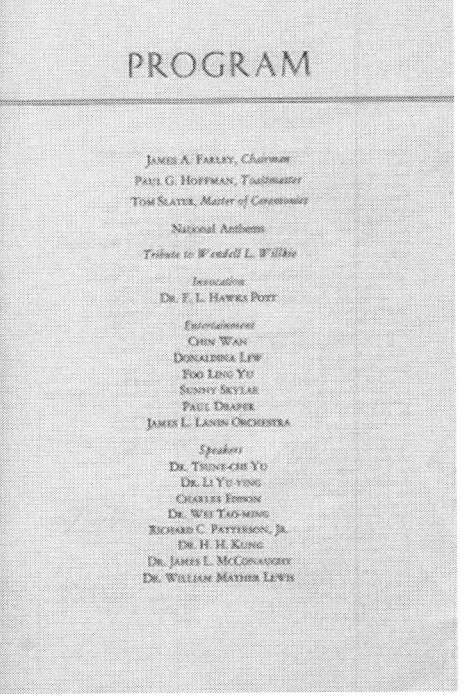

Because I was a war correspondent just back from China, United Press sent me out to speak at meetings to promote the sales of war bonds. On these occasions United Press asked me to wear my war correspondent's uniform with the CBI (China Burma India) patch. My first such speaking engagement to the Kiwanis Club of Salisbury, Maryland. In a letter dated October 16, 1944, I wrote:

> Yesterday I called up the Jelineks (Robert and Aunt Mary), and they got me about noontime and took me to dinner. Then we went for a ride around New York and out to Rutherford for dinner. I am going to stay with them now for the time being until I can find something more definite. I didn't get thrown out, but one of the other UP men is in town so as long as I had the bunk with the Jelineks, I said I could move out there and he could have mine. I will still leave some of my clothes here in the city and whenever I want will have a bed here to throw myself into, should there be late nights. Saturday night I was at a party at which there were a bunch of UP people.

We didn't get home until about four in the morning. So I slept late on Sunday.

I talked with Miles Vaughn today coming back from the lunch, and according to him I won't be back in Chungking until about next June, which gives me quite a time in the U.S. As long as I am going to be here that long, I have decided to get in some study and will probably go to school pretty soon. I figure on taking Russian at the moment, although by the time I am ready, I might decide on something different. The latest plan is that I am to study everything, including a little of the commercial side of UP. I am still green at the job but trying hard. The past two days have been very busy with the invasion of the Philippines, so that I get very little to do except the small stories. Next Tuesday I am going to Maryland to speak at a Kiwanis Club, so it looks like my tour of speechmaking begins once again. I am glad to get the practice.

I took the train to Maryland and checked into a hotel and spoke about my experiences in China. There was a small paragraph about my speaking engagement in the *Salisbury Times,* noting that I had been covering the Fourteenth Air Force in China. I still have the original letter, dated October 24th, and the clipping from the local newspaper announcing my appearance.

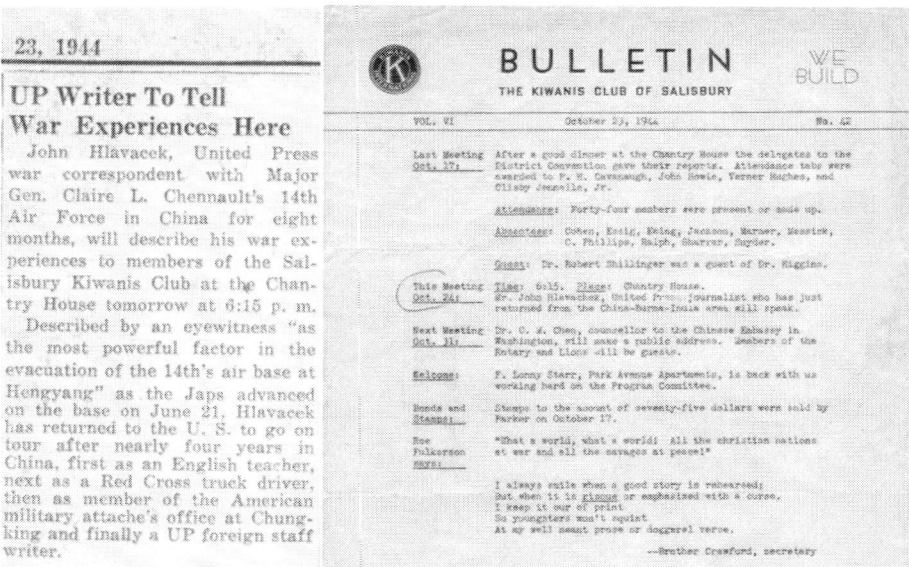

A few weeks later, on November 20th, I spoke to a meeting of the Equitable Life Assurance Society at their headquarters on Seventh Avenue. The announcement read that 1500 employees were expected to attend and that the purpose of the meeting was "to stimulate employees to sell War Bonds to the passing crowd and also to buy War Bonds."

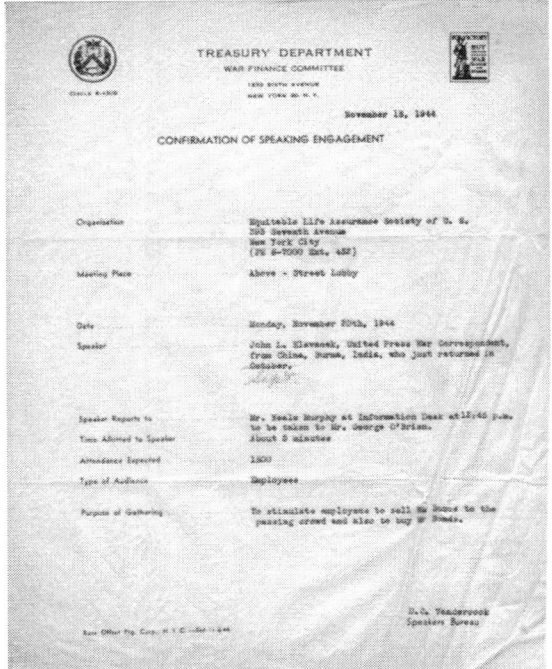

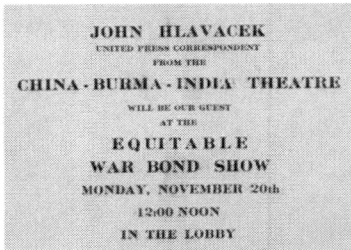

Having found a place to live with my relatives, my only worry was how to become a respected newsman. I was nervous as I introduced myself to the United Press vice presidents, Earl J. Johnson and Joseph L. Jones. The head of the United Press copy desk when I reported for duty was a white-haired Irishman, Charlie McCann. The first few days he assigned me to read official press releases and then rewrite them (boil them down). I would write my stories and take the copies up to Charlie for his approval, and then he would put them on the spike. (The spike was a file of all the stories written that day. Charlie, as the editor, was responsible for reading all of them.) The other regulars didn't bother Charlie as they slapped their stories on the spike. There were times when some of the complicated stories overwhelmed me. I remember one occasion when tall, handsome

Gene Gillette, the night news manager, had been watching me struggle. Gene walked over to my desk, took the book out of my typewriter, went back to his desk, and rewrote the story. That kind of help was standard at United Press, and it is the reason so many of today's media stars got their start at United Press.

The rewrite desk was a busy place. Many of the rewrite men (they were all men at the time) were former sports reporters. The editors believed that sports writers were the best journalists to write about the war. They had the sports words—slash, slice, round-up, race, smash, etc.—all the adjectives and verbs to describe military operations.

I reported daily to the desk at noon, and after a week of rewriting official releases, Charlie said to me, "John, you can just put your copy on the spike. I don't need to see it." It was a relief and a signal that I had arrived. The twelfth floor of the News Building was all United Press. There was a desk for domestic news and a desk for radio station news (no television stations existed yet in 1944). It took me some time to figure out where everything was, and I was so naïve that I even asked one of the reporters one day, "Which is the top desk in this room?" His answer was, "You're on it."

After writing the official releases, I soon began editing stories from China, Burma, and India because I was familiar with the geography of the area. The majority of stories came from Europe where the Allied Armies were advancing across the continent toward Berlin, and also from the Far East where American naval units were fighting their way across the Pacific toward Japan.

One day a story came in from Europe written by Collie Small, a United Press reporter who later went on to write for magazines such as the Saturday Evening Post. It was a story about a young American soldier talking to a young dead German soldier. It was beautifully written. All I had to do was add commas, periods, and paragraphs, then put the story on the spike. As I was leaving that night I walked past Charlie on my way to the door, and he said, "That was a great job you did on Collie Small's story." I stopped and said, "Hell, Charlie, I didn't do anything to that story. That's just the way it came in." As I walked away, I heard him say, "Well, at least you had the good sense to leave it alone." That was the day I was confident I could stay on the desk.

As the months went by, Gene Gillette talked about my staying on in New York for another six months. I was willing to stay, but that December two United Press correspondents were lost in planes in Asia and the foreign department decided to send me back to China.

I wrote home that although I was living in New Jersey, I had found friends in New York who had a bed for me if I wanted to stay overnight. I also wrote that I had made a visit to the Wright Aeronautical factory at Paterson and Woodbridge, New Jersey. Frank Buckner, a friend I had known in Chungking, was the public relations man for the Wright Aircraft Company, which made the engines for the famous "Flying Tiger" fighter planes, the P-40s.

One night I went out with a group of friends from China to a party in Harlem. We first went to a Chinese dinner party. At the party were Jim and Josephine Burke. I had just arranged with Josephine to take over their apartment on Central Park West if Jim had to go into the army. (As it turned out, Jim joined the Office of War Information and I returned to the Far East, so I never did get the apartment. (After the war Jim and Josephine moved to India, and they were our friends in New Delhi. Jim worked for Time-Life.)

My mother and father came to visit one weekend and I was able to show them around New York City. I had met a delightful girl whom I took on dates in the city. But the die was cast, and the United Press made arrangements for me to return to China on a troop ship. My last day in New York was December 22, and on December 23 I flew home to spend Christmas with my parents.

2

CALCUTTA AND BOMBAY

◆

(January to August 1945)

The first week of January in 1945 I reported to the army base at Camp Anza in Riverside, California and sailed on January 10th aboard a troop ship.

As a war correspondent, I had the simulated rank of an officer so I was billeted in officers' quarters aboard ship. I was in a stateroom with eleven other officers, and I lived in relative comfort for the 40-day transit to Calcutta, India. I wrote home that I had three meals a day, oranges or apples each morning, and ice cream every night. Also, there was an Army Post Exchange aboard where I was able to buy other amenities if I needed them. Three times a day we had fresh water for shaving and showers. At night it was stuffy because the portholes were closed as the ship was blacked out when traveling across the South Pacific. But we were allowed to go on deck, and I spent many a night sleeping on deck when the heat in the stateroom became unbearable.

In preparation for the journey, I bought a phonograph and the records to "Oklahoma" which was the most popular musical comedy playing on Broadway in 1944. I also bought Russian language records with the idea that I would have the time to study and could be speaking Russian by the time I reached India. However, I never did get around to playing the Russian language records because (I rationalized) the phonograph was in constant use playing "Oklahoma" and other records of the latest tunes which we found on board the ship. In fact, the record player finally wore out but then some of the ship's company came to the rescue and fixed the machine in the ship's machine shop. (I still have the Russian language records stashed away.)

For relaxation, I played a lot of poker, not for high stakes but to pass the time. I wrote home that we had variety shows and that I gave one lecture on China, recalling my experiences as a teacher of English. Also we had a number of "bull sessions" talking about everything and anything. I also played bridge, chess, and cribbage and a game called "Battle Ship" which, I wrote, "We used to play in grammar school." (At this time I have no idea what the game was like.)

Our route was across the South Pacific, and the ship stopped only twice during the 40-day transit to take on fuel, fresh water, and supplies. One stop was off Hawaii, and the second was off the coast of Australia. At neither stop were the troops allowed ashore. We griped loudly while being confined to the ship for 48 hours as we anchored off Sydney. All we could do was dream about going ashore.

On February 22nd our ship arrived at the port of Calcutta, where I was happy to see a number of friends from my China days. It was especially good to see Llewellyn Evans, a Welshman with whom I had worked in Kweiyang with the International Red Cross. He had managed to escape from Hong Kong to Singapore before the Japanese assault. He had news that his brother, Owen Evans, who was in the hospital when the Japanese attacked, had been taken to a Japanese concentration camp.

In Calcutta, I attended the Washington's Birthday party at the American Consulate. After only one night in the city, I flew to New Delhi to meet my new boss, Miles "Peg" Vaughn, the new Far Eastern Manager for the United Press. (My previous boss, John Morris, had committed suicide in the fall of 1944 by leaping from a window on the twelfth floor of the Daily News Building.)

New Delhi hotels were booked to capacity, but the United Press had managed to rent an apartment near Connaught Circus, the circular road in the center of the city. There I met a group of United Press correspondents who found a bed for me. Harrison Salisbury, the newly appointed foreign editor (and later a foreign correspondent for *The New York Times*) was in residence, as were Darrell Berrigan and Walter Logan, two veteran Far East correspondents. Both Berrigan and Logan were "characters." On one wall was a mounted deer's head, and Logan had wrapped a scarf around the eyes claiming that he hadn't been able to sleep because the deer was looking at him.

I had expected to meet with "Peg" and then fly the "Hump" back into China. The "Hump" was an air route from India over the Himalayas that served as the lifeline for bringing supplies into China. However, United Press had other plans for me. Before the war, India had been an integral part of the British Empire ("The Jewel in the Crown") and as a British Colony, the British had successfully kept out American businesses. Reuters, a British news agency, had a monopoly in serving Indian newspapers with foreign news. But when the United States began lend-lease to Britain and then entered the war after the Japanese attack on Pearl

Harbor, Winston Churchill had opened the Indian newspaper market to American-owned news agencies—United Press first, and later the Associated Press.

United Press, which at that time was the most energetic and "gung-ho" of the American news agencies, had opened a news bureau in Bombay in January of 1945 to receive international news to sell to Indian newspapers. "Peg" Vaughn asked me to go to Bombay to help get the service started. I was to be there only for a few weeks and then return to China. "Peg" and I and an Indian bearer (valet) named Danji took the train from Delhi to Bombay, my first train ride since my trip to India in 1940. It was a 26-hour ride on the Frontier Mail, a train I was to take many times in the future. We had a first-class air-conditioned compartment, which made for a comfortable journey. On Indian trains, each railway car is separate; you cannot walk from one end of the train to the other while it is moving. To get to the dining car, you wait for the train to stop at a station, walk to the dining car, and dine while the train continues to the next stop. Then you are able to leave the dining car and return to your compartment. The Frontier Mail served both European and Indian food. We ordered from the European menu. (On later trips I always ordered from the Indian menu because I found the Indian food to be much more palatable than the European.) While Peg and I were in the dining car, Danji remained in the compartment to prepare our sleeping arrangements.

Arriving in Bombay, we took taxis to the Taj Mahal Hotel, which was then (and still is) one of the finest hotels of India. Although we had many suitcases, Danji was able to organize our departure through the milling crowds at the station. At the hotel, we met the United Press Manager for India, Harold Guard, an Englishman who had set up a small office in Green's Hotel, which was adjacent to the Taj and owned by the same company.

Harold was my first boss in India, and during the months we spent together he became a great friend. He was a remarkable gentleman, a World War I veteran who had been a submariner in the Royal Navy. Harold walked with a slight limp, a wartime injury sustained while on a mission to mine the transit of the Bosphorus at Istanbul. Harold and another officer had swum from their submarine to place the charges.

Our United Press bureau was a fifth-floor room with a balcony. Harold had rigged up an antenna from the balcony for a wireless receiving station and hired two Indian radio operators to receive the news, which was sent from London by Morse Code. Our operators typed the news stories and we edited them. We then made copies on a Gestetner (a European copy machine) and sent the news to the Bombay newspapers by messengers on bicycles. For upcountry newspapers, we mailed the news bulletins to New Delhi, Calcutta, Madras, Karachi, Lahore, and Rawalpindi. (In 1945, India included all of what is now Pakistan and Bangladesh.)

Because there is a 12-hour time difference between Bombay and New York and a six-hour difference between Bombay and London, we produced an almost 24-hour service. We were serving the important English-language newspapers in Bombay, which were mostly morning editions. Also several Indian-language newspapers—in Gujarati and Marathi—had morning editions. But there were also afternoon newspapers in both English and Indian languages. Thus we were editing news stories early in the morning for the afternoon papers and late at night, sometimes as late as 3 a.m. for the morning papers. In addition, until the end of the war in August, all our outgoing stories had to be passed by censors—British and American. All Indian stories went to the British censors, and any stories about U.S. Army troops in India went to the American censors. Also, urgent cables from London went to the censors before they came to our office.

Harold Guard and I were responsible for editing the news from London as well as selling the United Press news service to Indian newspapers. In addition, we were responsible for reporting Indian news for UP's worldwide service. To acquaint the editors with our service, we provided the news for a few weeks at no charge so they could see the value of having another foreign news service in addition to Reuters. After a few weeks, I had to write up the contracts and then make monthly calls to collect the money. In 1945, these monthly calls were my way to meet Indian newspaper editors and establish my contacts in India. At the time, it was not really a "hard sell." The Indian newspapers, like most of India, were anti-British editorially and their editors welcomed an American. I had believed, when I joined United Press in China, that I would be mainly a reporter. In Bombay I became a salesman, although our office was also responsible for Indian news. (At the time, we had Indian "stringers" reporting in all the major cities.)

Harold had begun the service before I arrived, and most of the editors were well disposed to buy United Press. Many of the editors became good friends during my years in India. (In one of my letters home I noted that we had been putting out a trial service for Indian newspapers and that week we had signed three papers, "which means we have a total of five that we are serving in Bombay." I noted that we had been cheered up immensely by the sales.)

During the first few weeks in Bombay we concentrated on getting the office running. We had little time to see the city, although one Sunday, Harold and I took a day off for a long taxi ride. We rode along Bombay's Marine Drive and admired its white sandy beaches, drove into the suburbs to see its modern horse racing track, and went through the crowded market places. I wrote home that the ride cost 35 rupees, about eleven dollars, and the cost was going on our expense accounts.

On March 12th, I wrote home that the next day would be my 27th birthday. I wrote, "Strange things sure happen to one. Here I am in Bombay when I expected to be in China, and who would have thought even two years ago that I would now be in India. Join the UP and see the world. One never knows. I may yet be in Singapore or the Philippines."

Later in the month I told my parents that "I haven't been to China yet, which ought to relieve your mind." (My mother was very worried that I would be transferred to China and be tempted to marry a Chinese girl.) Also, I added that because of the assignment to Bombay I was further from the war and probably safer in Bombay than I would have been in New York.

I also wrote that after conferring with "Peg" Vaughn, I had my salary raised to $65 per week and I hoped that if the office continued to prosper I would be in line for another raise. I had been drawing only $20 per week for my expenses, and the rest was sent to my bank account at home.

When our office routine had become somewhat settled, I went swimming for the first time. Because I was still accredited to the U.S. Army and wore my uniform, I was able to swim at private clubs that offered servicemen temporary memberships. I wrote that I had to buy swim trunks and was embarrassed when I dived in and they came right off. I didn't dive again until Danji, our Indian bearer, was able to buy a belt to keep my swimsuit in place.

I had been in Bombay only a few weeks when I went to my first party. One of the British military press censors, Captain Ross Parker, who had become a good friend, was invited to a party and told me he would pick me up and bring me along. I found out that he, in civilian life, was a songwriter and had written, "There'll Always Be an England," among other songs. Ross was a big, jolly fellow. One of the guests at the party dubbed him "Pincushion." He also played a mean piano, which was the prime reason he was invited to the party. I had worked until almost 11 when he called, and off we went. The party was given by a wealthy racketeer, a Sikh, who (I was told) made all of his money on the black market and mostly in liquor. He owned a top-floor flat on Bombay's Marine Drive, which overlooked the Indian Ocean. The party was on the roof, with plenty of food and drink. When we arrived, they were just getting ready for the magician, who pulled different cards out of hats and did other tricks that magicians usually do. We found ladies to dance with, and I met some other guests who knew people I knew, which is about the easiest way of beginning a conversation. I didn't get back to the Taj until 3 a.m. and as a result slept late on Sunday morning. I explained to my family that sleeping late "didn't make much difference because there are no afternoon papers on Sunday and we don't have to get the news out early in the morning."

Also, with the two of us managing the office, we had time for golf. When I was growing up during the 1930s, golf was a game for the wealthy. LaGrange had one country club, and my family did not have the means to become members. When I was in China from 1939 to 1944, I lived in rural areas were there were no golf clubs, let alone golf courses. But in Bombay we had two golf courses. One was in the city at the Willingdon Sports Club, a short course with a par of 65. The other, the Bombay Presidency Golf Club, was located 12 miles north of the city with a par of 70. The Willingdon Sports Club had been established by Lord Willingdon, a former Viceroy of India. Until his time, the British had their private country clubs that refused entry to Indians. The Willingdon was open to all, provided they had the money to join. (At that time the entrance fee for new members was 1,000 rupees (about $330). When I first arrived in Bombay, there was a long waiting list for membership. Because I was accredited to the U.S. Army, I was given a temporary honorary membership.

With the help of my new British and American friends, I found a set of clubs, and I was able to get golf balls from the U.S. Army Post Exchange. I had always played team sports (football, baseball, basketball, and hockey) so I was fairly agile. I took up the game of golf and tried to play at least twice a week. I played mainly with my Army buddies because they had jeeps for transportation. There was a small group of Army officers stationed in Bombay for transportation duties at the port of Bombay.

The weather in Bombay that March and April of 1945 was hot and humid. In my letters home I mentioned having to lie down to cool off under the ceiling fans. We still did not have air conditioners in the hotel nor in the office. Although Bombay was terribly hot, it wasn't as bad as Chungking had been. I wrote, "At least here we have comfort and everything we want. Danji, my bearer, takes care of all my clothes, shines my shoes, brings me tea, and, in fact, I never have to worry about any of my personal belongings."

Toward the middle of April, we experienced our first monsoon rain. Harold and I stood out on the balcony in our underwear reveling in the cool downpour. I had only a few more days with Harold before he left for England. His replacement as Manager for India was M. Stewart Hensley, who had been the United Press diplomatic correspondent at the State Department in Washington.

To keep up with the political activists, I met the owners and editors of the Bombay newspapers served by United Press. I met them for business, signing contracts and then collecting the fees. One of our newspaper clients was the *Free Press Journal,* a rabidly anti-British paper owned by Mr. S. Sadanand, which was supporting the Indian drive for independence. The editor of the paper was Mr. S. Natarajan. "Nat" invited me to meet his wife, Sophie, as well as many of his friends. Nat and Sophie were unusual in that he was a Hindu and Sophie was a Muslim. I also became great friends with Sophie's mother and sister.

Nat also introduced me to leading members of the Indian Communist Party. Nat would invite me to join him on excursions to various islands in Bombay's harbor, where we would have heated discussions on the pros and cons of American, British, Russian, and Indian governmental policies. It was always an exhilarating evening, with everyone keeping his own opinions and no one changing anyone else's mind.

That spring of 1945 brought breaking news from Europe as the Allied armies pushed across France and into Germany. We were busy receiving the news and rushing it to our Indian newspaper clients.

Our first big story for our Indian newspapers was the sudden death of President Franklin D. Roosevelt. Because of the time difference, we received the flash late in the evening and I worked all evening and continued on through the early morning hours and into the afternoon of the next day. Editors of our Indian newspapers called us throughout the day offering their sympathies. The city of Bombay organized a mass memorial meeting that was attended by thousands of ordinary Indians. President Roosevelt had been revered by most Indians. Everyone wanted to know about President Harry Truman because at the time very few people knew anything about him. Our UP service during the next few days carried many stories about Roosevelt's funeral as well as news stories about the man from Missouri.

Our next big story for the Indian newspapers was the ending of the war in Europe: VE Day. We had been waiting for the announcement for 48 hours and when it finally came, we rushed the story to our Indian clients. But the announcement did not produce wild enthusiasm. Several British and American servicemen got drunk, but there were no wild celebrations. In a letter home, I explained that "Most of the Indians don't give a damn about the war in Europe. With their political leaders, Gandhi and Nehru, in jail and protesting against the war effort, there is little enthusiasm for the Allied armies."

That spring and summer was a time of furious political activity. The year before, in 1944, the British Government had released Mahatma Gandhi from his prison in Poona. He had been incarcerated at the palace of the Aga Khan.

Shortly after the war ended in Europe, the British voted out the wartime government led by Winston Churchill and replaced it with the Labor Government of Clement Attlee. Attlee's government immediately released Jawaharlal Nehru from his prison at the historic fort in Ahmadnagar, about 100 miles east of Bombay. Nehru had spent ten years of his life in prison, the last three years at Ahmadnagar, and for much of that time he had been in solitary confinement.

When he was released, Nehru came first to Bombay to a huge turnout with a long parade along Bombay's Marine Drive with masses of Indians on both sides of the road. As Nehru's open car arrived where Stew Hensley and I were waiting, Stew was able to crash through the crowds and get into the car with Nehru for an interview. There were no security guards at the time, and American newsmen were able to interview political leaders almost at will.

Not long afterward, the All India Congress Committee began meetings with the British Indian Government looking toward independence. Those meetings during the summer of 1945 were held in New Delhi, and when the weather there became unbearably hot, they were moved to the hill station of Simla, several hours by road from New Delhi. Stew Hensley, as the Manager for India, was the principal correspondent for those meetings while I stayed in Bombay to run the commercial service to our Indian newspaper clients. Once we had established a dependable service, we were approached by Bombay cotton merchants to furnish them with the closing prices of cotton on the New York Exchange. We charged a good sum for this service and would telephone the prices as soon as we got them in Bombay. They really didn't care what the prices were; they just wanted to use the numbers for their gambling. I never really understood how they made their money, but we had their business for several years. (When I was married in 1952, these businessmen brought beautiful gold saris as gifts for my bride.)

In Bombay, we were able to find Indian newsmen so that I could get out more to meet with Indian editors. Our Indian manager named Verraghavan was an orthodox Brahmin. Although he and I had a cordial relationship at the office, I was invited to his home only once. When I was away on trips, I always brought back gifts for his little daughter. As time went on we hired other Indian editors. Hiring English-speaking Indian editors was not a problem. Because India had been a colony of Britain for over 150 years, English had become the official language of the country. India is a country of many languages—in Bombay alone, there were two dominant Indian languages, Gujarati and Marathi—but the dominant language in government, on the railways, and in business enterprises was English. When a Bombay citizen traveled to Calcutta, for instance, he spoke with his friends in English because in Calcutta the dominant Indian language was Bengali. In Madras, the two dominant Indian languages were Tamil and Telugu.

3

BOMBAY AFTER THE WAR ENDED

◆

(Fall of 1945)

After Japan surrendered on September 2, 1945, life in Bombay quickly returned to a semblance of normalcy. For several months after the surrender, however, there was some apprehension of what peace would bring. I wrote about this apprehension in the following story for United Press, which was published at the end of November.

> Bombay—UP—Bombay, the Gateway to India, is worried the war is over and definitely apprehensive of the peace to come. And with good reason.
>
> Never before in its history has the city enjoyed such prosperity. Military and civilian personnel flocked into this port, spending money freely, and the city, far from the battle lines, suffered no war ravage except for the Great Bombay Explosion of April, 1944.
>
> Almost three months after the Japanese surrender, the city shows little change from its wartime life.
>
> Housing, one of the most acute problems during the war, continues to be a major stumbling block. Bombay is called the "10 persons to a room city," and it is usual to see the sidewalks lined with sleepers after 11 o'clock every night. The military authorities, who requisitioned buildings and built temporary structures on every vacant lot, have so far given up only twelve buildings and the future rate of de-requisitioning promises to be slow. The chance of finding business premises for office accommodations is even worse. To get business accommodation one must resort to sub-letting offices which are permanent—at fantastic rates. During the war the rent control ordinances issued by the government had little effect and the only way to get an apartment or business space was to pay "pugree" (bribe). Pugree sometimes can be as much as a

full year's rent and even more. House racketeering got so bad it was rumored that the rent controller himself had to pay pugree to get an apartment.

Practically all public utilities need overhauling. Requests for telephones dating from 1942 have not yet been filled and the General Manager of the Bombay Telephone Company says that were it not for military spare parts, the exchange could not have been kept running. There is little hope of any improvement for at least three months. Telegraph lines to inland cities too are overburdened and the end of the war brought no improvement. Strangely enough, the lines became more crowded than ever with messages about repatriation of war prisoners and the demobilization of troops. No telephone or telegraph lines have yet been given up by the military.

The city's streets are still as cosmopolitan as ever with soldiers and sailors of all Allied nations shopping and sight seeing. One noticeable feature is the gradual disappearance of American troops. Bombay, as a port of debarkation for American troops, closed more than six months ago and there has been a gradual movement of American personnel out of wartime offices. There is only one American rest camp occupying fives stories of an apartment house in one of the residential areas of the city. These men, too, expect to go soon and the end of the year probably will see the city completely bare of American troops.

British troops are also gathering here for the homeward voyage. The past week has seen the departure of the 2nd British Division, which carried the main brunt of the fighting in Burma the past three years. And more are due to go, possibly on the *Queen Mary* and the *Mauritania,* which are due here soon.

There is a great clamor on the part of troops and families waiting to go to England. Passages have been slow, and the recent dock strikes in British ports have hindered even this slow embarkation. Mr. Jack Lawson, the Secretary of War, was questioned in Parliament as to why he said passengers were better off in India than in England because of the food shortage and other difficulties in the United Kingdom.

John Gielgud, the Shakespearean actor, here on an ENSA tour, tried the same line with servicemen here—but he painted such a miserable picture of England that he was asked to please desist from further speeches.

Speaking of Gielgud, the present ENSA company which he heads, caused no less a sensation by performing a week's run of Hamlet. This is the first chance Bombay has had since before the war to see theater of this caliber. Bombay's civilians, who, under ENSA ruling, are barred from the performances unless they are the guests of servicemen, immediately cornered a good portion of the tickets and have been inviting servicemen to go with them. It is the best entertainment to hit Bombay for many years and the professional class of the community is taking advantage of it.

Most ENSA shows have been of mediocre quality, but the last two have been big-time. Gracie Fields, with husband Monty Banks and cast, packed the houses. Here again, civilians did their damnedest to crash the gate to see Gracie.

Movies are running to packed houses, which warms the hearts of the film agents. Part of their popularity is due to the few night clubs in Bombay which are too expensive for the average citizen. A dinner-dance at the Taj Mahal, Bombay's best hotel, costs nine rupees ($3.00 U.S.) per plate with Scotch whisky, when available, at three rupees ($1.00 U.S.) per peg. Other dine-dance hotels and restaurants are similarly priced.

Some of the most popular entertainment spots are the so-called dancing schools where servicemen learn to dance, ballroom style with some advertised jitterbugging. Afterward, if the serviceman has enough money, he may take his partner to Green's Hotel, or elsewhere, for more dancing, and after that, your guess is as good as the writer's. Dining in Green's Hotel daily (which I do), one sees the same attractive Anglo-Indian girls coming in night after night with different men.

For the moneyed Bombay citizens, the Cricket Club, the Willingdon Club, and the Yacht Club are popular rendezvous. The Willingdon Club, which also has the only 18-hole golf course in the city, has its membership filled by the influx of money into Bombay, and now has a waiting list of several hundred willing to pay the 1,000 rupee ($300) entrance fee. The club also has the best swimming pool, and Allied officers have been granted the privilege of using the club when stationed in Bombay on temporary duty.

The Cricket Club is also a popular place for lunch and a swim and has also opened its doors to Allied officers. The only other golf course, the Bombay Presidency Golf Club, is 12 miles out of town and not easy to get to without a car. The Cricket Club also has a long waiting list because Bombay is filled to overflowing with nouveaux rich from the black market or war profiteering.

Always a sporting town, Bombay will begin its racing season on November 10th. The season is ushered in with much apprehension, mainly because the summer meeting in Poona, three hours' journey north by train, was constantly interrupted by discoveries of doped horses. The whole meeting turned out to be one round of saliva testing with several trainers and jockeys being warned off. Race followers from Malaya and China coast ports, who have refugeed here, report that Bombay's racing is the crookedest they have seen, so more than a prayer must ride with your ten rupee to win.

There is also a great clamor for the military authorities to return the city's sports grounds. The military commandeered a majority of these green maidans (parks) to build temporary buildings and they are slow in giving them up. Local cricketers are swinging their bats in anticipation of the fall play, especially now that the Australian team, making a tour of major cricket areas and playing zone teams, is in India.

Bombay, a great commercial city and the home of Tata and Sons, the largest corporation, owning among other industries, steel mills, airlines, aircraft factories, hotels (The Taj Mahal and Green's in Bombay) and various other subsidiaries, is vitally interested in the Anglo-American financial talks and the final settlement of the sterling balances. India has come out of the war a creditor country, and these Bombay businessmen are anxious to put their money into post-war schemes. Almost every mill owner in this cotton town is trying to buy new machinery for his mills. New groups of people are trying to start newspapers to compete with Bombay's four English dailies, while the present publications are trying to get equipment to replace their worn-out presses and linotype machines.

There is great interest in the American surplus property disposal with everyone trying to pull all the strings he can to get in on the ground floor. It was announced recently that only bids starting from 50,000 rupees would be considered, which leaves the little man out and paves the way for the more powerful industrialists.

But politics is the big interest at the moment. Bombay is the scene of rapidly accelerating election campaigns in which both the National Congress and Mr. Mohammed Ali Jinnah and his Muslim League are the main political parties.

Mr. Jinnah, President of the Muslim League and an advocate of Pakistan, has just returned to the city from an extended election tour of the Province of Sind, north of Bombay, and Baluchistan. The Muslim leader is very optimistic of his chances, as the main issue of the election is the question of self-determination and Mr. Jinnah's claim to represent all the Muslims in India.

The A.I.C.C. (All India Congress Committee) touched off the election fever with Pandit Jawaharlal Nehru and other Congress leaders making impassioned speeches. Shortly afterward, there were communal riots—Hindus against Muslims—in the northern suburbs, with 34 persons killed and over 100 wounded before the police restored order. At the moment the area is peaceful, but the next outbreak could occur at any time, although the leaders of both political parties have appealed to their followers to fight the elections in a peaceful manner.

During the autumn of 1945, American businessmen began arriving in Bombay. Among the first to arrive were representatives of the American film industry. Because there were so few Americans in Bombay, I got to know most of them. I was invited often for bridge with Keith and Mary Goldsmith and many an afternoon I played golf with Keith, who represented an American movie company. The Warner Brothers representative, Mike Shathin, would invite a small number of friends to private showings of his films. One evening we saw *Saratoga Trunk* with Gary Cooper and Ingrid Bergman. Mike would screen his films in a little projection room at the Strand Theatre that accommodated about 20 persons.

Lee and Margo Kamern, in Bombay for Metro Goldwyn Mayer, also invited friends to see films at the Metro Theatre. Margo Kamern was a very talented amateur actress and dancer, so she directed the annual show for the American Women's Club. In one of these shows I and my two army buddies, Lt. T. J. Davis and Capt. Richard Boren, performed a dance dressed in Indian *dhotis*. A number of Indian friends were invited to these shows, and Roshan Batliwala, one of my Parsi friends, joined the three of us.

After the summer of meetings with the British government in Delhi and the hill station of Simla, in mid-September the All India Congress Committee held its first big meeting in Bombay at the city's famous Chowpatti Beach on Marine Drive.

Chowpatti Beach, 1945

At the time, Stew Hensley, who usually covered such meetings, was ill. Thus I had my first baptism of an Indian political meeting. Congress Party leaders from all parts of the country came for the three-day meeting. The main speaker was Pandit Jawaharlal Nehru, the leader of the Congress, who came to report on the results of his meetings in Delhi and Simla with the Viceroy and with the Muslim leader, Mohammed Ali Jinnah. Hundreds gathered on the beach—so many that security guards erected bamboo enclosures to keep members from rushing to the dais. I was issued a press pass by Mr. G. Patil, the General Secretary of the Committee. (The pass read, "Note: This ticket is issued to subject to the Congress President's right to control the meeting. The ticket-holder is required to observe peace and discipline and obey the President's order."

In a letter to my family from Bombay on September 24, 1945, I wrote, "The All India Congress Committee ended yesterday, and I spent almost seven hours of my waking day yesterday listening to speeches which I couldn't understand." I added that many were fiery speeches and my Indian colleagues generously helped me with translations. I, of course, understood Nehru's speech because he spoke in his impeccable English. Midway through the long meeting there was a tea break and Nehru came and sat across from me and talked with me. He was very friendly, but we only made small talk. He was soft-spoken, and I was such a cub reporter that I failed to ask him any headline-making questions.

In that same letter home I wrote, "Stew Hensley has been sick the past few days, again with boils. I think he will have to leave India, at least I think I would if I was feeling as bad as he does."

Just two weeks later, in October, Stew did leave India after a round of farewell visits to our newspaper clients and farewell dinners with our Indian friends. Upon Stew's departure, I became the acting manager for India. I expected to be in that position for just a few weeks until a new manager was appointed. However, I would not get a new boss for almost six months.

4

ACTING MANAGER FOR INDIA

◆

(October 1945 to March 1946)

Almost as soon as Stew Hensley left, I was faced with my first problem. One of our Indian editors, whom we trusted because he had been recommended highly, forged my signature to a check for 4,000 rupees (about $1,000.00). We discovered the shortage when figuring out our monthly statement. I went to our bank, and with their good offices, we got the fellow to admit he had taken the money. Much to my relief we got our money back. Losing $1000.00 would have been a very inauspicious start to my stint as acting manager.

One of my first tasks, a holdover while Stew Hensley was still in India, was to find an office. At that time I was living at the luxurious Taj Mahal Hotel while we were working out of a room in the hotel next door, but our office would get quite crowded. I began looking for a place with more room, but Bombay had few office spaces for rent and I was finding no takers.

I worried about being promoted, even in an acting capacity, because I had so little experience on newspapers. I thought that any day I would hear from Peg Vaughn that a new Manager for India was on the way. But the days and weeks went by with no message.

I continued to have a good time despite working at all hours of the day and night. Nat and Sophie Natarajan were extremely friendly and invited me to dinner and drinks. They often invited me to come along with them when they were invited out to dinner. I noted that their hosts didn't seem to mind that I was a "gate crasher." I chalked it up to the fact that I was a rare breed—an American—and Americans at the time were welcomed everywhere in India.

Among the Natarajans' circle of friends were two very pretty Indian girls—sisters. ENSA, the British equivalent of our USO, was putting on a week's plays in Bombay for British and American servicemen. The ENSA group featured famous English actors such as John Gielgud and Gracie Fields, among others. The only way civilians could attend was to accompany a serviceman. Because I was still accredited to the American Army, I was able to get two tickets for two nights. So one night I took one of the girls to see "Hamlet" and the next night I took her sister. (I wrote home to my mother, "Both girls are good looking, Mother, have lots of money, but for goodness sake don't start worrying.") Later the two sisters took me to lunch at the Willingdon Sports Club as a thank you.

Around this time, Nat introduced me to doctors Eddie and Piloo Bharucha, who became great friends. Eddie was a neurologist and Piloo a pediatrician. They had both received their medical degrees in London; in fact, they met and secretly married before returning to India. Eddie and Piloo were Parsis, a community that originated in Persia (Iran). Members of the Parsi community socialized with Westerners more freely than did most other Indians.

The Parsis had been driven out of Persia by Muslim rulers more than a thousand years earlier and granted refuge in western India by the local Hindu ruler. As followers of Zoraster, they worshipped fire, which was anathema to Islam. The Parsis settled mainly in the western provinces of India with a majority living in Bombay. They were limited, at first, to the areas bordering the Indian Ocean. Originally they had to show their allegiance to the Hindu rulers by wearing a black headgear shaped roughly like a cow's hoof. The Parsis brought their religion with them, and in Bombay's Malabar Hill section are the Parsi Towers of Silence where the Parsi dead are placed on platforms and the vultures consume the bodies. In Persia there was no place to bury the dead, and the custom was carried to India. Over the centuries the Parsis have lived in harmony not only with the dominant religious faith in the country (Hinduism) but also with the dominant political force. Despite being a minority in India, numbering only about 100,000, the Parsis have been a forward-looking community, and many of them became industrialists, educators, and doctors like my friends Eddie and Piloo. The CEO of Tata Industries, J.R.D. Tata, was a Parsi who belonged to the Willingdon Club, and I played golf with him occasionally. Indira Gandhi was married to a Parsi.

Drs. Piloo and Eddie Bharucha, two of my Parsi friends in Bombay.

Also in the Natarajans' circle of friends were Sharouk Sabavala and Roshan Batliwala, another Parsi couple who my Army buddies and I got to know very well. Roshan even joined us in a skit for the American Women's Club annual show. Later Sharouk ran for a seat in the Indian Parliament but lost his political race. (Roshan and Sharouk married in February 1947.)

At the beginning of November there was a three-day holiday to celebrate the Hindu New Year. I noted that I worked several shifts because my Hindu employees had the weekend off for the holiday. I was also invited to an Indian dinner at the home of one of our newspaper clients. I went with some apprehension but discovered that I really enjoyed Indian food. It was very good and I ate heartily.

Early in November I made a quick trip to New Delhi to negotiate the sale of United Press to the army newspaper, *The Roundup*. The contract was an important one, and since there was no one else around, it was my job to put the UP's case before the proper people. I wrote that because the newspaper was very friendly to the UP, I thought we would get the contract. But I worried because the Associated Press was also bidding on the contract. (In a later letter, I noted that we got the contract but that "much of the work was done by New York.") It was a whirlwind trip, leaving Bombay on a Tuesday afternoon and returning on Thursday morning. I spent the extra time visiting newspaper editors.

After returning to Bombay I attended a cricket match. I went quite by accident. I was Christmas shopping with Sophie Natarajan and then had lunch with her mother, Mrs. Sobani. At lunch I met more of the family and everyone was interested in cricket. So I wound up going to watch the match between the Australians and the Indians at the Bombay Cricket Ground. I wrote, "The Aussies were way ahead when they pulled stakes for the day but there are still two days of play to go. It's rather a silly game—maybe it's because I don't play it that I feel that way."

I continued to worry about the job although, I wrote, the only redeeming feature about working as acting manager was that I knew my limitations. I also began thinking of asking for a transfer to Singapore because I had many friends in Singapore urging me to come there. I gave it serious thought but realized I would be in Bombay for the foreseeable future.

Around the middle of November, as the U.S. Army continued to demobilize, three of my Army friends—Joe Murphy, T. G. (Stinky) Davis, and Richard (Dirty Dick) Boren—invited me to share their luxurious house, called "Hillcrest," in the Malabar Hill section of Bombay. I had my own room and was waited upon by Indian servants. To round it out, I had the use of two jeeps so I had transportation to my office at any time. Although I was putting in many hours at the office, there was always time for golf and swimming. What a change from having to take taxis or have friends pick me up for dinner dates.

We foreigners at the time lived what might be called an artificial life. Our social life was limited mainly to entertaining among our friends in the foreign community. The few Indians who were invited to our social gatherings were usually wealthy and non-orthodox. For the most part they also were involved in foreign business enterprises. Strict religious Hindus and Moslems did not imbibe alcohol and thus were not invited to cocktail parties where the Americans and other Westerners drank liberally.

The Bombay foreign community was very cosmopolitan. As a reporter for the United Press, I did not have the money to travel in the wealthy circles, but I was accepted because I was a bachelor newsman and the "Number One" of a very small company.

My letters home recounted my social life of cocktail and dinner parties at the Taj Mahal Hotel and at the luxurious flats in the high-rent districts of the city. It was a heady existence, and I reveled in golfing, swimming, sports, surfing at the beach. For me, it was a luxurious life style after five years of "roughing it" in China.

However, I didn't neglect the office. I noted that shortly after I moved into Hillcrest, I went to a press conference of Nehru's. I talked to him for a little while after the conference, which for foreign papers was not worthy of spending cable money, and he was very friendly. Of course for Indian newspapers, any time he said something it was front-page news. He was interesting to talk with because his English was British English. He had spent his early years in British public schools—Harrow and Trinity College of Cambridge University—before studying law at the Inner Temple in London. Returning to India, he practiced law for about seven years before joining the Indian National Congress. My Indian colleagues, who understood Hindi, said that he spoke better English than Hindi. It was also said that he dreamed in English.

One of my golfing partners was Ali Mecklai, whose father was the treasurer of the Ismaili Muslim community in Bombay. (It was Ali, some years later, who rented me the top floor of his family's home on seaside Warden Road when I was married.) Also a member of the Willingdon Club was the Aga Khan, the spiritual leader of the Ismaili Muslims. The Aga Khan, a heavily built man, played in golfing shorts. He wouldn't hit the ball very far, but it usually went straight down the fairway. The Aga Khan was married to a beautiful French woman. He was the father of Aly Khan, the handsome, polo-playing friend of Rita Hayworth.

With the end of the war and a new British-Indian Government in New Delhi, American companies soon began setting up businesses in Bombay and other cities in India. In a short time, the American community in Bombay grew with the addition of automobile assembly plants. Both General Motors and Ford Motor Company began turning out cars for the Indian market. All the parts were manufactured outside India and shipped for the assembly line.

Next came the tire companies. Firestone built a big plant in Bombay, and a large American contingent moved to Bombay not only for management and sales, but also to run the factory. Goodyear Tire had a large factory in Calcutta.

There were smaller companies as well. Rolf Arnason represented Abbott Laboratories. He and his wife often had me to dinner. Dexter Richards represented Eveready Batteries.

Genelle Moots, a TWA airline hostess (we called them hostesses in those days, but now they are flight attendants) came out to Bombay to train Indian young ladies to work for Tata Airlines.

During the summer of 1945, my Army friends had often invited me out to their mess for an "American" meal when they had managed to snare U.S. steaks or an American turkey. They also took me with them when they went out to Juhu Beach where the Army Transport Command had a rest camp. My "wonderful life" at the officers' mess continued into the fall. Almost every Sunday we would travel to the Army rest camp at Juhu Beach, play baseball or touch football and swim in the surf. We celebrated Thanksgiving at the camp with a turkey dinner at noon. I worked every day. My buddies took me in to work every morning when they went to work. They would pick me up at noon and bring me back for lunch and then take me down to work when they returned in the afternoon. The mess had two jeeps and I was able to use them at night if I wished. In a letter I wrote to friends, I said that I was living in a "fur-lined foxhole."

Our Cumbala Hill neighbors were prominent members of Indian society. Just up the block was the residence of Sir Benegal Rama Rau and Lady Rama Rau, and living with them at the time was their younger daughter, Santha Rama Rao. Santha was back home after attending Wellesley College, from which she had graduated Summa Cum Laude. Santha was the author of a bestselling book, *Home to India,* an account of her observations of her country after several years of living abroad. Sir Benigal had been a member of the Indian Civil Service, and Lady Rama Rau, a Kashmiri Brahmin related to Jawaharlal Nehru, was very active in Indian social circles.

My letters home tell of a dinner party at the home of J.R.D. Tata, the CEO of Tata Industries which owned airlines, steel mills, and other businesses. I had met him at the Willingdon Sports Club and had played golf with him. I noted that I had a wonderful time at his beautiful mansion on Malabar Hill with my friend, Santha Rama Rau, who was also one of the guests.

Santha had been a regular guest at Hillcrest, and in turn we—the army officers and I—were often invited to the Rama Rau residence for drinks and dinners. We had an amusing incident.

One evening as we were sitting down to dinner, Santha Rama Rao appeared at our door. We all said, "Santha! What a surprise! Come on in."

And Santha, bemused, replied, "Well, you did invite me for dinner, didn't you?" None of us could remember who had issued the invitation, but it didn't matter. She was one of us for dinner.

Later, we sent a formal invitation to Santha and her parents. And to make sure we didn't forget the date, we posted signs on all of the walls—"Remember, fellows, Santha comes to dinner tonight," which we removed after we all sat down to dinner.

Another neighbor was the Muslim leader, Mohammed Ali Jinnah, who lived one block away. As a reporter, I visited him many times and also got to know his private secretary, Ali Khurshid, who arranged the interviews and became a good friend. Mr. Jinnah was then mobilizing Indian Muslims for his political party and traveling to the northern and eastern provinces where the majority of the population was Muslim. Although Mahatma Gandhi and Jawaharlal Nehru were hoping to include Mr. Jinnah within the All India Congress Party, Mr. Jinnah was adamant to form his own party. His foresight was proven later as India was partitioned into the two countries of India and Pakistan.

I well remember one afternoon when I met with Mr. Jinnah. We were standing beside the large dining table when he remarked, "How can you negotiate with a man who won't even dine with you?" He then explained that when Mahatma Gandhi came to his house, he brought his own food as they sat across the table from each other. Gandhi was a strict vegetarian, and it was not unusual for Hindus to refuse to have dinner with persons of other religions.

Life for me continued to be one large party as the holiday season approached. Here is a sample of the letters I sent home:

> Saturday I worked all day while the rest of the house went to the races. Sunday was our last day at the beach since the ATC Rest Camp is closing. We had Mimi Bray, an American girl who is a secretary at the American Consulate, for lunch and she went with us to the beach. We had a swell time, playing ball, knocked ourselves out, and then for all the pounds I lost, made it up by drinking beer. In the evening, we went to Mimi's for dinner and played bridge while "Stinky" popped American popcorn.
>
> I check in with the office occasionally and do a little work, but mostly it's running by itself. There will have to be a great change soon and I'll have to get back into harness when Hillcrest is closed, but for the time being it's a very comfortable life.
>
> The boys are very good to me. I have no business living in the house since it's an officers' mess and I am no longer accredited. However, no one complains and they ride me to the office every day in the jeeps and even let me have a jeep to pick up my dates. It's all very comfortable. We have all sorts of supplies, have good American ice cream every night, plenty of beer, Coca Cola, and scotch. We have a radio, turntable, and all the records the Army special services can supply. We also have golf clubs, golf balls and go golfing regularly. On top of everything it's a very congenial crowd.
>
> Wednesday Dick Boren and I went golfing early. In the evening we were invited across to Santha Rama Rau's for drinks. The whole Hillcrest crowd was invited. What a party. It's getting funny now. Whenever I invite friends out to the house, they meet the rest of the gang. Now, when my friends are having parties, they invite me and include the mess.
>
> Tonight I'm going to baptize my new tux. I had a difficult time getting it made. Cost me one hundred bucks for a tux with an extra white coat. Also two dress shirts made which set me back some money. (I earlier had told my

family that my civilian clothes had been lost in Calcutta and I was replenishing my clothes with the local tailor.)

On Christmas Eve we had a quiet dinner at the mess. We had invited Mimi Bray to join us, and after dinner she wanted to attend midnight mass. I took one of the jeeps and stayed through the long two-hour program. After I took her home, I was awakened at 4:30 a.m. by a party of friends who had run out of gas. I took the seven of them home in a jeep and thought how lucky they were that the Army was here and had gas.

On Christmas Day we had a stateside turkey and invited a number of friends, American and Indian, to join us. We had a Christmas tree that the boys put up on the 24th, an artificial one because live Christmas trees were scarce in Bombay. I wrote home that it didn't seem like Christmas because of the lovely warm weather and the opportunity to go golfing. I also noted that it seemed strange to me that although we were in India where most of the people were Hindus, Muslims, or Parsis, everyone celebrated the Christmas holiday. All of the shops displayed decorated Christmas trees, and everyone had a holiday. The Indian Christian community was tiny, but after 150 years of British colonial rule with the government honoring Christian and British holidays, people of all religions took the Christmas holiday as well as their own.

On Christmas night we had an unexpected crowd in for evening dinner. We decided that we should put out a communiqué to all our neighbors apologizing for the noise we made with everyone making speeches and singing songs, loudly. After dinner the next night we were glad we had not sent the communiqué since we would have had to send out two. We had a riotous time on the evening of the 26th as well. I had taken the day off from work on the 26th, Boxing Day in Britain and India, and played golf. I was happy because I had set a new record of 85 on the par 65 Willingdon Club course.

American Women's Club skit, December 29, 1945;
left to right: "Stinky" Davis, Roshan Batliwala,
"Check" Hlavacek, and "Dirty Dick" Boren.

New Year's Day was a time for another celebration, and the American Men's Club of Bombay managed to have a New Year's Eve party that lasted until the wee hours. Then on New Year's Day, the Americans gathered again for a morning of Bloody Marys at the Willingdon Club.

During that week I had received two pieces of good news. First, my boss, Peg Vaughn, wrote me a letter with a handwritten note at the bottom saying, "I'm impressed with the fine work you are doing. Keep it up, old boy. Peg." In a letter home I noted that it was a good thing he didn't know about the "Life of Reilly" I had been living at Hillcrest. That same week the contract for the army newspaper, *The Roundup*, was finalized.

At Hillcrest we had a very quiet (for us) New Year's Eve. We invited Mimi Bray and George Small, a Vice Consul and a friend of mine from our days in

Chungking. On New Year's Day I spent the morning working at the office and then at noon, we picked up George and Mimi and together with Stinky went to the American Association Eggnog Party. It was an annual affair where the American community met to shake off the effects of late-night New Year's eve parties. We got there late and afterward retired to Hillcrest where the three of us took naps, leaving Mimi alone in the house making fudge. That evening we went to a movie, "Desert Song," and we took Santha along.

The first week in January I was the best man for the wedding of Joan Owen and Captain William Peterson, an ex-censor. I wanted to wear my new tux, but Joan wanted a military wedding so I got my war correspondent's uniform out of mothballs. After the wedding I took the two bridesmaids in the jeep to the bride's house for the reception. After the reception we took practically the whole wedding party back to Hillcrest where we had a good time eating, dancing, and joking. Then I took Joan and Pete to the train and saw them off on their honeymoon.

The next night, after a day of golfing, I invited one of the bridesmaids to dinner and then Dick and I took her to her train for Baroda. After seeing her off, Dick and I made a tour of Bombay's Red Light district. Dick was the Provost Marshal, so he knew the area. We stopped at some of the better houses and then toured Grant Road, the area of the infamous cages. None of it was at all pretty, and I thought "Just one hell of a way to make a living."

On the next Sunday after spending a very unprofitable morning at the office, I had lunch at the house and then went visiting. Stinky, Dick, and George Small went golfing in one jeep and I took the other one out to Bandra, a Bombay suburb, to visit Sophie Natarajan, who was sick. Santha Rama Rau came along with me, which made the drive a very enjoyable afternoon. After visiting Sophie, we stopped for tea at a friend of Santha's where we met new arrivals. One was a man who had been in China and had escaped from an internment camp near Shanghai. We found we had mutual friends, which always makes for good conversation.

That January was the last month for Hillcrest. My army friends were being demobilized and the last day for the house was January 30th, so we went golfing as often as possible because the house was so close to the golf club.

One night I went down to the office because I was expecting a call from our Calcutta correspondent, Bob Clurman, who had joined us after being hired by Peg Vaughn in Bangkok. I took the jeep and picked up Mimi Bray for the ride. But we never got the call. In India at that time, if one wanted to make a long-distance call, it was necessary to book the call ahead of time. You needed to give the operator the number, the name of the person you wanted to speak to, and then wait. It was particularly difficult and time-consuming for me because my name, Hlavacek, is usually difficult for Americans and almost impossible for Indians. It got so bad that I would spell my name with Indian words: H for Hardwar, L for Lucknow, A for Allahabad, V for Vishnu, A for Allahabad, C for Chakravarty, E for Ellora, and K for Karachi. I wanted to talk to Clurman because I was sending him down to Singapore to help Mac Wright, our correspondent there, who was sick. Clurman left that week, leaving me as the only American correspondent in all of India.

I had to work extra shifts that January because my chief Indian assistant was sick, as was another editor, and so we were working "under forced draft." But it didn't stop us from having parties. One of my notes said that Dick and Stinky managed to dig up several bottles of whisky so we would have enough for the guests. I added that I didn't know how many would show up, but there was "sure to be a crowd."

In a short note home, I wrote, "Last night Dick and Stinky caught two escaped Italian war prisoners who wandered into the house. Nothing exciting." And, "Today we got a staff car to add to our fleet of four jeeps, and the boys are happy as larks."

In the midst of getting ready to close up, I made a trip to New Delhi to see a couple of new prospects. It was a quick trip. I went up by Tata Airlines on a Wednesday and came home on Saturday on an Army plane. I hitchhiked on the army plane and recorded that I had saved the company sixty bucks. The weather in Delhi was very hot, and I was glad to get out. On the plane from Delhi, I met a young lady whom I invited out to the house for lunch and dinner. I took the new staff car for a sightseeing tour of Bombay as she had only one day to visit before leaving for home. My only record of the visit was "Nice gal, an Irish lassie named Murphy."

During those last weeks at Hillcrest, I had to make three radio broadcasts for Sophie Natarajan. I wrote home that I wasn't very happy with the results because it was the first time I had recorded the news for radio.

Around that time there was a sad tragedy at the office. My chief assistant, Veera, had lost his baby girl and was taking some time off to perform Hindu burial rites, so I was alone at the office.

After I returned from Delhi, it was just one farewell party after another. One night Stinky and I went to have a drink with Rolf and Ruth Arnason. Rolf was a graduate of St. Olaf and Ruth from my Alma Mater, Carleton. While we were there, Santha Rama Rau dropped in and we all stayed for dinner. Rolf was in

Bombay representing Abbott Laboratories. That same week the Hillcrest three and I were invited to the Rama Raus for drinks and dinner and we ended up at the Taj. On Saturday we had a farewell dinner for Dick. We took him to the train the next day and bid him good journey to Calcutta and home. With the closing of the house, we spent a couple of afternoons packing, and I acquired a lot of crockery and linen and even some furniture.

As a bachelor living on a small salary, I couldn't afford an apartment or a house on my own. But it was a sad day when I had to leave Hillcrest in February and move into the Ritz Hotel with George Small, a friend from my days in China. I wrote home that "living in a hotel again, after three months of Hillcrest, isn't much fun. However, the food is good at the Ritz." In leaving Hillcrest I had also lost my transportation, but George, being a vice consul, had an army jeep to drive. Also, because he had access to buying army surplus, he was able to order an Army surplus Chevrolet. I advanced him $250 as my half of the car's purchase price. We hoped it would arrive in the month of June.

In the middle of February I had to get back to work. The All India Newspaper Editors Conference was held in Allahabad, and I represented United Press. I had hoped to fly, but at the last minute I took the train. I had a hard time getting a berth and finally resorted to getting military priority through my British accreditation. Indian trains have two-berth compartments and four-berth compartments. I had an upper berth in a four-berth compartment. Below me was Mr. S. Sadanand, the editor of the *Free Press Journal* in Bombay. Opposite him on a lower berth was a spinster lady with her dog, an Airedale. She got in the compartment at Bombay and would not get out even though she was told the compartment was not for ladies. She accepted the compromise and agreed that the other three berths could be filled. The fourth berth was occupied by a "very very pukka Colonel in the Indian Army." We had a delightful time. Nor was that all. For the first four hours of the journey we had a young British army captain and his wife and their mountains of luggage. The train trip to Allahabad is a long one. We slept all night and then had to ride all the next day up until 10 p.m. before arriving at Allahabad. Meanwhile, during the day the colonel departed at a way station and in his place another couple boarded with their two babies and a dog. Our compartment was so full that I spent most of the day in other compartments that were less crowded.

At Allahabad we were met by a reception committee of the All India Newspaper Editors' Conference. Three of us foreigners were in attendance: Sir Francis Low of the *Times of India,* Preston Grover of the Associated Press, and me. We were taken to the Allahabad Club, a typical British institution where we were made quite comfortable and had the use of a car for our business.

Saturday morning Pres Grover and I went to see Nehru to get an advance copy of the speech with which he was to open the conference that morning. Nehru confessed that he had not written the speech, so after a few pleasantries we returned to the conference to meet all the editors. It was my first conference, so I had a number of editors to meet. They made quite a picture, some in beards, some in foreign dress, and others in the Indian *dhoti*.

Nehru opened the conference and then the outgoing and incoming presidents spoke. Preston and I ducked out after Nehru's speech to file a few words. The conference was held at Muir College, which had large, pleasant grounds. We had lunch together with the editors under a large tent. In the afternoon, Sir Tej Bahadur Sapru, India's foremost lawyer, spoke on press laws. His speech was marred by the fact that he was elderly and his voice didn't carry well. That evening the editors were entertained at a dinner hosted by one of India's Maharajahs.

The business sessions were interesting. I wrote home that it seemed that this was the one time in the year that all those who write had a chance to get up and shout to the rooftops. They introduced many resolutions, made fiery impassioned speeches and after all the hubbub, did very little. But they all had a chance to meet together and have fun. After dinner that night, I went straight to bed after a hot bath, my first since leaving Bombay.

The next morning, before the session, I stopped at Nehru's compound and although he was busy, talked to him for a short while. I must confess that I am not a sharp newsman or I would have got a statement from him about something. But somehow he has said so much and so often that it didn't seem to be worthwhile to repeat it. We got to the session in time to hear a lively discussion. The Government of India, a body the editors were continually attacking, sent down two men, a member of the Viceroy's Council and the Food Secretary. The former came down to ask the editors not to make the coming food shortage a political issue, which of course was the wrong thing to say. However, to an outsider like me, the dilemma had a humorous aspect. This minister said that India was already three million tons short and they would be another four million tons short. Then he recommended an austerity campaign. He said that he was cutting out bread at meals and that some of his friends were cutting out one meal a day. That from him sounded funny since he was about as round as he was tall. To make it even more ludicrous, one of the nationalist editors who was asking about the shortages accused the government of having primary responsibility for the shortage. This man, too, was equally big. To have these two corpulent gentlemen get up and talk of austerity was amusing to me. I had to duck out after these first two speeches to get to the telegraph office to file. While I was away, I missed more fireworks as the editors kept baiting these two government men. It was unusual, though, in that it was the first time the government had asked the press to "lay off."

On Sunday, most of the business was finished, and I caught a train for Calcutta. I then wrote: "It looks as if coming to Calcutta proved to be a mistake. I certainly picked the wrong time to leave Bombay. A mutiny in the Indian Navy is going on and I am 1500 miles away."

In Calcutta I checked in at our office and then got a room at the Grand Hotel, a misnomer if there ever was one. It was a perfectly lousy hotel but the only place to stay at the moment. The next day I made my rounds of visits to the newspapers. I didn't know any of the editors, so I spent the day introducing myself. In the evening I found Captain Lou Saban, who had been a high school football teammate of my brother. Lou was an all-American football star at Indiana when he was drafted into the Army and sent to a Chinese Language school. He was waiting to fly into China. I tagged along with Lou and his friends to a Chinese dinner.

The next day was another round of meetings. I had lunch with the editor of *The Statesman* and saw more Indian editors during the afternoon. In the evening I again joined Lou and his friends at the American officers' mess at Kanarni Estates. Lou was very anxious to get home and out of the Army in time to play for the Cleveland Browns later in the year.

I spent a third day in Calcutta and again spent the evening with Lou and his gang. He had just got his orders to go to China, and I was tossing coins about my travels. I already had my ticket to go to Madras, but I called my office in Bombay and decided I had better get back as fast as I could.

While I was in Calcutta, after the mutiny was put down, there was rioting in the streets of Bombay. I cancelled my Madras trip and took the train across India, a 36-hour ride. The ride, I wrote, was not too bad, seeing as how one of Lou Saban's friends found me a case of beer which was duly consumed on the trip. Riding Indian trains is not the pleasantest occupation, but I didn't mind this one too much because we had good food and fairly decent traveling companions. All the way across, I had the feeling I should be back sooner and at the same time wondered what would happen should I get caught in the middle of India if a full-scale revolt broke out. Fortunately, it didn't.

I arrived on a Sunday to find the office running well. They had had some rough days but managed to come out all right. We took a pretty bad beating the first couple of days of the Mutiny from the Associated Press but soon recovered.

The next day I had lunch with a large group of correspondents who had flocked to Bombay to cover the story: Paul Feng of Central News Agency of China, George Jones of *The New York Times*, Hal Boyle of the AP, and John Fisher of the *London Daily Mail*. This gathering was unusual in that Sharouk Sabavala and Santha Rama Rau had invited me to lunch and all the others just joined the party. Sharouk picked up the check.

At lunch, Paul Feng suggested I go with him to Poona to see the Mahatma. We had a Chinese dinner that evening and then took the midnight train to Poona, arriving in the morning. We shaved at the station and had breakfast and then went to see the Mahatma. He was in the middle of his morning walk—he walked daily for an hour between 7:30 and 8:30 a.m. After his walk he met us and just shook hands and we had some small talk. He said he was too tired to talk and that he had to get his morning massage. Paul and I went into town and visited the local newspapers, so the trip was not completely unprofitable. I decided to return to Bombay while Paul stayed on for the evening prayers in the hope of getting an interview. (He didn't get one.)

Coming back on the train, I met our company auditor and traveled in the compartment next to the Aga Khan. The Aga Khan was a big man—about 5'7" and about as round as he was tall. His private secretary sat in our compartment and was very quiet most of the time. However, the Aga Khan left the train at a station a half-hour before Bombay and as soon as he left, the private secretary broke out a bottle of scotch, which he shared with us. The followers of the Aga Khan are not supposed to imbibe, but it was good scotch.

Back in Bombay I had lunch one day with George Jones, Sharouk Sabavala, and Raja and Krishna Huthesingh. Krishna was the younger sister of Jawaharlal Nehru, and she became a good friend of mine.

One bad feature of the riots was that the car which George Small and I were going to buy was burned. It was a Plymouth and belonged to the Foreign Liquidation Commission. George received his authorization to buy it the same day it was burned by the mob. George then began trying to get another car, but he wouldn't know until the end of the month whether he could get one. So we were back to taxis and hitching rides with friends, and we were unhappy about it. We had been spoiled by the Army.

I had been asking my family to see about buying a car and shipping it out to me. But cars were also hard to get in the U.S. immediately after the war. If they could get one, I asked them to ship it in George's name. I also asked for some items of clothing that were not available in India: cotton sweat socks, a good pair of gym shoes, two pairs of suspenders—one black for my tux and the other for everyday wear—another pair of garters, a leather belt, and a couple of pairs of slacks.

In a letter to my sister, I asked her to send a package to Harold Guard in London: "It should contain, if possible, chocolates for his little girl—she is about 14—Lux soap for his wife, and cigarettes for Harold. Also anything else such as tea, or tinned food of any sort. P.S. and please find out about the possibility of buying an automobile."

In the middle of March, the Ismaili Muslim Community celebrated the Aga Khan's 75th birthday by weighing him in diamonds. (On his 50th birthday they had weighed him in gold.) The event was celebrated with a large set of scales at Bombay's Cricket Club grounds. The diamonds were sold and the proceeds donated to the charities that the Aga Khan supported. I wrote a story describing the event, and I received a cable from London telling me my story was great.

I continued golfing with friends, although I had to say goodbye to the Willingdon Club as I was no longer accredited to the Army. I applied for membership in the Chembur Presidency Club, which was located some 12 miles outside the city.

I continued socializing. The Natarajans invited me to dinners at which the talk continually turned to politics, especially about the maneuvering of the Congress and the Muslim League with the British Government.

During the week I had a date with Santha Rama Rau. We saw a movie, "The Valley of Decision," which I found disappointing because the Indian censors had cut it badly and removed the best parts. Afterward we drove to her home, which was across the street from Hillcrest, and her mother, Lady Rama Rau, and I had a long discussion about the political situation. She had hopes that the difficult situation could be resolved, but I was not so sure. I advised my sister, who was planning to visit me, that I was not optimistic.

On March 13th, I celebrated my 27th birthday, and I received the news that Gerald Rock, the new Manager for India, would be arriving in India on March 17th.

On the 16th of March, the British Prime Minister, Clement Attlee, delivered a speech before the House of Commons in which he emphasized the necessity for India to gain independence, while highlighting the problems brought about by this process. So early on the morning of March 17th, at 4:15 a.m., I traveled to Birla House where the Mahatma was staying to see if I could get him to comment on Mr. Attlee's speech. The answer was "No," but I had to wait two hours even to get that response.

5

THE FAMOUS PHOTOGRAPH

◆

(March to July 1946)

My new boss, Gerry Rock arrived in India just in time to begin covering the negotiations in New Delhi between the British Government and the two opposing political parties: the Indian National Congress, led by Jawaharlal Nehru and Mahatma Gandhi, and the Muslim League, represented by Mohammed Ali Jinnah. Clement Attlee, the British prime minister, had delivered his speech in the Parliament. Within days he had sent out his Cabinet mission, which arrived in India on March 23rd.

After Gerry reached Bombay, we had only a few days to discuss United Press business before he had to leave for New Delhi. I spent the time introducing him to our newspaper clients. Gerry had help in covering the story from P. D. Sharma, our New Delhi correspondent.

While Gerry was in New Delhi, I looked around for a place in Bombay for him to live. I found a three-bedroom apartment roomy enough for Gerry and his family, which included a wife and two children. The apartment was fully furnished, with a rent of 450 rupees per month ($150 U.S.). It near the sea and close to a swimming pool. However, Gerry would not be able to move in until the present occupant went home on leave, and then he and his family could have it for only six months.

At that time our UP office in Bombay was having trouble with our reception of news from London. I kept complaining to the Indian posts and telegraphs about the trouble, and I was told they would try to find out what was wrong. We were also having trouble with the land lines over which our news was going to newspapers upcountry. I had several conversations with Gerry while he was in New Delhi and he, too, was contacting the government for help.

I wrote a letter thanking my family for sending the parcels to London. Gerry had told us that he thought that outside of Berlin and Cologne, London sustained more damage than any other city in World War II. When Gerry returned from New Delhi, George and I met him at the train. Gerry brought a load of beer and other supplies he had been able to buy in Delhi. Gerry could only stay for one night and he then had to leave for Calcutta. We could not get him a seat on the plane, so he had to take the 36-hour train ride.

All during the month of April we were trying to get a car. George Small was able to get a jeep from the American Consulate but we could only use it to go to and from the office. After George dropped us off, the jeep had to be used for Consulate business. The weather continued to be hot during the rest of the month and well into May. I explained in my letters home that I was working many nights as some of our staff had days off and others had vacation time coming.

Gerry returned from Calcutta in the middle of May bringing with him three typewriters he had bought from the American Red Cross. On May 20th, George and I left the Ritz and moved in with Gerry as he took over his flat. So we had another luxurious abode until Gerald's wife, Penny, and their two children, Sharon and Terry, arrived in Bombay at the end of June. To celebrate leaving our rooms at the Ritz, we threw a housewarming party. The party was largely George's. We had 26 guests, and George reported that they consumed seven quarts of whiskey and four quarts of gin. Most of the American Consulate was at the party.

Our social life continued throughout the summer, and the welcome monsoon rains helped cool the hot, humid weather. With Gerry back from his trips to New Delhi and Calcutta, the office was running smoothly. I had to report to the family on two big parties. One was a picnic hosted by Don Wenzel, the head of Firestone in India, for Frances Page, a secretary at the Consulate who was leaving for home. The trip was on a large boat to the Elephanta Caves, which are on one of the islands in the Bombay harbor. Don supplied a wonderful lunch of cold chicken along with liberal cold drinks. Don had snared a 35-gallon drum and filled it with ice to cool the beer, soda, and gin.

The other big party was a swimming party at the Willingdon Sports Club hosted by Santha Rama Rau and a colleague of hers, Frene Talyarkhan, who edited a weekly magazine. We swam and danced by the side of the pool until 1 a.m. and then transferred to a flat on the top of Malabar Hill where there was more dancing, eating, and drinking champagne for the rest of the evening. I got home at 5 a.m. and heard later that the party didn't end until 8 a.m.

George Small sailed for home on the *President Polk* in the middle of June, so we had to give up the Consulate jeep. As the car George had ordered had not yet arrived, Gerry and I spent the next few weeks riding buses and taxis. I wrote that taxis were getting expensive.

About this time I was asking for another raise in pay, although I wrote home that I was earning enough to live comfortably in Bombay. I had been getting $150 per month for living expenses in addition to an expense account of about $70 per month for incidental entertainment and taxi fares. In addition I drew 99 rupees a month (about $30) and sent the rest of my pay to my family to be banked at home. Toward the end of June, Gerry's family arrived and I moved into the Taj Mahal Hotel, where I would live for the next month.

July was a busy month. After the negotiations in New Delhi and Simla with the British Cabinet Mission, both the Indian Congress and the Muslim League held separate meetings in Bombay. Both Gerry and I attended most of the Muslim League meetings, with Gerry writing most of the stories.

Sent to cover the meetings were two photographers, David Davis of Acme News Photos and Max Desfor of Associated Press. Dave and Max had been friendly competing newsmen in the Philippines, and they stayed at the Taj Mahal Hotel where I was staying that July. Acme Photos at the time worked closely with United Press, so I would pass on messages for Davis from his New York office and send Dave's pictures on to London. Both Dave and Max, like so many photographers I met over the years, were great people to be with. They were good newsmen and full of fun. The two would go together to cover the meetings, and as a United Press correspondent I found myself going with them. Both were slight of stature—Max about 5'6" and Dave only a little taller. So when I was with them at six feet and almost 200 pounds, they would get me to carry their camera cases, at the time heavy with Speed Graphic cameras. (It was only much later that photographers began using small 35mm cameras.) They kidded me that I was their gofer. But it also was, for me, a learning experience watching two professionals frame their shots and wait patiently for the angles they were looking for.

Max told me that in the Philippines, he and Dave had sometimes worked together. At one time, there was a story to be covered north of Manila at the same time that there was a story to be covered south of Manila. Dave and Max agreed to cooperate. Max went north and Dave went south, and each shot extra film. When they returned, they exchanged the extra shots. Max told me that the New

York office never figured out how he had managed to be in two places at the same time.

In Bombay, I usually accompanied the two photographers on the stories we were covering. When the Congress opened the meeting in July 1946 I went to the opening session with Max, who took the picture of Nehru and Gandhi that was to become the standard picture of the two Indian leaders. He took several shots, and one of the photos was later used as the design for an Indian postage stamp.

When I began writing these memoirs, I contacted Max, still hale and hearty at 92, to ask if by any chance Dave had shot the famous picture. Max sent me an e-mail to set the record straight:

> I dug through a lot of clippings I had stashed away and finally came up with the exact date, July 6, 1946, when I made the photos of Nehru and Gandhi at the All India Congress Party in Bombay. To make sure we are on the right page and an accurate account for your book, here is my recall of the events at the time. The report of the India Navy mutiny is what triggered my hasty departure from Manila to get to India. I arrived in Calcutta but couldn't get any further because all air transport was grounded. The old cliché about being in the right place at the right time happened to me. While anxiously sitting out the air traffic situation, fighting between Hindus and Moslems broke out and I happened to be on the spot when the slaughtering (in Calcutta) took place. When order was restored, I went to Bombay and then to New Delhi. Some time later, while in Delhi, I got the necessary credentials and arrangements to cover the AICP convention in Bombay. It was not that Dave couldn't get his visa to India but as a matter of fact he got to Bombay where we had a great reunion. He got here too late, however, to get his credentials and couldn't get into the meetings. That is when we did our "buddy" thing and I gave him a few of my negatives. He filed "his photos" only after I was positive my radio photo transmissions were cleared in my London bureau.

THE FAMOUS PHOTOGRAPH

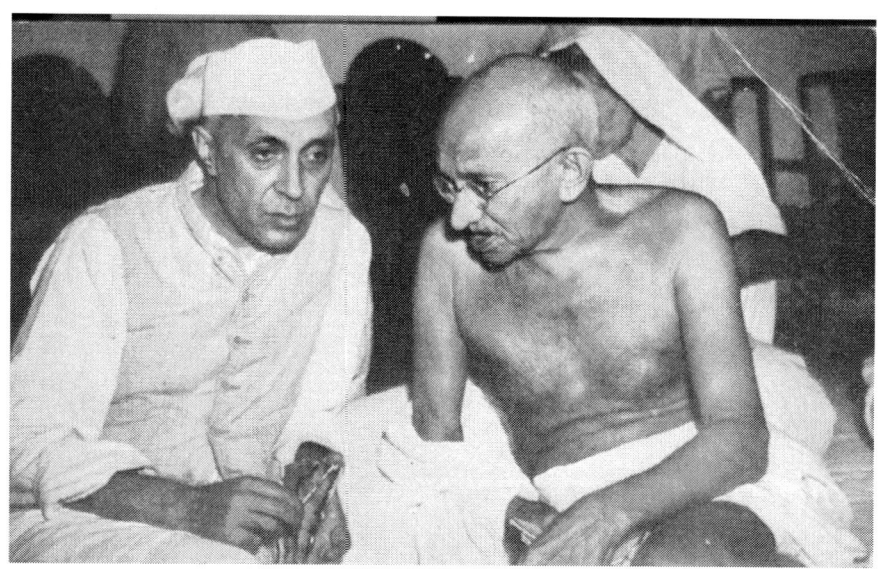

Jawaharlal Nehru with Mohandas Gandhi. Both photos were taken by Max Desfor, but Max gave the negative of the top photo to his friend Dave Davis of Acme News Photos.

CAMERA Angles

By IRVING DESFOR
AP Newsfeatures

The Pulitzer Prize for News Photography has always been considered the top honor for a photographer in the United States.

There is another, even rarer honor. That honor is for a government to design a stamp from a photograph.

It was with a great deal of pride, therefore, that I learned that my brother, Max Desfor, has now attained that double achievement. A photograph that he took as an Associated Press staff photographer in 1946 of Indian leaders Pandit Nehru and Mohandas Gandhi is the basis for a commemorative stamp recently issued by the Indian government. He was awarded the Pulitzer Prize in 1951 for his coverage of the Korean War exemplified by a scene of Korean natives, with their possessions on their backs, scrambling over the broken girders of a bombed-out bridge.

Only one other photographer has attained both plateaus of distinction. Joe Rosenthal, also an AP photographer, won the Pulitzer Prize in 1945 for his memorable picture of Marines raising the American flag on Iwo Jima. That same photograph was used as the basis for a U.S. stamp some years later.

Usually, governments give little credit or recognition to photographers when stamps are made from their photos. Unfortunately, in the case of the Nehru-Gandhi commemorative currently issued by India, there is presently no recognition at all of the source of the original photograph.

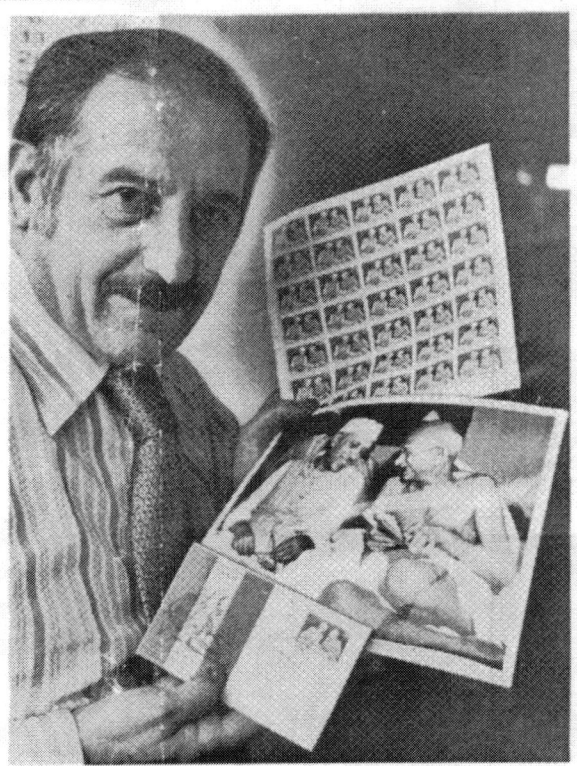

HONORED. The government of India issued a commemorative stamp designed from a photograph made by Max Desfor, AP Asian photo editor. He holds a block of the new stamps and the photo of Pandit Nehru and Mohandas Gandhi which he took July 6, 1946, at an All-India Congress meeting.

But an official government booklet obtained from the Indian Consulate describes the Nehru-Gandhi commemorative gether in the cause of national freedom and liberation," deserves itself to be freed and liberated from unknown identity.

Max Desfor in 1980 with his famous photo and the Indian postage stamp that was designed from it.

6

RIOTING IN CALCUTTA AND BOMBAY

◆

(July to August 1946)

After covering the Congress meeting, both Gerry and I attended the Muslim League meetings led by Mohammed Ali Jinnah. The speeches were quite spirited, bearing the theme that the Moslems trusted neither the British nor the Congress. Their meetings made good newspaper copy. Gerry wrote most of our stories, and I was merely a spectator at most of the meetings. However, with the police on alert for any disturbances, there were no serious incidents.

George's car arrived by ship, but it was so banged up when it was loaded that it had to be repaired and we didn't get it until the end of the month. The car had no spare tire and I spent time trying to find one, finally locating a spare tire in Calcutta. My friends at General Motors were helpful, and whenever the car needed repairs, I could always count on them. Because the car was registered in George's name, I got his consular gasoline ration. Gasoline had been rationed during the war and immediately after VJ day. I wrote home saying that the ration was to be doubled from the first of August and by the end of the year there would be no more rationing.

Gerry's car, a DeSoto, finally arrived during the first week of August. We spent several days walking the papers to the customs and tax offices. ("Walking the papers" meant literally taking the papers showing we had paid the taxes to the customs office before the car would be released.) It was the first DeSoto in Bombay and caused a small sensation.

At the same time new Fords began to make their appearance on the streets of Bombay. Five hundred of them had arrived in July and were just beginning to hit the streets. I learned that some were finding their way into the black market. The price from a dealer was 8,000 rupees (about $2500 U.S.), but the black market price was reported to be 18,000 rupees.

I posed for this picture with the Chevrolet I purchased with George Small in 1946.

During the first week of August, Columbia Broadcasting System (CBS) asked our office to get a three-minute interview with Mahatma Gandhi who had returned to Poona, some 90 miles south of Bombay. Because there was a telephone and telegraph strike going on at the time, we had difficulty acquiring the sound equipment and technical crew to record a three-minute interview.

Despite our troubles with the strikes, Gerry Rock finally managed to assemble the camera equipment and the technical sound and light men, and the news crew went to see the old man. But the Mahatma refused to be interviewed, so it was a lot of money wasted. We sent the bill for the expenses to CBS because they had asked for the story in the first place.

On August 16th, which the Muslim League had proclaimed "Direct Action Day," communal riots—Hindus against Muslims—broke out in Calcutta. Our

UP correspondent in Calcutta was Jim Michaels, and we, in Bombay, could get no messages to or from him via telephone or telegraph. After having had no contact with him for four days, I flew to Calcutta on Tata Airlines to make sure he was all right and to help where I could in covering the story.

While I was preparing this book for publication, I asked Jim for his recollections of the rioting in Calcutta. In an e-mail, Jim wrote:

> Back to Calcutta, 1946. To show its power in Calcutta, the Muslim League shut the town down—declared *hartal* (strike). The situation got out of hand. Muslims slaughtered a few Hindus, and the Hindus fought back with clubs, knives, fists, kicking people to death, slitting throats, bodies in heaps in the streets, males usually nude from the waist down. The mobs authenticated whether a male was Hindu or Muslim because the Muslims were circumcised.
>
> The police, unarmed and unsure of authority with the country on the verge of independence, simply stayed off the streets. It was mass murder, with both sides acting as much out of fear as out of anger. Martial law was declared by the Bengal government, but it had no means to enforce it. The Indian army was in the process of being disentangled between its Muslim and Hindu units, and the British forces were withdrawing in the ports for embarkation.
>
> On the second day I hitched on with a unit of the armed police and went on patrol with them in an open lorry. In those innocent days, there was no proliferation of firearms; the ordinary police constable carried only a lathi, firearms being a monopoly of the army and special police units. I was with an elite unit called the Army Police, gurkhas commanded by Anglo-Indian sergeants and carrying old Lee Enfields. I witnessed unforgettable sights—looting of dwindling grain supplies, large parts of the city burning, bloated corpses floating in the Hooghly, others decayed by the heat, being eaten by vultures in the city streets.
>
> One unforgettable vignette: A massed charge of 500 constables routed by bottle-throwing Hindus when the constables tried to clear the Howrah Bridge to let refugees (Muslims) reach the rail station where they sought safety in heavily Muslim East Bengal (now Bangladesh). The Hindus had the high ground, the roofs of the bastis (tenements) overlooking the bridge. The escape route remained blocked.
>
> The Armed Police NCOs would charge wealthy Hindus and Muslims to escort them to friendlier areas—1000 Rupees ($300), which was then a for-

tune. The poor folks simply stayed and died—pregnant women and children included. At last 10,000 perished, a tiny fraction of the number that would die in the next year's riots. A terrible foretaste.

I guess I was so excited I forgot to file frequently enough. I scarcely slept for two or three days—which is why you couldn't reach me by phone at the office or at my hotel. (The AP's Don Huth, my competitor, being more experienced, stayed closer to his office, his telephone, the cable office. He clobbered me on the news breaks, but I had much better color and sounds-and-smells stuff. I guess London UP had to pick the pegs from AP and they must have been furious. Harold Guard, wasn't it?)

I was on the streets, with these armed police. A city out of control, and the authorities helpless and hopeless.

Arriving at Dum Dum airport, I took the airline bus into the city. The bus traveled through areas where much of the killing had taken place. Although the most serious rioting had calmed down, there were still dead bodies, horribly bloated, on many intersections. The vultures were having a picnic. (I was told later that on the previous day the sky had been black with vultures converging on Calcutta.) The bus deposited me at the Great Eastern Hotel on Chowringee Street, and I was able to get to the office, which was only a few blocks away, to see Jim.

Of course, there is nothing like a riot to attract a bunch of newsmen. Among the correspondents were George Jones of *The New York Times,* Andy Freeman of the *New York Post,* Phil Talbot of the *Chicago Daily News,* Bob Sheplin of *Newsweek,* Dave Richardson of *Time,* Henry Keys of the *Daily Express* (London), Harry Standish of the *Sydney* (Australia) *Morning News,* and of course, Jim Michaels of the United Press and Don Huth of the Associated Press. We also had photographers: Max Desfor of the Associated Press, David Davis of Acme News Photo, and Margaret Bourke-White of *Life* magazine.

Fortunately Jim Michaels was working around the clock and managing without my help. I stayed at the Great Eastern Hotel for a few days. Then I met with photographer friends Max Desfor and Dave Davis, and we found a flat on Middleton Street. It was fairly comfortable living except that we had no cook and no food and we had to beat the curfew every night. We had all our meals at the hotels and restaurants that were open: The Great Eastern Hotel, the Grand Hotel, Firpo's Restaurant, and for three lunches a little Indian restaurant that served good Muslim food.

I wrote home saying that Calcutta was a "lousy place." The telephone system was old-fashioned, and during the troubles no one came to work so there was no telephone service. Taxi drivers, who were mostly Sikhs, refused to work for about five days, and then they would travel only in the predominantly Hindu areas of the city. Stores remained closed and the movies did only light business. Food got scarce but there was plenty of beer. In fact, the favorite pastime of correspondents was to gather in the lobby of the Great Eastern Hotel at 11 a.m. (when they began serving beer) and drink quietly until lunchtime. The beer was Canadian in quart bottles and very good. I remained in Calcutta, filing stories to back up Jim Michaels until the end of the month.

Although there was carnage all around us, American and British correspondents could travel freely throughout the city. The Hindus and Moslems who were killing each other ignored us. There were still some American troops in the city, but we didn't see many of them as they were restricted to quarters during the troubles.

After ten days, with the help of the British Army, Calcutta was quiet although the curfew would continue for several more weeks. I then returned to Bombay, taking the 36-hour train ride from Calcutta via Nagpur to Bombay. I arrived in Bombay on September 2nd, just in time to find the city erupting into violence.

Our United Press office worked day and night covering the story. The Police Commissioner ordered a curfew, but I had a reporter's pass and the rioters did not attack foreigners because we were not the enemy of either side. I patrolled the streets in the Chevrolet day and night with no one so much as threatening me. Occasionally I was able to see some of the actual rioting. One time I saw a wounded man lying prone on the street as his enemy, a Hindu youth, smashed his head with a bowling-ball-sized rock.

Curfew passes from the Deputy Commissioner of Police, Bombay.

Mostly we saw the results of a disturbance after it was over. It was very bloody. I visited the hospitals every day to watch the casualties coming in. Most of the trouble took place near Crawford Market and further toward the Victoria Gardens and then spread to the northern suburb of Parel where perhaps the worst outrage took place: a gang of about 300 Hindus burning a Muslim tomb and killing the seven men who were inside guarding it. At the time I predicted there would be more trouble in the near future in Bombay and unless the political leaders—Gandhi and Nehru for the Hindus and Mohammed Ali Jinnah for the Muslims—would meet to calm their supporters, the slaughter would erupt all over India. Fortunately, the Indian Army was being held in reserve.

After nine days of disturbances Bombay was quiet, although there was still a very noticeable tension. The Commissioner of Police extended the curfew for another two weeks. The curfew did not bother me, since our office had curfew passes. I wrote that Bombay was in really sad shape with "everyone looking over his shoulder. The rioting caused havoc among the business community and everyone is watching Delhi to see which way Mr. Jinnah is going to jump." I wrote that if the Muslims were responsible for the disturbances, they were pretty powerful to keep life in such a state. Crawford Market was a tough area, and everyone was going on short rations while prices were almost double. "All in all, it ain't healthy should you be a Muslim or a Hindu. We heathens seem to be in no danger at all" was my comment.

I still have the copy of the bulletins I sent the night of the first riots saying that the first reports stated that 40 persons were killed and 137 injured. I wrote home that we must have been doing something right on the coverage because we got cables of congratulations from both London and New York.

```
BULLETIN 1N 13 bulletin 2225 hlavacek bombay 31010 communal riots broke out
suddenly in bombay sunday night and first reports said forty persons were killed and
onehundred thirtyseven injured. MORE. UP LN 13.

RUSH L   14. rush 30226   hlavacek first outbreak came shortly after seven pm
police
       including full armed units were called out in full strength.


RUSH ln 15   rush 30225   h avacek third outbreaks came in usual trouble spots
of lal baug  lal baugh bhendi bhendi bazar null null bazar and round temple all
of which have been scenes of bloody encounters in past police fired on rioters nineteen
tim s using up fiftynine rounds of ammunition atop three cases of arson and one of
looting were reported para curfew was imposed from seven pm to seven am for seven
days in areas where trouble occurred.

OIL-PRESS.                         END.
0300?. JLR.
```

News bulletins describing the Bombay riots.

In the middle of August, before I had left for Calcutta, Gerry and I had finally managed to rent a fine new office after eighteen months of trying. We were pleased with the location, on Apollo Street in a building that had once housed the *Morning Standard* newspaper. I wrote that because of the riots, we had trouble getting it renovated and "it still looks like a barn, but we have a big sign out front and in a few weeks it will look like a million dollars (slight exaggeration)."

Pictures taken with Gerry Rock at our UP office on Apollo Street in Bombay. (The photographer was Dave Davis of Acme Photos.)

We had a growing staff. In addition to three radio operators, we had hired an office manager and three Indian copy editors plus our messengers who took the news copy to our newspaper clients on bicycles. Also, Gerry was negotiating with the new government in Delhi about getting land lines so we could buy surplus teletype machines from the American Army and begin sending our news throughout India on teletype lines.

7

BOMBAY AFTER THE RIOTS

◆

(September to December 1946)

After the serious rioting diminished, life in Bombay struggled to a nervous peace. The curfew remained in effect and there was another outbreak of rioting in October. The curfew applied only to areas of the city that had the worst of the rioting, which did not include the section of the city where the Americans and other foreigners lived. The only hardship—if one could call it that—was that the government had issued an order prohibiting the sale of intoxicating liquor which was blamed for helping to foment the trouble. I wrote home that the order really did not affect the foreign community because most westerners had a big cache of liquor and could drink in the privacy of their homes and at their private clubs. The Bombay Government also issued liquor ration coupons for foreigners. Foreigners could buy one case of beer per month, and it was possible to buy Canadian brands of hard liquor from time to time at the hotels and clubs.

We were very busy with United Press activities. Gerry Rock spent several weeks that fall in New Delhi negotiating with the Government to allow us to have land lines so we could better serve our client newspapers in the large cities of New Delhi, Calcutta, and Madras. We were also negotiating with the departing American Army to buy teleprinters at greatly reduced prices.

Our United Press office now was staffed with several Indian editors, and I spent many hours checking on the incoming files. As most of our newspaper clients were morning papers, we were busiest from nine o'clock to midnight, and I would staff that period several days a week. Also we were negotiating to receive news directly from New York because we were serving business interests with fast, accurate, stock market prices. I noted in a letter that "our commercial news business is booming."

Since I was working mainly nights, I began playing golf in the early mornings. I had become friendly with two Scottish bankers, Bill Rae and Bill Needham. Both were very good amateur golfers. Bill Rae was a scratch golfer, and Bill Needham played to a two handicap. I explained in letters home that in Scotland, they begin playing golf as soon as they can walk (much like the phrase at that time that Indiana boys begin playing basketball as soon as they can crawl). The two bankers had a small British car, and we would take off before sunrise, drive 12 miles to the golf course at Chembur, and tee off as soon as it was light. We could usually play 10 to 14 holes and then head back to the city. I wrote that playing with these two golfers improved my game tremendously. I rationalized that because I was no longer playing basketball and baseball in India, my exercise now was golf. In addition to playing during the week, I managed to spend most weekends on the golf course.

In a letter home, I explained that November is the beginning of the Bombay winter, the best season of the year. Each day is cool, the sun is out and the temperature hovers in the 70s. With the extreme heat subsiding in November of 1946, the political temperature also declined. The meetings between Nehru and Gandhi helped cool tempers—so much so that the Bombay government began lifting the curfew that had been in effect for months. I wrote that the curfew had lifted for a few hours and citizens could be on the street until 10 p.m.

The American Women's Club hosted a Thanksgiving Day dance with almost all the Americans in Bombay attending: about 250 persons. In a letter home, I noted that it seemed that the American parties in Bombay were the liveliest.

This was to be my second Christmas in India, and I spent both Christmas Eve and Christmas Day with Gerry Rock and his family. We trimmed the tree and greeted guests as they came by to wish us a merry Christmas with spirits. I stayed the night and was awakened on Christmas morning by a drum and bugle corps that went marching through the neighborhood. We all got up early to watch Gerry's two little ones, Sharon and Terry, tear open their packages under the Christmas tree.

In the afternoon, we made the rounds of visiting our American friends, feeling sorry for ourselves because our telephone calls to the United States did not go through. My call came through four days after Christmas. When it came through, no one at home could recognize my voice. My sister claimed I sounded like an Englishman. At the time, one booked his call to the U.S. and then waited until the operator made connections. The telephone company was so backed up that only a few calls made it on Christmas day.

New Year's was also a gala time. I spent New Year's Eve at the home of Al and Katherine Beaver. Al was the sales manager in India for Firestone, and many of the guests were also working for Firestone. In a letter to my Army friends, I recorded some of the guests whom they knew: Doc and Mrs. Palmer, Ralph and Mrs. Schaefer, George and Margaret Beatty, Don Wenzel—all of Firestone. And on New Year's Day, I attended the American Association's annual Eggnog Party at the Willingdon Sports Club. It seemed that no matter how late, or early, people had been up, they showed up for the party at 11 a.m. That afternoon, I played a round of golf with three of my friends.

I was looking forward to the new year—1947—because I had the promise of a home leave. I was hoping to be at home for three months in the spring.

8

THE SWAMI STORY

◆

(January to March 1947)

As we began the new year, the Bombay racing season was in full swing. I wrote that I rarely went to the races, preferring to play golf, but racing had been a big part of British colonial life and the Bombay Race Course would be welcomed anywhere in the world. I noted that I did bet one day on a "sure thing." The horse belonged to one of our United Press clients. (It came in last.) Because of the riots in the fall, the racing season was late starting so in order to get all the meetings completed, there were races every Wednesday and Saturday. It was next to impossible to get a taxi on Wednesday or Saturday.

With the New Year, more new American cars began appearing on the streets. The Ford Motor Company had got the jump on the rest, and Fords were seen all over the city. Occasionally one would see a new Packard, Plymouth, DeSoto, Chrysler, Buick, and others, but not very many. There were many new British cars which were much smaller than the American models. I wrote that they looked more like "roller skates."

The New Year also saw the arrival of the first TWA planes to Bombay. In the beginning there were two flights a week. The first planes were DC-4s. There was a big cocktail party to celebrate the inaugural flight. (TWA had the right to land in Bombay, while Pan American had the landing rights in Karachi and Delhi.)

We looked forward to expanding our United Press service. We expected to be able to get new land lines and to better compete with Reuters, which was the established news agency in India.

I continued to go to the movies with the American representatives. Arthur Doyle, the Twentieth Century Fox representative, invited me to a private showing of "Three Little Girls in Blue" followed by a good Indian dinner. The next night I went with Arthur, again, to see "The Green Years."

Although most of Bombay was quiet, from time to time, there were outbreaks of violence. In late January I reported that one Thursday afternoon I was out with the police and military in the disturbed area. I got some very good pictures of the mobs looting shops and also of the police firing as well as a good story that I filed later in the evening. I finished filing about 11 p.m. I told my family that at no time was I in any danger since the military and police were always nearby. I added that I was pleased with my news photos and shipped them to Acme News Photos. (In a later letter I reported that the pictures I had sent on the January 23rd riots had been bought by Acme. I had not expected to sell them, but I received a letter from Acme saying they were sending $25 to my account.)

My consulate friend, George Small, returned to Bombay in January so I went back to sharing the car with him. However, I wrote that we both usually went to the same places and we were sharing a room at the Ritz Hotel. We continued looking for an apartment, without success.

At that time I was hoping to leave in March to be home to watch my brother, Frank, graduate from Carleton in June. But it was not to be. In a subsequent letter I broke the news that I wouldn't be leaving in March as I had planned. Jim Michaels, our correspondent in New Delhi, had to go home urgently in May on family matters. It involved an estate, and if he couldn't get leave he would have had to resign, which would have made it impossible for me to leave. Gerry Rock was in New Delhi and arranged for Mike to fly home, finish his business, and return quickly. As soon as he arrived back I was to go on leave. We were expecting breaking news in India and it would be a busy time.

In the same letter, I had good news. I finally got a raise in pay. It was only ten bucks a week. I wrote that it would go into effect the week of February 3rd and the fact I got it at all was unexpected, since the United Press was on a "economy drive." I had been recommended for a raise for a year.

On February 12, 1947, I wrote to my friends "Stinky" Davis and "Dirty Dick" Boren describing the wedding reception for Roshan Botliwala and Sharouk Sabavala:

> The reason I thought of you two characters is that on Monday night the Chota Sahib (George Small) and I, along with about one thousand other guests, gathered at the little house on Ridge Road (the place where you two and I attained notoriety by appearing in dhotis) to attend the wedding reception for Roshan Batliwala and Sharouk Sabavala.
>
> The party had many aspects of the time a year or so ago when the three of us attended—by that I meant that good scotch was flowing just as freely this

time as last in spite of the recently imposed high prices because of prohibition. And this time there were respectable people there as well as the usual gathering of young folk. That lovely garden—the place where Dirty Dick almost disrupted relations with our British cousins (remember) was full of chairs, tables, and divans upon which sat the rich Parsi families of Bombay. There was a big platform, complete with colored lights upon which there was a performance of Indian dancing later in the evening.

The grounds of the house, the big trees, and the house itself were all gaily decorated with colored lights, which gave the whole place an aspect not unlike a Christmas tree. You could see the place from Marine Drive (about three miles away).

The bride, of course, looked beautiful, dressed in a silver sari.

This, mind you, was the reception. The actual wedding with Parsi priests took place in the morning. I gathered that Sabavala was not too keen on that part of the ceremony because he got to his own wedding about an hour late.

As for music, the family just about moved the Taj Mahal Hotel up to Malabar Hill. The Taj's orchestra was there, the Taj's manager was there to see that all went well, and several of the Taj's stewards and waiters were there to serve drinks to the thirsty guests. There was also a magic show.

Another difference: the Chota Sahib and myself arrived in a jeep. Our Chevrolet had a little trouble with the clutch and was in the garage.

We knew only a few of the guests. Our friend Santha Rama Rau arrived late and didn't stay long. We stayed until early in the morning, then a group of us left to Karaka's flat where we danced until some time in the morning. (George tells me it was about four when we arrived back at our suite at the Ritz.)

Roshan promised to get some invitations so I could mail them to you.

Best, Check (the bad one)

My sister Marie was planning to visit me in India after she graduated from college. In a letter to Marie in March 1947, I wrote the following:

India is still a country which is certainly not peaceful. I don't know how much you get in your newspapers but of late there was been widespread unrest in all parts of the country and Bombay has been under curfew now for almost a week. The curfew should end on Sunday, but there are still cases of stabbings going on so I expect the curfew to be extended. Up on the northwest frontier and in the Punjab it has been even worse this time with people getting killed right and left. The main danger is that fear is spreading and there are refugees now in almost every part of the country. In Bengal, the Hindus are leaving; in Bihar, the Muslims are leaving; in the Frontier, Hindus and Sikhs are leaving, and in Bombay and the Punjab nobody is leaving, but the poor of both communities don't dare to wander outside their respective areas. As yet, we foreigners can go anywhere at any time. In our last Bombay troubles the opposing communities had regular pitched street battles, throwing rocks and soda water bottles which make good grenades when they explode on impact. Also a more alarming feature was the appearance of homemade bombs. I haven't been able to find out how they are made but I have picked up a couple of the pieces of shrapnel that are enclosed in the bomb. I have a hunch they are made from cigarette tins. In any case, I don't mind them throwing rocks but when they start using firearms and bombs, that's another thing.

However, young lady, I think that we will continue to have a good time here. We have enough to eat, have a car, and can play golf as often as we can get away from the office.

In one of my letters home dated April 2, 1947, I wrote the following account of an unusual incident:

Weekends have been fun, especially the last two. There is a little story connected with it which really starts on Saturday the 22nd (of March). On that day George wanted to go racing so I got a taxi and rode to the Beavers' and they took me to the golf course for a game. I played with Al Beaver and we finished early. He happened to mention while we were sitting around having drinks that this was the day a yogi was to get buried for 24 hours. "This I gotta see," I said, visualizing a story that maybe nobody else knew about. So we left, meanwhile, taking Ted and Velma Ham, who live with the Beavers in the Firestone flat, in the car. Kay Beaver was sick that day so she didn't get in on all the fun. Anyway, we found the place where the Yogi, one Ramanand Swami, was to be buried. We found it because there was a mob of about five thousand people gathered to watch. Al parked the car outside a low wall which surrounded the field and we made our way to the dais from which speeches were being made. I had my camera along so was taking a few pictures. However, as we elbowed our way through the crowds, I noticed on the dais most of Bombay's local press coups plus Reuters and the Associated Press. So we climbed aboard and as we did so, the dais began to cave in. We stayed on it though since everyone else jumped off and we found ourselves right next to the swami, a nicely built guy with long hair and dressed in a brownish silk toga-like affair.

Below the dais was a cement pit, six by five by four feet and covered except for a small space for him to descend into it. As the swami left the dais to descend, the crowd went wild, pushing, shoving and yelling. One poor old man was pushed into the sacrificial fire burning in front of the cement-lined pit. (He wasn't burned badly.) The swami figured this was too much for his peace of mind, so he disappeared over the back fence. The promoters of the show said he might come back later so I made my way back to the car to tell Al (who had left before I did) not to wait for me, but by the time I got back there, there was no car so I figured they had gone. I found Duncan Hooper, the Reuters correspondent, and made arrangements to get a ride back to town in his taxi. Then about fifteen minutes later who should appear but Al in his car and the Hams had the following story to tell.

It seems that as the swami came over the wall with a couple of his disciples, the crowds, who revered him, wanted to get close to touch him. So they [the swami and his disciples] came upon the car and asked Al if he would let the swami in. Al said "Sure," and the swami and two of his disciples piled into the back seat on top of Ted and Velma Ham, both of whom were in golf togs. Velma, who is a beautiful Memphis gal, was dressed in shorts and sweater and I guess it's still a toss-up as to who was the more surprised, the swami or Velma. When the crowd saw the swami get into Al's car, they swarmed all over it, trying to get in. Velma said they piled over the wall like ants. The Hams succeeded in getting all the windows and doors closed, and Al drove through the crowd, luckily not hitting anyone. They took the swami to the home where he was staying and then they came back for me.

We decided that we had some time before the swami could regain his composure so we went back to the Beavers' for a drink. While there we checked by telephone to find out that the interment of the swami would be postponed until the next week.

Then I called George, who had been at the races with a ship captain, Reynolds Miller. He, the captain, suggested that we all go aboard his ship for dinner and the Beavers and Hams thought that was a good idea. So George came for me and then Duncan Hopper and I went down to our offices to file our stories. Then the ship captain said it might be a better idea if he went down to the ship and got the food and we ate at the Beavers' since their flat was much cooler than the ship would be. So we had the elements of a party. George and the skipper went to the ship in our Chevrolet, and Al's chauffeur drove me to the office to file the story. Duncan Hooper came with me and I dropped him at his office. Then we all gathered at the Beavers' for a big buffet dinner of American ham, baloney, cheese, American white bread, Coca Cola, ice cream and all the trimming such as olives, pickles, etc. Al played the piano, and we sang and danced the evening away.

Sunday, I took the skipper golfing with me, and then after golf we all went to Ray Crews' shack at Juhu Beach for lunch and the afternoon. Again we sponged on the skipper, he having his cook making seven southern fried chickens. After a big lunch, I took a nap, played a friendly game of blackjack and went for a swim. That night I got back to town to find out that my night editor had been in an accident and so I went to work at midnight.

On the next Saturday comes another episode in the swami story. The swami was to be buried at six, so I had to get my lunch quickly and Arthur Doyle and I went to the golf club for a quick round. I left Arthur at the club and went to the burying grounds which this time were well criss-crossed with bamboo fences to keep the crowd back. I had no trouble getting in—one of the advantages of the press—and got very close to the cement-lined pit so that I could watch all that went on. I naturally didn't believe that anyone, swami or not swami, could be buried in that pit for 24 hours and still be alive. There were a few speeches about the science of yoga and how it was an ancient art. The speeches were in Hindustani and spectators near me translated for me. They said that when a yogi goes into "Samadhi" he is able to stop his breathing, his circulation, and even his heart—mind over matter. At the appointed time the swami descends into the pit, sits down in yogi fashion, legs folded in front of him, hands resting on his knees, palms up and looking straight ahead with eyes closed. The masons arrive, place a board over the opening, and seal the pit with cement. And I mean SEAL.

I went to the office and filed a story.

On Sunday, I played golf at the Willingdon Club with the rest of the Americans. I hadn't had much sleep Saturday night because I worked at the office until 5 a.m. Arthur Doyle came barging into my hotel room at 8:15. After our golf game we had our lunch of chicken curry and rice. We then went to Juhu and George had invited another ship captain along. I spent the afternoon resting in the cool ocean breezes and then hurried to the grounds where the swami was to be disinterred. This time there were about 10,000 spectators, but the promoters had enough police and volunteers to keep the crowds from surging forward. Again, I had no difficulty getting in, and by this time the entire press corps knew me: "the big American from United Press." This time I had my movie camera to record the event. At 5:10, just 23 hours after the swami had been buried in his crypt, his disciple said he had a telepathic message from the swami that he should loosen one side of the crypt. The disciple said that it was to let air in to allow respiration. Promptly at six, the two boards were removed and I got a first look and there was the swami still sitting in the same position as when he was interred 24 hours previously. It was amazing. He looked much like a wax dummy. Four of his disciples entered the pit and held a cloth over him while the workmen removed the rest of the cement from the top of the crypt. They then lifted him out on the wooden platform he had been sitting on, the swami not moving and completely oblivious to everything. He remained sitting as the wooden platform was lifted to the dais so the crowd could see him. The crowd remained silent in awe. His brown silk toga, which was spotless and dry when he entered the crypt, was now wet and clinging to his body. As soon as he was placed on the dais, his disciples began gently rubbing the top of his head and his back while one felt for his pulse. Within five minutes he slowly moved, then opened his eyes and smiled at the crowd, which roared their approval. Women came forward and garlanded him and placed a reddish paste on his forehead—a ritual of the Hindu religion. It was the most amazing feat I had ever seen and, I believed, it was not a magician's trick. The swami stayed in that tomb without air, water, or food for 24 hours. Dr. Bharucha, a noted Bombay heart specialist and the father of one of my friends, was there, and I asked him about the feat. He said it was the first time he had seen it and that modern medical science could not explain it. He said that the swami was going to put on a performance for the medical profession of Bombay sometime in the near future. I plan to be there when he does it. I'm a believer now. I think the swami can stop his heart and breathing—at least slow it down—how, I don't know. But Dr. Bharucha said that an ordinary human being could not have lived more than two or three hours in that tomb.

With the swami back to life, I returned to Juhu Beach, picked up George and the skipper and returned to town to file my story. After filing the story I took the skipper and we returned to the Beavers'. This skipper had brought Kay Beaver out to India a year ago, so we had to have another impromptu party. And we did. I was full of my yogi story because it made a deep impression on me. We sang and danced and finally ate at almost midnight. Then I went back to the office to work the night shift.

I no sooner got back than I found that riots had once again broken out so out I went to the affected area. The police had things pretty much under control by that time, so I filed only a small story. But the disturbances were particularly vicious this time. The usual trouble spots which I toured had more debris than usual. Big rocks and broken glass littered the streets. A soda water bottle, when shaken and then thrown, explodes on impact and acts like a grenade.

I ended my letter with this paragraph:

The weekend of the first swami show I lost my camera. Usually I am careless with my things, but it seems that when I'm that way I never lose anything. This time I was taking care, so I thought, and I still lost it. I had Al Beaver's chauffeur that night, and he brought me to the office to file my story. While I was in the office (a matter of fifteen minutes), I left the camera in the car with him. However, one of those things happened: a crowd of drunken seamen came along and the chauffeur very wisely took the keys with him and got out of the car. I got down to find them sitting in the car. I got rid of them, but when I looked for my camera a while later, it had disappeared. Oh well, now I can get another one on my next trip.

BULLETIN LN 8 BULLETIN 1814. Hlavacek bombay 30194. Yogi ramanand swami disinter
red alive six pm six pm today after twentyfour hours in cement crypt . UP LN 8.

RUSH LN 9. rush 30182. Hlavacek add swamis disciples let first air into crypt
since sixpm saturday by lossening cement and only one of supporting wooden boards
stop they explaned that his was to allow respiration to begin again as swami had not
breathed during his interment para as other boards removed e looked into pit and
saw swami sitting motionless in same position he took yesterday before he was sealed
in stop his legs were folded with his arms resting on knees and eyes closed para swami
was still sitting in apparent trance as he brought out of crypt on platform in full
view of waiting crowd ten thousand stop after full five minutes while one disciple
gentley rubbed top his head and another felt for pulse swami showed signs life.

RUSH LN 10. rush 30183. Hlavacek third swami appeared none worse for his twentyfour
hours ordeal although his greyish brown robe which yesterday was dry and neat was wet
dash probably from crypts dampness para doctor phiroze phiroze c intila c bharucha
bharucha noted bombay heart specialist witnessed swamis disenterment stop he said
medical science could not repeat not explain feat which would have killed ordinary
person within two or at most three hours para swami has promised to demonstrate his
powers before bombay members of medican profession in near future para swami ramandand
came from ashram ashram at nan sarovar nan sarovar in himalayas on fund raising tour
to spread yogi training most persons doubted swamis claims he could stop breathing
and even cut off his heart circulation but after todays demonstration even eye who
went to see feat as scoffer came away believer. UP LN 10.

This is my story on the swami who survived entombment.

Clips from the swami story.

9

MADRAS AND COLOMBO

◆

(April 1947)

In the middle of April, I got away from the Bombay troubles for a business trip to Madras and Colombo. The Indian editors were meeting in Madras and Gerry Rock, who would normally go, wanted to stay in Bombay because his two little children were sick. I flew to Madras on Tata Airlines, a very pleasant trip because Tata has very good looking hostesses aboard to take care of the passengers. Our Madras correspondent had reserved a room for me at the Connemara Hotel. It was hot—in Madras, in the hotel room, everywhere. The Connemara was a good hotel, and it was built for air conditioning. But they had not yet been able to get the air conditioners, so there was very little air circulating in the rooms. Fortunately the rooms had ceiling fans. I took a bath and then went to lunch to meet the competition. The Associated Press had sent two men to the conference. (The United Press was usually outnumbered by AP, so it was really no surprise.)

On my first day in Madras I went to see two of our good clients, the *Hindu* and *Indian Express*. I visited with Mr. K. Srinivasan of the *Hindu* and then with Mr. Ramnath Goenka of the *Indian Express*. Then for the next three days I did nothing but see newspaper publishers and editors. My work was fruitful, as we gained another client in Madras and I sold some features and comic strips. (I also spent a lot of money: it cost the UP about $30 a day to have me go on this trip.)

Madras was not a very good city, at least from my point of view. It was spread out over a lot of territory, and I wrote that "it takes a long time to get anyplace and there is not much there when you get there." But it was a fairly clean city, as Indian cities went. The terrain was very flat, but there was a beautiful beach to compensate for the drabness.

After attending the session, I spent another two days visiting prospective clients and then took off for Colombo on the island of Ceylon. Now *this* was a good city—at least I thought so for the short time I was there. I went for business this time, but I planned to make another trip later for pleasure on the strength of what I learned.

The flight down was comfortable again. The Tata plane from Bombay to Madras continued on to Colombo. It took only two and a half hours to make the journey and then it took another two hours to go through Customs when I got to Ceylon. I had a rather funny incident. Being careless with my belongings, I never carried much money with me. When I arrived in Colombo I had only 167 rupees with me because I didn't expect to stay long. The young Customs officer, after examining my passport to check on my visa, asked me how much money I had and I told him. He said, "Oh, but that's not enough. You are an American. You must have 600 rupees (about $200) to come in here." I laughed and said, "Well, what do you want me to do, climb back on the plane and fly back to India?"

He laughed and said no, telling me that he would cut some red tape for me. The rules and regulations said I had to have 600 rupees, but he asked if I had any friends in Colombo and I mentioned a couple, one of them being the editor of the *Times of Ceylon,* so he was assured I would not be a derelict.

The airline helped me get a room at the Galle Face Hotel, the best one in the city. It was a beauty, a large red stone building on the sea. I didn't have much time to know it well because I was so busy.

I dined that first night with Frank Moraes, the editor of the *Times of Ceylon,* and then spent the rest of the night sleeping, as it was much cooler in Colombo than it had been in Madras. The Galle Face actually did not give me as good a room as I would have liked. It was an inside one instead of one facing the sea. The hotel had a swimming pool, but I didn't have time to go swimming. I decided to save that for next time.

The next day I worked hard for the United Press. Our string correspondent, Austin de Silva, came for me in the morning. We had breakfast together, and he brought me up to date about the newspaper situation in Ceylon. At that time the United Press did not serve any papers there, and we naturally wanted to swell our coffers.

I had to spend the morning checking with the medical officer—the country was strict about vaccinations—and then the passport officer because I had to get a visa to go back to India. Then I did some shopping and bought my sister some wooden dolls dressed in the costumes of the peoples of Ceylon.

Austin de Silva and I had lunch at the Great Oriental Hotel, the other big hotel of the city. The Galle Face was the more attractive of the two, but the

G.O.H.—as everyone called it—was the more commercial hotel. Then, with Austin, I went to see the Associated Newspapers, publisher of four papers, to pitch our United Press service. I thought that I sold them, but I wouldn't know for a week or so.

Then I met with Frank Moraes to try and sell him the service. He had a special problem and we hadn't yet figured out how to serve him, but we had a good discussion. Then I was off to the airline office to get my ticket to fly back the next morning. That evening I had drinks with Frank and some Firestone people—the Russ Jepsons—who were friends of his. We all went for a Chinese dinner and then to the Jepsons for coffee later. It was late when I finally returned to the hotel.

The next morning I took off for Madras, where I still had some business to complete. The hostess on the plane was very attractive—my roommate, George Small was dating her at the time—so we had a lot to talk about on the two-and-a-half-hour flight.

Back in Madras I had a lot of fun with the Customs officer. I had marked my declaration, "personal effects" but then decided that as long as the dolls had only cost me 55 rupees ($15 U.S.) that I would tell him I had them. He asked, "Are they of wooden manufacture?" I said, "Yes." "Well, then," he said, "you shall have to pay duty. How much did they cost?" I told him and he said, "You will have to pay 22 rupees." I said, "Oh no, not me. In that case they only cost 30 rupees." He said, "Then that will cost your 10 rupees. How's that?" "Still too much," I said. He finally told me, "You put down the value at 15 rupees and pay me four rupees eight annas" (about $1.50), and I agreed. It was all very friendly.

I did another afternoon's work in Madras, and the next morning I boarded the plane for Bombay. George and the hostess of the day before met me, and we went for tea. Then I saw Gerry for a while and went the office.

By this time George and I were living in a flat which we rented from Walter and Katie Langhammer. Walter Langhammer was the art editor of the *Times of India* and an accomplished portrait painter in oils. Walter's wife Katie was Jewish, and the Langhammers were living in India to escape Hitler. George had moved into the flat on April 23, and I moved in as soon as I returned from Madras. I wrote, "It's a great location and I'm sitting here now at home typing this letter with the cool sea breezes whipping the paper about. This flat overlooks the sea and we always have a cool breeze on the verandah." Then, too, we had our air-conditioned bedroom, which I found especially pleasant after trying to sleep in hot hotel rooms for the previous ten days.

No sooner had I gotten home, shaved and dressed than George's guests arrived. George had invited two American girls from the Consulate, a new couple in the Consulate, and the Lynn Clarkes, another young couple. The Clarkes had been playing golf with our friends the Beavers and the Hams, and they called from the golf course saying they would be late. Kay Beaver called and asked, "What are you doing?" and asked all of us to come to their house. So after dinner we all gathered at the Beavers'. And what a party it turned out to be! Dancing, singing, piano playing. Al Beaver was a good party pianist, and Helen Howden and Jeanie Fogg, the Consulate girls, also helped out. The party broke up at about two in the morning.

But it seemed that there always had to be some disappointments. Just as I was planning to have a really good two months of fun, I found out that I would have to go to New Delhi around May 10th and fill in for Jim Michaels while he went home for two months. Gerry said it would have compensation as it was a critical time and I would get my byline in the newspapers. I wrote, "I have no ambitions that way. I like my comfort. Still I shall be going up there."

10

NEW DELHI

◆

(May to July 1947)

I flew to New Delhi on Tata Airlines on the morning of May 12th just in time to join the farewell party for Jim Michaels hosted by the foreign correspondents in Delhi. I would be living in Jim's room at the Imperial Hotel, which also served as the United Press office for the capital. From that room we distributed the United Press service to New Delhi's newspapers. Jim flew home the next day, and the business of covering the news was in my lap.

Negotiations among the British, the Congress Party, and the Muslim League had been going on since March when Prime Minister Clement Attlee had sent his Cabinet Mission to India. Gerry Rock had been in New Delhi for a few weeks immediately after he arrived in India. He was ably supported by Jim Michaels and our Indian correspondent P. D. Sharma.

At the end of World War II, the British Government had decided that the situation in India was at a crisis stage. It had become quite clear that the time had come for British rule to end in India. But the British had been in India for 150 years, so the question was how to end the rule without causing catastrophic results. We know now that Mr. Attlee had been thinking about the problem at the end of 1946 and he was determined to find a man to preside over the procedure. That person had to have a deep insight into the problems of India as well as the necessary tact and diplomatic skills to deal with diverse groups.

The problems were many. India had a population of 400 million people who spoke 23 languages and two hundred dialects. They had lived under direct British rule in more than 500 semi-independent states that dated back many centuries. These 400 million were divided not only by race but by a caste system with three thousand categories for occupational, territorial, tribal, racial, and religious groups. In India there lived 250 million Hindus, 90 million Moslems, six million Sikhs, and a myriad of sects and cults, all united under British rule.

The country that sought its independence was itself torn by many conflicting interests. There were Indians who had fought on the side of Britain, and there were others who had actively opposed the British war effort. Among the main opponents of the war was the Indian National Congress, which had been formed in 1885 and which had been the most powerful exponent of the Independence movement. At the outbreak of World War II in 1939, it was the largest political party in India and had pledged to abolish British rule. Under the spiritual leadership of Mahatma Gandhi, the Congress Party's actions had been mostly non-violent. But in 1947, new leaders, led by Jawaharlal Nehru, attracted many young Indians who backed total non-cooperation with Britain even to the extent of using force.

To further complicate matters, the Muslim minority demanded freedom from the Hindus and called for the establishment of a separate Muslim nation that would be called Pakistan. The leader of the movement was Mohammed Ali Jinnah, a former member of the Congress Party, who now exhorted his followers to open violence. The disturbances in Calcutta and Bombay and other areas in 1946 were the result of tensions between the Congress Party and the Muslim League.

The big question was how to end British rule in an orderly manner. With the Congress leaders Jawaharlal Nehru and Sardar Patel, with the support of Mahatma Gandhi, on one side, and Mohammed Ali Jinnah and his Muslim League on the other, the country appeared to be headed for civil war. There had been meetings in London and also in New Delhi with virtually no progress. Prime Minister Attlee believed that a new approach should be made on a personal basis, and he felt there would have to be a change at the top. He recalled the resident Viceroy, Lord Wavell, and he called upon Lord Louis Mountbatten, a naval officer with connections to the British royal family, to take on the task. Attlee gave Mountbatten a deadline: an independent India by June of 1948.

Mountbatten had been the Supreme Commander of the Southeast Asia Command during World War II. In that role he had come to know Nehru and also he had Indian army units under his command. As Supreme Commander of Southeast Asia, with headquarters in Colombo, Ceylon, Mountbatten had Indian troops fighting in Burma and Singapore.

Mountbatten, accompanied by his wife, Lady Edwina, arrived in New Delhi in March of 1947 and was duly crowned what was to be the last British Viceroy of India. He immediately began holding daily meetings with the leaders of the Congress Party—Nehru and Patel in particular—and also with Mohammed Ali

Jinnah, the President of the Muslim League. As a result of these meetings, it became clear that the only practical solution would be the partition of India into two countries, with India being predominantly Hindu and Pakistan predominantly Muslim. It also became apparent to Mountbatten that the division could not wait until 1948. It had to be done quickly, and the target date was August 1947. It was only the voice of Mahatma Gandhi who was strongly against partition. Gandhi, who had immense moral stature, believed that Hindus and Moslems could live together, and he had lobbied against partition.

The meetings in late May moved back to New Delhi and Mountbatten fashioned the agreement for the partition of the country into two new nations, India, populated by a majority of Hindus, and Pakistan, populated by a majority of Muslims.

That was the situation when I arrived in New Delhi on that Monday in May. The talks among the major participants were on hold, as Mountbatten had returned to London to discuss the final plans with the government of Prime Minister Attlee. I was particularly unhappy because the temperature in New Delhi ranged between 112 and 115 and I was covered with prickly heat (an uncomfortable rash). The only way I could get any sleep was to take the sheets off my bed, dunk them in cold water in the bathtub and then put one sheet under and one over me and stay under the ceiling fan. At that, it took only a few hours before both sheets were hot pieces of cardboard, and so I dunked them all over again. At least this way I got a few hours of sleep. Everyone warned me that I would catch a severe cold, but it was that or no sleep. (It would be another year or more before air conditioning managed to make its way to the hotels in New Delhi.)

While Mountbatten was in London, the political parties continued having meetings in New Delhi and when the weather became too hot, some were transferred to the hill station of Simla. Shortly after I arrived, I managed to get an exclusive interview with Mr. Jinnah in which he demanded a corridor connecting the two parts of what was to be Pakistan. Muslim majorities resided in the west and north of India, the Punjab, and also in the eastern province of Bengal and the city of Calcutta. The plan was to divide both the Punjab and Bengal, which would leave a huge gap between the parts of India. This story aroused the ire of the Congress Party, and there were front-page articles with Nehru calling the idea "completely unrealistic" and saying that it "indicates that Mr. Jinnah desires no settlement of any kind."

I had been in New Delhi for more than a week when Mahatma Gandhi decided to return to the city. After the major negotiations had concluded, he had traveled to Bengal to try to calm the climate after the rioting. He arrived from

Patna on the morning of May 25th. He left his train at a station before Delhi and motored to his residence in the Bhangi (Untouchable) Colony. Gandhi had made it his practice to stay with the untouchable castes to try to remove the stigma of caste. That afternoon he had met with the leader of the Socialist Party for two hours. A reporter who was with him on the journey reported that Gandhi was sleeping that afternoon because he was exhausted by the heat.

That evening I went to his prayer meeting. Gandhi's prayer meetings were a "must" for correspondents, and either P.D. Sharma or I would attend. After the prayer meeting he would usually have something to say. Our correspondent reported that all along the railway line people had gathered just to get a glimpse of him. At one place, some 100 persons squatted on the railway line and his train was forced to make an unscheduled stop.

I took these pictures at one of Gandhi's prayer meetings in New Delhi in May 1947.

Although I hated the heat, I went golfing almost every morning with Bob Neville, the *Time* correspondent in Delhi. We would tee off at 5:30 a.m. and be back at eight in time for breakfast and the morning's work.

The lull in the negotiations offered an escape to the hills. My friend, Vice Consul George Small, came up to Delhi for a holiday. He said he could get a jeep to take a trip to Musoorie, a hill station close to Delhi. I called Gerry, told him I was full of prickly heat—which I was—and said I was going to take a couple of days off. On Monday George got the jeep and gasoline and early on a Tuesday morning, at 3:30 a.m., we took off for cooler weather. It was exhilarating to drive in the coolness of the morning, and we made pretty good time for a jeep. At that time of the morning traffic was not heavy, our only obstacles being ox carts and camel carts. All along the way we saw monkeys and here and there a peacock. I wrote that "I don't think I will ever get used to seeing monkeys running around. It always seems as if I'm in a zoo." The road was very good, and we reached Dehr Dun, about 160 miles form Delhi, about 7:30 a.m. and began the climb up the hill to Mussoorie, which is 6,000 feet up.

The road up the mountain is only one way, so one can only use the road at certain hours of the day. After arriving at the top, one must park his car, since no automobiles are allowed within the city limits. One must walk, ride a rickshaw, or go on horseback. At that time of year, with Delhi being so hot, the city was very crowded and George and I had come up without reservations. As a result we spent most of our three-day visit looking for a place to sleep. We slept under two blankets, and within 36 hours my prickly heat was gone. That alone was worth the trip. So Tuesday, Wednesday, Thursday, and part of Friday we walked about the city or rode a rickshaw. The rickshaws were either single or double. I wrote, "If it's a single, it takes four men to push and pull you; if it's a double, usually five men do the job since being on a hilltop, the roads are either up or down." George had some friends at the station, and we went dancing a couple of nights. The evenings ended early because we spent most of our time sleeping.

The hill station was crowded with Sikhs, most of them wealthy contractors and their families who had come there as refugees from the troubled areas of Lahore and Amritsar in the Punjab. Mussoorie also boasted an American school that was filled with the children of missionaries, businessmen, and diplomats. It felt good to be among American kids again, and they were unmistakably American. I could spot them in so many ways: dress, language, and actions. We returned on Friday afternoon so I could attend the meetings of the Congress Party on the weekend. Unfortunately, the prickly heat returned as we drove down to the plain.

Mountbatten returned to New Delhi at the end of May. He had spent several weeks in London meeting with Clement Attlee and working on the announcement in Parliament about the plan for the division of India into two dominions. The original Cabinet Plan had had to be shelved and Mountbatten had told Attlee that because of the possibility of more communal troubles, waiting until 1948 was untenable. Mountbatten felt that he had made remarkable progress in his meetings with Nehru, Mahatma Gandhi, and Vallabhai Patel of the Congress Party and Mohammed Ali Jinnah and Liaquat Ali Khan of the Muslim League. He believed that the division was possible.

On the second of June, Mountbatten met with the leaders of the opposing parties and laid out the government plan for the division of the country into two dominions. In an all-day meeting he got agreement from both sides to accept the plan. Only Gandhi, who always stayed out of the political negotiations, was against the division of India. Mountbatten, by inviting Gandhi to his Viceregal office, won Gandhi's promise that he would not disrupt the negotiations.

On June 4, in the halls of the Indian Parliament, Mountbatten and his staff met with some 300 Indian and foreign reporters. Speaking without notes, he lucidly explained the plan in 45 minutes. He answered most of the reporters' questions with tact and humor and only on two occasions did he ask members of his staff to answer the question. It was a stellar performance. I have attended many a press conference, and none compared to the eloquence and mastery of Mountbatten. In just the few months since he had arrived to be the last Viceroy of India, he and Lady Edwina had changed the Indian atmosphere from anti-British to pro-British. Mountbatten was the most popular Briton in India.

I was not the only reporter who was impressed with his performance. Both British and American correspondents on the scene reacted in the same manner.

The reporter for the Calcutta newspaper, the *Statesman,* wrote: "It was a remarkable performance, physical, rhetorical, as well as logical, and a great majority of the journalists must have come away deeply impressed by the Viceroy's evidently profound understanding of the Indian problem."

And Bob Neville, the Time/Life Delhi Correspondent with whom I went to the conference, said that Mountbatten's performance could be compared only with President Roosevelt in his prime.

The conference was followed by several weeks of negotiations with the Indian political leaders. Some of the meetings took place in the heat of Delhi and others in the hill station of Simla.

On July 4, the Mountbattens invited all of the Americans in New Delhi—there were 90 of us—to a party at their residence in honor of the American Independence Day. I wrote,

> The Viceregal Lodge is nothing less than a palace, and I wandered about the halls like a country boy come to the city for the first time. I went with Bob Neville and his wife (Time/Life) and we arrived at 8:00 to be shown into the huge ballroom where we met the rest of the Americans, a few Indian leaders, and Mountbatten's staff. We were offered mint julep, scotch, gin and just about any drink you would want. There were even soft drinks for the younger set and for the Indian leaders who did not drink. After a short period, we lined up around the room and the Viceroy and Lady Mountbatten came around to shake hands with each and every one. And then into dinner. At dinner there were five tables. At the head table with the Viceroy and Lady Mountbatten were Pandit Nehru and his sister, Mrs. Vivayalacksmi Pandit, and Mohammed Ali Jinnah with his sister, Miss Fatima Jinnah, and the American Ambassador and his wife. After dinner—consommé, fish, jellied chicken, ice cream with wines and champagne—Mountbatten spoke. He said that he had invited Nehru and Jinnah because they were the leaders of their respective parties and would be leading their people in the two new dominions which were to become independent. They now had a lot in common with the Americans who had gained their independence 170 years ago. After the speech we went into the depths of the lodge to see a movie, "Blue Skies." After the movie we adjourned to one of the parlors upstairs for more drinks and then the Viceroy and Lady Mountbatten took their leave—the signal that we could go if we wished. I wrote my story at 2 a.m.
>
> P.S. I wouldn't have noticed it, but all the ladies were in raptures about the choker Lady Mountbatten wore—emeralds separated by diamonds. Also, all of the women and the young ladies—who made a special trip from the American school at Mussorie—were just thrilled to meet the Mountbattens.

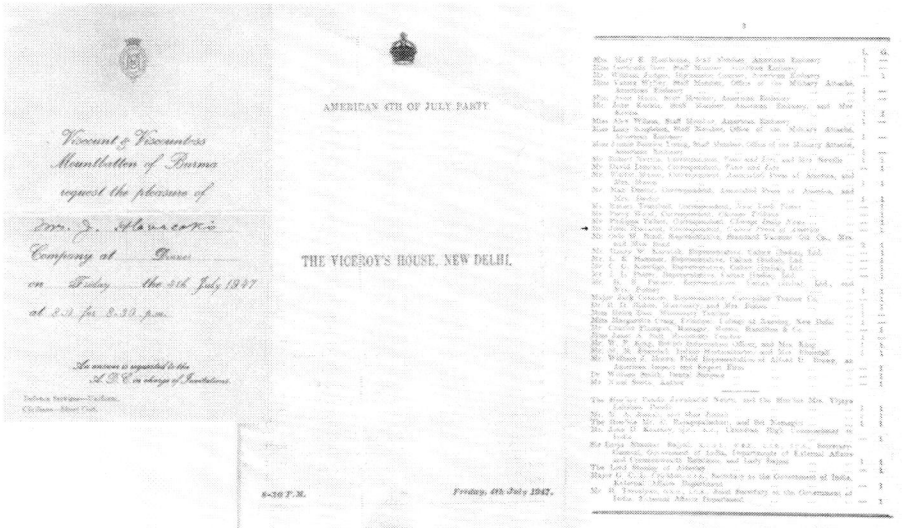

Invitation, program, and a portion of the guest list for the Independence Day party given by the Mountbattens.

11

HOME LEAVE AND AFTERWARD

◆

(August to December 1947)

At our first meeting in February 1945 I had told Miles "Peg" Vaughn that I thought correspondents working in Southeast Asia should be granted a "home leave" at least every two years. He agreed with me, so I was counting on making a trip to the U.S. in March of 1947.

Events conspired, and I was unable to leave while the political negotiations leading to the partition of India were going on. But I asked for a leave in the summer and my boss, Gerry Rock, agreed, provided "Peg" and New York authorized the trip. While I was sweating in the heat of New Delhi, the United Press instituted a new policy about home leave and it looked for a time as if going home would mean I would no longer have a job. I got the "go signal" on June 1 after a raft of telegrams among Bombay, Tokyo, and New York. I had dreamed of going home by ship through Europe but that was not to be. Flying home and back was preferable for United Press, because it was cheaper and faster.

Once my leave was approved, I made arrangements with General Motors in Bombay to buy a Buick. My good friend, Jim O'Connor, the sales manager for General Motors in India, made all the arrangements. I was able to buy a right-hand drive demonstrator at a very reasonable rate for delivery in New York in July. When my departure from India was delayed, I received authorization to take delivery of the car in the middle of August. I had hoped to get a Chevrolet, but Jim said I could get a Buick because delivery of a Chevrolet, Oldsmobile, or Pontiac was not possible. He also told me I could pay General Motors when I received the car.

I had originally reserved a ticket for July 21, but Gerry Rock had to make a business trip to South India that week so I agreed to delay my departure until the end of the month. On July 29 I left Bombay and flew to Karachi. The first night out of Karachi the flight stopped in Istanbul for the night. All the passengers were bussed to a hotel. In the morning, at breakfast, I could look down the hill at the Bosphorus in the sunlight. My next stop was London to see the United Press office. I stayed with Harold Guard at his comfortable home outside London. I met with all of the editors in the London office and urged them to find stories that would be of interest to the Indian newspapers who were our clients. Harold Guard would be sending stories for our Indian service. I stayed in London for a few days to visit the famous places I had read about. It was my first visit to England, and I had time to duck into the British Museum, see the Houses of Parliament and Big Ben, tour Westminster Abbey, and view the famous Tower Bridge.

Upon arriving in New York I met with the United Press vice presidents and other managers, who wanted to know firsthand what was going on in India. I gave them my reports and discussed our future plans. I took delivery of my gun-metal-colored Buick on August 15 in New York City.

My sister, Marie, on vacation from college, flew to New York to help me drive the car back to Illinois. We first drove south to Washington, D.C., to stay with Stew and "Bunny" Hensley for a few days. While we were in D.C. I met friends Ells and Bobbie Carlson and their two children. Ells and Bobbie had been Oberlin in China teachers at the same time I was teaching in Chintang, Szechwan province. We then drove to Illinois, stopping briefly in Martinsburg, West Virginia to see George Small's parents. Our Buick turned many heads along the way with its right-hand drive. My sister remarked that everyone noticed with surprise that the steering gear was on the "wrong" side of the car.

We continued on to Chicago and the Lemont Farm where my parents were living. They had sold the family home in LaGrange Park and had moved to an acreage in Lemont that had been bought by my uncles.

I had two months at home. While I was on leave, the Hindu-Muslim rioting erupted after the partition with the two new dominions of India and Pakistan. Jim Michaels and P.D. Sharma filed most of the stories, and Gerry Rock wrote that he supplemented their stories by telephone. In a letter Gerry sent me while I was at home, he indicated that when I returned I would be assigned to Karachi, Pakistan.

Being home after two years away gave me a chance to catch up with the few friends still living in my old neighborhood. I had been expecting to be in China, but now I began speaking to the service clubs about India. My father had delayed his vacation until my arrival so we could spend two weeks fishing in northern Wisconsin. Fishing was my father's favorite pastime, and we had not been on a vacation together for ten years. I also got a chance to see my brother Frank, who was now working in Minneapolis. We had not seen each other since I had sailed for China in the summer of 1939. He had recently graduated from Carleton, where he had finished college after his army demobilization. He had spent the war years in Europe, with his unit fighting in the Battle of the Bulge in Belgium. After our fishing trip I stopped briefly in Northfield, Minnesota, to visit the Carleton campus, the first time I had returned since graduating in June of 1939.

At home, I was busy every night. I had dates with several girlfriends. My mother encouraged me to find someone to take back to India, but the idea of living in Bombay somehow did not excite my dates. I also managed one weekend to watch Ben Hogan, Sam Snead, and Bobby Locke at a professional golf tournament. I always remembered that Bobby Locke, from South Africa, could hit a "wee hook" on his drives.

After packing my Buick—the trunk as well as the back seat—with clothes and other things I wanted to take back to India, I drove to New York at the end of October. I took my mother with me on the first leg of the trip because she wanted to visit relatives in Cleveland. I drove over the Pennsylvania Turnpike and stopped briefly in Jeanette, Pennsylvania, to have breakfast with Penny Rock's mother and dad. In New York I spent several days at the office and took a turn on the foreign cable desk when other men wanted a day off. I stayed at the Tudor Hotel (Stewart Hensley once called it "the hotel of clothes closets" because the rooms were about the size of closets), which was on 42nd Street just a block from the Daily News Building. I had several friends in the area as well as cousins Violet and Arline Knapp, and I spent several evenings visiting with them. Stewart Hensley was in New York at the same time covering the United Nations, and we had a breakfast together and talked about India and his job covering the State Department. I was driving my right-hand drive Buick to use up the gas because the tank had to be empty when the car was shipped. Irving Peck in the United Press office kindly arranged to ship the car back to India on the steamship *Mooncrest*. The car was unboxed so I was able to ship my personal effects in the trunk. I have the list of the items I shipped, which included "one golf bag, set golf clubs and golf balls."

HOME LEAVE AND AFTERWARD   85

My hotel bill from the Hotel Tudor in New York City, October 1947.

I spent the month of November working in the United Press office and discussing with the foreign department the situation in India as I knew it. They were mainly interested in the financial aspect and advised me to go slowly on expansion of the service because both India and Pakistan were new countries. The New York office wanted to be sure that we would be able to sell our service at a profit.

My stay in New York was made pleasant because a young lady in the foreign department, Virginia Stafford, accompanied me on several evenings to the Roosevelt Hotel Grill to dine and dance to the music of Guy Lombardo. And on the last Sunday in October, she went with me to visit a friend in the hospital in New Jersey and then to a professional football game that afternoon. We watched the Cleveland Browns because the captain of the team was Lou Saban, an old friend from my home town of La Grange, Illinois. Lou and my younger brothers had played on the same high school football team. I had not seen Lou since we met in the China/Burma/India theatre during World War II. Lou had been a Chinese language officer during the war. We met with Lou in the locker room after the game and then had dinner, a quick shopping tour, and a ride out to the airport.

I spent one day at the United Nations wandering about the corridors. I had no assignment so I enjoyed being free to look around. Also I got press tickets from Acme Photos to go to the New York horse show and took my cousin, Arlene Knapp. Another day, before I shipped the car, I took Stew Hensley and my cousin for a ride in Westchester County. And one Sunday, I went with Virginia Stafford to Yankee Stadium to watch the football Yankees play the Los Angeles Dons of the old American Football League. Virginia had managed to get press tickets. Later we went for a Chinese dinner and to a movie, "The Secret Life of Walter Mitty." Another night I had dinner with Dave Davis, my friend from Acme Photos. (As I mentioned in Chapter 6, Dave was the recipient of Max Desfor's "other" photo of Gandhi and Nehru.)

I was scheduled to return to India in the middle of November, but my visa for India was being held up. Several cables to Delhi were required before it came. But then it was close to Thanksgiving and the UP reluctantly agreed to let me take another week.

So the Saturday after Thanksgiving, I flew into New York, went to the office to say goodbye to everyone, picked up the young lady from the foreign desk, and we went downtown. First to the Commodore Hotel for dinner, but we didn't like the music of Stan Kenton, so moved to the Roosevelt Grill where we danced to the music of Guy Lombardo. It was a late night but we decided to get up early Sunday morning and go to New Jersey to see Jane Gaston Born, one of my friends from Junior College. Jane had called the night before inviting us to lunch. We returned to New York in time to see a football game, the Cardinals against the New York Giants. My date had acquired good seats from the sports desk. We had dinner at her apartment, went back to the hotel to pack, then to the airline office. Earlier we had purchased a lot of last-minute articles: flash bulbs and film for Acme Photos and bubble gum and "birds that drink water all the time." We had a long wait before going to the airfield and then another long wait while the plane was readied for take-off. My lovely date waited until I was safely aboard.

Now the "Murphy's Law" story of my flight back to Bombay on TWA:

Our plane was a DC-4 because TWA didn't fly the Constellations into Bombay. Take-off time was to be 11:30 p.m. but it was delayed and we took off at 1:20 a.m. The flight to Gander, Newfoundland, took five hours. I got a little sleep, although the heating system was not working and I was very cold because I had only summer clothes as I hadn't foreseen a need for cold-weather clothing in Bombay. We landed at 7:30 a.m. Gander was covered with snow and ice. It was snowing as we left the plane to have breakfast while the ship was being refueled. We reboarded for the flight to Shannon, Ireland. This was to be a ten-hour flight. About one hour out, I was reading the latest *New Yorker* when the flight engineer came back and sat down next to me. He told me that we had turned back to Gander because the plane had developed a number of minor troubles and the crew didn't want to take a chance on the long flight. It took an hour and a half to return to Gander, and we arrived about 11 a.m. We waited in the terminal, which was warm and comfortable, and we had lunch. Then we were told there would be a crew rest and we would be delayed another eight hours. At this announcement, Mrs. Vijayalakshmi Pandit, the Indian Ambassador to Moscow and also the leader of the Indian delegation to the United Nations (and the sister of Prime Minister Nehru), was furious with TWA and attempted to get a special flight back to New York and try again. All the rest of the passengers went to a hotel to get some sleep. Mrs. Pandit was unsuccessful and returned to India on the same plane as the rest of us. But before she gave up trying, she had shaken up TWA personnel at the airport with her demands.

One of the TWA planes from my long flight back to Bombay after home leave.

I had elected to stay at the terminal to see if Mrs. Pandit would be successful in getting an earlier flight to Bombay. I also telephoned the United Press correspondent in Gander. He came out to the terminal with one of his friends to get me and we went to the club for airport personnel, where we had drinks and played a game of billiards. Later we went back to the terminal and had dinner. One of the passengers from the plane, a Mr. Zazzara, an Italian from New York, joined us. He was on his way to Italy to build a group of factories. Our plane didn't take off until eleven that night, so we spent time talking, visiting the meteorological station and then having more drinks at the bar. The other passengers had enjoyed a good sleep while the two of us, Zazzara and I, had stayed up the whole time.

We took off for Shannon. Everything worked except the heating system, and we froze. I slept a little but woke up shivering, teeth chattering. Everyone else was the same. TWA made no friends. The trip was saved only by the fact that the passengers were a good bunch with a sense of humor. The wisecracks were many. Among the fellow passengers was an Italian American lady, a Mrs. Anita de Paulis, who was on her way to northern Italy to ski. It so happened that she was the next to last person to board the plane. I was the last one aboard, as it took us both a long time to say goodbye to our friends. At Gander, one has to walk down a long passageway and she kept dropping her odd coats and other belongings. I, of course, kept picking them up, so that by the time we got aboard I was one swell guy in her opinion. Another couple aboard were the Spignulis, who owned a restaurant at Fort Wadsworth on Staten Island. They were going to Rome to see relatives. Another passenger was a Jewish fellow from Detroit on his way to Jerusalem to visit his sick mother. He had a sense of humor, which saved many a difficult situation. Another passenger was a Mrs. Nakhleh, whose husband was a member of the Palestine Delegation to the United Nations. (In 1947, Israel was not yet a nation.)

I was still freezing. As soon as dawn broke, my friend the flight engineer took me up into the cockpit where it was a little warmer and I could watch the pilots guiding the plane. We finally landed at Shannon, where there was no snow but some rain. We had a good lunch in the terminal and then left Shannon for Paris. At Paris it was raining but we couldn't leave the plane because Paris had been closed in for three days and the terminal was full of passengers from flights that had been grounded. We stayed aboard the plane and tried to find a place to play bridge, unsuccessfully. After an hour's delay, we took off and then had a dinner of mostly French bread, which tasted very good. It was another five hours to Rome, where we had a meal of sandwiches and a little spaghetti.

At Rome, we had another four-hour wait because the airfield at Athens, Greece, was closed due to bad weather. The airport at Rome was not very good, and it was a long, dreary wait. In Rome, a number of our passengers left us. We finally took off at about four in the morning. I slept, and when I woke at dawn we were flying on three engines. There was a minor fire warning on one, so they had shut it off to be safe. We made it to Athens and had breakfast. I wrote that it was "not a good one, but then I guess no one eats very well in Greece." The air terminal was small and not very comfortable.

After an hour in Athens, we were taxiing on the runway when one of the other engines didn't sound right, so back we went to the terminal to check it. That took another half hour, and then we finally took off for Lydda, Palestine. Now we had a decent trip and landed at about four in the afternoon. Here we had the best meal we had eaten since leaving New York: lobster, soup, good meat, mashed potatoes, carrots, and for dessert, a chocolate-coated banana, with good coffee. But in Lydda, too, we had a long delay because the relief crew could not get in from Tel Aviv until 7 p.m. because they had to wait for an armed escort. It was early evening before we took off for Dharan, Saudi Arabia. On this leg we played bridge because by this time one of the flight engineers managed to change a seat around for us so we could sit facing each other. At Dharan there was a U.S. Army base and we had breakfast and I noted, ice cold chocolate milk.

Then we had another delay, but by this time we were used to delays. It was a minor mechanical glitch. Finally on to Bombay, playing bridge most of the way. My friend, George Small, was there to meet me. After a long delay going through Indian customs and the police registration, we went out into Bombay's glorious sunshine. I checked in at the office and George and I had dinner with Gerry Rock. Then I slept for 14 hours.

Bombay, after five months away, was different in that the city was flooded with Hindu refugees from Pakistan. Many of these refugees were wealthy, and they either found housing or stayed with relatives. Most likely they preferred to stay in Bombay rather than travel to other parts of India, because Bombay was a comfortable city with room to expand.

After taking a couple of days to catch up on my sleep, I soon adjusted to the office work, taking my turn at editing and making sure the news got to our client newspapers on time.

I was fortunate to be able to move in with George Small at his comfortable flat. My car had not yet arrived from New York, but I was able to ride with George every day. Although petrol (gasoline) was very scarce and rationed, George was able to get enough for our purposes.

The weather in Bombay in December is glorious, so whenever possible, I took time to play golf. Also, I had friends who had a "shack"—a beach house—at Juhu Beach, some 15 miles north of the city. Ray and Helen Crew were great hosts and welcomed guests. Ray was with the Western Electric Company. My letters tell of surf boarding and swimming.

I also became a baby sitter for Gerry's two youngsters. Gerry and Penny were in Hyderabad, and I stayed in their apartment and took the kids to Christmas parties. For my third Christmas in India, I stayed with Gerry and Penny and helped trim the Christmas tree. In the morning I was there to watch the young ones open their gifts. I noted that the Christmas tree looked pretty good. It was the same one they'd had the year before, and it had grown a little.

The Christmas season for Americans in Bombay was a joyous time. I noted in letters home that I was invited out to dinner every night. This was the year that the American Association of Bombay held its New Year's eggnog party on the day after Christmas, because January 1 was to be a "dry" day. Bombay had prohibition, and two days a week no liquor could be sold or served in public places. So the Americans had a great eggnog party on December 26 and I noted in letters home that the eggnogs were very good. After the party I played golf and later went out to dinner with friends and then to the Bombay Gymkhana Club for drinks and dancing.

Just after Christmas a group of my friends were scheduled to go on a hunt at one of the princely states. Unfortunately, I had to stay behind in Bombay because although the ship which was carrying my Buick was in port, it was not alongside so I could not clear the car through Customs. The ship arrived on a Saturday and I had to wait until Monday. Then there was a general strike in Bombay, but Gerry came with me to the dock and we managed to get the car through Customs with the help of an American Express representative who showed me how to save about five hundred dollars in Customs duty. It took all morning to clear the car, and after lunch we pushed the car from the docks to a gas station and then drove it home. Everything I had packed in the car came through without damage and I had only to pay minor Customs duty on my belongings. The car had several scratches but looked pretty good. The next day I went through the long process of getting the car registered which involved obtaining insurance, police registration, and finally, gas coupons. I calculated that getting my Buick landed in Bombay cost me about $3,300, but I thought I could probably sell it for twice that amount.

Because of the prohibition, I joined a small private party on New Year's Eve at the home of Lee and Margo Kamern. Lee was the Metro Goldwyn Mayer representative in Bombay. On New Year's Day I began the new year right by playing golf with Al and Catherine Beaver. Al was the sales manager for Firestone.

George Small's fiancé had arrived, and their wedding was planned for the first week in January. I moved in for a few days with Gerry and Penny Rock because we were expecting the Hyderabad contract to be finalized and I thought I would be on my way to Hyderabad soon. However, after George's wedding, at which I was the best man, all plans were changed and I found myself heading north to Karachi, Pakistan.

12

HYDERABAD

◆

(January to June 1948)

With the partition of India in the summer of 1947, the Indian political situation had begun to settle down after the terrible bloodbaths in the Punjab region caused by the movements of the Hindus from Pakistan to India and the Muslims from India to Pakistan. Most of the princely states had agreed to Mountbatten's plan that each state accede to either India or Pakistan. There were two major exceptions: Kashmir and Hyderabad.

These two princely states were similar in that Kashmir was ruled by Hindus although the population was almost entirely Muslim, while Hyderabad had a Muslim ruler, the Nizam of Hyderabad, and a majority Hindu population.

Kashmir became the focus of the dispute between India and Pakistan almost immediately and in a matter of months the issue was taken to the United Nations. There was a provision for a plebiscite to be taken, but it never came about. The dispute continues to this day, more than fifty years later.

Hyderabad opted to postpone choosing between Pakistan and India. The leaders of both India and Pakistan as well as Lord Mountbatten, who had become the governor-general of India, were so taken up with the problems of Kashmir that Hyderabad was relegated to the "back burner." Thus in mid-December of 1947, Gerry Rock, accompanied by his wife, Penny, traveled to Hyderabad at the invitation of the Nizam's government, to begin negotiating for the purchase of an American news service. Gerry spent a week in Hyderabad and negotiated a contract whereby the Nizam's government agreed to buy United Press news at a rate of US $48,000 per year. The contract stipulated that United Press would set up a receiving station in Hyderabad and that a United Press correspondent would be stationed there. I was to be that correspondent.

But first we had other business. In mid-January I flew to Karachi, Pakistan, to man the office for a few weeks. Our United Press correspondent in Karachi at the time was Mr. Tahilramani, a Hindu, and conditions were such that it was not safe for him and his family to remain in Pakistan. He said he would have to leave for India.

Tahilramani had a comfortable flat in a middle-class section of Karachi. The flat had a telephone, and it was well known to deliverymen and postmen. We decided to keep the flat in the name of United Press because we planned to have many managers in the next few years. After I arrived, Tahil and his family moved out and I moved in to keep the property. Karachi at the time was overflowing with refugees from India and as soon as they saw someone taking out luggage, like the Tahil family, they would move into the vacant flat. So I was there to prevent squatters from taking over.

For several weeks I lived in a vacant flat. I hesitated to hire any servants until we could hire another correspondent. I wrote home that my Muslim neighbors on the floor below were wonderful people and they provided me with a breakfast of tea, toast, and eggs every morning and also brought me tea in the afternoon. For my other meals I would go to the hotels and restaurants in the city.

During my first days in Karachi I made the rounds of the government offices to get the flat legally transferred to United Press. I wrote home that I had been trying to "nail down" an official for three days without any luck. I finally got the legal papers on the fourth day.

I wrote home that Karachi would be a good place to live if there were enough work to keep one busy. The political scene had calmed down in both India and Pakistan under the influence of Mahatma Gandhi. Devastated by the communal killings, Gandhi had begun a "fast unto death" to persuade the Indian and Pakistan leaders to meet and make every effort to stop the killing.

However, the question of Kashmir was being debated in the Security Council of the United Nations and I predicted that if the decision taken was not fair to both countries there would be more violence.

At the time, almost all of the Hindus and Sikhs (the Sikh religion is an offshoot of Hinduism) had either moved out or were in the process of moving out of Pakistan. Because it was the Hindus who had controlled most of the businesses in Karachi, their leaving had created a vacuum that was difficult to fill immediately. Almost all the clerical staff of all businesses were Hindus, and those slots were difficult to fill with Muslim refugees who came from an agrarian background.

I reported that Karachi had a nightclub as well as several athletic clubs where people gathered. I met a number of the American residents of the city. They included consulate personnel, representatives of Pan American Airways which had begun service to Karachi, and engineers of the Morrison-Knudson Company who were building roads and hydro-electric plants in Afghanistan.

On a Sunday I wrote that I went to the Boat Club with one of the American consulate girls and later called on Barrie and Anne Eldridge who represented Pan American Airways. I spent the next few days keeping our flat, and the following Thursday I had an interview with Mr. Mohammed Ali Jinnah, now the Governor General of Pakistan, and of course the "Father" of the country. I don't have the text of my interview, but I recall that he was hopeful that conditions between the two countries would improve although he was suspicious of India's intentions because of the two countries' dispute over Kashmir. (In my letter, I commented that the interview was unlikely to see the light of day.) I flew back to Bombay that same evening and on the next day, Friday, January 30, Mahatma Gandhi was assassinated in New Delhi while walking to his daily evening prayer meeting.

India descended into mourning—and fear—fear that a Muslim had fired the shots. Fortunately the word was passed quickly that Naturam Godse, a member of a right-wing Hindu organization (the Hindu Mahsaba), had fired the shot and was in custody.

Jim Michaels and P. D. Sharma, our United Press correspondents in New Delhi, were the first to report on the assassination and gave United Press a banner scoop. Excerpts from Jim's reports on Gandhi's death and funeral are included below. They are classic examples of excellent reporting.

Gandhi's Assassination: 'Bapu [father] is finished'
by James Michaels

New Delhi, January 30, 1948: Mohandas K. Gandhi was assassinated today by a Hindu extremist whose act plunged India into sorrow and fear. Rioting broke out immediately in Bombay.

The seventy-eight-year-old leader whose people had christened him the Great Soul of India died at 5:45 p.m. (7:15 a.m. EST) with his head cradled in the lap of his sixteen-year-old granddaughter, Mani.

Just half an hour before, a Hindu fanatic, Ram Naturam, had pumped three bullets from a revolver into Gandhi's frail body, emaciated by years of fasting and asceticism.

Gandhi was shot in the luxurious gardens of Birla House in the presence of one thousand of his followers, whom he was leading to the little summer pagoda where it was his habit to make his evening devotions.

Dressed as always in his homespun sacklike dhoti, and leaning heavily on a staff of stout wood, Gandhi was only a few feet from the pagoda when the shots were fired.

Gandhi crumpled instantly, putting his hand to his forehead in the Hindu gesture of forgiveness to his assassin. Three bullets penetrated his body at close range, one in the upper right thigh, one in the abdomen, and one in the chest.

He spoke no word before he died. A moment before he was shot he said—some witnesses believed he was speaking to the assassin—"You are late."

The assassin had been standing beside the garden path, his hands folded, palms together, before him in the Hindu gesture of greeting. But between his palms he had concealed a small-caliber revolver. After pumping three bullets into Gandhi at a range of a few feet, he fired a fourth shot in an attempt at suicide, but the bullet merely creased his scalp.

Cremation: 'Gandhi Still Lives'
by James Michaels

New Delhi, January 31, 1948: The body of sainted Mohandas K. Gandhi today was committed to the flames of the burning ghat as violence touched off by his assassination flared anew in Bombay.

The ancient Hindu ceremonial was carried out on the banks of the Jumna, one of the five sacred rivers of India, in a demonstration of national grief.

Devadas Gandhi, eldest son of the slain leader, touched fire to the pyre to consume the earthly remains of India's great soul.

For the moment India's capital was unified by grief over Gandhi's death.

His body was borne through the streets of New Delhi and Old Delhi in such a procession as India had never seen. As the cortege passed, the hundreds of thousands of mourners left their places and followed the bier in a procession that wound more than five miles long behind Gandhi's body.

At the banks of the Jumna, the huge mass of humanity, wailing and weeping, packed around the newly bricked burning platform for as far as the eye could see.

Gandhi's body was placed on the pyre with wood heaped below and around it.

While the crowd raised a cry: "Gandhi! Gandhi! Gandhi!" Devadas began the ceremony.

In Bombay, Gerry and I heard the news at about 6 p.m. We immediately got into our cars and drove about the city because we feared that there would be religious rioting. Because the word that a Hindu was the assassin had been broadcast, by 8 p.m. the streets were calm, with ordinary citizens in deep mourning.

Later that evening I joined a previously scheduled party at the home of the Standard Oil representative who had three lovely daughters. It was a very somber group with everyone quietly dining and wondering what effect Gandhi's death would have on the future of India.

The next day, a Saturday, we were at the office early receiving stories about the reactions to Gandhi's death from London and New York to send to our Bombay newspaper clients. We were writing stories about the situation in Bombay and receiving pictures of the Mahatma's funeral cortege and his cremation from New Delhi. The photos were sent to us in Bombay by plane and we then radioed them to London. At the time, there was only one post office in all of India to radio pictures to London, and that office was in Bombay. Jim Michaels and P. D. Sharma were sending down the photos, and Gerry and I would take them to the post office and see that they were sent for worldwide distribution. On Sunday the assassination was still the major story and Gerry and I continued sending radio photos to London.

Gerry and I had been scheduled to leave for Hyderabad on Monday, but we postponed our departure because we were not sure what the repercussions of Gandhi's death would be.

On Tuesday, Bob Miller, roving correspondent for UP, flew in from the Middle East. New York, fearing that the country would explode because of the assassination, had ordered Bob to reinforce our staff. That night Gerry had a party at his house and Bob was the center of attention as he told us of his reporting in Palestine. I had invited one of the Marshall daughters and Gerry had invited a member of the Consulate staff to meet Bob. We all sat on the floor as Bob told about meeting the various Arab sheiks. Bob told us that he always carried a cache of

American silver dollars from Las Vegas. He always presented a silver dollar to the Arab leaders when he interviewed them.

Bob left for New Delhi the next day and Gerry and I again delayed our departure for Hyderabad. Finally, on Friday, a week after we had originally planned to leave, we departed by train for Hyderabad. We had gathered up all of our radio equipment and also took our chief radio operator and a Western Electric engineer to erect the antennas for our radio station. After a 24-hour ride we arrived the next morning at Hyderabad. We were met by a reception committee from the government who escorted us to Percy's Hotel in Secunderabad, a twin city to Hyderabad, where we were welcomed as state guests. After having breakfast and depositing our gear at the hotel, we went right to work putting up our antenna poles. We worked all day, and after dinner we relaxed by going to a movie.

On the next day, a Sunday, we continued working on our radio station. In the evening Gerry and the Western Electric engineer left by train for Bombay. Our chief radio operator and I moved to the Rock Castle Hotel in Hyderabad which was only a few minutes' walk from the station. The Rock Castle Hotel, which was built on the highest hill in the area, was to be my home for the next several months.

I spent the next two days working to get the building ready, hiring workmen in to clean and whitewash the interior. It was slow going. On Thursday night I took the night train back to Bombay to get more equipment. The train arrived Friday noon and I spent the weekend in Bombay.

On Monday morning I took the train back to Hyderabad and spent the next three days continuing to get the building ready. On Thursday night I again took the night train to spend another weekend in Bombay. There were parties on Saturday. On Sunday I accompanied Gerry and Penny, their two kids, and one of the Marshall daughters to Juhu Beach where my friends, Ray and Mary Helen Crews, had a "shack." We had a fine time surfing at the beach and in the afternoon, we went out to the Juhu airport where a friend of Ray Crews' gave everyone a ride in an L-5 observation plane—that is, everyone but me, because by the time it was my turn he had run out of gas. On Monday I worked in our Bombay office and then spent part of the day buying gasoline to drive my Buick to Hyderabad. Al Beaver, the Sales Manager for Firestone, gave me letters to deliver to all of his agents on the route. That night there was a cocktail party at the American Consulate to celebrate Washington's birthday.

The next morning, accompanied by two radio operators and a messenger named Veraswami Naidu, I began driving back to Hyderabad. Our first leg was to Poona, where we stopped for lunch and bought gas. Then the next leg was a rough, hot, and dusty trek to our evening stop at Sholapur where we stayed with the brothers of our chief radio operator, Calmiano. The brothers were railway employees. At Sholapur we were able to buy more gas, and the next morning we drove the rest of the way to Hyderabad, arriving about noon. Because none of the roads between Sholapur and Hyderabad were paved, it was a dusty, hot drive.

Living in Hyderabad was a surreal experience. There were a number of western residents in this princely state, which was ruled by one of the world's richest men, the Nizam of Hyderabad. The Nizam was a direct descendant of the Caliphs of the Constantinople. As one of the preeminent princes, he was entitled to a 21-gun salute. The Nizam rarely left his palace and when he did, he drove about the city in his 1920 Rolls Royce. He usually made an evening drive to lay flowers on his mother's grave at one of the city's mosques. At the same time he was in a political standoff with the new Indian Government which had come into being less than a year previously. Negotiations had been going on for months, with the Indian Government pressuring him to accede to India and he, with his advisors, stalling for time. The Nizam had an army of 25,000 under the command of General El Edroos. It was a seasoned army, having fought with the British in their campaign to retake Burma when Mountbatten was Supreme Commander of the China-Burma-India Theatre.

The top three photos show the UP office in Hyderabad from the back (first two photos) and front. The bottom photo shows the staff members—back row, left to right: subeditors Apte (Hindu), Qamruddin (Muslim), and Sastri (Hindu); middle row: radio operators Menon (Hindu) to the left and Calmiano (Anglo Indian) to the right, with me in the middle; front row: messengers Swami, Ramloo, and Prabhu.

When I arrived in Hyderabad, as far as I could determine, I was the only American resident in the city. I soon made friends with the few westerners in the city and became a member of the Secunderabad Club. Secunderabad was the twin city of Hyderabad. Also resident in the city and members of the Club were four Polish airline pilots for Deccan Airways, flying Dakota twin-engine places from Hyderabad to major Indian cities such as Bombay, Delhi, Calcutta, and Madras. Three of the pilots were, like me, bachelors, and the fourth was married to a British subject. All four had been members of the Polish Wing of the Royal Air Force in World War II. When the war was over, they all had expected to become British subjects but were denied citizenship. Hyderabad gave them a home because they did not want to go back to Poland and live under Russian domination. We were seen together so often that the servants at the Secunderabad Club called me "the Polish pilot with the American accent" and the Polish pilots "the Americans with the Polish accents."

Living at my hotel was an Irishman, Desmond Sheen, who was the director of the Nizam's broadcasting station. Claude Scott, a British journalist, had joined the Nizam's government as Director of Information. During my months in Hyderabad, I got to know these two men as newsmen and as friends.

When I arrived in Hyderabad that February, it was the beginning of the hot season and I found myself spending many daylight hours in the swimming pool at the Secunderabad Club. There I met an Australian family, the Greenes, and their two lovely daughters. Mrs. Greene was prominent in the YWCA and she invited me to the dances at the Y. The Secunderabad Club held dances twice a week, which I and the Polish pilots regularly attended.

At the Club I played some bridge. I wrote home that the first time I played, I won. During the game I had no idea that we were playing for money—that the winnings and losings were calculated and put on your Club bills. I wrote that I had not been playing for much, and since I had won anyway, I didn't worry about it.

Left: standing next to Gerry Rock at the UP office in Hyderabad; middle: with Menon, one of the radio operators; right: with a customs man at the Hyderabad border.

From time to time, I was able to meet with Muslim families. Mr. Ansari, the Firestone agent to whom I had been introduced by letter from my Firestone friends in Bombay, invited me to dinner. I noted that it was a real Muslim dinner—spicy—but that by this time I was accustomed to Muslim meals.

When the elder Greene daughter was leaving for England, a Muslim family friend gave a big farewell dinner for her and I was invited. The dinner was Moglai style except, I noted, that both men and women sat at the table. Even in 1948, most Muslim families still kept the women in purdah, or in the zenana, the women's quarters. Some of the more western-educated women did go out in public, but they were few. At this feast, we all removed our shoes and then sat on the floor eating from a table about a foot high. We ate without utensils and the food was very tasty and highly seasoned, so I drank huge glasses of cold water.

With my Irish friend, Desmond Sheen, I was invited to a Muslim wedding. We first went to the home of the bridegroom, who was a friend of Desmond. The groom was dressed in a Moghul uniform and covered with garlands of flowers. We went with him to a second home where all of the men attending the wedding had congregated. From there we all moved to a second house where all of the women were together. This was a zenana where all the women had to remain and would not be seen. When the time came for the wedding, the bridegroom, alone, went into the home to claim his bride.

As the only American in Hyderabad, I met a number of families. In the first part of May, I was involved, accidentally, in an unfortunate human situation that happens all over the world. The story concerns a young couple whom I had come to know in Hyderabad. The young couple eloped and threw the girl's family into a tailspin. It so happened that I had been invited to the girl's house for dinner that night and arrived to find the family out looking for the eloping couple.

The young man was a lieutenant in the Hyderabad Army named Krishna Reddy. His mother was Swiss, and were it not for the name one would never know he was Hindu because he looked like an Englishman, talked like one, and for the most part, acted like one. His family was very well known in Hyderabad. The girl was a 19-year-old Australian whose parents had lived for 24 years in Hyderabad because her father worked for the Nizam's government. Her mother, guessing that something might have been up between the two (this happened before I arrived in Hyderabad) had been keeping a tight rein on the girl and would never let the kids go out alone. At that time it was considered natural for a mother to worry about her daughter marrying an Indian, even if he happened to be a good-looking one from a good family.

The upshot was that the young couple secretly married. Since none of the local British ministers would marry them, the girl converted to Hinduism and went through the Hindu marriage rites, which were considered legal in Hyderabad. The family, being Anglican Catholics, were horrified. The family found the young couple and took the girl home. Since then there had been nothing but bad feelings among everyone. I was caught in the middle because Krishna Reddy introduced me to the family and both sides had been confiding in me. I felt sorry for the young couple because it took a lot of guts to plan the elopement, only to have the bad luck to be caught.

The girl had an older sister who was leaving for England at the end of the month to get married, and the family also included a younger brother in Australia. The girl promised not to run away and was reconverted to Christianity. After a week had passed, there was still no resolution of the situation. I played billiards with Krishna Reddy at the Secunderabad Club. He told me he wasn't sure whether he was willing to become a Christian, and that was about the only way the girl's mother would consent to the marriage. I never did find out what happened because a few weeks later I was transferred back to Bombay to take over as Manager for India and Pakistan.

While my private life continued to be comfortable, the political tension between Hyderabad and the Government of India was growing more and more difficult. Because the Nizam continued to stall in making a decision, India began an economic blockade that forced the rationing of gasoline. I had to sell my Buick, which used more gas than I was issued, and bought a Czech motorcycle, a Jawa. With the weather growing warmer I was able to travel around the city with the four gallons of alcohol I was given. A friend of mine who worked for Deccan Airways managed to find a gallon or two of gasoline to mix with the alcohol. Because of the blockade, the Nizam's Government had begun producing alcohol. I wrote home that I was happy riding around on the motorcycle because there was no rain falling in the daytime.

I noted that a Muslim organization called the Ittehad el Muslimeen wielded an influence on the Nizam. The organization had a private army called the Razakars (volunteers) who were young and fanatical and who maintained a high profile around town with their parades and drills. They wanted to keep Hyderabad independent, and their presence was a distraction in the negotiations between the Nizam and the Indian Government.

During my first two years in Bombay and during the negotiations for the partition of India, Acme News Photos stationed one of its own photographers in India. In Bombay it was Dave Davis, and I accompanied him on many of his assignments. At the time Acme was a related agency to United Press. Later, United Press bought Acme and renamed it United Press Photos. During the time I was in Hyderabad I began sending pictures to Acme News to accompany the stories I was writing. I pleased to find that my efforts were appreciated, which became clear when I received a letter from R.P. (Bob) Dorman, the foreign director of Acme, acknowledging receipt of a seven-picture layout I had sent and asking where he should send the payment. Bob wrote:

> I certainly appreciate your thoughtfulness in sending this stuff as it is right up with the news. Be sure to keep up the good work. Incidentally, the pictures were excellent. If you made them yourself you certainly are getting to be a regular cameraman. Also it was a relief to obtain intelligent captions with the pictures. Some of our cameramen are lacking in that.

When I was promoted to Manager for India, I always carried a camera with me on my stories. (Later, when United Press began a television service, I bought a 16 mm camera and carried it along with my still cameras. It got so that for each story I would write a report, take a still photo, and also send along television copy. Much later, I added radio reporting when I worked for NBC in the Caribbean—but that's another story for my next book.)

In the middle of June I got a letter from Gerry Rock saying that I should not make any definite plans. He said he was planning to depart from India about July 15 for home leave with his family and that there was a possibility he would not be returning to India. At the same time I was getting letters from friends in New York suggesting that I was going to take Gerry's place.

Mountbatten, Governor General of the Indian Dominion, had been advising Indian leaders on their negotiations with the Nizam. Because of his position as the last British Viceroy of India, he hoped that his presence in the negotiations would persuade the Nizam to come to terms. But Mountbatten left India in June, and on July 1 the Indian Government imposed a complete blockade of Hyderabad. The Indian Government banned even air services, and Hyderabad's only link with the outside world was the railway. I had written that if they stopped train travel by July 15 I would have to stay in Hyderabad for a while.

In July I saw the Nizam for the first time. The occasion was the laying of a foundation stone for the new legislative assembly building. The Public Works Department, which was responsible for the ceremony, built a temporary pavilion to make sure the Nizam would not get wet if it rained. Inside there was a plush easy chair plus a big couch covered with gold brocade on which the Nizam would sit. All of the invitees were to be in their seats at 4:30. It was a select gathering, mostly government officials. The Army Commander arrived at 4:35, the Prime Minister at 4:40, the Prince of Berar at 4:45, the Nizam's brother at 4:50. Then there was a 15-minute wait until the Nizam arrived. The road from the palace to the new ground was lined with policemen and as soon as the Nizam left the palace, the police began blowing their whistles. First we heard the whistles in the distance, getting louder as the Nizam approached. His car drove right up to the pavilion and out he stepped, a little old man dressed in a golden coat and wearing a gold "dusti," a ceremonial headdress. He turned and faced the Fort Golconda Infantry Guard of Honor and took the salute and then stood while the band played the national anthem, "God Save our Gracious Nizam." Then he marched in and sat on the divan. The Prime Minister gave a speech of welcome and the Nizam answered him, speaking in a loud voice that was carried throughout the state by Deccan Radio. Then off he went to lay the foundation stone. Afterward he was presented with a casket in which his speech was enclosed, a silver trowel, and a silver salver. He picked up the trowel and turned it over to see the hallmark, appeared satisfied, and then took the salver and made sure it, too, was of good silver.

Next, the Prime Minister and about four others presented "nazar," the ceremonial offering. It consisted of silver rupees presented to the Nizam on a white handkerchief. The Nizam took the coins calmly and put them in his pocket, jingling them to make sure they were of good silver. Then he had tea with everyone watching him. After ten minutes he left. The Nizam was usually mentioned as being the richest man in the world.

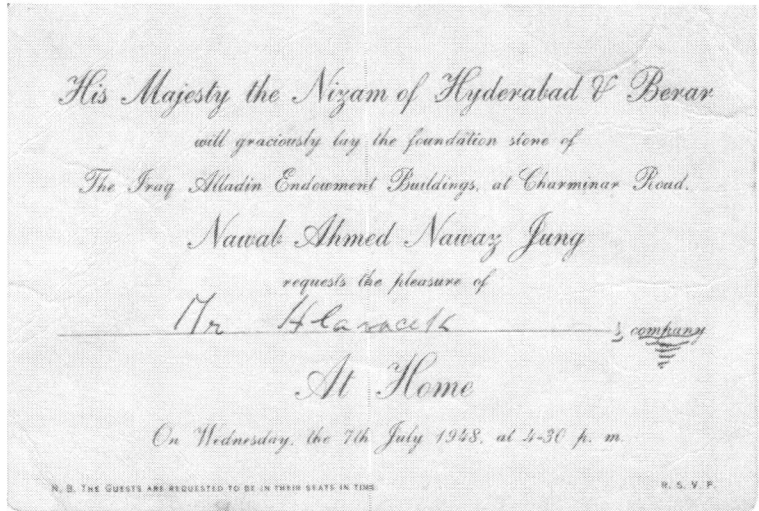

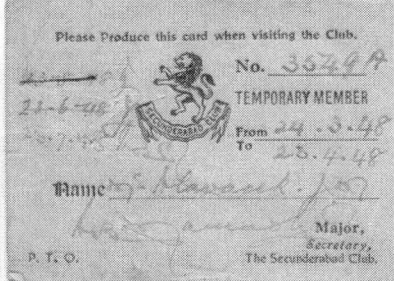

Top: Invitation to the event where I saw the Nizam for the first time; bottom left: riding the Czech motorcycle I bought after selling the Buick; bottom right: membership card for the Secunderabad Club.

13

BOMBAY MANAGER FOR INDIA

◆

(July to September 1948)

Gerry Rock and his family left Bombay on July 22, 1948, and as of that date I was named Acting Manager for India. I had moved to Bombay from Hyderabad in the middle of the month and spent several days with Gerry going over the files and the business prospects that were in the pipeline.

I had no place to live, so I moved into the Taj Mahal Hotel on a temporary basis. New York had advised that Bob Branson, a young United Press correspondent from Manila, was coming up to take my place in Hyderabad. When Bob arrived, I made a quick one-day trip to Hyderabad to introduce Bob to my contacts in the city and brief him on what he could expect in view of the Indian blockade of the state. I transferred the Jawa motorcycle to him so he could have transportation. When I returned from Hyderabad, I moved from the Taj Mahal to the Ambassador Hotel.

I started my new job at the same time the Indian Newspaper Editors were meeting in Bombay. I did not attend their meetings, but I kept in touch with their activities because many of the editors were clients of our United Press news service.

Having sold my Buick, I once again found myself without transportation. While I was in Hyderabad, my friend George Small had been transferred to a consulate in Spain and so I did not have the use of his car. However, one of my friends from General Motors came to the rescue and promised to help me buy a car from GM. (The General Motors people proved to be great friends, arranging to let me buy at least three cars from them during my stay in India.)

On the Monday of the first week of August, I flew to New Delhi to meet with Stew Hensley, who had been the Manager in India before Gerry Rock. New York had asked Stew to come to India for a few months to help me navigate the changeover from Gerry.

After lunch, Stew and I interviewed Howard Donovan, the Charges d'Affaires of the American Embassy. He invited us to dinner that evening, and I was pleased to discover that most of his home was air-conditioned. In the heat of Delhi in August, it was pleasant to dine in comfort.

On Tuesday, we made a round of visits to Indian Government offices and the New Delhi newspapers. We met with Devadas Gandhi, editor of the *Hindustan Times* and, incidentally, the son of the Mahatma. In the evening, P.D. Sharma, our New Delhi correspondent, took us to the Gymkhana Club for drinks, dinner, and dancing.

On Wednesday it was our turn to serve as hosts, and Stew and I entertained our New Delhi correspondents, P. D. Sharma and Jim Michaels, and Jim's wife at dinner at the Imperial Hotel Grill. (I made a note that it was quite pleasant although it cost us a mint of money. Working for the UP, we were always worried about money. Jim Michaels was the United Press correspondent in New Delhi who had reported on the assassination of Mahatma Gandhi.

The next day we met with the Deputy Prime Minister, Sardar Patel. Next to Nehru, he was the most important leader in the government. In fact, Patel was probably even stronger than Nehru when it came to many of the negotiations that led to the partition of India into the Dominions of India and Pakistan. Sardar Patel had quarreled with Mahatma Gandhi, and he was devastated when Gandhi was assassinated because he had not yet made his peace with the Mahatma. It was reported that, although ill, Patel had walked the entire distance in the funeral procession to the cremation of the Mahatma's body.

On Friday afternoon, Stew had an exclusive interview with Prime Minister Nehru which I, with the help of P.D., had arranged. The interview was given great play and brought United Press great prestige among India's newspapers. After filing the story, we attended a cocktail party for one of the foreign correspondents who was leaving India. After the cocktail party, Mr. Wei, a Chinese correspondent, Jim Michaels and his wife, and I took in a movie. Afterwards we went to a Chinese restaurant for a midnight dinner that Wei and I ordered together.

On Saturday we flew back to Bombay after what we considered a successful five days. Back at the office, we spent the next several days fixing several loopholes in our news operation. I noted at the time, "We will be able to fix it. I say 'we' reservedly because it's about 90 percent Hensley and 10 percent Hlavacek."

At that point I felt better about being appointed the next Manager for India and Pakistan. Stew told me that there had been other candidates for the job but that I was his and (Vice President) Joe Jones' first choice. I also was happy that I was to get a raise of about $25 per week. I would be making about $7,500 per year, which, I noted, "ain't bad for a newspaperman." (For comparison's sake, my 1948 annual salary of $7,500 would be worth at least $50,000 in 2006.)

After a week of working in Bombay, I left Stew in charge and flew to Karachi, Pakistan, to spend several weeks staffing our office and selling our service to Pakistan newspapers. I began a sample service and then was able to negotiate several contracts. I had to fire the correspondent we had hired to replace Tahilramani, and I planned to send up a young American from Bombay. I had hired two former Army men who had elected to stay in India because they had married Anglo Indian wives. One was George Rice and the other Jim Berry, and I made arrangements for Jim to come to Karachi.

After Jim arrived I was able to make a quick trip to Lahore, Pakistan, and then flew back to Bombay. Taking over as the manager, I inherited a smoothly running office. The manager, Verraraghavan, took care of all of the details such as salaries, bills to be paid, and advice on which clients were behind in their bill paying. He was not a reporter, but he was essential to our operations. Verra was also a Brahman, and consistent with the caste system, he was friendly in the office but we never had a close relationship with his family. I never met his wife or visited his home. When I traveled I always brought back a small present for his daughter and Verra always had a request for a small gift—a transistor radio, a special wristwatch, etc.—which I would bring to him.

On the editorial staff, we had three radio operators, all of whom had got their training with the Indian army or the Indian post office. The news came in Morse Code from London. The copy they took down was sent to the editors we had hired.

The chief editor was Ernest Dharma, a Ceylonese who had been in Malaya and escaped to India where he worked with the American army in Calcutta. He had an excellent command of the English language and was married to an Anglo-Indian lady, Islet, and the couple had two little boys. My relationship with Ernie and his family was very close. Later, Islet and the two boys left India to live in Manchester, England. Ernie stayed with the United Press for a number of years and I managed to get the United Press to send him to cover the Olympic Games in Helsinki for our Asian newspaper customers. (Our relationship continued after both Ernie and I had left the United Press. My wife, Pegge, and I visited him in Manchester on several trips to England.)

Assisting Ernie were three sub-editors. Govindan Unny, whose home was in Kerala on the southwest coast of India, spoke Telegu in addition to his knowledge of English; Shastri, from South India, spoke Tamil, and he, too, had excellent English. Both Unny and Shastri later transferred to the United Press office in Singapore at the request of the Singapore Manager, Wee Kim Wee. After working in Singapore for a number of years, Unny left to become a regional reporter for Agency France Presse (the French news agency) and Shastri left to become a correspondent for the *Times of India* in Cairo, Egypt and later in London. I had two other Indian sub-editors: Lakshman, who was from Bombay, and Swamy, an Indian who had been in Malaya.

Finding good editors in India was not a problem because everyone who wanted to be a newsman had studied English in school. English was the major language in India and served as the "bridge" language among all the indigenous Indian languages.

And of course the United Press had good correspondents in Calcutta and New Delhi. Jim Michaels was hired by the Far East Manager, Miles (Peg) Vaughn, in Thailand, where he had been working after serving as an American Field Service ambulance driver in Burma. Also hired for a short time was Robert (Bob) Clurman, who had been in the China Burma India Theatre as an American Field Service volunteer.

For a time Ernest Dharma was in Calcutta before coming to Bombay, and when Jim Michaels was transferred to New Delhi, we hired an Anglo-Indian newsman, Ronald Rolfe. We had competent "stringers" in Madras and also in Ceylon and Burma: Austin de Silva of the *Lake House Newspaper* in Colombo, and Ed Law-Yone in Rangoon.

With such a staff to back me up, I was free to travel and to indulge in my pastimes of golf and baseball. I took full advantage of my spare time away from the office.

That September, Mohammed Ali Jinnah, the "Father of Pakistan," died in Karachi. He had spent the previous months mainly in Lahore with trips into the hills. He had been flown to Karachi on September 13 to Karachi but died the same day he arrived at the hospital.

In Hyderabad, the Indian Government, tired of the Nizam's delaying tactics, ordered its army to march into the city. General K. S. Thimmaya led the Indian troops. Bob Branson woke up one morning to find Indian troops in his office. A few days later, Bob left Hyderabad and came up to Bombay.

14

MARIE'S VISIT TO INDIA

◆

(October 1948 to May 1949)

In 1948, my sister, Marie Jean (who for no apparent reason had the nickname MacGregor) was a senior at Indiana University. I wrote to her from Hyderabad suggesting that after her graduation, she should take time out and visit me in India before she married and settled down in the United States.

For several months we had letters going back and forth frequently as I provided tips on how to travel, what to bring, and what she might expect when she arrived.

Here is a sample dated May 1, 1948:

Dear MacGregor,

How is the visa coming? I'm still waiting for a letter from you or Mother about that, since I understand that it might be difficult. I've written to Dorcas (Small) about writing to you and she has said she would. In the same letter George (Small) wrote that either the Isbrandsen Line or Isthmian Steamship line were the best. So I'll be writing to them but you might also contact their Chicago offices to see what can be had.

I've been thinking more about the car angle and I believe that the best bet, thinking over everything, is to get one of those Crosley's if you find the people that have them are satisfied with them. They are economical on gasoline and if my guess is right, money may be tight here about the time you arrive and a Crosley will bring you more profit than a larger car. If, however, by this time you have the Oldsmobile by all means bring it.

It's been hot here lately and I've been spending most of my time in the swimming pool. Was there all day yesterday and then in the evening went out to dinner with a Mr. Ansari, the local Firestone dealer, and he fed me a real Muslim dinner. At that it wasn't too spicy even though I can take anything they serve up nowadays.

Last week I was out twice to dances, the regular Thursday evening dance at the club and I was invited by the Greenes who have two daughters. The older one, in fact both of them, are a lot of fun. Unfortunately, or fortunately as the case may be, the older is engaged and leaving for England to get married next month. Too bad because she's loads of fun. The Greenes are Australian.

Friday night I went to a YWCA dance with the Greenes again. Mrs. Greene and both her daughters are big wheels in the local YWCA.

Swimming we have been having a lot of fun. I believe I told you there are a group of Polish pilots here with whom I've become quite friendly. So much so that the servants in the club call me one of the Polish pilots. So we've been kidding about, and I call myself the Pole with the American accent and the Poles the Americans with the Polish accent. I'd like to find some excuse to get away from the office and go swimming today. Maybe I'll do it yet. I was supposed to visit Osmania University but I think I'll get out of it.

Time is fleeting or have you noticed. I only hope we can get everything ready by the time you are ready to come. In August now, I think.

I still have the Buick. It's still running very well so I'm not too worried. I have had a few interested bids but none of them that want to pay my price—yet.

My girlfriend in New York is still writing. I think that the romance with Jock is over. So much for my love life.

I'm trying to find an excuse to get to Bombay to see George and Dorcas before they leave, but I don't think it will be possible. I'll send this off now. Keep your fingers crossed and we'll get everything worked out yet.

Love, John

When I first began writing to Marie about her upcoming visit, I believed that she would join me in Hyderabad where I had a comfortable lifestyle with quarters in the Rock Castle Hotel and a membership at the Secunderabad Club with its swimming pool. There was also a Boat Club where there was sailing on the Hyderabad reservoir, which served as the water system for the cities.

But when the unexpected occurred and I was transferred back to Bombay as the Acting Manager for India, I was living at the Ambassador Hotel and that is where Marie got her first Indian experience. The Ambassador Hotel was managed by two Greek citizens, Jack and Socrates Voyantzis, who became great friends. Also, my Polish pilot friends were now living in Bombay waiting for the political problems of Hyderabad to settle down.

Originally I had suggested Marie come out to India by ship. But when the reservations became too uncertain, she flew from New York on TWA, arriving in the first week of October. She had a similar experience to mine in that her flight was delayed at several stops on her route from New York to Shannon (Ireland), Paris, Rome, Athens, Cairo, Dharan (Saudi Arabia) and finally Bombay where I met her and shepherded her through Customs and Immigration.

Before taking her into the city and the hotel, we made a detour to Juhu Beach, which is near the airport, to show her the "Shack" which was to be her new home. The "Shack" was the beachfront living quarters for my friends Ray and Mary Helen Crews. Ray was with Western Electric, and he and his wife were departing for a six-month leave in the United States. They had agreed to rent out their "shack" while they were away. We would have the Shack during the best time of the year—from November to April. However, the "Shack" was not yet ready for us to move into, and thus our home for the next two months was the Ambassador Hotel. I told my sister that having arrived in India, she was to be the correspondent to keep our family up to date on our activities. For much of the next nine months she took the role seriously, faithfully chronicling her (and my) experiences for our parents.

In her first letter home, she included a couple of paragraphs that reflect her first impressions: "When I landed we came here so I could get a shower and change clothes. The hotel is just a half block from the sea so it's quite cool. The room, which is next to John's, has an overhead fan which is wonderful. Without it, it would be very uncomfortable. John's bearer (valet) came over this afternoon and brought some coat hangers. It's wonderful—Whatever you need, you tell the bearer, and he brings it. What a life this is going to be."

When Marie arrived, I already had the Chevrolet that my General Motors friends had sold me, but if we were to live at the "Shack" we would need another car because the "Shack" was 13 miles out of town and we didn't want Marie to be there alone while I was in the city managing the United Press office. During the months that we were writing about her travel plans, we discussed the kind of car she should bring. We finally decided on a Crosley station wagon—a small car that was produced just after the war. Crosleys had good gas mileage, which was essential because gasoline was rationed in Bombay. Marie bought her Crosley in Chicago and drove it to New York and, with the help of the New York United Press office, shipped it on a freighter called the "Silver Plane." It was not due to arrive in Bombay until the middle of November so until then, Marie stayed in the hotel although we spent many a weekend at the "Shack" at Juhu.

Her letters home during this time were virtually diaries of her day-to-day activities. One of the first letters told of swimming, cocktail parties, dinners, and dancing. She included this sentence: "People seem to be quite surprised that I don't drink or smoke and wonder if I have any vices."

One letter, written ten days after her arrival, relates her activities one weekend.

> Friday afternoon I went swimming with Ralph Bird, Reg Sutton, and Alex Toser. They were three fellows from Hyderabad who were friends of John. That night Stew Hensley, John's United Press colleague, came in from Delhi so we all went to the Taj Mahal Hotel where the fellows are staying and then came back to our hotel for dinner.
>
> Saturday afternoon I was swimming again. This time with two of the three Polish pilots. That evening John and I went to a cocktail party at the flat of three girls who work at the American Consulate. It was a farewell party for two of them. They have an apartment on the fifth floor and the elevator was not working so we climbed the 110 steps. The apartment is quite nice and I might move in with the third girl after the other two leave. The apartment has two bedrooms and baths plus the living room, dining room, and kitchen.
>
> From that party we went to the apartment of some of the fellows who work for an oil company. There we had more drinks before going to dinner. The dinner party was given by Joan Spielman and her fiancé, Jack Burns, who are to be married in December. Joan is the sister of Harry Spielman who is one of John's best friends. The dinner party was at the Ritz Hotel, which had just opened its rooftop restaurant. Lots of ordouvres, and plenty of champagne. We danced and ate and then went back to the apartment for more dancing and drinking. Got home about 2 a.m. In Bombay they stop serving liquor after 10 p.m. in public places and then, too, there are three "dry" days each week when no liquor can be served.
>
> On Sunday, we went to Juhu. There were 12 of us: Ralph Bird, Alec Toser, Reg Sutton, Harry Spielman, Joan Spielman, Jack Burns, Mr. Lee and Dr. Wright from the American Consulate, Stew Hensley, one of the Polish pilots, John and myself. The Spielmans' brought fried chicken and potato salad and

we had some lunch from the hotel and the Hyderabad boys brought some bread so we fared pretty well. We got to the beach at 11:30 and then played ball in the heat of the day. After lunch we all took swims and naps and then played more ball in the afternoon. We got back into town about eight o'clock.

In another letter, written a week later, Marie wrote:

On Tuesday we had quite a party!! The three Polish pilots, Stew Hensley, John and a Polish girl and myself. We went on the roof for dinner and had lots of good seafood and lots of food in general. I think I danced every dance so, of course, had a good time. The dance ended about 11:30 and then we went to the Polish boys' room and had more drinks. We started singing and went through everything from Old MacDonald to the Sweetheart of Sigma Chi, including some Polish songs. About one o'clock we went back to the roof and I proceeded to play the piano. It was the first time I had looked at a piano since I'd left home so I was pretty rusty, but we had fun.

Marie was an accomplished pianist and played both piano and organ. Living in the hotel, we spent many an evening having dinner on the roof and dancing. Often, after the diners had left, we would go to the roof and sing to Marie's playing.

About another Sunday, Marie wrote:

John played golf. I went out to the Shack with the Polish pilots, Stew Hensley, and "Spike" Merfield, a British engineer who works for Western Electric. He has been out here 20 years. John came about one and the Spielmans', Harry and Joan, came soon after. They brought with them Doug and Elli Ornstein. Doug represents the United Artists. We had a good time surfing and playing ball. In the afternoon we were playing bridge and some of the men were playing a dice game. They were all kidding us that we should open up a gambling joint. Next week Doug and Ellie are going to get a Beachcraft Bonanza so we can have sightseeing flights over the city. Next Sunday is Halloween so we probably will have a party. At night we came back to the city and went to a private showing of "The Time of Your Life," a United Artists picture which Doug invited us to see.

When we came to the end of October, and Halloween, Marie wrote about going to the market to buy a pumpkin.

Saturday I went shopping with Joan Spielman. John let us have his car so we got around very well. I had my first experience in the market. We bought apples and a pumpkin. The market is the place where you are supposed to bargain over the price, but seeing as it was my first time, we didn't do too well. We had a little trouble trying to explain that we wanted an orange pumpkin on the outside but we didn't care whether or not it was orange inside. There are many coolies with wicker baskets who want to carry your loot, and, of course, if you have a large quantity, you are expected to buy their basket and, of course tip them. It was quite fascinating to me. We didn't have much time to stay so I'm anxious to go back.

Stew Hensley carved the pumpkin into a very good-looking Jack-O-Lantern. Saturday night we went on the roof again. There was a very happy crowd and we always add to the merriment so we took the Jack-O-Lantern and set it on the piano on stage. The Spielmans were there with another party and asked us to join them after the roof closed, so we were out till two drinking and dancing some more.

Then Sunday we rode out to Juhu: the Spielmans, the Ornsteins, and the Eisenbergs plus the Polish pilots, Stew Hensley, John and I. We decorated the shack with crepe paper and the Jack-o-Lantern. We played ball and swam and played poker in the evening. At midnight, one of the Polish pilots, Stefan Zygnarsky, set off all the fireworks we had bought. We—Stew, John, the two Polish pilots and Harry Spielman—stayed overnight. The next morning we were up at 6:30 to see the Polish pilots as they left for Hyderabad. After they left we had a dip in the sea before breakfast. Later in the day, the Ornsteins and Russ and Phyllis Hadley and their small son came back out to the Shack. Russ Hadley represents Paramount Pictures and as I wrote before, Doug Ornstein represents United Artists. We had a grand time and again, we stayed overnight.

In another letter, Marie wrote,

You probably wondered about the fireworks. This past weekend—Sunday, Monday and Tuesday—was a big Indian holiday, Divali. It's the Indian New Year and all the financial books are to be closed and all debts paid and then new books are begun. There was no business so John could stay out at the Shack, which he did. The custom is to shoot off fireworks so it sounded like the 4th of July around here. I'm hoping that my car gets here soon because it will be so much easier to get around. John thinks we will move out to the beach soon after the car arrives. There's nothing much to do but swim and sleep or read. Otherwise it's heaven on earth. In the evening, it's beautiful. You look out across the water and watch the sunset and with all the coconut palms around, it's just gorgeous.

The first week of November was a very busy time for the UP office. The American election with Harry Truman and Thomas Dewey was big news in India, and our Indian newspaper clients were calling all night long. Because there is a 12-hour time difference between the U.S. and India, we were still receiving the election returns late into Wednesday morning and even into Thursday. Because our radio operators were taking down the news from London, I was in the office continually because once he took down the story, we—our editors and I—had to type it on the Gestetner (early Xerox) and send it by messengers to the newspapers. The final returns came in late in the evening and I was at the Taj Mahal hotel having dinner with one of my editor friends when the news came in that Dewey had finally conceded.

In a letter to one of her friends, Marie described the "Shack":

> The Shack has a cement block floor, solid walls that come up about three feet from the floor, and then shutters made of thatched palm leaves. And the roof is made from palm leaves. There are two bedrooms, and one extremely large room that serves as living and dining rooms. The kitchen and bathroom are in a separate building immediately behind.the Shack. The Shack itself is about 200 yards from the sea with nothing but a sand beach in between, so it really is comfortable.

The Shack at Juhu, October 9, 1948.

The Shack was so close to the ocean that at high tide, the waves came almost up to the front door. During our six-month stay, we had a cook, Jerry, and a hamal—a servant who kept the place clean and who was on duty when we were not there. The stove was a solid bank of cement with three holes about six inches deep and 10 to 12 inches across. The fuel was charcoal, and there was no oven. My sister wrote, "It's not much of a kitchen and I wonder how Jerry, the cook, does what he does."

The Shack was a great meeting place for our friends who lived in the city. Every Sunday, without fail, there were always ten or more friends out for the day. We would swim, play baseball on the beach, and in the evening, there would be bridge games, poker games and cribbage. We always managed to have lots of food, and drink although Bombay at the time had prohibition. There was a loophole in the regulations that allowed foreigners to get a permit to buy a few bottles of liquor. Also, many of our friends worked at the American Consulate General and, with diplomatic privileges, they were able to help with the bar needs. It is fair to say that we were not deprived.

Most of the food was bought by Jerry, the cook, who would leave each morning for the market in the village of Juhu. We had plenty to eat, and our parents wanted to know the prices of food. My sister provided the following information:

> Butter is a dollar a pound. Eggs about 57 cents a dozen, beef about 40 cents a pound. Bread is six cents a loaf but the loaf is half the size of the ones at home. Bacon is a dollar a pound. Canned ham about $1.65 a pound. Grapefruit 6 to 10 cents apiece depending on how well one can bargain. Milk is 33 cents a seer, which is roughly a quart. Oranges, 33 cents a dozen. Tomatoes about 16 cents a pound. Sugar about 16 cents a pound. Lettuce about six cents a head. Lamb also about 40 cents a pound. Beer is one dollar a bottle for a 26-ounce bottle (and you're allowed three bottles to a customer). Whiskey runs from $12 to $17 a bottle. American cigarettes are $4 a carton. The bread man and the egg man both come to the shack to sell their wares. The egg man carries the eggs in a large round basket on his head. The bread man rides a bicycle with two large baskets hanging from the handlebars.

We supplemented the above with fish and lobster that the fishermen would bring to the shack. We would bargain with them as to the size, but the price was always low. The fishermen would go out in their little boats and then drop their nets in a large arc and the men on shore would slowly pull them in. Sometimes they would get a very small catch, with minnow-sized fish, sometimes almost nothing, and then at times the nets would be full of flapping fish.

At times my sister would drive into the city to buy food as well. My sister's Crosley had arrived from the United States. The Crosley was a small car—we claimed it had a sewing machine engine—built by the Crosley Radio Corporation. The Crosley, a mini car in today's terminology, was actually born in 1939 but World War II intervened. It had a four-cylinder engine and was very economical, one of the reasons I advised my sister to buy it because in India we had severe gas rationing. Twenty-five thousand Crosleys were sold in 1948, including ours. The company ceased production in 1952, but today there are still a few Crosley Auto Clubs in existence. Two are listed on the Internet: one in New Jersey and another in Ohio.

In a letter to Jennie Hlavacek (secretary in the Acme Photo office—no relation) dated January 26, 1949, Marie wrote:

> My present house is a shack on the beach. And it's really a shack. It has a thatched roof, no windows, but thatch shutters, and it nestles between coconut palms. It has a tile floor which is divided into two bedrooms, and one big room which we use as a combination dining and living room. We have modern conveniences such as a flush toilet, shower and an electric refrigerator so it is very comfortable. A cook and a hamal (boy who cleans and makes the beds) makes everything comfortable.
>
> Most of our friends live in the city in very modern flats but they like to come out to the beach so on weekends we usually have a crowd of people. Lunchtimes the cook fixes curry and rice in great quantities for the voracious appetites of we who have been playing baseball on the sand, then surf riding before lunch. Afternoons we sit about playing bridge and drinking beer or maybe taking a walk up the beach to watch the native fishermen bring in their nets.
>
> The shack has wicker furniture with cushions and three couches. One bedroom has a double bed and the other twin beds. All the beds have mosquito nets, which are mandatory. There is a good-sized table for eating and several cupboards and bookcases.
>
> John managed to borrow an electric roaster, and it has been wonderful because we don't have a decent oven in the kitchen. I am going to attempt a cake this afternoon so I hope it turns out all right.

In addition to electricity, the Shack had a telephone, which made it possible for me to remain in contact with the office.

At the American Women's Club dance on March 8, 1949, we won a case of scotch. On the next Sunday we had an even bigger crowd than usual because everyone knew we had won the scotch and they came out to help us drink it.

Left photo: Marshall Holbrooke (Marie's future husband), Marie, and Harry Spielman.
Right photo: Marie and I.

Left: The Crosley station wagon.
Right: Enjoying my leisure time at the Shack.

120 United Press Invades India

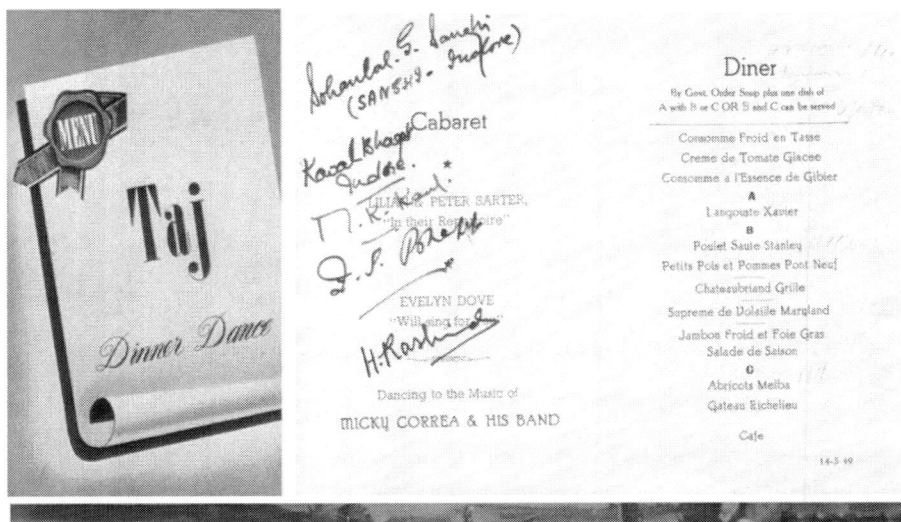

*Dinner Dance at the Taj Mahal Hotel in Bombay, May 14, 1949.
Marie is second from left.*

15

AFGHANISTAN

◆

(November to December 1948)

In late November 1948, at the invitation of Al Beaver of Firestone, I traveled to Afghanistan because it was part of my United Press territory. He was making the trip to check on his Firestone agents and also to visit the Morrison-Knudson operations in Afghanistan. It was a great opportunity to visit the country at little expense (always appreciated by United Press).

Traveling with the two of us from Bombay were two other Firestone men, Archie Blackwood, Firestone's chemist, and Jim Stansill, an expert at vulcanizing and tire retreading. While I was away my sister, Marie, stayed with Katherine Beaver at her luxurious flat.

On November 27 we flew to New Delhi. We were met at the airport by the Firestone dealer and taken to the Imperial Hotel, where we had difficulty getting rooms. Stew Hensley was in New Delhi at the time so I got a bed in his room and the other three got a room at the hotel later in the evening. That evening, Stew and I went with P. D. Sharma, our United Press Delhi correspondent, to the Delhi Gymkhana club for dinner. Later we went back to the Hotel Imperial's Grill Room where we met the Firestone men and stayed until closing time. Delhi weather in November is perfect in the daytime but very cold at night. We had fires in the fireplaces to keep our hotel rooms warm.

The next day, a Sunday, Al and I had planned to play golf but the car we had arranged never appeared so we stayed in the hotel. That evening, Joseph Bobinski, one of the Polish pilots flying for Deccan Airways, came to the hotel to see Stew and me. Bobinsky was in Delhi overnight and was flying back to Hyderabad the next morning.

On Monday, the 29th, we went to the Pakistan Embassy to get our visas for Pakistan, and Al had to get his Indian registration completed. It took us all morning, but we got our permits. In the late afternoon I called on Devadas Gandhi, editor of the *Hindustan Times*, on United Press business. (Devadas was the son of the Mahatma and had become a good friend as well as a United Press client.) That evening I went to a party given by the Firestone dealer in Delhi, a Sikh name Suchar Singh. Stew Hensley didn't want to go, so I invited another Deccan pilot, Kasik Garstecki, to come along. Kasik was one of my Polish pilot friends from Hyderabad. The party was held some miles out of New Delhi at an old palace that had been deserted. We had plenty to drink (scotch) and also plenty to eat. Suchar Singh had invited many government people as well as some army officers. It was a very good dinner.

The next morning, Tuesday, we flew to Lahore. Stew Hensley also left that morning for Hyderabad, flying in the plane that Kasik was piloting. We arrived in Lahore at 9:30 and spent a good hour going through Customs and police registration. In the "small world" department, going through Customs ahead of me were Mr. and Mrs. M. T. Kennedy, Sr. They had been in the plane with us, but I had not met them. I introduced myself as "Check" and they said that Mel, their son, had given them orders to look me up. (Mel Kennedy had been an Oberlin in China teacher when I was at the Carleton school, and later he was an officer at the 14th Air Force headquarters in Kunming, working with General Claire Chennault.) Mel's parents had been with the YMCA in India during the war and now were traveling about the country visiting YMCA locations in India and Pakistan.

When we cleared Customs, Ozzie Hardy, the Firestone district manager, met us and took us to Faletti's Hotel, the only good hotel in Lahore. We obtained good rooms and then went our separate ways. Al and the Firestone men went to the Firestone office and I called on the newspapers. The United Press had just started service to a number of them, and I wanted to see how it was working out. We had lunch at the hotel and in the afternoon I went to see more clients. That afternoon I attended a meeting of Pakistan students who had returned from the United States. After the meeting I had drinks with Merritt Cootes, the American Vice-Consul in Lahore. (Before the meeting I happened to meet Charles Booth, one of the vice-consuls who was in Lahore. Charlie was at the American Embassy in Chungking during the war when I was at the Military Attache's office.) That evening I had dinner with Phil Heal, the manager of the *Civil and Military Gazette*. Phil was a Canadian and the C&M was a client. (C&M was the newspaper where Rudyard Kipling worked.) Phil and I talked of many things while sitting in front of a fireplace. It was so comfortable that I dozed a couple of times.

Wednesday morning, December 1st, we began our trip north. We had the Firestone Chevrolet, and Ozzie Hardy joined our party. That morning we drove to

Rawalpindi and arrived at lunchtime. We stayed at Flashman's Hotel and as soon as we arrived we ordered firewood for our rooms. The Firestone men had some business with the Pakistan Army so we stayed the night. We visited one of the Firestone dealers and managed to buy some Scotch. There was prohibition in that part of Pakistan, but only for Muslims. Non-Muslims were allowed to purchase up to six bottles of liquor each month. We, being travelers, had been given a quota of four bottles each, and I used only half of my quota. The price for scotch was only about Rs 22 a bottle ($7.00) while in Bombay the price had gone to about Rs. 37 ($13.00) if you could get it—but mostly you couldn't. That afternoon there was a slight drizzle, so we played some poker. Late in the afternoon I had an interview with Col. Wilson, aide to General Gracey, the Commander in Chief of the Pakistan Army. General Gracey was in Karachi. Col. Wilson spent an hour with me explaining the Kashmir situation from the Pakistan Army's point of view. At that time the Indian and Pakistan armies were facing each other in the complicated Kashmir problem. (Almost sixty years later, in 2005, the Kashmir problem had not yet been resolved.)

Thursday morning, the Firestone men had a business meeting with the Pakistan Army and I went to see General MacKay. We had a long talk about the Kashmir situation. At the moment there was a delicate ceasefire but every now and then each side would fire a round or two. After lunch, our party left for Peshawar. The road to Peshawar—in fact, the entire road from Lahore to the frontier—was very good. It was a macadam road built by the military, and it was very comfortable driving. We arrived in Pehaswar, the capital of the Northwest Frontier Province, about 6:00 and got rooms at Dean's Hotel. As we drove up I met Eric and Margaret (Parton) Britter, who were in Peshawar on a news trip. Eric was a correspondent for the *Times of London* and Margaret for the *New York Herald Tribune.* They were leaving that evening to go back to New Delhi, and I had a farewell drink with them before getting ready for dinner. The Firestone dealer in Peshawar sent over firewood for our rooms along with a large basket of fresh fruit, nuts, and dried fruit for us. It was very cold at night and there was no hot water, so none of us took a bath. We played poker in Stansill's room, and his room was quite a mess by the time we got through, with nut shells all over the place.

Friday morning we checked in with the police. This being a frontier area, they were very strict about who came and went, and a permit was needed to travel the road to Kabul. Ozzie Hardy, who had applied for his visa from Lahore, found that it had not yet arrived at Peshawar. (We went on without him.) That morning I met my string correspondent, Mr. Shah, and we had a pleasant time talking.

He kept United Press covered on any big goings-on in that part of the world. After lunch we walked about Peshawar and toured the bazaar area. We bought some fur hats. The hats were made from American synthetic caracul, which was shipped to Lahore where the cloth was made into hats and shipped to Peshawar where it was sold to people like us. Actually we knew what we were buying so we weren't suckers, but I was amused by the situation. In the evening we repaired to Jim Stansill's room and ate dried fruit and nuts while playing poker.

Saturday morning we were up early for the drive to Kabul. We had to leave Ozzie Hardy behind because his visa had not yet arrived. We promised to get him a visa as soon as we arrived in Kabul so he could join us. The first part of the drive was slow as it had rained and the macadam rods were slippery. But later we got into the country leading to the Khyber Pass where the roads were dry and we were able to make better time. It was rugged country through that part of the journey.

The drive through was much the same as the time I had made the journey in 1940. The roads were the same, the only difference being that most of the troops had been pulled out. In 1940 British troops occupied all the forts and there was constant fighting between the British troops and the tribesmen. After the partition of India, most of the troops were withdrawn and there seemed to be little fighting. Most of the region was a tribal area and there was really no jurisdiction either by Pakistan or Afghanistan. At the moment all was peaceful, but one never knew when trouble might occur. We had no incidents on our way to the border, where we went through passport inspection and showed our permit to drive the car. We had to pay a toll, since the road from Peshawar to the border was a toll road. That took some time, but we finally got them to open the barrier and in we went to Afghanistan. (I had only gone as far as the border in 1940.) Once we crossed into Afghanistan, the road got rough. The drive from Peshawar to Kabul took some nine hours driving time for only 180 miles. At about 11:00 a.m. we stopped at Jalalabad where there was a camp belonging to the Morrison Knudson company with ten American employees. We drove in to say hello, and they offered us coffee and cake. Then their mechanics fixed the brakes on the Chevrolet and by then it was lunch time so we had lunch with them. The ten were only a few remaining workers from what had once been a large camp. They were surveying the river and the road in preparation for construction work later. It felt good to get into their American-style buildings, even though they were construction type. Screens were on the windows, and there was running water, hot and cold. We had a good meal.

After lunch we continued our drive into Kabul. All along the way we passed camel trains belonging to the nomads. These nomads traveled in large caravans, sometimes as many as 10,000 strong, complete with camels, horses, donkeys, dogs, chickens, and kids. The dogs were especially formidable—big and very fierce. I took one look at them and decided to give up any plans I might have had about traveling through Afghanistan on foot. When we crossed the border into Afghanistan there was a big encampment and then we were to meet the nomads throughout the country. It was the time of the year when they were moving south into Pakistan for the winter, and in the spring they would move back north. They carried food and clothing for bartering. It was interesting to see their chickens on top of the camels, tied so they couldn't get away. The nomads were rough-looking individuals and not too friendly. Every once in a while one would make a pass at the car with his stick when we had gone too fast near one of his camels. We drove on from Jalalabad through a river valley where the local people had irrigated many of the hillsides for terrace farming. It reminded me of the China that I had been in. Most of the country is mountainous, so they had to do terracing to get any kind of food production.

We arrived at Kabul after dark and had dinner with the Morrison Knudson people at the far edge of town. The MK people had no room for us, so we went to the Hotel de Kabul where we had wired ahead for rooms. The hotel could put up only two of us in the hotel but had arranged for a room across the street. We flipped to see who would go across the street, and Al and I won and were able to stay at the Hotel de Kabul. Jim and Archie moved across the street to the accompaniment of some good-natured complaining and remarks about the coins I used. We got firewood and coal bricks and went to bed. It wasn't as cold as we had heard it would be, although we got a frost that night and others. But we didn't have to drain the car radiator, so it couldn't have been too cold. The hotel was not too bad but we found that the manager was a brother of the manager of the Ritz Hotel in Bombay where I had stayed for some time a couple of years earlier. He had just come from Italy to Kabul and his wife was helping him modernize the hotel. We heard tales of what the hotel had been like before they arrived from Bombay: stories of no food, no water, no wood and the like. The hotel was better when we were there, but there was still plenty of room for improvement. I wrote that I would not advise anyone to go to Afghanistan for a pleasure trip. For one thing the food was pretty bad. Mutton was the only meat, and most of it was cooked in mutton fat which permeated everything they cooked. The taste became tiresome after a while.

Sunday morning after a breakfast of omelets, toast, and what they called coffee, Al and I took the car to see Al's Firestone dealer, Mr. Hafazullah Khan. Kabul was one of the first cities I had been where a knowledge of English didn't help very much. The night before we met people who spoke French and German but no one who spoke English until we found the University of Kabul where I routed out an assistant professor of chemistry who guided us to the Morrison Knudson camp. We finally got the name of the place written down—Sherkat Service—and with that we found the place. Mr. Hafazullah Khan spoke quite a few languages and enough English to be fluent. He was glad to see Al and then piloted us around to the American Embassy where I found Elliott Weil, the Chargé d'Affaires. Hafazullah left us there, and we a long talk with Elliott. It was Sunday, but he was working because the diplomatic pouch was being sent that evening to Peshawar. The pouch goes went once a week by car to Peshawar where a courier picked it up to send on to Washington. There was no airplane service into Peshawar from Kabul.

We had a long talk with Weil, who gave us some of the background about Afghanistan, mainly about the recent charges made by the Russians that the American were trying to include Afghanistan in the Marshall Plan and how the Afghans (according to Weil) stood right up and denied all the charges. I also got some background on the Morrison Knudson operations in Afghanistan.

In the afternoon, Al went to see his Firestone dealer and I took the car and went to see Mr. James Hays, the man in charge of Morrison Knudson activities in Afghanistan. Hays told me he had arrived in April and that the present work of the company was concentrated in the south where they were building diversion dams and getting ready for irrigation projects in the Helmand River basin not far from Kandahar. Hays didn't want to tell me too much until I had seen the Public Works Minister since MK was working under contract to the Afghan Government. However, I got the idea that the MK operations had been more than a little fouled up when they had begun more than two years earlier and it was only when Hays came that they had a complete house-cleaning and things began to move. Evidently the Afghans had been taken for somewhat of a ride for the first two years. Hays mentioned that there were many difficulties what with the partition of India at the time, difficulty in getting construction equipment and transporting the equipment once they could buy it. He also said the Afghans didn't know too well what they wanted done. But all in all, it smacked pretty much of a mistake on the part of the Americans. At least it looked that way to me. Hays told me that since he had come the Public Works Department minister had been out to inspect the work down in the south and taken along the finance secretary, and both were pleased with the way things were going. I spent an hour and a half with Hays and then went to pick up Al. His man, Hafazullah, took us for a tour of the city, which at that time of the year was not very pretty. Most of the roads were gravel and dusty. Also because of the strict purdah in Afghanistan, most of the houses had thick walls protecting them. From the street the houses looked ugly and it was only when one got past the gages that one saw the lovely bungalows hidden behind. This reminded me of China and the China compounds behind the walls. We rode through the newly planned city where trees had recently been planted. Late in the afternoon we returned to the hotel and Hafazullah joined us for a drink. We were back to welcome Ozzie Hardy who had arrived from Peshawar. He had secured a seat on the Afghan Mail truck and it was a rough journey—hard wooden seats on a two-and-a-half-ton truck over rough mountain roads. He was one tired individual when he arrived.

By this time we had two rooms with a bath connecting them so Jim and Archie had moved into the main building. However, we needed another bed for Ozzie, so he moved in with us.

That evening we had a mutton dinner—we had mutton for every meal—and we had slices of pears for dessert. We walked along one of the streets of Kabul where there were small shops. We must have looked a sight because we stopped at each one to try to find out what they sold, how they made their food, and how much it cost. Of course, none of us could speak the Persian the Afghans spoke, and the shopkeepers knew no English. Afghanistan was well known for its fine melons. The important trade with Pakistan was dried fruit, and the shops were well supplied. Also they barbecued small pieces of mutton roasted over a charcoal fire. What interested me most was the making of Afghan bread which, when finished, looked like a snowshoe. In making the bread, as far as I could tell, they mixed the flour with water until they had a dough they could work with. Then the dough was shaped and pasted on the inside of a huge oven. One man did nothing but slap the dough to bake and then with a long iron fork removed the loaves for the customers who waited for the "hot" ones. The ovens were of two kinds—one above your head and one below. In either case it was quite a feat to keep from falling in, but the bread kept rolling out. It was the staple food in Kabul.

Monday morning, December 6, Al and the Firestone men dropped me at the American Embassy because I had to use the Embassy telephone and interpreter to make some appointments. There was a Cabinet meeting in session, so I had no hope of seeing anyone until Tuesday. I spoke with Eliott Weil and also with Dave Wharton, the commercial attaché, who told me something of the system of business in Afghanistan. In the country they had what was known as sherkatz, or joint stock companies. Each of these companies—about 130 of them in all—had a monopoly on a business. These were begun in 1933 because the Afghans found that most of their businesses were in the hands of Indian businessmen. First they formed a national bank and then they began setting up the companies. At the end of 1948 they had no competition.

The monopolies were very interesting. Petrol pumps (gasoline stations) sold sugar, since the sugar monopoly and the petrol monopoly were under the same sherkat. That was just incidental. Monday lunchtime found us at the hotel. In the afternoon we took a long (three-hour) walk through one of the bazaars. Most of the bazaar was covered, and each of the little shops displayed its wares. There were many shoemakers since people walked everywhere in Afghanistan. The narrow paths were crowded and full of traffic—camels, horses, donkeys, carts, and even automobiles from time to time. I saw many hats made of caracul (unborn lamb). At another shop they were roasting popcorn and several kinds of nuts. We finally wandered back to the hotel and took a bath—at least, I did. That evening we played poker using our stock of matches as chips. We played for very small stakes and had a lot of fun.

Tuesday morning, the 7th, I was finally able to begin my work although it was a struggle. At 10:00 I had an interview with Mr. Richtya, the president of the Press Board of Afghanistan. The Afghan Press was completely controlled by the government, and I wanted to see the head man before going further. We had a short chat during which I learned nothing, and then I left after getting an appointment with the head of the news service, one Mr. Feroz. After talking with Richtya, I wandered around to the Ministry of Mines where I found a young American named Walsh who was an advisor to the ministry. Walsh had been in Afghanistan for two years and knew as much about the physical aspects of the country as anybody did, including the Afghans. We had a productive talk. I remembered that this was the official day for lighting up fires, so he didn't have one in his office yet but promised that the next time I came back, there would be one. (In the winter, the Afghan government decreed that one could begin to light fires in the fireplaces on a certain date—this year it was December 7th. So his office was cold.) Walsh told me about the geology of Afghanistan, where the mineral deposits were, and how the Afghans were interested in exploiting everything they could in the southern part of the country but they were wary of doing anything north of the Hindu Kush, the mountain range that bisects the country. North of the mountains there were oil outcroppings but the Afghans didn't want to try to develop anything because they were afraid that once they began developing the areas their neighbors to the north (Russia and China) might take over. Walsh told me there were ammonium and talc deposits, and he explained how the new building and construction program was tied in with his work. He had found old traces of early travelers and through them had located ancient mines that the Afghans didn't even know about. He spent half of each month traveling throughout the country.

I left him to meet Mr. Feroz, the head of the official news agency of Afghanistan. We had written many letters to each other and I tried to do business, but he was not prepared to pay for our news service. Otherwise we got along fine. When we parted I made my way to Eliott Weil's for lunch. He had also invited the Firestone men. The lunch was excellent. He had what was probably the best house in Kabul, I was told, and the meal did it justice.

I left a little early to see the Minister of Mines for a short meeting and then returned to Weil's. The minister didn't provide much information, but he talked of the good work that Walsh was doing for Afghanistan.

That evening, I left the poker game to visit the radio station where the Bakhter News Agency copied its news. (After I returned to Bombay, we made a deal with the Agency to pay for our service.)

Wednesday, December 8, was a busy day. Al and the Firestone men went with Havazullah Khan, the Firestone dealer, for a ride about the city while I tried to see various people in the government. I had another conversation with Elliott Weil for background. Also, I visited with Hays of the Morrison Knudson group, but he wasn't too helpful. I think that too many people had been sponging off the group, and he was a little cold to visitors. We all had lunch with Havazullah and I again had to leave early to see the P.W. D. Minister, a Mr. .Mohammed Kabir Khan Ludin, who was the moving spirit behind the modernization of Afghanistan. We had a fruitful meeting. He was a graduate of Cornell University and thus understood Americans. He was frank in telling me that much of the early trouble between the Afghan Government and Morrison Knudson had been due to bad management on the part of MK. I left late in the afternoon to return to the Hotel de Kabul.

That night we had one last poker game, as we were to leave early the next morning.

Thursday morning after an early breakfast, we received a new station wagon from the Firestone dealer in Kabul. The trip to Kandahar was a killer over rough roads, and a passenger car would have been more comfortable. But the Firestone Chevrolet that we had driven had to be returned to Lahore. The road from Kabul to Kandahar followed a river valley and there were no mountain passes to climb. However, the road was dusty and rough with frequent chuckholes. All but one seat in the wagon were comfortable—the back seat was the problem. We decided among ourselves to trade off sitting there. I sat for the first couple of hours, bouncing around. Then Jim Stansill took over, then Al Beaver, then Ozzie Hardy, and finally, Archie Blackwood. Archie had the best ride, since the road seemed to get smoother as we got closer to Kandahar. We stopped for lunch about three hours from Kabul at a small town where there was a government hotel. It wasn't much of a hotel and we had to eat what we brought from Kabul—sardines, tuna fish, and bread plus a couple of tins of toddy (an American leftover from the army days which the Firestone men had found in the bazaar). Then the journey was just dusty and long. We checked the mileage: from Kabul to Kandahar was 334 miles. We were a very dusty bunch when we finally arrived.

We had one incident en route. Driving late in the afternoon with the sun in our eyes, we began to overtake a small pick-up truck belonging to the MKA (Morrison Knudson Afghanistan) people. Evidently, the driver of the pick-up also had trouble with the sun because at one point he almost drove the pick-up into a ditch. He swerved in time, but one of the men sitting at the rear of the pick-up was thrown off the vehicle. We stopped and picked him up. The pick-up stopped as well. In the pick-up were three Americans, one MKA man, and some American teachers who were going on vacation from Kabul. The Afghan who was thrown from the pickup suffered a cracked shoulder, we found out later.

At Kandahar we had a makeshift meal. The hotel had received a telegram that we were coming but as the telegram didn't specify that we wanted food, the hotel had not prepared any. However, the hotel got to work and prepared a meal—not very tasty but it filled us up. At Afghan hotels, one paid separate fees for the room and meals. In India, meals were included in the room charge.

We got rooms, and mine was the only one with a fireplace so we all gathered there. Al and I found a checkerboard and I proceeded to teach him how to play after I had gotten beat a couple of times. The room was cold, but I kept warm since I had a fire and I also slept in my clothes with my overcoat on top of the lone blanket provided by the hotel.

Friday morning, a holiday in Afghanistan, the station wagon came for us and we went to the MKA camp. Al and Ozzie wanted to find out why Goodyear had all the business. I went along. It being a holiday, they didn't conduct much business. The MKA people invited us to stay for lunch but since we had left Jim and Archie at the hotel, we went back. At breakfast that morning Al was so disgusted with the food that he told the hotel we wouldn't be wanting lunch. He thought we could pick up some canned goods in the market. On the way back from camp, which was a couple of miles out of town, we tried to find some food but there were no canned goods anywhere. We gave up and had pomegranates for lunch. I guess it was good to fast for one meal. We ordered dinner that night.

Friday afternoon, it was warm and sunny in the courtyard and we played poker. We were all tired from the trip of the day before but too tired, I guess, to sleep, so we sat and played. Friday evening, after dinner, which was mutton and rice, we gathered in my room, lit a fire, and played poker until midnight.

Saturday morning, we all went to the MKA camp. I found the dispensary, talked to the doctor, talked to the radio man, and then went to the doctor's house where I had coffee with him and his wife. It turned out that he had been an army doctor in China, and he knew Colonels Barrett, DePass, and McCoskrie. His wife was the unofficial newswoman for the camp, and for that matter, all of Afghanistan. She listened to the radio every evening, took down the news, mimeographed it and sent it to all the MKA camps and to most of the Americans living in Afghanistan.

At lunch we ate at the regular mess of the MKA. It was good American food, and we had our fill. After lunch we found an MKA man who was driving to Chaman on the Afghan border and to Quetta in Pakistan and would give us a ride. We returned to the hotel, packed our bags, and said goodbye to Hardy, who was to go back to Kabul by station wagon. We then left for Chaman, which is on the border of Afghanistan and Pakistan.

The road from Kandahar to Chaman was a new one being built by the MKA people. It was a four-lane highway, gravel-surfaced and still under construction. There were several bridges which were not yet finished. We had a little bad luck with a flat tire about halfway there, but with all the tire people we had with us, it was fixed quickly and made our way to the border for the inevitable Customs examination of passports and visas. Ours were all in order and we crossed into Pakistan where we had trouble with the Pakistan officials because we had crossed the border after the 7 p.m. deadline. However, we talked our way into the country and went to the MKA bungalow. The MKA kept two men at Chaman to do all the forwarding of their supplies, which came from Karachi by rail.

We had a good meal provided by the MKA, sat near the fireplace talking, and then retired. It was cold, but we had plenty of warm bedclothes.

Sunday morning we had breakfast and then moved quickly to Customs to get our permits to travel by road to Quetta. In this border country, one needed a permit to travel. We sent a message to Quetta to get reservations on the plane to Karachi. Then after viewing the MKA man's fish pond—a big water tank near the railway yard where he kept fish he had caught up country—we took off for Quetta. This was an easy journey because the road was a military road which traversed some mall mountain passes but nothing exciting.

We arrived at Quetta in time for lunch. We stayed at a small hotel where the food was very good. After lunch we wandered downtown to see the city. Quetta was once a large army cantonment but by that time most of the British had gone and there were lots of empty spaces. The Pakistan Army kept a number of troops at Quetta. The town was clean and the shops were full of goods. It was quite a nice change from the dusty Afghan towns.

That evening we went to a bingo party. We played for a while. The bingo party was at the local railway institute and patronized by all the railway people, most of whom were Anglo-Indians. There was a bar and an orchestra of sorts that played between games. It was good fun. We left early to return to our hotel for dinner and then the four of us played poker.

Monday, December 13, we had a late breakfast and then went to town to make sure of our plane tickets. A Firestone man flew up from Karachi in the morning to make sure we had enough money. We wandered around town all morning, I to look at the newsstands and the bookstores, the others to see tire dealers. We had good coffee and cakes at a restaurant and then returned to the hotel for lunch. The MKA people gave us a car to take to the airfield and we waited about an hour for the plane, which flew us to Karachi.

As we boarded the plane in Quetta, a Muslim woman was boarding with us. She was completely covered with a burka. As she entered the plane, she whipped off the burka and threw it on the floor and sat in the plane in her western dress. The scene was one I will not forget.

In Karachi, we again had trouble getting hotel rooms. We went to the Beach Luxury Hotel where we found one room. Jim Stansill and Archie Goodwin got the room. I phoned the Palace Hotel, where I knew the manager, and obtained a room for Al and myself. At the hotel we had beer and oysters before dinner, and after dinner we retired early.

Tuesday, the 14th, I went to my United Press office to see Jim Berry, my manager. Jim and I spent the morning going over our local problems and then went to see a Karachi newspaper editor before lunch at the hotel. In the afternoon, Jim and I visited all our clients. After dinner, American Embassy friends Orpha Soine and Harry de Kine came by and took us to the Boat Club where there was a dance. We had a good time and after the orchestra left, we persuaded Al to play the piano. We got back to the hotel at 3 a.m.

Wednesday, the 15th, the Firestone men left for Bombay but I had another day's work ahead of me. Jim Berry and I visited newspaper editors all day. I had lunch at the hotel with Orpha Soine and then moved my bags to the office. That afternoon Jim and I had tea with a Lahore editor who was in town. He wanted to buy United Press service but wasn't prepared to pay the price. That evening Jim and I went out to dinner and I spent the night at the office.

Thursday morning I caught a plane for Bombay. My sister met me at the airport and I got back in the Bombay routine. That evening there was an American Association meeting where we saw movies of our Calcutta sports trip. We then went out to dinner at the Taj Mahal Hotel with many of the members.

Now for some incidental information about Afghanistan:

The money was called Afghani. The official rate was 421 Afghanis to 100 rupees, but the black market rate ran from 480 to 500 Afghanis for one hundred rupees (100 rupees was equivalent to 30 U.S. dollars).

Afghanistan was a Muslim country and had prohibition. You could not buy liquor openly. The hotel in Kabul, run by an Italian recently hired, was a government hotel. The manager told me he was trying to get the government to let him sell liquor to foreign visitors. I was told that one could buy liquor in Kandahar, but we didn't try since we brought most of ours along from Lahore.

There were no railroads in Afghanistan. Transport was all by road.

Afghanistan was a kingdom. Its royal family controlled what went on in the country. Also powerful were the Muslim priests, or mullahs, who were the ones who decreed that women stay in purdah.

One saw no women in Afghanistan except the nomadic women who went about with their faces uncovered. Women were just not allowed out.

Here is a dispatch I sent to United Press about Afghanistan:

Kabul, Afghanistan, November 1949—(UPA) "Companie Morrison" is the name for Morrison Knudson Afghanistan, the much criticized construction company working for the Afghan Government, which will probably continue building roads, dams and irrigation projects for another five years.

That's the opinion of Mohammed Kabir Khan Ludin, Afghan Public Works Minister, who is responsible for the American company being in Afghanistan.

But it hasn't been easy for either the Afghan Government or "Companie Morrison," as the Afghans call MK.

MKA signed the contract—a cost plus percentage deal—in 1946. American construction men and engineers began arriving in Afghanistan early in 1947.

Money for the project came in American dollars which the Afghan Government had billed during the war years by the sale of Afghan caracul (unborn lamb) when the Afghans enjoyed a virtual monopoly because her only real competitor, Soviet Russia, could not export during the war.

The Afghan Government had been thinking of modernizing its country in 1939, but World War II interrupted all its plans.

After the war, with a surplus budget and a big reserve of dollars, the government entered into the contract.

Prime mover behind the contract was Ludin, a Cornell University educated government scholar. Ludin, after spending 1932 to 1938 at Cornell, moved over to the U.S. Bureau of Reclamation for a year and it was there he got to know Morrison Knudson, which is one of the major construction companies doing work for the bureau.

Both Morrison Knudson and Henry Kaiser Construction firms were asked to come to Afghanistan and make recommendations. Kaiser, busy with his automobile venture, dropped out and MK began the job.

But Afghanistan is a mountainous country, land-locked, and lacks modern communications and industry. It has no railroads and its irrigation dams were built many years ago by German and Japanese engineers. To improve the lot of its people, it needs better and more roads, efficient dams for irrigating its valleys and the proper exploitation of its mineral resources.

To do just that, Morrison Knudson Afghanistan, a subsidiary of the Morrison Knudson Company of Boise, Idaho, signed a contract with the Afghanistan Government to implement a scheme to make Afghanistan a modern country. Two years ago they began their work in this backward country.

At first there was little news of their work. But last year, rumors began circulating that Companie Morrison was not doing its job. Stories spread that the Americans—between 200 and 250 of them—were building air-conditioned houses, brick canteens, and were making life comfortable for themselves on Afghan money. And that work on the roads and irrigation works and dams that they had come to do was being forgotten.

Opposition to the Morrison Knudson Company grew, with prominent ministers in the Afghan government openly criticizing the spending. The stories were enlarged by interested foreign governments—openly by the Russians who did not want to see American influence grow, and indirectly by western democracies who were jealous of their past influence upon Afghanistan.

The sad part about most of the stories was that there was a good deal of truth in them.

Ludin, himself, admits the first two years of MKA management in Afghanistan was bad. The American Ambassador to Afghanistan at the time, Mr. Ely Palmer, who was instrumental in getting the Afghans and Americans together, took a trip to the U.S. and informed Morrison Sr. that something had to be done.

In early summer, an entirely new team came out to take over, led by James B. Hays of Boise, Idaho, a veteran MK employee.

With Hays' arrival, work went forward and the Afghan Government is slowly being won over to a continuation of the work.

I talked to Hays about MKA. Hays said that much of the trouble during the first two years was due to three factors: (1) delays in shipping because of circumstances beyond control; (2) inability of the Afghan Government to make up its mind what should be done first, and (3) lack of proper organization of the work by MKA.

Under the first, Hays explained that the original shipments of construction equipment were held up in the United States by strikes. Then, during the summer of 1947, the division of India into the new dominions of India and Pakistan and the dislocation of populations which followed blocked all shipments from the port of Karachi, Pakistan, the entry port for goods going to Afghanistan. Also, rail connections between Karachi and Chaman, the border town through which most MKA equipment is shipped, were blocked by refugee trains and lack of railway equipment.

Secondly, Hays said that part of the difficulty was the uncertainty on the part of the Afghan Government as to what they wanted done. Hays listed many small jobs which MKA did which had no connection with the overall construction work.

Hays admitted that MKA did not plan the job correctly. Too many men came out for the job and the company was just not ready for them. Hays feels that if smaller groups had come there would not have been the dissatisfaction and dislocation they found.

When the first workers came, there were no quarters for them to live and they had to live in tents. Afghan has no movie theatres and there is no night life. A Muslim country, there is strict prohibition. And women are in purdah. They are not allowed to be seen out in the city.

Turnover on MKA personnel ran at one time as high as eighty percent with construction men quitting their jobs and going home. Contracts are for two years and only a few men have stayed their full time.

Pay is good and all living expense is borne by the company. Quarters are now built, there is good food in the mess, but still Afghanistan is a godforsaken place to most of the men. By working twelve months they get paid for thirteen.

16

BOMBAY TO COLOMBO BY AUTOMOBILE

◆

(May to June 1949)

In May of 1949, although I had been in India since 1945, I had not been able to travel through South India. In my reporting and United Press business, I had been to Madras where there were important English-language newspapers, and I had been to Goa and Ceylon. My friend, Harry Spielman, an American Consul, Agricultural, assigned to the Consulate General in Bombay, also had not been able to see the Malabar Coast. As Harry was soon to be transferred, he and I made plans to make the trip before he left India. It fit in with my plans as well, as I was to attend an All India Editor's Conference to be held in Bangalore in the middle of May.

While we were discussing the trip at the India Coffee House one day we were joined by Dick Brecker, an Information Officer of the United States Information Service attached to the American Consulate General in Bombay. Dick said he would like to join us, and as an incentive, offered to take his new Chevrolet.

We mapped our plans to drive down India's west coast and then cross into Ceylon on the ferry from South India, and on the morning of May 14, 1949, the three of us took off on our journey of almost a month.

The diary of this trip was written by Harry and myself while we were returning from Colombo on the President Jefferson. Both Harry and I had kept daily journals. Dick Brecker had left us in Colombo because he had to get back to work in Bombay.

Henry W. Spielman, known as "Harry," was a graduate of Oklahoma A & M. He was an expert on coffee, having spent four years in Brazil for the State Department. Also, he was a recognized expert on cotton. He had traveled extensively throughout India.

Richard L. Brecker, nicknamed "Dick," was a graduate of Yale University and was on his first foreign assignment with the State Department.

What follows is the story of our journey as it was written in 1949.

BOMBAY TO COLOMBO BY AUTOMOBILE 139

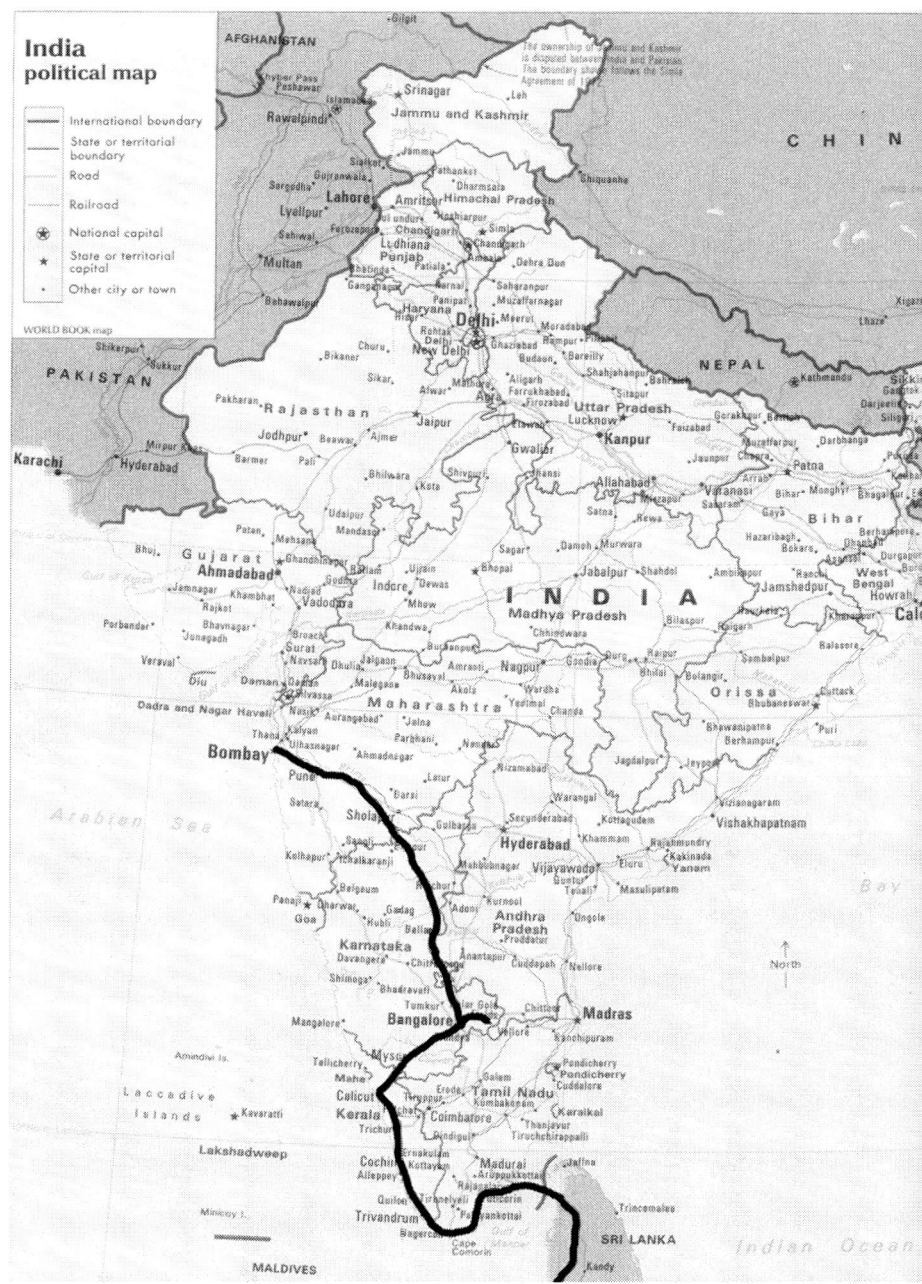

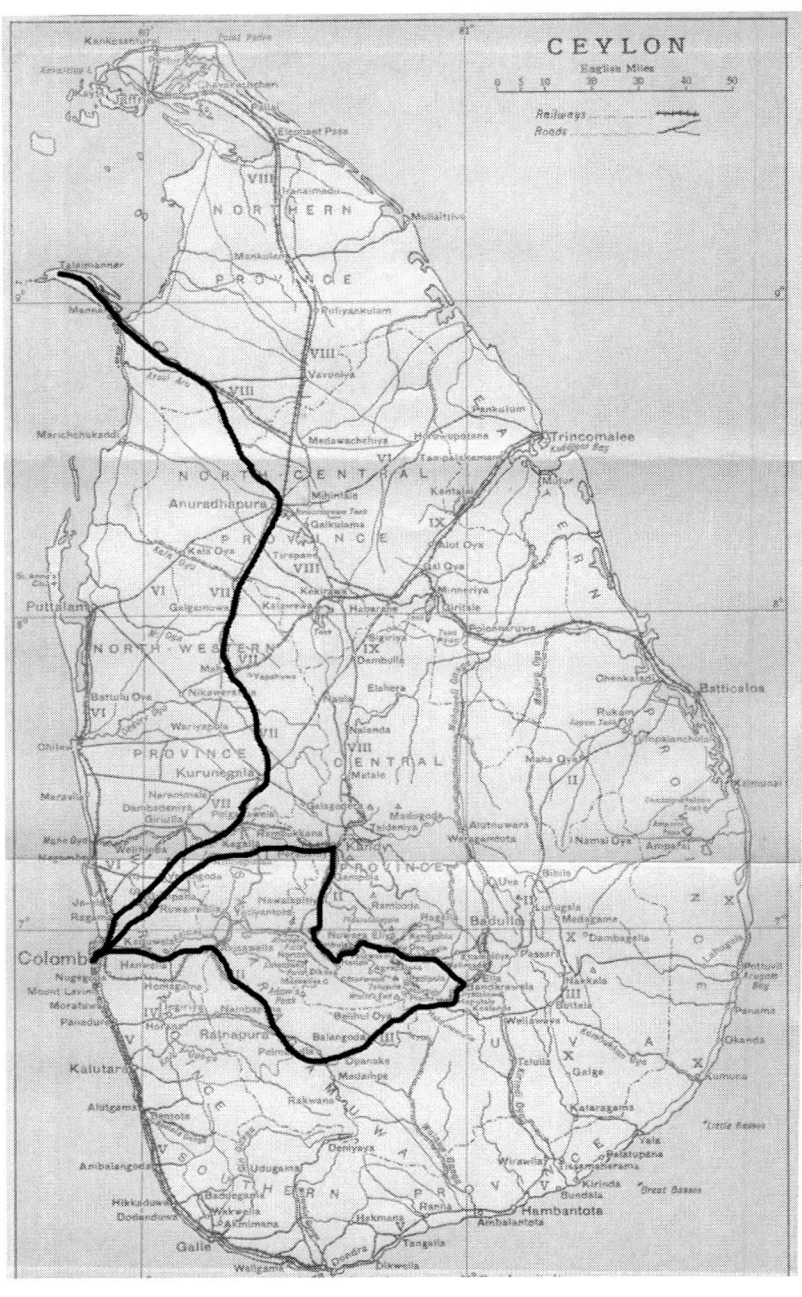

May 14, 1949 (Harry)

Check arrived about 8:30 as planned. He had been to his office and was ready to go. Brecker arrived a little after 9:00. Marie (Hlavacek), Check's sister, Joan (Spielman) Burns, Harry's sister, and Marshall Holbrooke, a tech rep with Pratt & Whitney Aircraft, helped us pack the Chevrolet. By ten o'clock, we were ready to go but first had to cool off a bit and tank up on water. We drove out on Marine Drive and then headed on to the Caltex station in the suburb of Worli. It was a little after 10:30 when we actually started on the Poona Road. We made good time and stopped for lunch at the Public Works Bungalow just beyond Poona. We continued on, buying gas at the city of Satara. Beyond the mountains behind Satara there had been showers which cooled the air and dampened the dust. About thirty miles south of Kholapur at dusk we saw our first elephant lumbering along the side of the road. Elephants are amusing to watch. They are so big, and yet they put their feet down softly, almost squashy. Their trunks sway back and forth.

When we arrived at Dharwar, we found no reservation had been made for us at the inspection bungalow. The Minister of Agriculture was due on Sunday and there was no room for us. We bought gas and drove on to the city of Hubli. There at the travelers' bungalow, we had our supper. The caretaker brought a loaf of bread and made tea. He also had drinking water which we again tanked up on. By the time we were ready to leave, it was eleven o'clock; consequently we were not able to find a service station open. We had planned to drive all night. We took turns driving and sleeping on the back seat. Check and I got acquainted with the Chevrolet's spotlight. It was very effective in getting people, ox carts, and trucks to move over. Check spotted a wildcat and I three or four jackals. Since we found no filling stations open along the way, we ran out of gas about daybreak. Fortunately we had passed two trucks. We stopped the first one, which was almost out of gas, but the second one gave us two gallons for ten rupees. That gas got us to Tumkar, where we bought twelve gallons after waking the attendant. It was fortunate for him that we woke him as the two trucks arrived while we were getting our gas so he made more sales. Tumkar was a bright, clean town with many individual houses, most of them painted white and some trimmed in red. We saw a number of Brahmins taking their morning constitutionals.

(Before I forget it, about four in the morning Dick was driving when he met a truck coming from the other direction. There was the usual turning out of lights. As the back wheel of the truck passed, the tire hit the rear fender of the Chevy, denting it slightly, but in inspecting the bumper, we found that the bumper had also taken a hunk of rubber out of the truck tire. The truck kept going, much to Dick's disgust. The driver probably did not know he hit the car.)

Check drove from Tunkar. When he stopped in the country, I woke up to find him taking movies of a colony of moneys. Monkeys are always interesting to watch. Remember the crowds at the zoo. In their native habitat they are even more fun. They have not learned to entertain crowd but merely go about their business the way they want to. The one-quarter grown monkeys jumped on a half-grown one—such goings on and such noise! It was difficult to tell whether they were in earnest or just playing. Like children, the fight was soon over, and the three were running off toward the lake like bosom pals. The must amusing moneys were the mothers with their babies. Some of the youngsters were quite young. They would nurse while the mother picked up seed from the ground. Some of the larger babies would go three or four feet from their mothers looking for seeds. If we approached too closely, they would run for their mothers. Actually the monkeys paid little attention to us other than to keep eight or more yards away. The place where we stopped must have been the meeting ground for the group before they started across the dam, since monkeys came from all directions to this spot. Many of them kept going when they reached the dam. The big bull monkeys were less friendly and kept at some distance. As one mother thought it time to leave, her youngster ran and jumped on her back like a little boy riding a horse bareback. Most of the young clung to the mothers' underside. Some of the little ones had tails three or more times the length of their bodies. All of them ran on all fours. One about half grown turned cartwheels. He wasn't watching us, so it wasn't for our entertainment.

The country around Tukar was something like that northwest of Lawton, Oklahoma. More or less level with stone hills rising. Some of the hills were being used as a source for rocks, both slab and crushed form. Apparently some of the rocks were formed in sheets (when the earth cooled) so that slabs three to four inches thick, about two and a half feet wide and six or more feet long could be made. Some cultivators make pens for storing grain from these slabs. There must be a lot of wild pigs in the area. (Oh yes, during the night we saw lots of rats on the road. All of them were fat, and fast. They were the most common form of "wildlife" we saw.) When I woke up again, Check was asking someone where the West End Hotel was. We had reached Bangalore. I have never seen so many flowering trees. Many of them were brilliant red and deep orange. There were also yellow trees and bushes and many primavera or bougainvillaea.

When we reached the hotel, the manager said he had no room for us even though he had received our telegram. We talked for a while and he gave us a room for one night. We cleaned up, had breakfast, and went to bed.

May 15, 1949, Bangalore (Harry)

About two that afternoon we had lunch. Before I got downstairs, Check and Dick had met Joachim Alva, editor of a weekly magazine in Bombay, and in his presence they talked the clerk into letting us stay until we were ready to leave. Alva had lunch with us. I took three colored pictures of the trees on the hotel grounds. While Check and I were walking around, we decided to play golf. Dick was agreeable but he wanted to see a couple of people to whom he had sent letters. Check and I played twelve holes of golf. The ground was almost like concrete, and the greens were hard sand, locally known as browns. I consistently knocked the ball out of bounds. I had a chance to par five holes but took my usual three or more to sink. After the twelve holes we were ready to do something else. So we had a beer. Then we went looking for the BUS (British United Services) Club and a friend of Dick's on Residency Street. The numbers on the street were a bit confusing—at the beginning No. 1 was on the right-hand side and the last number on the left. We didn't know that until we had gone to the other end. Of course, we were looking for the largest number. We found Dick's friend away. We returned to the hotel, cleaned up, and went down for a drink. It was amusing to buy all one wanted on a Sunday evening. We met five of Check's friends from Hyderabad. One worked for the British American Tobacco Company. That company has a plant in Hyderabad but gets its tobacco from northeast Madras. He said that most of the good quality tobacco is sent to England, but even so, some good cigarettes are made in India. About nine o'clock we had a good dinner and went to bed about ten-thirty.

May 16, 1949, Bangalore (Harry)

In the morning we went to the Indian Dairy Research Institute where the GOI (Government of India) is training government officers and technical men for private industry. It is the only dairy school in India, although the Allahabad Agricultural Institute gives a degree in dairy science also. Most of the cattle in the dairy were Red Sindhi, although there were a few white Sindhi and Gir.

The Institute had attempted a cross between Ayrshire and Red Sindhi which was not too satisfactory. The original Ayreshire stock died within three years after arriving in Bangalore. Attempts were made to save them by sending them to Ootacamund high up in the hills. Their lives were prolonged but they died anyway.

Some of the crosses were still in the dairy and giving good results. One cow gave 11,000 pounds of milk in 300 days. Now the only bulls on the place are Zebu so that more and more the Ayrshire blood is going out of the herd.

While we were watching the cattle, one of the calf boys started feeding the calves by putting his fingers in the calf's mouth and pushing its head into a bucket. Check had never seen this operation and was fascinated by it. In fact, I fed one of the calves while he took a picture of the process. It is amusing to watch a calf follow a person's fingers after they have been dipped in milk. One of the really funny things was to watch the calf get its face washed. Like little boys all of the calves objected to both the washing and drying.

Also in the herd were about 25 water buffalo cows and a couple of bulls. They were included mostly to give the students practice in handling buffalo.

It was surprising that the milk herd did not include any South Indian breeds. One would think that one of the functions of the Institute would be to develop one of the milk breeds of this part of the country. I guess there aren't any breeds that have possibilities. The local oxen are small but fast. The oxen cows give little milk, hardly more than enough for their calves.

Another interesting part of the Institute was the experimental feeding of rats. The standard Norwegian rats were used. They are cute and respond to attention. Some rats were fed Madras and Bengal diets. Others had various types of fat added, and one group had milk—the equivalent of eight ounces for humans. The latter group made normal growth. Those fed some fat showed some increase in growth but not nearly as much as the milk fed. Of the fats, butter showed the greatest growth but only slightly better than peanut oil or hydrogenated peanut oil. There were no harmful effects of the latter type of fat.

They were experimenting on how to improve the village methods of making butter ghee (clarified butter) without using different equipment or added expense. The method used is boiling the milk twice, once shortly after the cow is milked, and the second time, four to six hours later. By this double boiling both the usual bacteria and the spores are killed.

The creamery seemed very clean and the method of handling milk appeared to be the most sanitary. We drank two quarts of morning milk among the three of us and we probably ate at least a half pound of cheese. The milk is sold for five annas a pound, yet the cost of production is about eight annas a pound.

It was a little surprising to see so many graduates of foreign universities on the staff of the Institute. The dairy husbandry man was a graduate of Glasgow and at least four were graduates from American universities.

I took a few pictures of the bulls at the entrance but decided that I had better go back tomorrow and take more.

We returned to the hotel for lunch but were not hungry since we had had so many dairy products. Rather than pass up an opportunity to eat, we had lunch anyway. After lunch, Check and I slept about an hour while Dick went out to see some friends. He came in about two-thirty and woke us.

We went to see Mr. Mani of Firestone who told us something about the countryside we planned to visit. By that time, it was time to start for the editors' meeting. On the way we were stopped by the police to let Sri C. Rajagopalacharier, the Governor-General of India, go to the meeting. Check talked the police into letting us go on through. I drove Check and Dick to the Town Hall down a long line of police. After letting them out, it was necessary to park until after Sri C.R. arrived. I waited with the other drivers and onlookers across the street. The crowd was a motley group made up of more curiosity seekers; others knew the names of many of the people arriving.

Town Hall is also called Sir Puttannachetty Hall. On top were flying the Indian and Mysore flags. The columns in front of the building were wrapped in green leaf streamers, while the street in front had a number of colorful three-cornered paper flags. It was an impressive sight to see all the police keeping the crowd back for almost an hour before Sri C. R. arrived. In front of the hall was a fountain spraying precious water. One thing one can say for Indians putting on a show, they know how to do it. One man who arrived posed for a number of pictures, then had all of the cameramen stand around him while one of his assistants took a picture of the group.

It was easy to tell when Sri C.R. was coming. Two motorcycle cops preceded several cars by three hundred yards. Sri C.R. was in the second car. As he approached, there was mild clapping but no other cheering. He did not wait long for his picture to be taken. As soon as he was inside, the traffic was permitted on the street. I returned to the hotel to call my Bombay office to find out when I was to go on home leave. It cost forty-two rupees just to find out.

Check and Dick returned about seven. They were enthusiastic about the Indian dances they had seen at the conference. There were two girls in the dance who added to the enjoyment. One of the girls was the daughter of an editor attending the meeting. Check made some contact with old customers and friends with a couple of prospects. Dick met the Dewan and the Finance Minister of Mysore Province. The latter promised to arrange our trip to the Kolar Gold Fields and for the lights to be turned on at Krishna Raja Sagar—the dam at the great reservoir in Mysore. The lights are turned on only on Saturday and Sunday evenings but will be turned on Wednesday for us. Darn nice concession.

In the evening we had a couple of drinks with a Caltex man and his wife who wanted to go to a movie. Kasik Garstecki, a Deccan Airways pilot friend of Check's, joined us for dinner. We turned in early.

May 17, 1949, Bangalore (Check)

We were anxious to get up this morning. We had a lazy tea and managed to get shaved, bathed and down to breakfast. I decided to skip the business meeting of the editors' conference since there is usually nothing to do except meeting editors, and I had done most of that the day before. I went instead to see the editors of the two local daily newspapers. After breakfast Harry and Dick left me at the office of the *Deccan Herald*. I had a good hour with the manager of the paper and with the news editor, but Mr. Pothan Joseph, the editor, was in the hospital. After the *Deccan Herald* visit, I called on the *Bangalore Daily Post* for a good talk. I want both of these papers as customers for the United Press, but the *Post* is an old established paper and relies mostly on local news while the *Herald* is a new paper and is still losing money.

I got back for lunch at the hotel to meet Harry and Dick. Before lunch, however, I met Mrs. Giles, wife of the Intercontinental (Hotels) man, Mrs. Kumar, wife of the owner of the Ritz Hotel, and E.J. Kuruville. I had a beer and they had soft drinks until Dick and Harry arrived. We arranged to go swimming with Mrs. Giles that afternoon. After lunch, the three of us went swimming with Mrs. Giles and her little boy at the BUS (British United Services) Club, which has a small pool. The water was refreshing. While there, we met Dan Molina, an American selling books, whom we had been told to see. Dan gave us information about whom to see in Colombo when I got there in regard to Radio Ceylon.

Back at the hotel I met J. Natarajan, the editor of the *Ambala Tribune* and an old friend. Nat was the Principal Information Officer in Delhi and was also the Information Officer at the Indian Embassy in Washington in 1947–48. Nat, being an unorthodox Hindu, had some drinks with me. We sat in the bar and Harry joined us later. Dick had drinks with his friends from Madras who were leaving the next morning. Mrs. Giles joined us for dinner, along with the Curleys and Nat. Nat, Harry, Mrs. Giles, and I decided to see "Easter Parade" at the local movie house. The show at 9:30 was almost empty and we wondered how the movie companies were making any money. There were only twelve of us in the high-priced seats in the balcony and about the same number downstairs in the "cheap" seats. The movies in Bangalore have the intermission in the middle of the main feature, a different procedure from Bombay, where the intermission comes between the shorts and newsreels and the main feature.

Dick and Harry had spent the morning in the offices of the Coffee Board arranging our visit to coffee plantations.

Clockwise from upper left: Inspector's bungalow; Check getting a haircut; horseplay at the pool; the Indian Dairy Research Institute.

May 18, 1949, Still in Bangalore (Harry)

The room bearer came in a half-hour too early, at 6:30 but Check was up and at 'em just as if he had good sense. Dick was as enthusiastic as I was. The water did not run well. In fact, Check got halfway through shaving before the water ran out. We yelled loud enough to get ten gallons of hot water, but no one wanted a bath, just a shave. It never rains but what it sprinkles—must be the monsoon season.

We were ready to leave on schedule at eight but found the right rear tire had a nail in it. When we arrived at the garage, the employees were there but no one would begin work until the bell rang at 8:15. When the men did decide to go to work, it only took nine of them to take the tire off the car and put in a new tube. The nail was imbedded at least two inches into the tire, but, fortunately, it was a self-sealing tube so that it did not go flat immediately. We left the tube to be fixed and started for the Kolar Gold Fields before nine.

We arrived at the gold fields after ten. Mr. H. showed us a map of the mine we were to visit as well as a scale model. The gold vein is in a reef which slopes gently for a ways and then drops steeply. The "ways" is about 4,500 feet. We were to go to level forty-eight, which was level for over 6,000 feet. It is at the bottom of the first shaft. From level forty-eight there are three and a recently complete fourth shaft going down to 7,300 feet below the surface. And now they are drilling three more shafts going down, how deep no one yet knows. The depth will depend on the amount of gold in the reef and how difficult it will be to force air down there. The rock temperature varies from 125 to 145 degrees Fahrenheit. Before men can work in these conditions the air must be cooled. Even at 7,400 feet the rocks are nearly that hot and with the cooled air the temperature is still in the 108 to 120 degree range.

Before going down we were shown the wheel house, the air compressors, and the air conditioning system which is a separate plant by itself. The wheel house is thirty feet high and the towers for the lifts are seventy-five feet high. I mention this because it is necessary to carve similar structures out of the granite underground.

At ten-thirty, we donned our helmets, checked our cameras, except the one with the flash attachment, and went below. The first trip down was to No. 44, which was several hundred feet above No. 48, our original destination. We stopped there because ore was being loaded. There were some electric lights, but it was necessary to use cyanide lights as well. Mr. Godoin showed us the vein or reef which was being worked, which at that point was about a foot wide. Actually it varied from a foot to thirty feet with the average about five feet.

I halfway expected to see mules pulling the carts (bandies) around but it was done by men, or in the case of long hauls, by an electric engine. We dodged carts as we went down one "hall" and ducked our heads as we went through fire doors. Twice I found out what the bamboo helmets were for—to keep from bumping one's head. After wandering around for a while, seeing something new at almost every stop, we returned to the elevator shaft to wait for the lift to take us to No. 48. There I tried to take pictures, but I found out the damn flash gun would not work. Were we unhappy! Especially after Check had left his flash gun in Bombay. Everyone took it good-naturedly and down we went to No. 48. As time was getting short, we went down only one "hall" but found out the crew was not ready to use their drilling equipment. Then we went down to No. 73 which was 7,300 feet below the surface. The actual depth was 7,159 feet. Because of the shortage of time, we did not see the workings of the mines, but we did see the new shaft which was going down to possibly 10,000 feet. It was already 300 feet down. To do the work, four men are lowered in a basket which can also be used for bringing up the material dug out of the shaft. The bucket has a top so that nothing can fall on the men as they are being lowered or lifted, or while they are working. This top is not a lid but a steel sheet about ten feet above the top of the bucket.

We walked around a bend in the tunnel, only to have dust hit us in the face. As we got closer, we found workmen filling the push carts full of material which had been blasted out of the ground. When we got closer, the dust was really thick. It wasn't from blasting or digging but just from picking up the material (ore) and putting it into the carts. The work was being done to build the room for the underground wheel house. It was to hard to realize that underground, out of rock, a space big enough for both the wheel house, the wheels (overhead) and the cable runs had to be blasted.

By this time we did not have time to see the actual mining operations. Instead we took the express to No. 48, shifted to another lift, and rode up with the miners to the surface. I did not notice the heat down in the mine; it was a very dry heat and since I was doing no physical work, I did not mind the high temperature. Also we did not get over 100 yards from the shaft which is also an air vent. But as we were lifted at thirty-five to forty feet a second up the main Henry shaft, we felt cold. That was understandable because we were moving at a rapid clip into the downward flow of cool air which was being forced down the shaft. After we reached the top, we did not notice that the air was either cool or hot. In fact, for a little while, the sun felt good.

Now to lunch. Mr. Gadoin gave us the bamboo helmets which we had worn. We had lunch with Messers Tayler, Morrison, and Morgan in Taylor's mansion. As Check said, it was easy to see how Communism could get a hold on the workers: the managing director living in a luxurious house with at least twenty servants while the miners received a rupee fifteen annas a day for six hours below ground with no sanitary facilities. In addition, the miners receive twenty-two rupees eight annas dearness allowance. These managers (they call themselves superintendents) point out that the cost of living is 300 rupees now compared with 100 in 1939. But they admit wages have not gone up in that ratio. Each mine has its own union, or as they are called in Mysore, associations. As far as the managers knew, the unions are not controlled by Communists, but there are Communist workers among them. This regional Communist headquarters is Hubli according to Morgan. Altogether there are about 20,000 miners. Nearly all of them are married and have families. Most come from Madras. About sixty percent are furnished company houses for five annas a month. What we could see of them, the houses were built of local brick and plaster with tile roofs. There are community water taps and community toilets. There is no objectionable smell in the company villages, not even at the toilets. There are about 600 Europeans and about twice that many Anglo-Indians. There are a number of recreational clubs, including a golf course, tennis courts, and swimming pools for this group. The Indians have their own recreational facilities which they have developed themselves, such as football (soccer) fields and reading rooms.

John A. Taylor IV is a country squire type of an Englishman. Tall, about 6'2", slender but strongly built, blond, blue-eyed, he talked with a slight impediment in his speech which added to his charm rather than detracted, and was a charming, gracious host. As a hobby, he plays golf, tennis, and like most Englishmen, has a keen interest in this garden. He was proud of his one orchid which was a pinkish-red with a sweet odor. He is planting cannas in beds which must be dug out each year, the soil sunned and aired, fertilizer mixed and the cannas planted. They bloom about ten months of the year. He is also planting bougainvillaea as a hedge to screen the garden. Trees were carefully planted to cut out the view of the mines and the slag dumps.

Morgan, the Superintendent of two mines, looked like Harry Caray, was proud of his machinery which was by far the biggest we saw at the mines. [Harry Caray, for younger readers, was a popular radio and television sportscaster in Chicago.] He took us to a shaft which went down 6,996 feet in one drop. The wheel was forty feet in diameter at the outside and thirty-six where the cable began to wind. The axle weighed fifty tons. Morgan, Check and I walked between the two moving wheels. One had to hold on tight and not look too long at the moving wheels, or he might fall into one of them. The outer rims were not over two feet apart, just room enough to squeeze between them. They stirred up quite a breeze, too. The cables were two inches in diameter and over 7,000 feet long. They were good for 100,000 miles or about two years' service. They were carefully inspected once a week. The wheel house was tremendous. Just the lubricating system would fill a large room with pumps, coolers and cleaners. This engine room was spotless. All power was electric.

The power comes from the hydro-electric development on the Cauvery River, ninety-five miles away. When it was built, in 1900, the transmission line was the longest in the world.

The mines were started by a British officer who got a concession to develop coal mines or any other he might find. He found some gold and went to England to get financial help. An engineer was sent to survey the property and he reported favorably. The first attempts were partially successful but soon failed. In 1885, the present company was organized and has been operating every since. It has never missed a dividend. Nearly all of the capital is owned in England.

As the mine goes deeper, the cost will increase, but if the reef contains more gold, which seems to be the impression of the owners, it should continue to be profitable. The management has no idea how deep the mine can go. As long as the gold content is sufficient, the company will continue to go deeper. The Champion Reed mine is already to 10,000 feet.

The gold extraction operation was as interesting as the mining itself, the main difference being that here we were merely spectators while in the mine we had the feeling of being with the miners and sharing some of their difficulties. "Silent" Morley Williams showed us around. He had cards which explained in simple terms what each operation was doing.

The ore came from the mine in carts and was dumped into a series of pounders crushing it. There was a feed which limited the amount of rock entering each of the crushers. The crushers were a series of pounders about six to each crusher. These pounders were hard steel about six inches in diameter and about fourteen inches long with a handle on the end to fit into the drive. When the ore left the crushers, it was about the size of crushed stone used for building. The crushed ore was fed into revolving drums which had small boulders inside. These boulders helped crush the small pieces of ore into what "Silent" called face powder, and a soil scientist would call pure clay. It would pass through a mesh of 20,000 to 40,000 a square inch. We did not have time to count the openings in a square inch, so we had to take his word for it. From the drums the face powder flowed over carpets where seventy-five percent of the gold collected on the fleece—in the olden days sheep's wool or hides were used, hence "Golden Fleece." The amount of gold in 100 tons of ore is now reduced to four tons. The clay containing the remaining twenty-five percent goes through the process again along with the larger pieces of quartz.

The four tons is treated with cyanide and clarified. The gold goes into solution with the cyanide, or rather chemical combination. Zinc shavings are then added to the solution and the cyanide, liking zinc better than gold, not like most women and a lot of men, drops the gold for the zinc. The gold goes to the bottom and is removed about once a week. It is then mixed with, since it is black and not too pure yet, lime, niter, and four other chemicals and fillers, put in a crucible and heated. It is then poured into a settling form where the gold settles to the bottom and the sand mixed with manganese forms a type of unusable glass. The gold is in a cup-shaped form. Samples are then taken from the top and bottom of the gold cup to be analyzed for its purity. Generally it runs 90 percent gold, about nine percent silver, and the rest the chemical picked up in the assaying process, but generally copper and traces of iron. The gold cups are sent to the Bombay mint where it is further purified and made into blocks for sale on the bullion market. The present price of gold in India is about Rs. 300 an ounce. None of it goes out of the country since the present Indian price is by far the highest in the world. Gold is the little man's bank. He can buy a part of a gold brick and bury it in his backyard and when he needs money, dig it up. Wealthier Indians can keep it in safes. There is no danger of this type of bank closing its doors. The market in India is wide as the people are more interested in protecting their savings than earning a return on them. Whereas the "little" man in the United States will buy stocks or bonds in hopes of making money on an increase in price or earn money from his investment, the "little man" in India will invest in something he can watch. Of course, Americans are prohibited by law from holding gold.

After spending an hour with "Silent," it was easy to understand how he got that name. He loved to talk, and all of what he said was interesting. Maybe after one had heard his stock of stories several times, it would become you know what.

He is not just the head assayer. He keeps trying to develop better methods of recovering gold The clay containing twenty-five percent gold is handled in bulk of course. It is dumped into large vats where it settles to the bottom. It is run into large cylinders where it is treated with a ten times weaker solution of cyanide than the seventy-five percent mix. Air is blown through the solution. After ten hours, the solution with the slag is pumped to a battery of filters. The filters are vertical pieces of canvas separated by coils of wire. Thus when pressure is applied, the canvas is held apart. The wire serves no other purpose. The gold-bearing solution passes through the canvas, leaving the mud behind. The mud is washed out of the filters and carried to the piles of slag a couple of miles away.

The solution is taken below to another building where the real fun begins. The place is well guarded because this is the place where the gold metal is produced. The solution is run into vats where shavings of zinc are spread across the bottom. The gold and zinc trade places in the solution, with the gold settling out in a black compound. "Silent" told us the following story about this chemical process. Gold might be considered a man who is in love with cyanide. The come together to form a union. After they are together for a while, the couple meets zinc. Cyanide falls madly in love with zinc and drops gold. Poor gold is then left to himself and decides to purify himself to become a unified person. He then is mixed with purifying agents and goes through fire. He is then poured out into a settler where the gold goes to the bottom and the glass forms above. The gold is in a small cup shaped mass.

In order to keep the appointment Dick made for us in Krishna Raja Sagar, we had to leave although Check and I would have liked to stay longer. As we neared the town of Kolar, which is about eighteen miles from the mines, we began to look at the gas gauge. It showed "Empty," but we had driven less than 150 miles since filling the tank. We started out of town when Check decided that we should go back and look for a station. Just as we reached the edge of town, the gas gave out.

Dick was unhappy and kept saying, "I told you we should get more gas. Next time we will buy gas every time we pass a station." Again we got some coolies to push the car to the station which was about a half mile away. Dick and I walked through the business district after the car. If it had been moving under its own steam, it would have run over someone because there were so many people on the street they could not get out of the way. This time we knew the tank was empty so we filled it completely. We then took off for Bangalore. We reached town just after the filling station closed. One man was present, but he did not have the key to the storeroom. He did not know how we could get the tube we left for repair. We left a forwarding address in Trivandrum care of Volkarts: little did we know there was no such agency there.

We stopped at the hotel to see if any mail had come for anyone, but none had. On we went on the Mysore road. It was an excellent concrete, two-lane, paved road all the way. As darkness settled in lightning played in the clouds. We arrived at the hotel in Krishna about nine. The lights in the garden were still on. The place did look beautiful with all the lights on the fountains and under the water. In fact it looked like a World's Fair display but nothing particularly unusual or out of this world. I am glad I did see it with the lights on but would not particularly care to see it again except with a fair young person. The hotel would be a good place to go for a honeymoon. There is the pretty setting with nothing else to do. The only thing I had against the hotel was the number and size of the cockroaches.

May 19, 1949, Krishna Raja Satar to Coorg and back (Check)

We planned to leave this morning by eight o'clock, but it was after eight thirty by the time we had our tea and breakfast. It had rained a little during the night. The gravel road was spotted with pools of water. But the big advantage was there was no dust. Harry was driving. When the sun began shining we decided to make a movie of part of the road. It was a pretty spot with overhanging trees. I got out the tripod and shot the Chevy roaring over the hills. Then we drove for a couple of hours.

Harry and Dick had received instructions (detailed) on how to find the man who would show us the coffee plantations. Harry said it was either the first fork to the left and the second fork to the right or vice versa. In any case we went whipping along with occasional stops to ask passersby if they knew the way to "Heron Estate." None of them had heard of it. (We found out later that the place we were looking for was "Heroor Estate," but even that wouldn't have been familiar to the people we chose to ask.)

Finally we came to a barrier where an officer asked us for a toll to travel over his road. We asked where the road went. He told us toward Tellicherry which was about ninety degrees in the wrong direction. We said thanks, but we didn't want to pay the toll, and swung back along a country road due north to hit the main road. We kidded Harry that after this he better wear his garter seeing as how he didn't know which was right and left. About this time we were worried about running out of gas. I assured Dick and Harry that there should be enough gas, but as I had already told them that before we ran out of gas the first two times, they didn't have much confidence in my statement.

We finally hit the main road and after a small council on which way we should turn, correctly decided to swing west. In a short time we reached the Coorg border. We followed along and we finally found our host, Mr. A.C. Thimiah, standing by the roadside where he said he would be. We were almost an hour late, so we had to move fast. "Tim" (who incidentally was a cousin of General K. S. Thimiah, the Commander in Chief of the Indian Army) took us immediately to his estate office. From there he took us on a short walk along one of the plantation roads to where a gang of workers were spraying his coffee trees.

The plantation fascinated me. Huge eucalyptus and acacia trees shaded the smaller coffee trees, which stand four to six feet high and about six feet apart. At this estate the water for the spray was brought in by bullock carts and women workers carried pails of the water to mix with the copper sulfate for the spray guns. A small gasoline motor supplied the power for the spray guns which had small nozzles. The coffee tree is sprayed from below to protect the leaves from a fungus. After watching the operation, we hurried back to the estate office where we enjoyed good coffee. While we had been watching the spraying, one of "Tim's" employees had put a couple of gallons of gas in the Chevy, which relieved our worries about running out of gas.

"Tim" had a busy program planned for us and hurried along to the estate of Mr. and Mrs. Webb. It was a long climb from the main road, with the estate road winding up around coffee trees to a large bungalow overlooking a lovely valley. The Webbs, both large, friendly people with Mrs. Webb almost as tall as her husband, welcomed us with a cool drink. Harry talked coffee with Mr. Webb and "Tim," comparing conditions for growth, costs, and what-have-you with Harry's experiences in South America. I talked with Mrs. Webb, who showed me pictures of the elephant round-ups in Mysore and then mentioned that she had a pet spotted deer just a few weeks old which her workers had found on the estate.

She brought it out so we could get pictures. It was nervous but feeding it milk from a bottle calmed it down. It even let me feed it.

Mrs. Webb mentioned that this was the third young doe she had had. I asked if she had the same experiences as the story in *The Yearling* and she said it was about the same—that after they grew older, they got very destructive in the garden.

The Webbs' children were all in England and Mrs. Webb said she planned to leave about the end of June to join them.

We went with the Webbs to see some of their coffee trees and also to visit the workers' quarters. We saw the drying beds for the coffee and also saw our first pepper vines. Webb said that the busiest time for him was in December when they began harvesting the coffee, the pepper had to be brought in, and also he had to buy food for his workers for the year. He sold the pepper on a contract basis, the pepper buyers coming up in the spring to estimate the fall production and paying part of the contract price. The buyer has the responsibility of harvesting the crop. Mr. Webb has only a few acres of pepper and this is the best way of marketing it because all the risk falls on the buyer. At the moment, though, with the price of pepper so high, the risk for the buyer is also a pretty good one.

We then went to the labor lines. Labor on coffee plantations in India works out roughly one laborer to an acre. The Webbs have about 350 acres in coffee, and thus about 350 laborers. Webb said that most of the workers came from the Tamil areas of Madras Province. The labor lines were of one story, long, low bungalows nestled on a hillside. The estate has a school for the children of the laborers and also a small hospital with a nurse in charge. Mrs. Webb said they had a herd of twenty Red Sindhi cows and all the excess milk was given to the children, pregnant and nursing mothers. Webb mentioned that the cost of putting up buildings had gone up greatly. Each labor family had a small room about 10' by 10' with a small kitchen about 5' by 10' attached. As far as we could see there were no sanitary facilities except the jungle behind. Although we didn't go into the quarters we could look in. In one of the small apartments there was rice spread over the mud floor to dry. Although these quarters looked poor by our standards, they were quite good in relation to what most Indians live in. The workers got these quarters free. They are paid at the rate of about one rupee per day—slight over that for a man and slightly under for a woman. They work an eight-hour day and a six-day week. Food is bought for them by Webb in bulk amounts and he sells it to them at what he pays for it so they are assured of an adequate supply the year round.

Besides coffee, which is the main crop, the Webbs also have small cash crops of pepper and oranges. Because we were late in our schedule, we reluctantly took leave of the Webbs and drove about the hills of Coorg to the estate of Mr. B.S. Bucknall, where we were to have lunch. "Tim" told us that this would be the best-run estate in the area and as far as we could see, it was. Harry wanted a lot of facts and figures and all he had to do was ask and he had figures on what he wanted for the last fifty years. Bucknall not only had the information in books, but in his office was a graph which clearly showed how production on his estate had increased through the years.

After Harry had exhausted Bucknall's clerk getting information, we had a short drink or two and took a stroll around the estate which is all coffee and all business. Bucknall has 247 acres of Arabica and seven acres of Robusta coffee.

Bucknall showed us some old coffee trees and then some young trees which had just been planted. Also he showed us his spray system which completely covers his whole estate and which gives him efficient carriage of water and does away with the old-fashioned method of hauling water in bullock carts. The system is fairly simple. He divides the estate into three sections and then lays a pipeline up this line to the farthest edge of one section. He then connects this line to his water supply for this area. From the pipe end he spreads "T" shaped pipes where the workers spray with rubber tubes. By doing it this way he decreased the amount of friction on the metal tubes and gets more pressure for the spraying at the nozzle end. As each section is sprayed the pipe is removed by section and started off on the second direction. Thus, as one section is worked back to the base, another is being set up for spraying. When the second section is sprayed, the third is being prepared. In this way Bucknall is able to spray his whole plantation better and faster than the other planters. Bucknall sprays three times each year and on each spraying covers the estate one and a half times, thus his coffee gets sprayed four and a half times to other planters' three.

After watching the spraying operations, we came back to his bungalow for lunch and then hurried off again, this time to drive with "Tim" around Coorg. We drove to the city and up on the ridge where on a clear day you can see the lovely valley below. It was clear but cloudy with a threat of rain. From there we drove to the old palace of the Maharajah of Coorg. "Tim" explained that in the olden days one of the Maharajahs was an excellent shot and one of his favorite pastimes was taking pot shots at prisoners. The prisoner was given a chance to spring a distance of about fifty yards, making for a narrow gate in the wall. The Maharajah then took his stand and the show was on. Tim said that only two or three ever made it. In the same courtyard were two plaster elephants which looked real from a distance. On the spring from the palace to the wall gate, I had Harry try it out while I "shot" him with the movie. We hope the pictures turn out.

Tim then took us to his home. He owns several places spread about the hills of Coorg, but this home is called "Green Hills." Driving up to it reminds one of an old southern plantation (at least the way I have pictured them from the movies)—a long drive with big lawns in front with white columns emphasizing the red brick southern plantation type of building.

We met Tim's mother, his daughter, wife and numerous friends and relatives who were visiting. He treated us to a delicious meal—chicken pilau—and all we could eat. Then he displayed his hunting trophies which lined the dining room: elephant tusks, head of deer and bison, and stuffed, mounted panthers looking down from each corner.

We had a small walk over his plantation. Here at his home he had valuable rice fields. He also was experimenting with molasses grass which he had received from South America and which he planned to feed to his cattle. We saw his small herd of Red Sindhi cattle. We also saw his arica nut trees and he also has some pepper.

Tim explained that he was a jagirdar—a position he inherited from his father and grandfather. A jagir is a land grant given to a high government official. Tim's grandfather was a Prime Minister of the old Coorg State before it was taken over by the British government. Tim admitted that in time he would have to sell or else pay taxes on his land. His land at the moment is tax-free.

Back at his home we went upstairs where Dick entertained us with his piano playing. Tim's daughter, Pamela, is a dance music fan and plays excellently for a girl of thirteen. Dick carried on until about nine o'clock when it was time for the dozen assorted children to retire. We never did figure out where all the kids came from, but they were Tim's and children of his house guests. During the evening Tim showed us his album of hunting pictures which made us envious, especially pictures of hunts on elephants for tiger.

We were sorry for the evening to end but we still had a good two hours' driving ahead of us. It had begun to rain. This was disappointing because Tim had told us of a herd of wild elephants which were in the vicinity and that we might see them as they had been on one of his estates that morning. But in the heavy rain we couldn't have seen an elephant even if it was lit up.

I drove about halfway back and then handed the wheel to Harry. I took a comfortable position on the back seat and went to sleep, letting Harry and Dick find the way back to Krishna Raja Sagar. We didn't arrive until after eleven but the hotel staff was still up and had a short meal for us, so we ate.

The hotel at Krishna Raja Sagar was very good in all respects but one. It had large cockroaches which we tried to destroy—without success.

I forgot to mention that we asked about the health of plantation labor. Bucknall said that since the advent of DDT, he had had no trouble with malaria. He hadn't had a case of malaria among his workers since the war when he began using DDT. (He also slept without nets in his home, a pretty good advertisement for the manufacturers of the insecticide.)

[*Editors note:* This memoir was written many years before the publication of "The Silent Spring" which effectively did away with using DDT.]

May 20, 1949, Krishna Raja Sagar—Ooty (Check)

We tried to get an early start again, but it was after eight by the time we had collected our laundry and packed. Before leaving the dam site, we rode over to the dam to take pictures while the sun was shining. By the time we had taken our pictures it was after nine when we headed for Mysore City.

Dick wanted to see the palace. We went first to the government house. We were a little worried about a permit to carry our liquor although with two diplomatic passports (Harry's and Dick's) worry seemed a little silly. However, we decided to get the permit, if possible. (Mysore, like many Indian municipalities, had a prohibition against hard liquor.) From the government house where we could raise no one, we went to the office of the head clerk who tried phoning for someone to give us the permission. What with one thing and another, we had a long wait, so much that it was afternoon and we still had not received the permits. Just about this time we found that Mr. V.P. Menon, a high Indian government official, had arrived at Government House and was talking to three Indian newspaper reporters, so we joined in the questions and answers. V.P. was quite friendly and ordered soft drinks all around He said he was in Mysore mostly on a personal visit and that his seeing the Maharajah of Mysore meant nothing politically, just a social visit. V.P, off the record, had some hard things to say about prohibition in India, but he could not explain why the Indian railways had began prohibition when the central government was taking a soft attitude on it. He talked about Madras' attempts to enforce prohibition and the amount of money the province was losing. (All this was great for me and my United Press reporting—and went a way to rationalize his taking time to travel.)

It being lunchtime, we went to the Hotel Metropole and were having a beer at the bar when my friend, Russ Hadley, walked in. Russ, who was the Paramount Pictures representative in India, said he was mainly in Mysore to see it on his way back to Bombay from Colombo, Ceylon. Russ joined us for lunch, after another beer.

It was 2:30 before we finished lunch and filled the car with gasoline. We then drove to the Maharajah of Mysore's palace. The signs said "no pictures" but I distracted the guide's attention while Harry snapped one or two. This section of the palace is usually open to visitors in the mornings and afternoons. We were shown about, looking at beautifully carved ivory doors, silver doors, and huge durbar rooms, some hung with large crystal chandeliers imported from Europe. Other rooms had painted ceilings. One room was filled with hunting trophies: mounted tigers, bison, elephant heads and tusks. Another room was crammed with silver boxes which the maharajah had collected when attending social functions such as opening schools, temples, roads and what have you. The custom is for him to be presented with a written speech which is in the box. The box usually rests on a silver tray. On each was engraved the place and date he received it. In this room, too, were chess sets in which both Harry and I were interested. There were also three thrones where the Maharajah, and before the British left in 1947, the British viceroys and British Residents, sat to receive people. These thrones were usually placed in the durbar halls, the rooms where a Maharajah receives visitors—the smaller and more private the durbar hall, the more important the visitor.

In the courtyard opposite the largest of the durbar halls was what appeared to be a boxing ring. In olden times the Indian version of gladiators put on spike iron gloves and went at each other. We haven't been able to find out whether they just made passes at each other until one or the other drew blood or whether they really went at it until they mauled each other into bloody shreds.

Time getting short, we stopped at the government souvenir store which had works of ivory, inlaid rosewood tables and sandalwood work. We bought a few rosewood trays inlaid with ivory and Dick bought some tables. We also bought sandalwood fans. This store is a cooperative run by the government. The workers make the products in their homes in the villages and bring their work to the shop for sale. The workers receive eighty-five percent of the sale price. We found items extremely well made and reasonable. We only needed more money. Dick solved the problem by having our purchases put aside to be paid for on his return to Bombay.

Clockwise from upper left: Gold mine shaft; inspecting pump for spraying system at coffee plantation; palace at Mysore; elephant statues.

Getting late again and we still wanted to see the sandalwood factory two miles out of town. We found the right road although almost running down half the local population. A little man greeted us and guided us through the factory which had the pleasant smell of sandalwood, so much so we couldn't smell much else for a good while after leaving.

Our guide took us first to the room where the sandalwood is cut into pieces three feet long. All of the wood is shipped from the northern area of Mysore State which has practically a monopoly on sandalwood trees. These three-foot lengths are shredded into small bits on much the same principle as a vegetable shredder goes to work on a cabbage. Whirling steel circular saws with small cuts reduce the three-foot lengths into wood chips in just a few minutes. The lengths are handled by a worker who throws the butts of the wood on the floor for later shipping. We wanted to grab a small piece for a souvenir for Harry so he could work is wood carving wonders on it but decided we would get it later. The wooden chips are now blown to the second floor to form big piles of sandalwood sawdust. This is dumped into large cylindrical boilers into which is forced live steam. The sawdust is cooked, giving off the oil with the steam. The mixture goes into a cooling system to condense it. The mixture is allowed to settle with the sandalwood oil, being lighter than water, drawn off the top. The oil goes through one more refining process and is then poured into one-ounce bottles, one-ounce aluminum tins, and into five and ten-gallon tins for sale. The remaining sawdust is fuel for the boilers.

Harry and I bought a couple of ounces of the oil for souvenirs. While buying the souvenirs we asked for a sample of the wood for wood carving. The plant manager said it was against the rule and he just wouldn't do it. We asked to se the general manager who wasn't any more helpful. It just wasn't possible to get a sample. (Harry was an amateur wood carver.)

The general manager said that most of the sandalwood oil in the U.S. was made from the raw wood sent from India. He said that the roots of the main trunk of the tree contained the largest percentage of oil. It was those parts of the tree that were exported. Most of the oil in India is sent to soap makers. U.S. perfumery industry uses the oil for a base for perfumes.

There are only three other sandalwood oil plants in India: two in Madras Province and one in the United Provinces. The one we saw was government owned and the largest in India.

We were still a little apprehensive about the amount of liquor we had in the car and we went to the magistrate's office to get a permit on the chance it might make things easier at the border if we had it. Madras Province, in which the hill station of Ootacamund is situated, is dry, while Mysore State has no prohibition. We had heard tales of how the border guards search cars, confiscating all liquor found without permits. We found the magistrate who just wasn't sure whether he could give us a permit for a territory over which he had no jurisdiction. We finally left without the permit.

The first forty miles of the road to Ooty was a good paved or metalled road. We have been able to figure out why an asphalt road is called a metalled road in India. Dick was driving. A few miles out of Mysore we brought him to a stop with a shout: "a windmill!" The first one I have seen in India. It was dusk already but we took a chance and took a time-exposure picture. Then on to Ooty, trying to beat the rain which threatened but the closer we got to the hills the more rain. I took over from Dick about halfway for the drive up the mountain. It was through wooded country which we had heard was full of wild game, so-o-o-o I had the spot on most of the time and my eyes peeled for what we wanted to see: "wild game." We didn't have much luck, seeing only two spotted does which bounded onto the road and off on the other side out of the glare of the headlights. It rained most of the way. It was a long ride up the thirty-eight miles of winding hill road. We arrived at the Hotel Savoy at about nine in plenty of time for dinner. We had good rooms, Harry and Dick taking the double and I the single adjoining.

It was pleasant to be in a cool climate, almost cold. We put on suit coats for the first time on the trip.

The Savoy is on the Swiss style with the dining room, lounges and offices in the main building and the residents' room in small bungalows ringing the main building. After a good dinner of chicken, for which the manager, Brian Love, apologized, we were entertained by Dick at the piano. We finally crawled into our rooms after warming our systems with a good slug of bourbon.

May 21, 1949, Ooty (Check)

I slept soundly until awakened at seven a.m. by a little man who insisted I have some tea. I poured a cup and went back to sleep, finally arising about eight-thirty for breakfast. Dick and Harry were up earlier and wandered around looking for horses to go riding. Dick was the rider and Harry and I planned to golf.

They came back with the news that all the nags would be racing that afternoon so Dick decided to come golfing with us. We had our usual big breakfast. In fact all our meals were large. We usually took one look at the menu and told the waiters to bring all of it. They usually did.

We found the golf course despite the slow drizzle which continued most of the morning. The golf club let us become visiting members for three rupees per day and also furnished a couple of sets of clubs for the three of us as well as caddies and fore-caddies. For golfers of our caliber we needed someone down the fairway to help find our balls.

The Ooty course is, to say the least, hilly. But it's a sporty course with lots of chances to lose golf balls in the rough on either side of the narrow fairways—at least they looked narrow to us. We lost most of the balls we had brought—the "we" refers to Harry and Dick. I was lucky and used the same ball all the way around. It took us a while but we finally finished and headed back for warm, dry clothes and lunch.

At the hotel at lunch we found a note from three American young wives: Gladys Ryan, Anne Spaulding and Mary Jane Barnett, all from Madras and all at Ooty to take their children out of the Madras hot weather. Check had known Gladys Ryan, whose husband Vince was with Caltex in Bombay before moving to Madras. After lunch, Gladys and Anne arrived planning to go to the afternoon horse races. Dick decided to go along while Harry and I opted out to go back to the golf course to try and find some of our lost balls. We took Dick and the two ladies to the race track promising to get them after the races and then Harry and I decided to take a little rest before attempting physical exercise. Besides, it was raining hard.

In mid-afternoon we decided to give golf another try. We were joined by Brian Love, the hotel manager. It was still raining when we arrived at the course, so we had coffee. When the rain became a drizzle we teed off. We had a good game but only played twelve holes and I broke my record of not losing a ball by putting one squarely in the tank on the last hole.

It was already six so we figured that Dick and the ladies had found their way home. We had another cup of coffee and when we got back to the hotel we found a perturbed Dick. We had the only key to the hotel room and the hotel didn't have a duplicate so Dick had been waiting for us in the lobby for three hours. It was raining too hard at the races so the group had come back to the hotel to play bridge.

We then learned about plans for the evening. The ladies had to go to a dinner first, and we were to join them later. Mary Jane was not invited to their first party so we invited her to have dinner with the three of us. Gladys and Anne drove with us to get Mary Jane and we all went back to the hotel for diner.

We were late finishing so took Brian Love along to the club where the Saturday night dance was in full swing. The four of us joined one party, Brian joining his own party. It was a good dance. I can't remember the names of all the people at our table, but in addition to the three of us were the three ladies from Madras, a young fellow with Standard Vacuum Oil Co., a Mrs. Shah from Bombay, The Rajah of Vizianagram, and a couple of others whose names I never did get.

When the orchestra tired, Dick took over at the piano and did much better than the orchestra. He usually was better than any orchestra we heard on this trip.

Later another fellow from Bombay insisted we go to his bungalow where he had a better piano. We went. Dick played till five a.m. at which time we all went home because a few of us wanted to go to the hunt the next morning. The hunt was advertised on the bulletin board of the golf club. I've never seen one. We collected the names of persons who wanted to go with us. (It's too bad Harry didn't wake up soon enough the next morning.) I still haven't been to a hunt.

May 22, 1949, Ooty to Calicut (Harry)

I was designated to wake at six a.m., wake Check, go pick up Mary Jane, and go to the gathering of the hounds for the hunt. Dick insists the alarm went off with no effect. He rewound the alarm three times and held it near my ear and still got no response. After shaking me a few times, he decided I was asleep for a while longer. Actually it was nine before I managed to wake. Even then it was only after I heard Gladys and Anne talking to Check outside that I realized it was time one should be up and about. It seems the girls were invited to breakfast and since they had to be at the flower show at ten, it was high time they began eating. Dick rushed to dress and he and Check took them to breakfast.

We decided we would play golf if the rain was not too heavy. On the way to the course we stopped to pick up Mary Jane. When she got home the previous evening, she put on her clothes for the hunt and slept in them. She, too, had awakened at nine—too late to see the hounds. It was raining too hard to play golf so we had coffee and played bridge until lunchtime. We began with a couple of drinks while Dick played the piano and after lunch we returned to our hotel, packed and started for the city of Calicut.

I slept on the back seat until five-thirty. Check said we had passed two work elephants going down the ghats. The road was being widened by cutting down part of the mountainside. The work was being done with pick and shovel and the earth moved by basket. It was amazing to see how much and how well the work was done. Of course, the road was a little muddy since the gravel was covered with the dirt removed from the side of the road. There was no difficulty, however, The workmen wore large hats made of what I would guess to be woven bamboo. They were at least two and a half feet across, sloping from the center to the edge. They sat about two inches above the head on a crown made of stiff material but lined with cloth so as not to scratch the forehead. The hats were protection from the sun, rain and falling objects. When a car passed and was likely to splash mud or water on the worker, he would take off his hat to protect himself from the splash. Check said they were very similar to the hats worn in China. They resemble the pictures I have seen of Chinese hats. We passed one bus that was packed. From the outside all we could see were faces. Don't know what people did with their bodies—there wasn't room for them. Big hats were hanging on the back of the bus. It seems that everyone in the bus had a big hat which he fastened to the back of the bus. Of course, there would not be enough room inside for their hats, too. Unfortunately it was too dark to get a picture.

As we drove through the lower ghats we noticed many of the people were aboriginals. Many had bushy hair which stood on end. Most of the men, women and children wore only a loincloth. Some of them wore hats. Since we were in the jungle on a rainy day at six o'clock it was too dark to take pictures.

The road wound along a valley with paddy fields on either side. The seed beds had been started in the higher parts of the valley. The bright new green of the young rice always is a pleasure to see. Further down the valley some transplanting had begun. All of the paddy fields were terraced or bordered but each had an overflow which let the water run into the next field.

Since the rice was produced in the valleys, the people made their homes there too. Much of the way was lined with villages, giving the impression that a large number of people lived in the area. Actually, probably few people lived outside the valleys. The hills and mountainsides were covered with forests. As it got dark we expected to see wildlife, but there were too many people around for wild animals to venture on the road.

The road was good despite the rain. I have driven on much worse roads in India during the dry weather. The monsoon has not started but pre-monsoon rains have begun. Fortunately, the rains have cooled the air although it is still sticky. We found the Sea Beach Hotel at Calicut without trouble. As the name implies, it is on, or rather near, the beach with only a road between. It is better than the usual Indian hotel, but like most, has no running water.

May 23, 1949, Calicut (Check)

The rain started about eight o'clock and continued much of the morning. There was considerable debate about its being the monsoon or just rain. Many of the locals call any rain monsoon. A writer for the Madras Hindu newspaper claims it is an early monsoon. Calicut Europeans call it rain from inland and not from the sea as the monsoon should be. The monsoon has not started in Colombo and the weather department in Poona claims it is just rain.

Calicut is a "has been" port but still a busy and industrious town. There is a lot of activity in agricultural products, both for domestic consumption and for export. Coir yarn seems to be the largest export but does not represent over twenty-five percent of the Indian export. Coir yarn is used for making rugs and door mats. There are two methods of preparing the fiber. Both are taken from the mature coconut shell. The better quality is soaked in water, either fresh or sea, for about five months. The shell, after the nut has been removed, is put in the water without any further treatment. After it has rotted for this time, it is removed and beaten to remove the non-fiber parts of the shell. Most of the shell trash is removed, leaving a clean fiber of from three to six inches in length. It looks like it averages about four inches. It is then spun by hand with the aid sometimes of a crude wooden twister. The yarn is generally of two strands. The entire process is a cottage industry with most members of the family, but especially the women, doing the work. The yarn is prepared in skeins of fifty to a hundred feet, depending upon the amount of fiber a family has on hand at the time of working. This type of yarn is used for rugs.

The second type of coir yarn is made by beating the shells soon after the nut is removed and spread in the sun to dry. As soon as it is dry, it is hand spun into yarn. This type of coir is much weaker than the rotted. It is red in color and for some strange reason is called red coir. It is used in making mats.

Both types are cottage industries. Generally there are two middlemen between the producer and the exporter. A village storekeeper will buy much of the yarn from the villagers. He generally does a number of other things as well as buy yarn so that he merely collects the quantity locally produced. The second buyer comes around and buys from the storekeeper and makes crude bales, more or less by quality. He also brings the yarn to the exporters who are in the port cities like Calicut and Cochin.

Coir yarn, which is made from the fibers of coconut shells, is exported to manufacturers of rugs and doormats.

The exporter prepares piles of similar qualities and if the yarn is damp, dries it. Since a higher price is paid for lighter colors, much of the yarn is bleached with sulfur fumes. The yarn is hung on racks in an airtight chamber. Sulfur is heated and the fumes bleach the yarn. The bleached yarn is spliced by hand into hanks of three to four hundred yards. No attempt is made to be accurate. As long as the hanks are within that range, the yarn is saleable. For the U.S. market, three strands of yarn are loosely twisted. This twisting is done with a wooden twister turned by hand. The local merchants do not care to sell to the U.S. market because of the U.S. specifications and most of the yarn can be sold to Europe.

After splicing and twisting for the U.S. market, the yarn is baled into bales of three hundred weights. The bales must have a density of thirty-five to forty pounds a cubit foot. On the top and bottom, in the press, are placed woven bamboo covers. Then the bales are completely covered with burlap supported by strips of bamboo.

From Calicut, coir is loaded into lighters which carry it to ships off shore. The amount of coir produced depends upon the price. When the price is high, the villagers process more fiber. If the price is low, they throw away the coconut shells or burn them. Production varies with price. The amount depends, of course, on the number of coconuts shelled.

After visiting the coir yarn factory, we made our way into town to see the local newspaper. It was raining hard. We visited the office of the *Matrabhumi,* the leading Malayalam newspaper of the Malabar Coast. While I talked with the editor, Dick and Harry went out to buy umbrellas. When they returned we went back to the hotel for lunch and then headed for Cochin in the rain.

We made good time and didn't lose our way, though we had to ask at about every crossroad to make sure we were going the right way. It was late when we finally pulled into the Malabar Hotel in Cochin—late enough to have dinner in the dining room. We managed to buy some cans of vegetables and a canned ham (Hormel), and the hotel managed to scrape up some bread so we didn't go hungry. It was a good hotel and we had excellent rooms overlooking the harbor. It was still raining.

May 24, 1949, Cochin (Check)

The sun was shining when we woke up. Dick and I had a double room and Harry a single but they were the best rooms in the Malabar Hotel. I say the sun was shining because Dick, in the gloom of the downpour at Calicut, had made a bet that we wouldn't get two hours of sunshine on the trip down the coast. True, the sun only shone for about fifteen minutes when the clouds came over, but there was every promise of a good day.

We had our morning tea, collected all the dirty laundry for the dhoby (the laundryman) and went to breakfast. The Malabar Hotel stands on a small island which belongs to the Cochin Port Trust, and the road to the island is a toll road. Each car pays about 15 cents (U.S.) per day. We followed the road over a large bridge to the port of Cochin called "The Fort," an area about a mile square in which all the big business houses are located. Here we found Volkart Bros. and met Mr. O. Kappeler, the manager of the Cochin branch and an expert on pepper. He had just returned from a trip to the U.S. on business (pepper). Harry got information on pepper production for this year and for previous years.

The price of pepper is very high—eighty-four cents a pound—and probably going higher. There are only two major producing countries, India and Indonesia, and Indonesia at the moment is in the midst of political trouble and only small amounts of pepper are being exported. India, thus, virtually has a monopoly on the world's supply.

Kappeler said that all the grinders and buyers of pepper in the United States could not understand why the price is so high when all the other consumer goods prices in the U.S. are coming down. Kappeler said the price reflected the supply being low and the demand high.

Harry also asked about coffee, ginger and coir yarn, but in general we stuck to discussions of the pepper situation. I was impressed that Volkarts had complete records and graphs about any subject we asked for which made it easy to gather the information we wanted. We made a date with Kappeler's assistant, Mr. Venkatramen, for a tour of Cochin countryside to see pepper gardens as well as the rest of the produce that grows in the area—and practically everything grows in the Cochin area.

We returned to the hotel for lunch and Kappeler joined us. He came across the harbor in the company launch, a matter of five minutes, while we drove around the long way—seven miles.

We had a couple of drinks in the bar while Harry and I invested our usual five rupees in the hotel's slot machine—called fruit machines over here. This one was the best we had hit yet—for the house. We put in twenty slugs and didn't win once, so we quit. Harry and I usually divide the slugs and see how long we can play.

After lunch, Mr. Venkatramen joined us for our tour of the area. We first drove to Ernakulam, the capital of Cochin. I like the name of that town which inspired me to do a verse à la Nash:

> "Newspapers published in Ernakulam
> Are written in the Vernakulam."

Along the way we saw mounds of coconut fibers drying on the roadway in the sunshine. Venkatraman explained that this was a cottage industry. We took pictures of little girls beating the husks with sticks. Afterward they would rub the fiber in their hands and twist it into a strand of rope.

The weather was alternately rainy and sunshiny. Usually when we would get to a pepper grove, the sky would be overcast. The roads were good, a little wet and bumpy in spots, but good. We finally stopped at one farm where we saw the telltale smoke of a lemon grass still. We made our way up the bank of the road, through coffee, pepper and coconut trees to a little hut where the still was producing lemon grass oil.

This was much the same process as the sandalwood only more crude. The lemon grass was put in the still, steam passed through it, and the mixture of steam and oil passed over a vat where it was allowed to cool The oil comes to the surface and is scooped off. Lemon grass grows pretty fast; the farmer can cut it every three weeks. Thus it makes a good cash crop.

The cultivators in this area all wear a little cap made from a leaf of a tropical tree. It looks somewhat like a rowboat upside down when perched on their heads, but it keeps off the rain and sun. Whenever one wears out, they just cut another leaf off a tree.

We stopped at another farm because Harry wanted to see how pepper grew. Part of this farm was supposed to have a plot where pepper was being planted, but the cultivator couldn't find it—on his own land! However, saw some ginger. The cultivator explained that it was planted like potatoes. The ginger roots have eyes, and each eye or bud is broken off and planted.

In this part of the country the staple food, next to rice, is a root from which tapioca is made. It grows everywhere. The local people eat the root which is cooked like potatoes or made into a flour. This farmer had just about everything on his property: rice, pepper, lemon grass, ginger, tapioca, a few head of cattle, bamboo, coffee, cashew nuts, and even a couple of boats to go traveling in the backwaters.

The farmer came with us into a little town where we met his father who was one of the local merchants from whom Volkarts buys. In his store and in his warehouse across the street we had to see his wares. Lemon grass oil, ginger, tumeric, merotti seed (used in a leprosy cure), cashew nuts, sesamum—all these he bought and sold. Evidently the advent of foreigners in this little village was an event, for we soon had a crowd of friendly faces peering at us from all sides. I tried to take a picture of the store and the owner, but all the little boys and girls wanted to mug the picture. Then they got interested in the aerial for the radio and wanted me to tune in a station, but I couldn't find any on the dial. All of them knew the word "radio" and kidded me when I couldn't find the Cochin station. Harry sneaked across the street and took a picture from the warehouse when the crowd had all their attention on the car.

I forgot to say that when examining one of the pepper gardens, the Chevy stalled and we couldn't get it started. Being expert mechanics the two of us being fortunate to have the car on a downhill grade, we put it into gear and pushed it and sure enough it started.

On the way back to Cochin, we went through the town of Alwaye and stopped to see the fertilizer factory. We had heard about it, it being built by the Inter-Continent Company, which is an American firm. We found the place after a couple of stops when the engine stalled and we again used our mechanical knowledge and got a bunch of people to push until the engine started again. One of the stops was in the middle of a pontoon bridge which interrupted traffic until we were pushed off.

We found Mr. Van Ness, the American manager, and Mrs. Van Ness at their bungalow on one of the hills behind the factory. They gave us a welcome drink—after twisting our arms—and then Van Ness took us on a quick tour of the factory, a much bigger plant than I had expected, so much so that we tentatively decided to come back the next day for a longer look, and also to accept Mrs. Van Ness' invitation to lunch and a swim at their pool.

It was getting late and we still had an hour's drive so back we went to Cochin, Harry pulling out the dash throttle every time I stopped on the clutch pedal to make sure the motor kept going. We made it back into Cochin, breezing through Ernakulum to Cochin city to take Ventatramen home and then back to the hotel. We made it to the dining room before it closed for the night.

(For the benefit of those who have never traveled in India, I might say that all the hotels are on the American plan—three meals each day—and that most of the hotels we stayed in lost money on us, because the three of us never missed a meal and when we did eat, we ordered everything—repeat, everything—on the menu.)

We stayed awake all of about five minutes after dinner.

May 25, 1949, Cochin to Alwaye to Trivandrum (Check)

We slept late, although we knew we should have been up early for another long day. After breakfast and paying our bill, we packed and headed for the city to visit Pierce, Leslie and Company, the largest shippers of cashew nuts.

We met Mr. Holloway, the manager, and Mr. Northey, who gave us information about cashews, about the road to Trivandrum and an invitation to visit their factory at Quilon. The also told us how to find the old Jewish quarter in Cochin, which can trace its ancestry to 68 A.D.

Just around the corner from Pierce Leslie, we found Mr. S. Koder, the leader of the "white" Jewish community. He has a general store (later we found a chain of general stores along the Malabar Coast). He looks a typical Jew and he could be from anywhere in the world.

Koder said he would be glad to take us to see his synagogue but first wanted to tell us he was worried about the position of the Jewish community in the new political administration. He said that in the last Cochin elections, the Jewish community found itself without any representation for the first time. We asked if there hadn't been other times in the almost two centuries the Jews had been in India that times had been tougher but he didn't seem to think so. He said that always before the maharajahs and ruling princes had given them a voice in government, even though it was a small one.

En route to the synagogue—and again three pairs of eyes were on the gasoline gauge because it was reading "Empty"—we stopped to take pictures of the old Portuguese church where Vasco de Gama was first buried. His remains were taken to Portugal shortly after he died, but his grave is still in Cochin.

After several turns through narrow streets, we came to the narrow lane leading to the synagogue. It was about 100 yards long, lined with the houses of Cochin's white Jewish community, numbering about 100.

There are two Jewish communities in Cochin—the "white" who have never intermarried with Indians, and the "black" who at some time in the past or present have intermarried. The two communities are at loggerheads. We didn't have time to meet the leaders of the "black" community to hear their side of the story.

Koder escorted us to the synagogue. It was a relatively small one but with beautiful Chinese tiles, each one different, covering the floor. These had been brought from China some time in the 1700's. The synagogue was about 200 years old. Koder explained that in this synagogue, unlike the modern ones, the men and women sat on different sides of the room. Not having seen a synagogue before, I was interested in the square platform in the center from which the rabbi chants the prayers. There is also another pulpit on a small balcony over the entrance where the rabbi sometimes preaches.

We bid goodbye to S. Koder and headed, after taking on gas, for Alwaye. Again we had to retrace our steps through Ernakulum along the Alwaye road. Just a few miles outside the city a culvert was out and we had to take the diversion to the right of the road. Across the little stream was a one-pontoon bridge. The ramps, however, went up at a sharp angle and coming down I took off one of the rear bumper guards and the backing light. We stopped long enough to pick them up and then continued on our way, arriving at the fertilizer factory.

Mr. Van Ness met us and took us on a tour. The Fertilizer and Chemicals Travancore Ltd. (FACT) was built by the Intercontinent Company. Intercontinent also built the airplane factory at Loy Wing in China just across the Burma border during the war years (I had been there) and also managed the Hindustan Aircraft factory at Bangalore.

The factory here makes ammonium sulfate fertilizer by mixing ammonia (NH_3) and sulfate (SO_4). I have been away from chemistry too long, but they also make sulfuric acid to produce ammonium sulfate which they bag and sell.

The chief ingredient for all this, strangely enough, is wood. The wood is floated down the river near Alwaye, cut into three-foot lengths and sent up a long conveyor into a cooker where it goes through a process of partial distillation. This results in wood tar, which is drained off and thrown away leaving producer gas and nitrogen, which is the final product they need. The sulfur is imported from the United States. We watched the cranes and shovels pick up large gobs of it from the river lighters.

While we were inspecting all this, two of Van Ness' mechanics were working on the Chevy by cleaning and adjusting the carburetor. The car started when we turned the key.

After the inspection we returned with Van Ness to his bungalow for a swim and a drink before lunch with the Van Nesses. Then it was off again to Trivandrum.

Back along the road to Cochin, but this time the motor decided to conk out just before we hit the one-pontoon bridge. Luckily one of the cars from the other way stopped—he had to, we were blocking the way—and the chauffeur got out, unhooked the gas feed line to the carburetor, stepped on the starter, and the car ran. He then connected the feed line and the engine continued to run and we were on our way.

As we proceeded we came to the customs barrier between the states of Cochin and Travancore. At this point, Travancore nearly surrounds Cochin State. Leaving the barrier we almost ran into a large Rolls Royce station wagon. We drove around the Rolls and all of a sudden the Rolls was full of persons waving to us. Fifty yards up the road, we stopped and the driver came running toward us. He stuck his face in the window and, breathless, said, "Will you fellows come to my wedding?" It took us a few minutes to realize this was a boy we had met in Bangalore. He then told us about the wedding. It was to be on Sunday, but there was to be a big party Saturday night. (This was Wednesday.) If we could come, we would have to be at Alleppy at four on Saturday afternoon where a launch would take us forty miles through the backwaters to an island where he lived. It was to be a big show—a Syrian Christian wedding with all the important people of the Indian Navy, Cochin State, and Travancore State there.

The invitation tempted us, and in a few mintues we had decided to change our route, drive to Trivandrum, Cape Comorin and back, and then to Alleppy, and after the wedding drive to Madura on the east coast of India.

It wasn't until after we left them that we decided it would be too much, and later, reluctantly, we called it off.

We drove through Cochin State making our way to Alleppy. We had to ferry across the river which is the boundary of Cochin and Travancore. The ferry was a platform on two wooden scows and poled across by four ferrymen. They had long—about 25 feet—bamboo poles.

Across the river, the Travancore Customs noticed our car radio. It seems it was against the law to import a car radio into Travancore. I told the customs officer that we were going to Trivandrum and that if they wanted to detain us, he could call up the police chief there and we would settle the case at Trivandrum. That did the trick and we were waved on.

We continued our drive along the coast road. The sea was on our right and on our left bits of land surrounded by water. This coastal region is interlaced with what are called the backwaters. The only road is the one we were on along the coast, but one can go anywhere in the region by boat. It looked like descriptions I have read of the Florida everglades.

All along the road, especially from Cochin to Alleppy we saw evidence of filarial (elephantiasis). It was especially noticeable in the legs, huge swelling in the legs which makes the legs look like tree trunks. People in this area wear very little, both men and women bare from the waist up.

Near Trivandrum we again had rain and drove the last hour in a driving rainstorm. I had taken over from Dick at Quillon, about 45 miles from Trivandrum. The road was good, if a little narrow in spots, and all asphalt.

We arrived at nine at the Mascot Hotel with the three of us all in one large room. Harry was not feeling well so we bedded him down after taking a couple of aspirins and hot tea and let him sleep. Dick and I went for dinner. It had been a long day, and I was asleep in about sixty seconds.

May 26, 1949, Trivandrum (Check)

I was the last to awake, and when I got to breakfast Dick and Harry already had been looking at ivory souvenirs in the little shop in the lobby. The fellow in charge wanted to take them to his workshop, but first I had to find my United Press stringer correspondent, Dharmarajan, who was to have my mail. The last I had heard from Bombay was in Bangalore and I was a little anxious. Dharmarajan had mail for me and also a slip saying that my flash gun had arrived. In Bombay I had left it behind because Harry had one and we were trying to save space—not very smart. On the way back from Dharmarajan's we visited a few souvenir shops. We were looking mainly for chess sets, but we ended up just looking. We stopped at the Air India office to ask them to bring the package with the flash gun from the airport customs. (Travancore State has its own customs.) We then visited the ivory workshop of the hotel man.

We watched the workers carving elephants and palm trees aided by pencil drawings and using cutters, chisels, files and feet. Each carver used his feet as a vise, each one squatting on the ground and using toes to hold the pieces of ivory in place. Harry, being a wood carver, was interested to see how they held their tools and he learned a few things about how to work ivory.

Back into town we stopped at the Chevrolet dealer. He said the shop was busy, but as a favor he would grease the car and check the carburetor. We also asked him to replace the bumper guard and the backing light.

Dharmarajan came to the hotel about noon and I had discussions with him about the newspapers in the area. All of them are printed in the Malayalam language and none of them has any money. All the English-language newspapers are brought from Madras by air express. We invited Dharmarajan to join us for lunch, but he declined, saying he already had eaten. (We surmised that the main reason for his refusal was that he was an orthodox Brahmin and thus a vegetarian.)

In the afternoon I went to the Air India office to get my flash gun. We tested it and it worked. Now we hope for some place to use it.

Dharmarajan again came in the evening, this time bringing his brother who was on vacation from his job at the fertilizer factory. Dharmarajan told me about the plans for merging the two states of Cochin and Travancore being negotiated by V.P. Menon, the adviser to the States Ministry at New Delhi, with the maharajahs of the two states.

Meanwhile, Dick had investigated the roads from Alleppy to Madura and decided that we would have to skip the wedding.

That evening we went to the only movie in town, "Home Stretch," and we took Dharmarajan and his brother with us. In the movie the gambler wins the girl from the State Department man, but otherwise it's an entertaining picture. Dick wanted to know why the State Department always lost out in the movies. Said something ought to be done about it.

After the movie we returned to the hotel, headed for the bar, and found another slot machine. Harry and I invested another five rupees apiece and in time, of course, lost everything. After dinner we retired early because we had a long drive on the morrow.

May 27, 1949, Trivandrum to Cape Comorin (Check)

Our first stop this morning was at Quilon to visit A. Thangal Kumju Musalier and Son, Ltd., the largest cashew nut sheller in India. We spoke with the son since the father spoke no English, only Malayalam. The Indian production this year is about 300,000 bags of one and half cwts. (168 pounds), while the imports from East Africa will amount to about 500,000 bags. The shelling percentage is about is about one-fifth: five tons of nuts produce one ton of kernels. We soon realized that we were not going to get much information here, so we politely thanked them and drove to the Pierce Leslie compound a few miles away.

From Quilon we drove up a jungle road expecting to see wild animals along the way. To our surprise the road was crammed with pedestrians walking up and down the road going about their business, much the same as Americans drive madly about cities.

We found the railway station at the village of Kundara, as we were told we would, just six miles from where we started. We then found the side road and after two miles we came to a fenced, enclosed compound. Sure enough, there was the sign "Pierce Leslie" The gate seemed to open automatically as if we were expected. On the other hand the gatekeeper probably assumed that anyone in a car coming up that road was looking for the cashew plant. Mr. Bolland accepted us as if he had received a letter from Mr. Pierce himself. This is one of the nice things about traveling in India. Most Europeans are so pleased to see a white face that they will take another European on face value. This condition puts responsibility on the traveler not to betray that trust. Very few people do.

Mr. Bolland told us the present Indian crop of cashews was about the same size as last year, about 30,000 tons. Imports this year are about the same as last year, or perhaps a little larger because of the large African crop. The total amounts to thirty to forty thousand tons. Most of the African nuts are imported by Bombay merchants who also keep in close contact with the kernel market in New York and try to get the maximum price for the raw kernels.

Cashews are harvested from March to May, but the best time to visit would be during April. It will be easy to see the fruit on the trees. Harvesting must be seen by flashlight and the stronger the better. There are only a few groves of planted cashews. They were planted about 1933/34. It was found that the trees did not respond to civilized treatment like pruning, spraying or fertilizing. The trees preferred to grow on laterite rock soils and receive as little treatment as possible.

The harvesters sell their nuts in the mornings to a local merchant who generally gives them about twelve annas a pound for the nuts. Middlemen then collect the crop from a number of merchants and sell to the companies that have shelling facilities. Since the trees require little care and grow on poor soil, the cost of production is low and the harvester sells for a relatively low price.

At Pierce Leslie, the nuts are dried on a factory drying ground and put in storage for six months for curing. The nuts are then shelled. The shelling process is complicated because the American consumer wants whole nuts. The cashew nut is kidney shaped, making shelling a difficult process. To this date no machine has been developed to shall the nuts without breaking the kernel.

The raw nuts are roasted in a cashew shell oil bath, a process which removes some of the oil from the shell. At the same time it makes the nut easier to crack and remove the kernel. After the nuts are roasted, they are put in a centrifuge where the oil is further removed, mostly from the surface. The nuts are then sprinkled with dirt to absorb more of the oil and then taken to the shellers. Most of the shellers also coat their hands with dirt to keep the oil from damaging their hands.

On the day we visited, there were 529 shellers at work in the first process. Even in this plant there was a caste system. The two lower castes did the first shelling. After the nuts are shelled, they are allowed to dry for one day and then sent to chambers where hot air is blown over them for eight hours. During this process the parchment protecting the nut from the shell dries and makes it easy to remove. The next morning the nuts are given to a second group of shellers who remove the parchment. This work is all done by women. A good worker can shell twenty-eight pounds a day but the average is twenty-two pounds. They receive one anna a pound. No payment is made to either group for brokens because American consumers do not like broken cashews.

The shelled nuts are then sorted by size and all the off-colored and "bad" nuts are removed. The sorting take place on a sheet of green felt which permits dust to pass through. The nuts are graded—the 240s are put in one can, the 320s in another. The number indicates the number of kernels that make a pound. The cans are carefully weighed—each weighs 25 pounds. Two holes are drilled and CO_2 (carbon dioxide) is pumped into the cans, which are then sealed. The CO_2 creates a vacuum and also kills any insects that might be present and preserves the kernels. The kernels meet the requirements of the pure food and drug act of the

U.S. The cans are now put in cases with each case printed that it contains a product of India and the name of the shipper.

All of the factory workers are agricultural labor. They report to the factory when they do not have other work to do. In the shelling department there are about 3,000 people on the list, but only 950 are needed to do a day's work. During the past two years there have been seven strikes. The workers have demanded two rupees a day where they now make only one rupee (about 33 U.S. cents) They have no objection to being paid by their piece work. They just want more money. The strikers pick an opportune time, like ten o'clock in the morning or two in the afternoon, after a large quantity of nuts have been cooked and are ready for shelling. If they are not shelled, the nuts will spoil. The industry gives the appearance of combining rural work with industrial work so that income from each will increase the standard of living.

The highest-paid Indian in the establishment receives 120 rupees a month. A good clerk makes 70 rupees a month, and according to Bolland the clerk is a top-notch worker who makes no mistakes and does neat work.

Bidding goodbye to the plant, we headed for Cape Comorin at the extreme south end of the Indian continent. We made good time and arrived in time for dinner at our hotel for the night.

May 28, 1949, Cape Comorin to Madura (Harry)

Last night we arrived at the end of the world. We looked straight south into nothing but sea, a sea that continued for thousands of miles. According to the map, there was no land between us and the South Pole and we were eight degrees above the Equator. Cape Comorin is one of the few places in the world where one can stand on the end of a continent and look across the ocean and know there is nothing but sea.

The manager of the hotel told us that the three seas that come together at the Cape are the Bay of Bengal, the Arabian Sea, and the Indian Ocean. We expected to see some differences in the color of the three seas (of course, we did know better), as if someone might have drawn a line on a map and indicated which sea was which. As it was, the junction showed mixed waters which resembled any other point jutting out into one sea.

This morning, in better light, we fancied we could sea how the waters were mixing. The Arabian Sea at Bombay has a dirty brown color. Sure enough there was a streak of brown water coming from the west. From the hotel this water appeared to hug the shore right up to the point of the cape. The tide seemed to be coming from the southwest, or was that the direction of the wind? There was a streak of blue-green which must have come from the Indian Ocean.

Clockwise from upper left: Jewish synagogue at Cochin; Check with Dharmarajan, UP correspondent in Trivandrum; Harry Spielman, Dick Brecker, and John Hlavacek at the "end of the world" (Cape Comorin); cashew processing at Pierce, Leslie and Company.

Early this morning, Check and I went for a swim off the cape. The water was considerably cooler than the Arabian Sea at Bombay. By why shouldn't it be cooler; hadn't it come all the way from the South Pole? The fact it had crossed the Equator did warm it a bit. I said swim. That is not quite the correct term.

The coast at the cape is rocky with considerable coral and granite. Someone will tell me the two do not go together, but the rocks looked like coral and granite to me. The coral was about six feet thick on the surface and as the sea washed the soil out from under it, it fell onto the beach. We did find a sandy place about 100 feet long. It was a mixture of sands. Near the shore the sand was reddish-black and fine. Where the water hit with force the sand was coarse quartz, or was it granite? The beach was steep, much more so than we expected. We waded into the water to catch a breaker. A nice one, five or six feet high, would hit and we would try to ride it in. Much to our surprise we found ourselves trying to drill a hole in the coarse sand with our noses. It was fun for about five minutes.

After breakfast we went to the Hindu temple on the Cape to take pictures. There were a number of Indians bathing in the protected area in front of the temple. Bathing at this point seemed to be the holy thing to do. Guess Check and I did the right thing by going swimming, or bathing. We were more undressed than the Indians. I wonder if baptism in the Christian religion isn't another form of the Hindu rite of bathing. Both have as their basis cleanliness. Before the modern water system in western countries, baptism no doubt had something to do with cleansing the body as well as the spirit, the same as bathing in the Hindu religion today. I never cease to marvel at the similarity of religions, basically.

The big Brahmin temple was painted red with white vertical stripes. Since we were not Brahmins we were not allowed to enter the temple.

The hotel manager told us there would be a petrol pump twelve miles up the road. We went sixteen miles to the border between Travancore and Madras, only to find no pump. (We found out the petrol pump was twelve miles in the opposite direction.) After much persuasion we got a police officer to give us one gallon from his jeep. Check borrowed a hose from a police truck and used Dick's two-gallon thermos flask to carry the petrol from the jeep to the Chevy. The operation took so long that we could have driven back to the petrol pump and saved time. On the other hand we furnished entertainment to about thirty Indians as well as ourselves. The police officer was so afraid of violating the regulations that he did not want to give us one gallon of petrol. He was unlike an American official. Had foreigners been so insistent, the American would have been more insistent in not giving it.

It was thirty-six miles to the next petrol pump, which was in Tinnevelly. I bet Check five rupees that we would not make it. As we drove down the road, Check kept checking off the miles and as we got closer, the furlongs. If we ran out, that would make four times in two weeks. It couldn't happen to us. It didn't. In fact, we only got twelve gallons in the tank when the tank holds a little over thirteen.

After filling the tank, we went to the India coffeehouse for our usual two cups of coffee, cashew nuts, and a few cookies. It is difficult to say which coffeehouse was the best, but this one was certainly attractive and clean.

We began looking for the telegraph office and sent a telegram to Alleppy to tell Mr. Kuruville that we could not attend his wedding. The telegram went to Madura, Madras, to Cochin to Allepy. He might receive it next week.

When we arrived in Madura, we first tried to arrange to ship the car to Ceylon. After finding the railway freight office, we learned that it was Saturday afternoon and we would have to go to the home of the superintendent, which was in the railway colony. After several inquiries we finally found Mr. Chandy, who said he would do his best to arrange a freight car to take the Chevy to Ceylon. However, he suggested we go to a company called TVS which did a lot of trucking business.

Fortunately, we also had a letter from Ralph Schaefer of Firestone to their agents in Madura, TVS. When we arrived at the TVS offices we presented a copy of the letter from Ralph. We were told the owners were away on leave but to take a seat and we would be taken care of. An assistant manager appeared to find out what we needed. He, like a number of others, thought we could drive directly to the ferry terminal at Dhanushkodi. He made a phone call only to find out it could not be done. Soft drinks arrived, and a little time later the business manager, Mr. B. Vijendra Rao, met us.

Mr. Rao was very cooperative. We told him we wanted to get to the ferry tomorrow, if possible—the quicker the better. He said he knew the railway people and would arrange a car if one were available. To get us from under foot, he took us to the English club where he had reserved a room for us. After making sure we were settled he left us to see about the transportation. Dick tried the piano. It sounded like it should have been in a circus, and Dick played it that way. We cleaned up and I began writing. We had a drink from our own bottle. Check and I went to the pool room and began playing billiards. A little after seven, three members arrived and we watched them play "slosh." Two of them took Check and me as partners and we jointly played a game. We messed around until eleven when the cook was getting nervous. So we stopped and had dinner while the members drove off home. This was a wild Saturday night in Madura.

TVS is a famous firm in South India. It has the agency for a number of European and American companies. The company is the agent for Firestone, Dunlap, General Motors, spare parts for Fords and Jeeps. It also operates several bus and trucking companies. It operates 42 buses in Madura alone, and in addition operates interurban bus lines. The firm began 40 years ago as T.V. Sundaram Iyenger.

Later it was changed to T.V.Sundaram Iyengar & Sons and later to T.V. Sundaram Iyenger & Sons, Ltd. With every change in names the firm was expanded. The expansion also coincided with a son taking over part of the business. One son is in charge of the bus line, another the truck line and a third, the "garage."

May 29, 1949, Madura to Kodai Kainal (Check)

I slept late. As far as I know so did Dick since he was in the same room. Harry reported he was up early and trying to write a little of the diary. Just as we finished breakfast, Mr. Rao arrived with the news that we could drive to Kodai, but we had to be back before ten on Monday morning so the car could be loaded on a railway car for the crossing into Ceylon.

We started for Kodai, which is a hill station 75 miles from Madura. The road crossing the plains was only so-so, mostly gravel, wide and bumpy. It took us a good two and a half hours to drive.

The drive was uneventful except for seeing the construction of a new sugar factory and passing a convoy of bullock carts, each one carrying one long steel I-beam.

The road up to the hills was a good one. It's one moderate climb to the top. There are elevation signs every 500 feet. Dick said it could be too far because Kodai was not as high as Ooty; it probably was only 5,500 feet. We kept passing the elevation signs. Harry said he thought Kodai was 6,800 feet. When we passed the 5,500-foot sign and were still going up, Dick figured that maybe it was a little higher than he thought. Kodai's elevation is about 6,800 feet, though some of the surrounding hills may be higher.

We were in time for lunch and stayed at the Carlton Hotel. We were the only Americans in the dining room. The weather was cold and threatening rain, but otherwise Kodai was a delightful hill station. A small lake fronted the hotel. Harry and I decided to play golf while Dick went to find some friends he had been told to look up. We found some clubs and we had a good time. The course itself is hilly which makes it nice to look at. The fairways are green but rough. Here the greens are "browns." It's a nine-hole course and the members made it an 18-hole by having different tee placements using the same "browns." At some holes one must ring a bell after putting out to let the following players know the hole is clear. The "brown" is out of sight from the middle of the fairway. We were lucky it didn't rain during the afternoon. Once in a while we would have to wait on a tee for a few minutes to let a cloud roll by. No foolin'.

We were having good coffee in the clubhouse and reading about Bobby Jones when Dick came to get us. He had with him Dorothea Ness. She teaches in Madura. Her parents teach in the American College in Madura. Small world—I found out her parents were American Board missionaries and she had played as a child with Mel Kennedy, an Oberlin in China English teacher friend of mine in China.

We stopped at her house to meet her father and mother. Dick and Dorothea were going to an oratorio—a song fest. Harry and I begged off, promising to meet them later for dinner at the hotel. We asked Dorothea to bring a couple of her friends so we could have a party.

Despite the hurrying of the hotel staff, who said dinner wouldn't be served after eight, we went into the dining room after nine and still got dinner. Dick and Dorothea were already there with another girl, Cornelia Sanders, who teaches at the American School in Kodai. (There is an American School in the hill station for the sons and daughters of Americans who work in some of the large Indian cities like Madras.)

After dinner we moved the hotel's small piano into the lounge near the fireplace to keep warm. At the other end of the lounge a group of Parsis were playing some sort of a community guessing game which all seemed to enjoy, judging by the loud laughter. We knew Dick's piano playing would not disturb anyone. It didn't.

Later, another girl, Mary Argenbright, joined us. She is another American school teacher at the Allahabad Agricultural College. We sang every song Dick could think of until Dick tired of playing.

May 30, 1949 Kodai Kainal to Madura to Ramnad to Mataban (Check)

We got an early start. We wanted to be back in Madura by nine-thirty. I drove down the mountain road, Dick taking the back seat to sleep. We were at TVS by 9:15. Mr. Rao went with us to the railway station. While he went to arrange for the transport, Harry and I walked on the station platform. Later Dick joined us for some coffee and ice cream cakes in the railway restaurant. Rao came back with the bad news that we couldn't ship the car because the electricity that was needed to work the switches was out. The alternative was to drive to Ramnad and load the car there. We said that would be okay. Then the railway at Ramnad were informed to expect us.

From the railway station we went to the Imperial Bank where Dick was expecting money. It hadn't arrived. Mr. Rao took us to see the TVS workshops, a truly impressive sight. It had five acres of repair shops, body building shops, rows upon rows of lathes and other mechanical equipment. I was most interested in their manufacture of charcoal gas plants to be fitted on their trucks. I had driven some of the Chinese charcoal-burning trucks during the war.

TVS pays good wages. Also each year the company sends students from the garage to Bombay for training in the General Motors factory. Harry said it was a "damn good garage" and that he had seen very few garages, even in the U.S., to compare with it.

Mr. Rao then took us to the large Hindu temple in the city, the largest in South India. It has four huge towers, one on each side of the temple, which covers an area the size of a large city block. Upon entering, one removes one's shoes, so we went in barefoot. At the entrance is a large area filled with stalls selling food, pots and pans, flowers, clothing, candles and everything connected with Hindu customs and rites in their temple worship.

Before entering the next room, we passed through an archway in which there were hundreds of little receptacles where oil wicks were lit at night. Continuing we came upon a large bathing pool which lay under one of the large towers. The walls were painted with legends of Hindu history. The ceilings and arches had carved figures of Hindu gods.

We were not allowed to enter the center of the temple, which was reserved for Hindus only. On our way out we saw the temple elephants and a camel, as well as the temple bull.

Back to the English club for lunch. We packed quickly because we had 70 miles to drive to Ramnad. As we approached the car, behold, the left rear tire was flat. Mr. Rao's driver and I quickly changed the tire and we went roaring to the TVS workshop where they removed the damaged tube and replaced it with a new one. It took only a few minutes and we were on our way.

Harry drove while I curled up in the back seat, so I didn't see much of the drive, waking up only at intervals. The railway people at Ramnad knew all about our coming so we drove the car immediately onto a railway car while Dick made out the necessary shipping papers. We then took over the railway waiting room, Harry and I playing chess, while Dick shaved and read. One of the many railway people brought tea and bananas and we had plenty of water in the thermos to mix with the bourbon.

Our train for Mataban came at nine o'clock, and we arrived at Mataban, about twenty-eight miles away, a couple of hours later. The dining room at the railway station had a meal ready for us but there was no place to sleep. Dick learned that there was a railway officers' rest house not far from the station, so after dinner, leaving our luggage at the station, we walked the two furlongs to the rest house and parked ourselves on the beds without changing clothes. We slept!

May 31, 1949, Mataban to Ataban Camp to Dhanush Kody to Taliamanar to Anaradapura (Check)

When I woke up, I found we were in a rather nice little rest house. We met the two railway officers staying there and they informed us we would have to walk back a mile and a half to Mataban Camp to get our health clearances for Ceylon. As the rest house was only 100 yards from the sea, we went for a swim and because there was no one around, we didn't bother with suits.

After romping in the surf, we dried off in the sun and had a cup of tea at the rest house. Then we walked back to the railway station for breakfast: chicken, fried potatoes and onions—a good breakfast!

The walk to the Mataban Camp was pleasant if you like mile-and-a-half walks. We hurried because we wanted to be sure to catch the train back to Danush Kody at eleven o'clock. While we were walking along, a goods (freight) train came by and we saw the railway car which carried the Chevy.

Mataban Camp is a large area run by the Ceylon Government. It's a quarantine camp where all Indian laborers who work in Ceylon, second and third-class train passengers, and others must stay for six days before they are allowed to leave for Ceylon. In the case of first-class passengers like ourselves, the camp just examined our inoculation certificates and let us go. We also had to get a permit from the Protector of Immigrants (Indian) to allow us to get on the ferry. But this "red tape" was done in good time.

Ceylon is a health-conscious island, and it takes every precaution to keep all communicable diseases under control. Ceylon has a large staff of doctors and administrative staff to keep the approximately five thousand persons who go to Ceylon each week properly inoculated.

The Indians in the camp are charged a nominal fee of one rupee per day for food. Special trains run right from the camp to the ferry.

We caught our train, which stopped momentarily at Ramnad to pick up our baggage, and then continued to Dhanush Kody, the Indian terminus of the ferry connecting India with Ceylon.

We made preliminary enquiries with Customs about the car and then walked to the dock with our baggage. We had to wait for an hour or two because the passengers on the morning ferry from Ceylon had not yet left the ship. We watched them depart. The Indian Customs officers dug through every piece of luggage. The incoming passengers were all Indians, most of whom were workers from the

Ceylon tea estates coming home for vacation. They sat on long benches, moving up one at a time. About 100 were allowed to leave the ferry at a time.

We three were hot and sticky so decided to go swimming. We found a small room in the Customs shed, changed clothes, and walked to the end of the pier which was at least two furlongs long. (One eighth of a mile to you who don't know what a furlong is.) We left our luggage in the Customs shed with the Customs officers promising to keep an eye on it.

We dove off the end of the pier into cool water. It was only then that we found there was no ladder and that we would have to swim around the ferry to shore. We didn't attempt it immediately, preferring to rest on the anchor chain. Dick went on ahead and Harry and I lolled around in the water. Harry thought he saw a couple of fins swimming, which deterred us for a little while. But when we figured he couldn't have seen sharks, we swam in. Two furlongs (l/4 mile) is a long way swimming when one is not in condition.

We were hungry, so we opened some cheese and some Parles biscuits (like Ritz crackers) and cold water. We waited until all the passengers had left the ferry and then watched some of the passengers embark.

Leaving India the examination by Customs is only perfunctory since the restrictions of what can be brought from Ceylon are more strict than those on what can be taken out of India.

All the women laborers wear all their jewelry, huge golden earrings which stretched their ear lobes all out of proportion. Most of the passengers carried a papaya for food on the ferry.

We had lunch aboard the passenger train. The young Englishman who controlled the ferry had his workers unload the train slowly so we could finish our lunch.

On the train we met a young Englishman from the Madura Company who told us we could come aboard and make ourselves comfortable. Nothing but soft drinks in the bar, but we settled for them. It was a very hot day.

Dick, meanwhile, had gone back to the station to finalize papers for shipping the Chevy to Ceylon. It was finally moved onto the dock and was the last car to be taken aboard. Dick drove it out of the boxcar onto a sling supported by blocks. Then the ship picked up the sling and deposited the car on deck. It dipped a little on the way up but made it, much to our relief.

The ferry run is two hours. We sat and talked most of the time, although Harry tried to do a little writing for this diary. We found out when we were almost across that prohibition extended only to three miles from the Indian shore, so we broke out a bottle of gin and had a couple of drinks with the

Englishman and one of the police officers checking passports. Dick, the old bird dog, had found the only two gals on the ship and was on the bridge talking to them.

At Taliamanar, the Ceylon terminus, we had some dinner aboard the train taking passengers to Colombo. We invited the police officer and the Englishman to sit with us, and latter brought a half-bottle of scotch along, which we killed. By the time we finished dinner, the car was unloaded and we were ready to drive.

Clockwise from upper left: Riding on an elephant; view of Hindu temple in Madura; temple bull; shipping the car.

Harry curled up in the back seat, Dick drove, and I tried to help by spotting the direction signs to keep us from taking the wrong road. We drove about twenty miles to Mannar, where there was a rest house. It was full. The manager said he'd like to help us but what could he do? We said we needed gasoline (again) and he came with us to wake up the owner of the petrol pump. We needed enough gas to take us to Anuradhapura, the ancient capital of Ceylon.

On our way out of the rest house, two of the guests came to ask us if we had wanted a room. We said, "Yes." One of the guests said he wanted to write a letter to the Colombo papers telling about these bone fide travelers (us) being turned away. He said that many persons who had no business staying at the rest house kept the rooms; hence travelers like us had to move on.

One of the two said that if we were driving on to watch out for "Jumbo" who was a rogue elephant loose in the vicinity. Rogue elephants are beasts with an inferiority complex. They go about the country uprooting everything in sight. Generally, a rogue elephant was once leader of the herd but a younger bull has kicked him out and the rest of the herd will have nothing to do with him; thus the inferiority complex.

But we met no elephants on our drive. I took over from Dick about halfway and we arrived at the Grand Hotel about midnight. It was dark, but we woke up a little boy who opened up two rooms, and then we tumbled into bed. We were too tired to even unpack the car.

June 1, 1949, Anuradhapura to Colombo (Check)

After a hot bath and breakfast we hired a guide whom the hotel recommended. Mr. Pereira evidently had memorized his lines a good many years ago. Most ancient cities leave me cold, and this one was no exception. We drove through the city viewing all the granite stone pillars which at one time supported huge Buddhist buildings and monasteries. Most interesting were the huge reservoirs which the ancient peoples used to irrigate their lands. They were restored under the British rule and today provide the water supply for the city. No swimming is allowed. In addition it would not be healthy because alligators live in them.

We had lunch at the hotel and began our long drive to Colombo, Ceylon's capital. The roads were good and unlike India, people in Ceylon move off the road when one blows the horn.

Immediately upon arrival in Colombo we stopped at the health office. The doctor asked us to come and see him before we left the island. Then to the Galle Face Hotel, a grand red brick edifice overlooking the city, and our room which the American Embassy had thoughtfully reserved for us. (It's always pleasant to have diplomatic personnel in your party.)

Almost immediately we began to meet old friends and acquaintances. The first person I met was the Reuters correspondent, Graham Barrow, whom I had known in Chungking during the war. Then I ran into young Billy Patrick, who took me to see his mother and sister. Billy's father had been an American banker in India who had died of a heart attack. Sylvia Patrick and the children were staying in Colombo before returning to the United States. We asked Sylvia to have dinner with us that evening.

Back at the room Harry and Dick were going over plans with Horton Schoellkopf of the Embassy. They had plans made for our future trips to the interior. We invited Horton and his wife, Eleanor, to have dinner with us at the hotel. Instead we wound up having a fine dinner complete with fine scotch at the Schoellkopfs. Dick had discovered, as far as he knew, Colombo's only nightclub. The Schoellkopfs opted out but the three of us, with Sylvia Patrick, found our way to the Silver Fawn.

We arrived too late for the floor show but in time for a couple of dances. When the orchestra went home, Dick took over at the piano and was later joined by an Englishman who could play the drums. Everything was friendly and one drink led to another.

As we were almost ready to leave I found Russ Jepson, the Firestone Agent, at the next table. He invited us for old-fashioneds the next day at noon.

Somewhere along in the early morning, Harry left us and went out to the car to sleep. We followed a little later and didn't bother to wake him up—just shoved him over and drove to the hotel. Sylvia helped me walk Harry to our room and get him to bed, and then I helped Sylvia get home!

(Neither Sylvia nor Harry remembered this in the morning. What a spot for blackmail!)

June 2, 1949, Colombo (Check)

Our first stop this morning was the Embassy where I used the phone to make some appointments and Harry planned for more of our trips while Dick talked with the ambassador. My first appointment was for two in the afternoon, so Harry came with me to see my United Press correspondent for Ceylon, Austin de Silva, who also worked for the Lake House Newspapers. Austin had my mail and messages from my office in Bombay.

Harry and I returned to the Embassy. Dick was still with the ambassador, so Harry and I went to the hotel. With Sylvia Patrick we converged on Russ Jepson for the old-fashioneds. Horton and Dick arrived together. A number of guests were already there: Lynn Porter of the Morrison Knudson Company, Mr. and Mrs. Keane from Calcutta (he is the Studebaker representative), Joe Norwood of Muller and Phipps, and Mr. Smith who was with a company that sells machinery to Morrison Knudson.

I had to leave early, at two, to see an official in the Ministry of Communications and then was busy with my newspaper people all afternoon.

While I was on my newspaper meetings, Dick took the car to the garage for servicing and Harry continued at Jepson's, finally having lunch at about 4 o'clock.

From the newspaper office I tried to call Lady de Mel, a lady I had known in Hyderabad, and then Harry and I stopped to see Eleanor and Horton Schoellkopf, They were going to dinner with the O'Donnells. Charles O'Donnell is the First Secretary of the Embassy. Eleanor phoned, over our protests, and in no time we were invited to come along. We let Horton pick up Dick at the hotel while Harry and I drove with Eleanor to the O'Donnells'.

Dick left early, having a secret rendezvous somewhere. Harry and I followed later but went to bed—alone!

June 3, 1949, Colombo to Kandy to Newara Eliya (Harry)

We planned an early start for Kandy, but it was nearly ten before we were out of the hotel and had said goodbye to Sylvia and the children. We stopped by the Embassy to see if Dick had received any more mail and to find out if we should do anything else before leaving town. We impressed upon the Embassy our need to get passage on the *President Jefferson,* a President Line ship which was scheduled to sail to Bombay. We hoped to get passage for both passengers and car. We had been to the shipping agent who had no information about us getting passage. While Dick and I were at the embassy, Check went to the police to get his passport and also to register. It was after eleven before we were finally on the road to Kandy.

The road to Kandy was paved, as are most roads in Ceylon. On the way we noticed a number of signs: "Drink More Ceylon Tea" and "Have You Had Your Tea Today" and "Tea Served 300 Yards."

We saw eight elephants working along the road. We reached Kandy in time for lunch at Queen's Hotel—a long, rambling old-fashioned hotel that served good food. For lunch we had soused fish—at least that's what it said on the menu. Check wondered if it would be stewed, and Dick suggested fried. Actually it was pickled.

After lunch we drove by the Temple of the Tooth and by the lake in the center of the town. The lake adds charm and beauty to this old city. We stopped at the Botanical Gardens where we found the Superintendent who was our guide for a brief tour. The gardens had a great variety of tropical plants from all parts of the world. In one section there was a large grassy area bordered by bright blooming flowers. Leading off to the right was the avenue of tall coconut palms. At the end of this avenue was another leading off to the left of Royal Palms, which appeared to be stunted compared to the ones I knew in Brazil. These palms were only 50 to 60 feet tall. Unfortunately the orchids were not in bloom. Ceylon is famous for its great variety of different sizes and colors of orchids. We did see a few of the medium size brownish orchids in bloom. There was a collection of most of the spices of the world but not in their commercial types. Cinnamon was a tree and not the bush which is cut for bark production. We saw allspice and nutmeg, which are grown primarily in the West Indies. We were shown some of the original rubber trees which were brought from Kew Gardens in England, but the main grove was in Colombo. While riding around the gardens we passed a river where an elephant was taking a bath. We also met some students studying the different tropical plants. The superintendent could give us only an hour so we were soon on our way, much to the relief of Check and Dick.

As we drove up the mountain to Nuwara Eliya, as in the case of driving to Kodai, it seemed we would never reach the top. The more we climbed, the more tea groves we saw. Whole mountainsides were covered with tea bushes. In Brazil there are seas of coffee, but here in Ceylon there are mountains of tea. The always white tea factories stood out in the deep green tea groves. About five o'clock we began to pass trucks and buses loaded with tea pickers returning to their homes after a hard day's work of picking tea leaves. I should think tea-picking would be among the hardest labor jobs in the world.

Tea drinkers are lucky that there are people who will do this hard work. If they received a "fair" wage, tea would be a couple of dollars a pound wholesale in the raw tea market.

We reached Nuwara Eliya about six and tried to drive into the Hill Club thinking it was the Grand Hotel. (Certainly, there were a large number of Grand Hotels on this trip.) An Englishman driving out stopped us and seemed to read our minds, saying he would lead us to the hotel. The Grand Hotel is a large building that gives the appearance of a hotel in a truly cold and snowy climate. It is a two-story rambling hotel. Many people call it "The Morgue" because in the off season so few people stay. There were 20 to 30 guests in the dining room when we dined.

After dinner, Dick and Check browsed around while I called Singleton Salmon at the Hill Club. I got him out of his bath but he was a good guy and asked us over for a drink and to discuss our plans for seeing the tea and rubber estates. We drove to the Hill Club to find Singleton Salmon waiting for us in the bar-library. We discussed what we intended to do and then joined his wife in the community lounge where we met two more tea planters. Mrs. Singleton Salmon is fun. She is of French origin, has lived in the United States, mostly New York, and in Ceylon on tea estates.

After drinks, we excused ourselves and returned to the hotel for dinner. As in India, the dinner hours in Ceylon are from eight to ten. We usually made it before closing time because we hate to miss a meal. After dinner, Check and I played "slosh" in the billiard room with an Englishman. The billiard room closed at eleven.

June 4, 1949, Nuwara Eliya (Harry)

Check and I got up early and went to the golf club. We found the caddy master who found two sets of clubs for us and two fairly good caddies. We also took a forecaddie to help us lose golf balls. The Nuwara Eliya club is famous in Asia because its tees, fairways, and greens remind one of playing in Switzerland. In fact three holes on the course are labeled the Swiss holes. We played twelve holes and were back in the hotel before nine o'clock.

Then it was off to a tea estate. Dick drove, and we reached the estate on schedule to find the director in conference. While waiting we talked to the botanist. We learned that most tea bushes are planted from seed. Except for experimental purposes there is no budding of the bushes. Usually a tea bush is planted in the hole where it will spend the rest of its life and not transplanted except for replacements which are few. In the older plantations the bushes were planted up and down the hill but on the new ones, some effort is made to plant them on the contour. Erosion is a serious problem in tea since nearly all the bushes are planted on hilly to mountainous land. In fact some of the slopes are so steep that I do not see how a man could go up them. It would be easy to come down. The tea pickers begin at a road, or lane, and work up the mountainside. Until most of the bushes are planted on the contour they must continue working up from the bottom.

The estate does some breeding work to try and find fungus-resistant varieties. Work is done at the station in selecting plants that have resistant qualities and isolating them for experiments. If one selection does well, it is increased and the seed, years later, distributed to estates.

The estate makes recommendations for pruning which must be done once every two to three years. The bush must be kept small and as near a uniform height as possible. It makes picking easier and gives a better appearance.

The estate also does work on spacing. After speaking with the botanist, we walked out into the grounds to see what was actually being done. While there, Dr. Norris, the estate manager, walked up and confirmed the information. Dr. Norris led us inside and told us about the leaf blight that was causing considerable trouble in the industry. The tea planters were worried. After all, the coffee industry in Ceylon was ruined by a leaf blight and the tea industry was started on the ruins of the coffee. The leaf blight is found in areas where the clouds hang in the air and only a small amount of rain falls. Where there is a heavier, more uniformly distributed rainfall with some sunshine, the blight does not occur or causes little damage. Most of the damage has occurred in the lower levels of the plantation.

Speaking of lower levels, tea-growing regions are divided into three regions: lower level (up to about 3,000 feet), medium level (3000 to 4500), and high level (above 4,500). The quality varies with the different levels. The low country produces more tea per acre but like most bulk production the quality is not good compared with the other levels. As the tea is planted on higher levels the quality goes up, with the best quality produced on the highest levels. Darjeeling tea is considered by Ceylon planters as the best in the world because it is grown at such high levels (above 5,000 feet). When you buy tea in the store you do not get any one growth but a mixture, the same as with coffee.

Each estate has its own factory for processing the tea leaves. As the leaves are plucked, they are put in a basket and taken in the evening to the factory where they are cured. The leaves that are plucked are two leaves and the new leaf at the end of the stem. These leaves grow in about six to nine days depending upon the fertility of the soil. Most bushes are picked about every nine days. To make picking easier the bushes are trimmed or pruned to keep them low and a uniform height. On pruning some of the bushes, the stems are cut level, leaving only the larger stems but with fewer leaves. If the plant is not too healthy, not all of the stems are cut back. On one pruning some of the outside stems are left growing; on the next pruning the inside stems are left. This type of pruning makes an irregular-shaped bush but at least keeps the tea bush healthy. Many of the pickers do not care, anyway. Nearly all of the tea workers are Indians, as the Ceylonese do not care to work at high elevations nor do they like the back-breaking work of tea picking. The pickers must bend over all the time they are picking while carrying their baskets on their backs but strapped around their heads. A good picker will make a rupee to a rupee four annas a day depending on how many pounds of leaves he picks. Unlike the rubber workers, there are trucks to pick up the tea leaves and to take the workers to and from the areas being picked. Such a system is necessary since the tea grows up the steep mountainside and if the workers had to walk to the area being picked they would be too tired to continue climbing to pick tea.

The green leaves are taken to the factory for processing. The curing appears to be fairly simple. The leaves are spread on burlap shelves which are spread about eight inches apart. They remain there for eight hours. Drying take place in ordinary air, but two six-foot fans suck the air out of the drying rooms. This draft dries the leaves sufficiently even in wet weather. The leaves are then sent down a chute to the next floor where they are run over screens and separated by weight and size. Only the smallest are discarded along with the lightest. They will be used but not with the better qualities. The partially dry leaves are then sent to rolling machines. There are three separate machines. The leaves are dumped into a large vat which has an open bottom. The bottom touches a plate that has small ridges. The vat moves over the plate in a rolling motion which rolls the leaves. After twenty minutes of rolling, the leaves are dumped and carried over sifters. The well rolled leaves pass off the end of the sifter and are ready for fermentation, which takes four hours. The rolled leaves are then transferred to trays about four inches deep and permitted to stand. The employees can tell by smelling whether the leaves have fermented sufficiently. They are then taken to a dryer where they pass through heat of 140 degrees. The dried leaves are taken to a grading room where the tea is spread out on boards and Indian women can pick out sticks and other foreign material. Tea should not have more than three percent water in the leaves.

After grading the tea is packaged in chests made of special wood which is both light and strong and will not absorb moisture. The inside of the chest is lined with aluminum foil and paper and sealed. Before sealing, samples are taken from each lot. The estate keeps one sample and sends the other to its agent in Colombo. Tea is sold to exporters on auction days, which are usually Monday and Tuesday. The exporters buy their tea and ship it generally in estate lots to importers in England, the U.S. and other importing countries. Lipton now owns only one or two small estates. Lipton buys most of its tea from other producers and are not considered important buyers of the best-quality teas. In addition to the large estates, there are a number of small producers of tea, especially in the lowlands. These small producers have only a few acres which do not produce enough leaves to justify the expense of a factory. Thus a number of factories have been built in the lowlands to buy leaves. A few of the factory owners may also produce tea but their main business is generally buying and processing the leaves of small growers. Since the low country tea is low quality, the process is not as strict and does not require as much skill as for the better quality.

Clockwise from upper left: Ruins at Anuradhapura, the ancient capital of Ceylon; Dick Brecker, Mr. Gourlay, and Harry Spielman; tea drying on burlap shelves; Harry talking with an Indian worker.

After visiting the factory, we left for Newara Eliya (without being offered a cup of tea!). Dick's new girlfriend had already had her lunch, so the three of us ate and then scattered. Check went to play golf. I decided I would rather sleep. Check played 18 holes, part of them with the caddy he had in the morning. My morning caddy also went along. Between the two caddies they improved Check's game and he came back to the hotel in good spirits. We dressed and went for a drink with Singleton Salmon at the Hill Club.

We again met in the library where we asked more questions about tea over a couple of scotches. While we were on the second scotch, Mr. Gourlay came in with the results of the Derby. None of us except Singleton had known a derby was being run, but we quickly developed interest and even knew the names of some of the horses running. We had a couple of drinks and then Singleton and Gourlay decided we should meet their wives before the two of them were shot. We wound up in the Snake Pit of the Hill Club. The pit was a small bar with bench seats around the sides with a bar on the left as one entered. The walls were all wood-paneled and looked cozy, especially when all of the younger (under 40) women members of the club seemed to be in the room, all seven of them. Singleton and the others were not in the room so I went to look for them. Gourlay's wife was in the pit talking with a fairly attractive woman and I wanted to remain, but since Singleton was our host I thought I had better join the others. Mrs. Salmon was unhappy with us for keeping her husband so long, but we parted good friends a little later. Mr. Gourlay invited us to his place for drinks at noon on Sunday, the next day.

We returned to the hotel, had dinner, and Check and I played slosh until 11, the closing time, and turned in. We never knew where Dick had disappeared to.

June 5, 1949, Nuwara Eliya (Harry)

Check and I were up early and over to the golf club. We got our same two caddies. By the seventh hole I had lost all but one of my golf balls, most of them in the spiny brush. By the fifteenth I had to buy two more so I could finish. The Nuwara Eliya course is without doubt one of the prettiest courses in the world. It has everything. Narrow and wide fairways, hills, lots of them, water holes since a stream meanders across several of the fairways, and then one has a combination of all the obstacles. After a while, when we came to a narrow fairway or one with a water hole, I used a three iron and usually did not get into trouble. Altogether I lost four balls and I think Check lost one, maybe two. When we reached the clubhouse, we found Dick, who said he got up just after we left. During the night he wanted to play with us, but since he did not tell us we left him behind.

At noon we met Gourlay, who is also the captain of the golf club. We stopped in the bar where Singleton Salmon met us for a quick drink before leaving for Gourlay's home. His hillside home has a lovely view. In the distance is a mountain with two waterfalls. One is called "Lover's Leap." The story goes that a boy and girl fell in love. The father found out so they ran away toward the mountain. The father organized a posse to go after them. As the men approached, the young couple locked themselves in each other's arms and leapt over the falls.

Directly in front of the house was an artificial lake at least a half-mile wide and two miles long. The house, on a small hill, had no tall trees to obstruct the views. The lawn was seeded with Australian bluegrass, which seemed to do well in the mountains. The house was designed and built by Singleton and his wife. It was a well-built brick structure with three bedrooms on the second floor and the usual rooms below. We returned to the hotel for lunch, and in the afternoon Dick and Check played golf while I went to the dairy.

The dairy is 15 miles east of Nuwara Eliya and at a higher elevation. The dairy is important because it is one of the few places in the tropics where drinkable milk is produced and also where European cattle are present. All of the cattle are purebred Ayreshire which came from Australia during the war. Unfortunately the Aussies sent many of their poorer animals. The average production is only 5,000 pounds of milk a year. A good heifer should do twice that amount. The herd manager is a graduate of the Dairy Institute of Bangalore and seems to be a capable Ceylonese. He has obtained a good bull from Australia and a young one from Scotland to improve the milk yield. He said he wanted to eliminate about 40 cows but because Ceylon is a Buddhist country, cattle cannot be killed. Of course the dairy can give the cattle away and is not responsible for what happens afterward. The local people do not seem to want the cows. If the 40 were disposed of, the average of the herd would increase to at least 8,000 pounds of milk a year which would be a great improvement since more milk would be produced with less food. In addition to the cows that cannot be disposed of, there are 165 bull calves that are useless. The locals will not take them as gifts. With over two hundred animals that do not pay their way, the dairy is not making money. But it is breaking even.

The dairy is nestled in the hills surrounded by green rolling pastures. It could have been in New York state. The buildings were of European design, and when I went inside the cattle looked familiar. Gosh, it was good to see well-cared-for animals that looked prosperous! The two cow sections ran parallel and were joined at the road end by the bull and calf pens and food storage sections. The inside was not whitewashed but clean, nevertheless. There was no silo nor hay left. The cows are fed fresh-cut grass the year round, so why make hay whether the sun shines or not? After all, green grass is better than the best hay made from grass. The cows are given feed that most American or European dairymen never hear of: coconut meal, rice polishings and bean bran. They do well on this diet. The morning milk is taken to nearby towns and sold as fresh milk. All of the afternoon milk is skimmed and the cream sold as fresh cream or made into both sweet and salted butter. I arrived after all the milk had been skimmed so I drank a glass of cream that was thicker than whipping cream. The skimmed milk is given to the calves.

It was after dark when I returned to Nuwara Eliya by a mountain road which I had been over only once. Part of the way was foggy, but it was fun to drive anyway. Check and Dick were already at the hotel. After Check and I cleaned up, we went in the lounge to listen to Dick playing the piano. An engaged couple, Paddy Newton and Diane Haley, and a Mrs. Creasy were also listening. When Dick left to change clothes, Check and Mrs. Creasy took turns playing the piano. Olive and Tony Riley came in on Check's invitation. Dick had hinted to Singleton and Gourlay that we would like to go to the dance at the Hill Club that night, but the hint did not take. He also hinted to the Rileys, but that did not work either. However, Dick came back and played well and we sang for a while. Each man present bought a round of drinks, and by the time the last round was consumed we decided it was time to eat. The Rileys returned to the Hill Club and we took Paddy and Diane to dinner with us. Check loaned Diane his coat. It was darn chilly that night. After dinner Paddy returned to his estate which was an hour's drive away. Check and I played slosh in the billiard room and were joined by an Englishman and Dick. The room closed at eleven and off to bed we went. What else was there to do?

June 6, 1949, Nuwara Eliya to Colombo (Harry)

By nine this morning we were up, packed and breakfasted and began our return to Colombo. Dick wasn't sure we should take the long way which Singleton Salmon had suggested but thought we should return the way we came, via Kandy. We took the long way by driving southeast from Nuwara Eliya. The pass we drove is considered the highest in Ceylon. On the other side of the pass was a valley which must have been 75 miles across. The valley was not level but had hills dotted about. Some were bald while others might have had tea growing on them. Far to the east was a tall peak upon which there was snow as the clouds seemed to hang around the peak. After driving a while we kept to the mountains on the right and began to climb. After reaching Bandarawala, we turned south toward Hupatale. We drove through town and as we came out on the south side we saw why Singleton had sent us this way. The road came to the edge of a cliff which dropped at least 4,000 feet. Directly ahead was a flat coastal plain reaching all the way to the north shore of the island. Unfortunately there were clouds which prevented us from seeing the Indian Ocean. We saw two lakes in the distance. To the right were more mountains, some of which appeared higher than the one we were on. I thought the road would make for the plain and then to Colombo. Dick was inclined to agree with me. Check thought we should keep to the mountain and gradually work our way out. As usual he was right! Dick was driving and made good time down the mountains. As we passed Adam's Peak, clouds hid it from view. Still we saw no elephants. We reached Ratnapura right on schedule. Just as we drove into the club compound rain began to fall. It was a nice heavy rain that soaked everything in sight in two minutes and then kept raining. At the club I gave the note from Singleton to the butler. He asked what we would have to drink and said that lunch would be ready in a half-hour. The club had a bowling alley and Check and I rolled one ball each. It was too much trouble to set up our pins to have a game. We read magazines until a delicious meal was ready: lamb chops and more of the sweet pineapple for dessert. After coffee, we paid the bill and started for Colombo with Check driving.

A word about clubs. There is an old saying that when two Englishman get together they form a club. In a country where the white man's customs are so different from the natives it is only natural that the white man should form clubs where he could have something resembling his prior life. This Ratnapura club had two private sleeping rooms with two beds and bathrooms. Behind the bar were more individual rooms with community showers and toilets. There was a library with several shelves of books, some of the latest magazines from England and several tables with upright chairs for playing bridge or other card games. Two tables could be used for bridge and one large table for six or eight to play poker or other community card games. Next was a pool room with one pool table. (All of the clubs seem to have a pool table and a bar even if they have nothing else.) The next room might be called the dining room, which was separated from the bar by a portable screen. On the veranda was a fence marking off the bowling alley. The bar was on the far left side. It has stool and a rail! One could order any of the more famous Indian tropical drinks as well as straight whiskey (scotch) There was a staff of five. We were the only ones for lunch. Club life begins after five and continues until midnight if anything interesting to do develops.

As we continued toward Colombo we saw two elephants lumbering down the road—one large one and a small one. We saw two more elephants as we drove over a narrow bridge. In the water to the left was a large elephant playing in the water. He was having fun just lying on his side and running his trunk through the water. The second was down stream being scrubbed by his handler.

We reached Colombo in late afternoon and checked into the Galle Face. We changed clothes quickly and headed for downtown. Going down toward the clock tower we ran out of gas—again.

We coasted to the tower and then were told the nearest petrol pump was about a half mile away near the Regal Cinema. We began pushing and were soon joined by four coolies. They got the car moving fast, so we let them push. When we reached the corner near the Embassy, I left and let Dick continue to the petrol pump because he had the key to the gas tank.

As I walked in, Horton told me the bad news. The *Jefferson* was full and would take no passengers to Bombay. Dick was ready to take Air India the next morning until he remembered he did not have an Indian visa. We talked with Miss Thurgood, an Embassy secretary, about other possibilities but there seemed to be none. It looked as if the end of our trip would be the only part which did not go as planned. I almost decided to fly on Thursday. I knew that I wanted to see the rubber plantation after coming this far and another day would make little difference.

Dick agreed to bring our passports to the office the next morning to get the Indian visas. Then he remembered that if he were to ship his car to Bombay he might need the car to get it on board. This decision left us without a car to go to the rubber estate. Horton offered to take his little Austin, which would be very crowded for four persons. He made Dick an offer to use his Austin while we went to the estate in the Chevrolet, and Dick accepted. About this time Check drove up and we returned to the hotel. Check went to see another newspaper, Dick went swimming, and I did a little writing. Check was back in time to go for a drink with the Salmons at seven.

Soon we began discussions: Check and I with Horton on tea, rubber, coconuts and Ceylon economy in general while Dick was talking about New York, art and Paris with Eleanor. The phone rang for Dick, and he had to leave to meet his date. Check and I then left to go to dinner at the hotel. Neither Check nor I were wearing suitcoats, and the chief steward, a Frenchman, would not let us be seated until we got our coats. (It was the usual custom in hotels that one had to be properly dressed for dinner.) Check and I retired after dinner. I have no idea where Dick ate or what he did, but there was a rumor that he was out with a girl name Carlotta. That evening he acted as if he didn't want the two of us around. The next morning he talked as if he were truly sorry we were not along to help him out!

June 7, 1949, Colombo (Harry)

Eleanor and Horton came by for us at eight and we headed for the rubber research institute. On the way out of town we bought gasoline from the filling station (petrol pump) where Horton buys his. Because he is an Embassy officer he pays only the actual cost of petrol; no tax which represents about 45 U.S. cents per gallon or a little more than half the price we had been paying. Check drove like he ordinarily drives but, after riding in the tin Austin, both Eleanor and Horton were more than a little disturbed at driving at 35 miles per hour through traffic and challenging other cars, trucks and buses which wanted their half of the road in the middle. The research station was 45 miles south of Colombo. At the 10-mile marker we passed Mount Lavinia, a beach resort near the city. The hotel is on the beach, and its grounds are shaded by tall trees.

The road here was a six-lane highway. The only trouble with a wide road is that more oxcarts get to use it. There were also sidewalks in the more thickly populated section but some people preferred to walk in the street. It wasn't nearly as bad as India, even so. A blue-green Austin passed us. After the road narrowed the Austin seemed to go even faster, but Check kept up with him. He was going over 65 at times. At that speed a motorcycle which had been following us gave up. The road was lined with coconut trees, most of them in groves of varying sizes from plantations to small holdings. Usually a thatched hut nestled in the center. Along other stretches there were rubber plantations neatly planted in rows that reminded one of the pattern of an orange grove. Of course the trees were much taller and the ground around the trees was well shaded giving the impression of a tremendous, well shaded lawn free of bushes and undergrowth. No, goats are not used to keep down the under growth.

The two-lane road curved gently through the green growth of trees. The Austin continued to keep ahead of us. A time or two we were going too fast to see completely the direction signs for the side roads. We stopped to ask the way. After asking twice and getting agreement we found that our side road was on the other side of town. We had gone only a hundred yards when we found the Austin waiting for us. We asked the driver where to turn off and he agreed to show us. Actually it was a couple of miles.

Leaving the main road, we drove through more rubber plantations, nearly all of which were on the hillside. Only a few were on level ground. That land was planted to rice. The road continued to be blacktop, wide enough for two cars, easily.

After a few more enquiries we found the estate road which was gravel. After the morning rain there was no dust and the road was smooth. For a short distance there were small bushes which looked like coffee growing under the tall rubber trees. This land must have been owned by small farmers because the large rubber estates do not grow other crops under their trees. As we wound down the lane, we came to a fork in the road (please, no jokes) and took the drive going to the junior officers' bungalow and the laboratory.

At the laboratory we found Dr. Rhodes who was expecting us. Yes, he was called "Dusty." He was very thin, slightly stooped, about medium height, blondish with blue eyes and most friendly. Dusty told us the farm was divided into two parts. The one where we were was used to study diseases and insects of the rubber plants as well as to experiment with different methods of tapping or bleeding the trees. A large number of trees were old, and new methods for spacing were also being tried. On the other estate was the nursery and stock for improving the varieties of rubber.

He said it was difficult to get men to work on the estates because of the increased cost of living and a widespread feeling that the rubber industry of Ceylon was uneconomic for the future. He had been in Ceylon and was leaving at the end of June because he could not get young officers to carry on the work.

He suggested we see the processing plant, go to his bungalow for a drink, and then on to see the plantation. Processing rubber on an estate is a simple process, possibly more technical than tea or coffee. The latex is brought in as the tappers fill their buckets. It is received at the plants in the same manner as milk from the milk shed. The plant is screened like a milk house. The latex is poured into vats where acetic and formic acid are added to make the latex coagulate and to separate from the water of other material which accumulates while the collecting cups are hanging on the tree. Since rubber trees prefer some rain every day, there is bound to be considerable rainwater in the collecting cups. Also the rain washes the trees carrying bits of bark, dust, fungus and old rubber into the cups as well. After the latex settles for eight to 12 hours it can be separated into different qualities depending upon color and density. The color various from black to white and the density up to that of cheddar cheese. After the latex has coagulated it is run through ringers to squeeze out the water and acid and form the latex into paper-thin sheets, much of it full of holes, to dry. It is hung in a drying room for one to five days depending upon the dryness of the air. After drying some of the sheets are scraped while most of it is smoked. The sheets are baled and sold to exporters in Colombo.

In a separate building liquid latex is prepared. Each day's collections are stored in a vat. On this estate four days' collections fill one vat. A chemical is added which causes the latex to rise to the top just as cream rises on milk. After four days the "cream" is ready to skim. A preservative is added, the cream taken off and put in drums. Liquid latex sells for considerably more than smoked sheets but is a more technical process and does not produce as much saleable rubber. Much of the liquid form is used for making foam rubber for mattresses and upholstery.

From the laboratory we visited another set of offices where we saw examples of the different types of knives used in tapping rubber trees in different parts of the world. Here we met Clement da Silva, the botanist at the institute since 1934. He was English educated and had spent time studying in Trinidad. Before working on rubber, he was a soil scientist at the tea institute. He was obviously well educated and spoke beautiful English and was sincere about his work. (I'll bet one day he soon he will head the rubber institute.) Da Silva was with us from then on until we returned to Colombo.

We drove up the hill through the rubber estate to see the spacing experiments as well as some tapping. By this time rain, or showers, had stopped and some of the trees were dry enough to tap. If rubber trees are tapped while wet or during the rain the latex will run down the side of the tree and not in the cut groove. In the grove of trees the ground was moist, the air damp, and it was easy to realize how fungus might grow on the trunks of the trees causing great damage, not only to the tree itself, but also to the latex as it ran toward the collecting cup. In the new plantings all of the trees had been budded so as to produce more latex than the old first-planted trees. On some of the new high-yielding trees a new fungus has developed. It can be treated by scraping the bark and applying a chemical By the time a new bark has grown the fungus has been killed.

Clockwise from upper left: Rubber tree with cut bark; gathering latex; Harry Spielman looking at sheets of rubber with with Singleton Salmon; Ceylon street scene.

Da Silva is also experimenting with spacing. Many of the Ceylon rubber estates plant only 90 to 120 trees an acre. In Malaya as many as 250 trees are planted. Two of these methods which show promise have been tried in Ceylon. The more common planting and one which is especially suited to fertile and almost level ground is to plant trees 9 feet apart.

After the trees are about seven or eight years old, they are thinned by removing the runts on the low yielders. Rubber trees grow to 40 or 50 feet high, spreading some at the top forming a heavy canopy if planted too closely. The object in spacing is to give some sunlight to the trunks and plenty of ventilation so the trees will dry and the air will not become too moist.

Readers of *Weeping Wood* by Vickie Baum, and students of rubber, know that Ceylon was the first country to cultivate rubber on a commercial scale. The original seeds were taken from the Amazon Valley of Brazil to Kew Gardens near London about 100 years ago. Some estimates indicate at least 30,000 seeds were taken. From this seemingly large number only a few thousand survived. When the survivors were seedlings, twenty were taken to Ceylon and planted in the local botanical garden. At that time Ceylon was one of the world's most important coffee producers. The rubber plants did remarkably well which resulted in a large number of seeds being planted on the island. From Ceylon, seeds were taken to Malaya, later to Java, Sumatra and still later to Indo-China.

Large fortunes were made from the rubber estates during World War I. During World War II Ceylon was the main Allied source for natural rubber since the larger areas further East were held by the Japanese. As in many countries which have a good source of income from agricultural products, little attention is given to research for the improvement of the varieties grown or cultural practices used. Most of the groves in Ceylon were planted before 1910. As yet no one knows the full life of a rubber tree. One of the original trees brought to Ceylon is still living. It is called No. 2. On the other hand, there is a point beyond which it is unprofitable to continue tapping. In Ceylon that point seems to be between 30 and 35 years, but it might be earlier if the soil is as poor and rocky as much of the soil in the rubber groves of Ceylon.

Only a small percentage of the rubber trees in Ceylon have been replanted. Most of the trees are old, producing less and less rubber each year. In the past most of the rubber estates made at least 40 percent on the investment. Like people the world over who make easy money, nearly all of it was spent as it was earned. Little thought was given the depreciation of the land and trees. The day of reckoning has arrived when the trees must be replaced or the state go into the production of other products. Difficulties are encountered because of the lack of reserves with which to meet the cost of replanting and more importantly the loss of income until the new trees come into production seven years from the time they are planted. Some of the better estates are in a position to modernize. Many of the small producers will be able to meet the crisis because they have only a half acre to three or four acres of rubber and in addition they grow coconuts, oranges, pepper, cinnamon and probably rice for their own use. The loss in income from rubber will not hit them hard.

In order to meet the crisis the government has made a detailed study of the rubber-growing regions and made recommendations for improvement. The report recommended that one third of the rubber be taken out of production and other products planted. The government has offered to buy the land for 200 rupees per acre. After the land is acquired plots of five to ten acres will be sold to small cultivators—all Ceylonese and not Indians. The government has also prepared lists of crops which could be grown on this old rubber land. In some areas cocoa will be grown. Now that a blight has hit the cocoa in West Africa some officials think they will be able to enter to cocoa market by the times are of producing age. Unfortunately there is not enough land suitable for cocoa to make Ceylon a major market for cocoa.

This one third of old rubber land is the poorest and will not materially reduce the total production if the remaining two thirds are properly taken care of. Much work will be required and at the end it may not pay since costs are continuing to rise. If the owners are satisfied with six percent interest they could likely complete with Malaya and possibly with synthetic rubber. Like most predominantly agricultural countries the owners want at least 25 percent a year and if they do not receive it they think that the world is against them. Not much rubber land could be used for growing food grains because the land is steep and rocky. Cultivators in both Ceylon and India insist on growing rice in water, which requires level land. There would be little possibility to increase rice production by planting rice in the rubber estates even though Ceylon imports one third of her requirements from Burma and Thailand.

Ceylon rubber is important to the United States for two reasons: (1) It is the oldest supplier, was about the only supplier during the war and still produces a good product. The argument against that reason is that Ceylon is a high-cost producer compared with other rubber-producing countries. If she cannot compete, why should she be helped. But who knows, we might need her rubber again and need it badly as in the last war. (2) Rubber is Ceylon's largest source of dollars. If the U.S. is to sell manufactured products to Ceylon she must have dollars. If we do not buy her rubber she cannot buy our goods. Perhaps we should give technical assistance. We do have rubber experts who have been assisting Brazil and Liberia for a number of years and who could do Ceylon much good, perhaps.

After a glass of beer and much discussion we went to the second estate owned by the institute. Both Rhodes and da Silva agreed that *Weeping Wood* describes accurately the story of rubber production in Ceylon. We had a little trouble getting Rhodes to leave his bungalow as he insisted we have more beer. He agreed to go if we agreed we would have a beer before lunch.

We then took some pictures of rubber tapping. By the end of the day the latex on the tree has hardened. The daily cutting, or every other day's, is done largely to remove the dried latex. It also slightly cuts the tree. The tree immediately begins to bleed and the latex literally runs down the cut into the coconut shell container. Coconut shells are the most satisfactory collectors since they cost little and no one is interested in stealing them.

Nearly all of the rubber tappers and most of the other workers are Indians. There are more Ceylonese working rubber than tea, however. Low rubber prices will be more felt in India than Ceylon as far as labor is concerned.

At the second estate we saw the budding of rubber trees. Generally the bud is taken from a tree of high production. Much of the bud stock comes from Malaya, where high yielders have been produced and where budding has been practiced for 25 years.

The buds are grafted on year-old seedlings. After three weeks the wrapping around the bud sprout is removed and the wood nicked to see if it is green. When green, it shows the bud has taken and it will grow. Transplanting takes place in February during the northeast monsoon and before the really hot weather. Just before the budded seedling is planted the original seedling is cut just above the bud. The bud then grows for a couple of years but it eventually straightens up. The only way to tell the tree has been grafted is the "sell butt" or heel at the base of the trunk. In tapping cuts are never made as low as the graft scar.

Tapping of rubber trees is interesting in that it is one of the few times when non-doctors can make money by cutting a living organism. There are many systems for tapping trees: the most common is to cut half way around the tree on one side one year and cut the other side the following year. The cuts begin about three feet about the ground. During one year six to eight inches are cut on one side. Each side gets cut three times. By the time the bottom cut has been made, bark has grown out on the first cut so that tapping can begin again.

One of the major difficulties of the Ceylon rubber industry is the large amount of labor required. A rubber worker in Ceylon can tap 90 to 120 trees a day while in Malaya, Sumatra, Java and Indo-China, a worker taps 200 to 250 a day.

The rubber industry of Ceylon is in a bad way. It needs modernization quickly if the industry is to earn dollars. Any improvement will take 10 to 15 years before it will affect the Ceylon economy. In the meantime there will continue to be what is locally called a crisis.

From the second institute estate we repaired to a rest house for lunch. We all had beers but "Dusty" insisted someone join him for a pink gin. Check did, and on the second round, I joined in while Eleanor shared a beer. The lunch was delicious: fish and chicken with potatoes, green beans and a pudding for dessert.

On the way back to Colombo we stopped to buy two gallons of gas just to be sure we did not run out the fifth time.

At Colombo, Check went to the Associated Newspapers and I to the Embassy. At the Embassy I learned that Dick had arranged to ship his car the next day and that he was to leave by plane the next morning. If the car left the next day, Check and I would be left without transportation. One of the reasons for taking a car was that we could get around Colombo. The Embassy had obtained our Indian visas during our absence. When we returned to the hotel Check went for a haircut and I went to see Dick. He told me of his plans to fly first to Madras to see the Consulate General and the USIS office there and then on to Bombay by Friday night. When Check returned we talked him into writing a letter to Cooks, the travel agency arranging to ship his car, to keep it until the last minute before it should go on board. With that settled, we all three repaired to the bar and later to the dining room for our last dinner together before Dick left the next day.

June 8, 1949, Colombo (Harry)

The room boy brought our bed tea at the usual hour of seven along with four bananas. Before we could go back to sleep another room boy brought Dick's extra baggage. Still another room boy brought the morning newspapers. We remembered that our task for the day was to find passage on a ship, and two American ships were due in today.

At breakfast, Paul Van der Lippe, an American advisor to the government on irrigation and reclamation, came to our table. We told him about our visit to the rubber estates and our thoughts about the possible revitalization of the industry.

After breakfast we went directly to the jetty to see what ships had arrived. The *Steel Architect* was in, so we went immediately to the Isthmian Steamship office in the McKinnon Mackenzie building. There we learned that the ship was headed for Savannah with no chance of stopping in Bombay. However, the agent checked the list of ships that might be going to Bombay. He found an Italian ship and said that Mr. Thomas was the agent. We hurried to the Times Building but Mr. Thomas gave us very little hope since the captain was a "no" man from way back. However, he would speak to the captain to see if he would take the Chevrolet. We then learned that the *President Jefferson* was due later in the afternoon. We went to see Mr. Smith, the agent for the *Jefferson*. He said he would speak to the captain and tell him our story. We then went to Cooks to see about shipping the car. Cooks said they planned to put the car on the Italian ship provided the captain would take it. Check asked him if we could get on the *Jefferson,* could the car go with us? He checked and found that although American President ships do not take cargo to Bombay they would take the car if we got on board. We asked when Cooks needed the car and were told not before tomorrow morning and we could check if they needed it then.

We had done all we could do for the time being so returned to the hotel. Next a trip to the Air India office to get a package for Check, only to find it was at Customs. At Customs he had little difficulty and had the package in ten minutes. In Bombay it would have taken all morning. While Check was at Customs I went into a travel bureau in the building to pick up more brochures on Ceylon. When Check arrived, one of the Sinhalese girls asked what nationality we were. Check beat me to asking her what she thought. She replied, "You are not British, but you don't act like Americans." When asked how Americans acted, she replied, "They have a lot of dash and are full of pep. The language they use is different. You do sound like Americans, though." Both girls were friendly and pleasant, as tourist bureau people should be.

We went to the Embassy to find a note from Van Der Lippe asking if we would see the Permanent Secretary of Agriculture at three that afternoon. Horton called to tell him we accepted. Horton, Check and I rode with Charles O'Donnell to the Ambassador's residence for lunch. Before lunch, the Ambassador had a tall glass of beer, Horton a lime squash, while Check, Charles and I had gin tonics. The Ambassador was interested in Check's problems on setting up United Press service in Ceylon and how Check was going about it. He also asked how the Embassy could be helpful.

After lunch and before coffee we had a stroll around his garden to see his collection of small orchids, some of which were in bloom. He also had a number of coconut trees. Over the first cup of coffee we discussed the possible future of Hong Kong and came to the conclusion that if the Commies wanted it, they could get it in either of two ways—direct attack or infiltration. The latter would take longer but cost less in both equipment and men and not turn the world against them. Hong Kong cannot be held if the shore is in the hands of the enemy. Most food must come from the mainland. Since Hong Kong is an island it could not be supplied from the sea since the ships dock on the land side. On the other hand it is doubtful if the Chinese want to take the city. Who knows when the present leaders might be looking for a safe haven nearby. In fact that is one of the main reasons for having a city like Hong Kong so near the mainland.

We mentioned Ceylon's rubber crisis. The Ambassador jokingly said that the U.S. and other northern countries should expend more effort developing synthetic products to substitute for those grown in the tropics. After the new products had been developed the tropical countries would be able to solve their own problems. White men have never been able to live in the tropics and compete with the natives on an equal footing. The white man has always had an advantage or he could not survive.

By this time it was nearly three and Check and I rushed to the office of the Permanent Secretary of Agriculture in the Ceylon Government, only to find he was out. So Check left me and went to the newspaper office. I waited until the secretary came. He asked about my general impressions of the island. He asked about artificial insemination, especially how long the semen could keep when shipped. I told him and he said he was thinking about getting semen from Karachi from Red Sindi cattle for use with the cattle in Ceylon. He was interested in improving both the milk-producing capacity and the workability of animals in the countryside. I said he could get the semen flown in from Karachi but he might better get the semen from the Dairy Institute in Bangalore, India. He had not thought of that. I also told him that one of his farm managers was a graduate of the Dairy Institute and could easily help him obtain what he needed. It seems to be human nature the world over, including the U.S., to look elsewhere for something which we have at home. That trait is true of individuals as well as nations. Both Paul and I tried to get him to talk about what technical assistance the U.S. might provide, but he preferred to talk about other subjects. He made it clear that he was more interested in the estate side of the rubber problem than the workers. After all, most of the workers could go back to India.

After an hour of discussions, I excused myself. On the way out of the building I bought two books on Ceylon and went back to the Embassy. At five Check arrived at the Embassy and we decided to visit the zoo. But then the rains began so heavily that we gave up and went to Horton's for tea. We left Horton's about midnight after playing several rubbers of bridge.

June 9, 1949, Colombo (Harry)

After breakfast Check and I went by Whital's, the *Jefferson*'s agent, to see if Mr. Smith had heard anything from the *Jefferson*. We learned he was on board the ship. We went to Cooks, who had heard nothing. We had only one alternative: go to the ship. As we were walking on the jetty we met a group of Americans going ashore. We stopped one and asked if he was on the *Jefferson*. When he said "yes" we asked how many were aboard. As soon as he said "eight," we ran for the launch. First, though, we had to get police passes, so we ran to the head port police officer. When we told him we were trying to get passage to Bombay he gave us the passes and wished us luck. We were the only passengers in the launch which made straight for the *Jefferson*. Even without an agent's pass we had no difficulty getting aboard.

The captain was in his office. Captain Jack Windus was pleasantly cheerful with more the look of a businessman than a ship's skipper. He wears glasses which may help give the impression of the executive. Yes, he had four cabins and three bunks in each. Unfortunately, three of the cabins were occupied by married couples and the fourth cabin by two ladies, one of whom was getting along in years. She was the wife of a Congressman from Oklahoma or Kansas, he thought. Consequently we would not want to stay, either of us, in that cabin. He would like to take us but there was no other place we could stay. Check suggested we were willing to stay in any kind of place, crew's quarters or otherwise. He replied he had a full crew and there were no other bunks. We talked about a few other things, like fuel, where he had been, the Shanghai situation. He thought there should be several ships going to Bombay, considering the number of ships in the harbor. (There were 25.) We told him about trying every source we could think of, even agreeing to ride on an old Italian ship which would not take us. The next ship would not leave before June 20. Check said we would sleep in a linen closet or a smoking room. A little later the captain excused himself. When he returned he said if we did not object he would let us sleep in the hospital. It is two decks below the main deck but has a porthole. It would be hot but we could sleep on deck. It is against regulations to have well passengers in the hospital. If anyone got sick we would have to move out. From Colombo to Bombay there should be no difficulty. We were most eager to accept and thanked him much. He would also take our car, which was a great help since Cooks told us that the ship they had hoped to use would not accept it. Cooks did not know when they could ship the car but it would be at least 10 days and probably not until June 27. Thus by getting on the *Jefferson*, we were saving Dick considerable inconvenience by not having his car until the first of July.

Check and I took off for shore to get our tickets, put luggage in the car, clear with the port doctor, tell the Embassy we were leaving, turn over the car to Cooks, and check out of the hotel, which we planned to do after lunch. We walked to the Jepsons' to tell them good-bye. After a few gimlets, we agreed to meet the Jepsons about six thirty to go to a lecture and dinner. Russ put us in his car to send us to the hotel. We had lunch and then telephoned Eleanor Schoellkopf to say we were at the hotel. In ten minutes Horton came to our room and said he would send his car back to take us to the ship. After he left, we had a row with the room servants about where my army blanket was. No one knew anything about it. After much brow beating, ranting and raving, the room boy came in and pulled the blanket from under one of the tables where it had been covered completely with a cloth. Purely accidental, of course. We managed to get everything into the bags although some bulged more than normal. When one travels for a while his things get spread around a bit. It is only when one tries to get everything into a few containers that he realizes how much freedom he has traveling by car. At the jetty we had no difficulty going through Customs nor the police. A launch was waiting. After we were settled, twelve more persons got into the launch. They were headed for the *Napoli*, an Italian passenger ship at the berth just beyond the *Jefferson*. Fortunately, the same man was on this launch as the one we had had earlier. Check had given him a generous tip in the morning. He and his buddies helped get our luggage aboard. The first officer took us to our "cabin." It has four bunks, a lavatory, shower, toilet, and three locked chests for medicines. We dumped our suitcases on two of the bunks and the rest of the "stuff" on the floor. The "stuff" consists of this typewriter, two briefcases, the camera equipment bag and four cameras and a tripod. By this time it was five o'clock and dinnertime. We tried to eat but since we had had lunch at three we weren't very hungry. We did go for iced tea, having at least four glasses apiece. It was the first iced tea I had seen in some time. Wonder why hotels in tea-producing countries do not serve more iced tea. With lemon and sugar it is an excellent hot weather drink, even in the tropics. We ate some fruit Jello, American cookies and a cup of American coffee. It tasted different from the good coffee we had in the Indian coffeehouses, but just as good in a different way. Four of our fellow passengers came in and introduced themselves and vice versa. One couple was going home from Japan after two years in the American occupation army. The other couple was from Honolulu on their way around the world. After dinner Check and I went ashore on the agent's launch with several members of the crew of the *Jefferson*. Also in the launch were several mailbags. Check noticed that on one it said "Karachi via Colombo." He asked the ship's agent why it was being unloaded in Colombo. He said that was the way the bag was routed and according to regulations it would be unloaded here, sent to the post office, and then resent to the ship, probably the *Jefferson*.

Ashore, we took rickshaws to Lake House, the newspaper office, for John to see his correspondent, Austin de Silva. We watched the editors preparing news for the morning paper. After bidding Austin goodbye, we took rickshaws to the Jepsons'. After we paid the men one rupee apiece, they asked for more money. We doubled their fee and they seemed pleased. We feel sorry for the poor devils because it is not easy pulling their passengers in Colombo, which has a number of hills.

At the Jepsons', we were fortified with a drink before going to the 80 Club to hear a lecture by Lt. Commander Hall of the British Information Service. His subject was the economic situation in the United Kingdom and how the government was meeting the problem. To me, much of what he said was new. To the British present, it must have been old news. It was encouraging to hear that industrial production and exports had reached new heights during 1948. One must admire the British for doing so well under such adverse conditions. More power to them.

The speaker left shortly after the lecture and the rest of the group settled down to a little drinking and conversation. Mr. and Mrs. Fonseca were friendly and seemed anxious to talk to Americans. They had been in the United States for eight months in 1947. Both used a lot of American slang. Mr. Fonseca had combined a business trip with a visit to the Mayo Clinic for an eye operation. While they were in the Chicago they saw a baseball game which they enjoyed, went to a convention by accident, and were welcomed with open arms. The president of the group invited them to her estate outside Chicago where they enjoyed a weekend in typical American fashion. While in the United States she wore a sari, which did create much interest. In the States they found that nearly all Americans knew nothing about Ceylon nor where it was located. They gave up telling people they were from Ceylon and started saying they were from India. Mr. Fonseca is an agent for a large number of manufacturers of American consumer goods like refrigerators, Mix Masters and Firestone products. When the Firestone name came up, Russ Jepson brought the Firestone catalogue which was as large as a Montgomery Ward catalogue except for the cover. We did a little wishful shopping through the book, especially the fishing equipment and sporting goods. Tires were actually advertised but not prominently. We came to a vibro tool which prompted me, at that stage of the drinking, to take off the belt I made about a year ago to show off the brands which I had drilled on it with a vibro tool. A number of people came to see because they had never seen an actual brand.

Left: Harry and Check on the deck of the President Jefferson; *right: Harry at the typewriter aboard ship.*

The Fonsecas came with us and the Jepsons to the Silver Fawn for dinner. It was our last night and we had prawns and steak, which was especially good and just the right size to keep us from getting drunk. Of course there was dancing between courses. With only two women and four men, two of us ate our food rather quickly. Before we had finished our steaks we were joined by Smith and his date, Peggy. Peggy is a British girl from Jaffa in North Ceylon where her husband works for a cement factory. Check and I tried the slot machines with our usual five rupees. The first time through we were well ahead, having about 30 slugs for our original 20. Peggy came over on the second time through our pile and helped us lose them. Later Ernie and Bea Stevens joined our party. Ernie works for Standard Vacuum Oil Company in Madras, and he and his wife were on a short vacation in Colombo.

It was after midnight when the orchestra finished playing. There were several men who played the piano so the music did not stop. Soon there were only two tables of revelers in the club. The Jepsons knew the man hosting the other table so we joined them. We were now a group of fifteen and we all gathered around the piano to sing. We soon ran out of liquor and the club refused to furnish any more, saying it was all locked up and no one present had the key. Russ Jepson, Smith, and Peggy went for another bottle of scotch. We continued to sing and when the music was danceable, Check would dance with Peggy and Doris, and Mrs. Fonseca and I would join them. About four a.m. the liquor ran out and the three pianists became tired so we called it a night. We took Peggy back to the

Galle Face where Check escorted her to her room. He was back shortly and the Jepsons took us to the jetty. No launches were available, but a rowboat was waiting. After saying many farewells to the Jepsons we took the rowboat back to the ship. All the ships riding at anchor were well lit, but even so the water looked dark and it would have been possible for motor launches to run down our small craft. Our boatmen made it to the Jefferson and we were aboard just before five a.m. Check and I made it to our hospital beds and had no trouble sleeping.

Traveling by ship is always fun. One has time to rest, read and think. On this trip to Bombay, Check and I wrote up most of this diary. The officers of the ship were a great group. They answered all of our foolish questions and asked us to join them for a drink every night before dinner.

At night on board one can watch the stars better than most any other place in the world. Last night the Southern Cross stood out like a diamond necklace in the southern sky. I think the Southern Cross is the most interesting constellation in the sky. Of course the Big Dipper is the most famous and somehow always reminds me of home. When I am away from the U.S. I can always look at the Dipper and know that it is above the states. The Cross, on the other hand, is not visible in the States. It is a symbol of travel, adventure and romance. It is more delicate and dainty than most constellations. It is the jewel of the southern sky.

Officers on the *President Jefferson:*

Captain Jack M. Windus
1st officer P.N. Bergerson
2nd Richard Harter
3rd Marion Haynes
Jr. Kenneth Johnson

Passengers:

Jeff and Margaret Boling
Mrs. Ruby Ridgeway
Mrs. L. Kapelman
Dr. and Mrs. Boyd
Mr. and Mrs. Milbauer

17

KLM PLANE CRASH

◆

(July 1949)

After returning from Colombo on the *President Jefferson,* I quickly caught up with a few things at the office and resumed my (by then) usual social life. There were eight other Americans on the *Jefferson* and so we took the men passengers and the ship's officers who were not on watch with us to an American Association meeting. I gave Joan Burns, Harry's sister, my car so she could take the ladies from the ship on a tour of the city. Afterward we all had dinner at Harry Spielman's and later we took everyone back on board about midnight and stayed a while drinking coffee. On board a freighter, the coffeepot is always on and there is sandwich meat in the icebox and plenty of bread, butter, and jam.

After the *Jefferson* left the next day, Harry Spielman, Dick Brecker, and I began working on our diary of the trip. I recorded that although we had some rain, the monsoons still seemed to be light.

Then it was time for the Fourth of July party, which had been postponed to July 5th because the 4th fell on a Monday, which in Bombay was a dry day. There was a Navy ship in port and we had a baseball game with some of the chiefs and younger officers. The party was at the home of one of the Consular officers, and I noted that it was a good party since I got home about 3 a.m.

The next day we had another game with the crew and after the game we invited everyone to my flat for a party. We had a bathtub full of iced beer (courtesy of the Navy). Harry invited all of the Anglo-Indian girls from the consulate. Only three of the eleven Navy men at the party passed out, and no one was rowdy. I carried one aboard the ship at one o'clock and then had to take four of the girls to Bandra (a suburb of Bombay) where they lived.

The next week the monsoon really broke, and it rained every day. I was in the office one afternoon when I got the first message that a KLM plane carrying

American reporters had crashed. I filed two quick messages and then put George Rice on the telephone, grabbed my camera and made my way to the wreck. It took a long time to find the plane and it was raining hard the whole time. It was a mess. Although the scene of the crash was only three miles from the Bombay municipal area, access was difficult. The region was a quagmire from the lashing rains. I slogged through the rain with the workers as they uncovered parts of bodies scattered about the hillside. Pieces of typewriters, cans of food, packs of cigarettes, and splintered suitcases were everywhere. The fuselage was about 100 yards from the point of impact. I got back to the Santa Cruz airfield to call the office with my story. I then came back into town and filed more stories and took my film to the *Times of India* to develop and print my pictures. Fortunately they were good.

The next day, I went to the airfield to meet the American Ambassador, Loy Henderson, and his party from New Delhi. I then went to the tower to get the story from the tower operator. Then I went to the morgue where the first bodies were being brought in. I managed to get a lunch and then worked all night. I brought Bob Trumbull of the *New York Times,* Bob Lubar of *Time* magazine and my old pal, Max Desfor of the AP, back to my office to file their stories. That done, we all went to the home of "Tim" Timberlake, the Consul General, for a drink. Then the correspondents and I went to dinner at Gordon's Restaurant, where we had a fine steak. The next day was more of the same. I got to the office early, then I went to the morgue, attended a funeral, and filed more stories. There was a memorial meeting at the Town Hall and I had to worry about pictures. This time I arranged for some Indian photographers to take the pictures. I found myself working long hours at the office because we were short two editors.

I have another note in my letters written the first week of August. Max Desfor, the AP photographer, had come to Bombay en route to his new post in Rome. He was supposed to get there in a hurry but he had to remain in Bombay until he could take the one TWA flight that flew over Iraq. Max, who is Jewish, could not get a visa for that country. He had to wait six days for his flight, so we had several lunches and dinners at the Taj Mahal Hotel where he was staying.

18

COLOMBO CONFERENCE

◆

(January 1950)

In the middle of January, I traveled to Colombo, Ceylon, to cover the British Commonwealth Foreign Ministers conference.

For my Indian newspaper clients, this was an important meeting because Prime Minister Nehru would be attending and India was, at the time, one of Britain's free commonwealth countries, along with Pakistan, Ceylon, and Burma.

It was at this conference that views concerning the recognition of the Chinese Communist Regime were discussed. However, since Britain, India, Pakistan, and Ceylon had already recognized the Peking regime, the only divergent views came from Malaysia, which at the time included the city of Singapore.

At the conference, Malcolm MacDonald, the British commissioner for Southeast Asia, warned the foreign ministers that they must expect an attempted Communist infiltration, which, if not checked in Indo-China, would seep into India and Pakistan. MacDonald told the conference that the communists were anxious to gain control of the Rice Bowl because the country that controls it controls Asia.

MacDonald told the foreign ministers that a government such as that of Emperor Bao Dai in Vietnam was absolutely necessary to prevent communist influence spreading to the region.

At the conference, Nehru called on the United States to withdraw its occupation troops from Japan. He warned that prolonged occupation might drive the Japanese toward communism. Nehru had made similar statements in the Indian parliament and was quoted as saying, "You cannot keep 80 million people under military occupation forever."

At the conference I had the help of our Colombo stringer correspondent as well as the reporters from the Lake House Newspapers. Lake House Newspapers was a client of United Press as a result of my trip to Ceylon the year before.

On January 2nd, a holiday in Bombay, I boarded the P & O Coastal Ship *Carthage* late in the evening for a two-day cruise down the coast of India to Colombo to report on the Commonwealth Conference being hosted by the Ceylonese Government.

Also aboard the Carthage was Don Thomas, a reporter for the *Times of India* and a good friend of mine. We had no trouble going through Customs, Immigration, and Health. I wrote that all I was carrying was one suitcase, a typewriter, and most important, my golf clubs. I wrote that I expected it to be a "swell" conference.

I wrote my next letter home on January 25, 1950, aboard the P & O *Stratheden* during my return trip to Bombay after the Commonwealth Conference:

> I had a pleasant trip down on the Carthage but didn't meet many people. I was the only American male on the ship and British are just naturally hard to get acquainted with in a hurry. On arrival in Colombo on Thursday morning, January 5th, Don Thomas (Times of India) and I went through all the formalities of police and health with ease: all we had to do was mention that we were coming to the island of Ceylon to cover the conference and all the usual red tape was waived. So we walked off the jetty, customs didn't open anything, and across the street to the Grand Oriental Hotel, referred to in Colombo as the G.O.H. Of course, we had no reservations, but Hlavacek's Lucky Star was still working. We asked for a double room, were told to wait about 15 minutes, and then were given a double room with bath—but on condition that we would only occupy it for one night. Don and I had lunch at the hotel and in the afternoon I went about the city trying to find out what happened to all my applications to the Ceylon Government about a news service. I finally tracked down the papers and I spent a couple of days before the conference began and a whole week afterward trying to get something moving. People out here don't like moving fast, especially governments. That night Don and I went to see a movie—a film about the time of the French revolution.
>
> Friday, January 6th—More of the same except that we had to move from our room in the morning, bring all our bags to the lobby and wait to see if we could get another room. The desk clerk—a lady—was very good about all this. After all, we didn't have reservations and there were a lot of people com-

ing to Colombo for the conference. But she gave us another room, this time with only a wash basin—no bath, but we were satisfied.

That afternoon I called Russ Jepson, the Firestone manager, and we arranged to play golf that afternoon. (I had met Russ on my previous trip to Colombo). After the golf game we stopped to meet and have one drink with the Vlacos', Ray and Kay, who are with Caltex Oil Company. It was funny. We drove up to the house in complete darkness. Someone had blown a fuse or the electric company had turned out the lights. So we had a drink by candlelight. Then Hlavacek decided to see if he couldn't fix the lights. And, by luck, by taking out all the fuses and putting them back in different places, all the lights came back on. I'm sure the Vlacos think I'm quite an electrician. Well, after that we naturally had to have more drinks—and we finished up by having a snack dinner at a quarter to twelve. Lots of fun.

On Saturday the 7th, it being a half-day of work nothing much could be done. We were moved out of our room again in the morning but the nice lady clerk gave us another one, this time with only a wash stand. But still it was a room and in the GOH which was necessary once the conference started. Of course, during these early days delegates to the conference were arriving and we were filing some stories but nothing much of real importance. In the afternoon I played golf with Russ Jepson again and in the evening I dressed and joined him for a round of the pubs of Colombo. First to the Galle Face Hotel bar to see if we would meet anyone we knew—we didn't. Then to the GOH club, a good dinner dance club where we had dinner. We were joined by the Vlacos and another couple named Nichols. We danced, ate and drank. The Vlacos and the Nichols went home but Russ and I decided to have a look at the Silver Faun, Colombo's nightclub. This was at 2 a.m. and we left about four.

Sunday the 8th, I was up early, had some breakfast and then Russ picked me up and we out to play golf again. After golf we came back to Russ' flat and had waffles and bacon for breakfast. Then we relaxed until lunchtime, when we went to the Vlacos' for drinks and a curry lunch. That night I had dinner with Russ at his flat. Russ' wife, Doris, was up at the hill station of Newara Eliya the whole time I was in Colombo, so we went about together quite a bit. It made it very comfortable for me because I had the use of his car.

Monday, the 9th of January, the conference began. We were still in the room. I don't know how much you read about the conference, probably not much, but in brief here is the way it worked. On Monday morning, all the delegates met in the garden opposite the Senate House for pictures and to meet the press. Afterward they retired to their meetings, the details of which were supposed to be kept secret. However, the Canadian delegate was staying at the GOH and we had met him the day before. Therefore, whenever a meeting was over, we would find our Canadian friend and find out what went on and file our story. The "we" in this case refers to Steve David of the Associated Press and me. Usually, we never work together, but in this case the Canadians said they would only talk to the wire service men representing news services which served Canadian papers. So we had to work together and it made for a pleasant conference. Also, we had the news before anyone else and we were always first with the news. I understand that the U.S. newspapers were not interested in the conference much but people out this way were. And I got good play with my stories in the Indian press and also got a message from Tokyo that my stories were being used there so it worked out fine.

Press conference in Colombo (I am the balding man near the center of the crowd facing the camera, wearing a bow tie).

From Monday to Friday we worked hard. There were two meetings a day and after each one we had to find out what happened to file our stories. Also we had to find out news from other delegations and this was mostly at night after the meetings were over.

On Tuesday we again had to move but late that evening the hotel gave us another room, this time with bath, and we kept this one for the rest of our stay at the hotel. It was room 444, and we called it press headquarters because in addition to Don Thomas and myself, we had reporters coming in at odd hours to use typewriters and file stories: Bob Trumbull of the *New York Times*, Bob Lubar of *Time* magazine, Allington Kennard of the *Straits Times* of Singapore, and others.

Don Thomas came in handy because I was covering the conference by myself and he covered Nehru and the Indian delegation for me. I, in turn, gave him all the news we got from the Canadians so he had a good story each day for his paper, which is a United Press client. Actually on stories there were only two sessions, out of ten, that we didn't know immediately what went on at the meetings. One of those two we tracked down, but it took a couple of hours. Usually we were well ahead of everyone else.

Most of the correspondents couldn't understand me. I played golf every morning of the conference except the first day. Austin de Silva, our United Press string correspondent, offered me the use of his car, which I took. That gave me a way to go golfing every day. I would always get back in time to meet the delegates as they left the meetings for a word or two. And my lucky star was with me because I happened to get in on a lot of meetings just by accident and happened to have good stories. Everyone else was worried and busily hopping around and I, thanks to the Canadians, didn't have to worry.

During the week, too, I managed to get out a couple of times with Russ Jepson though I had to pass up several luncheon dates and couldn't make any dates for dinner. Toward the end of the week though it was a little easier and we got to attend a few receptions for the delegates and saw our fill of Kandyian dancing.

Also, at these receptions we met the delegates and other people connected with the conference. I went only to the Governor General's cocktail party. The others I had to pass because they came at times that wire service reporters have to be working.

I must say that the Ceylonese treated everyone fine. They were very anxious to make a good impression and everything possible was laid on.

We all hoped that the conference would end on Friday, me especially, because Russ was going up country and I had planned to go with him. But there was an open meeting on Saturday, the 14th, and I had to stay in town. So that night I went out with Joe Norwood and some of his friends.

Of course, I played golf every day that week. On Tuesday I played with a caddy but toward the end of the round met another golfer, introduced myself and found out that he, too, was from Bombay and in Colombo on holiday. He played every morning too so we arranged to play together. He was an elderly Indian, a Mr. R. D. Morarji, who owns a chemical factory and textile mills. He must be at least 60 but he plays a much better game of golf than I do. He gives me five strokes and we came out about even after playing together for two weeks. He is on the ship now going back to Bombay so we plan to have more games in Bombay.

Once the conference was over, I spent practically all of Sunday sleeping. I was reading too but would fall asleep over the book. It was a pleasant way to spend Sunday.

On Monday I moved over to my friends the Schoellkopfs. Horton and Eleanor had asked me to stay with them when I first arrived in Colombo but during the conference I had to stay in the hotel for contact reasons. With the conference over, I only had to follow up on the business side of United Press, and could stay with them. (I had met the Schoellkopfs when I made the trip to Ceylon with Harry Spielman and Dick Brecker.) They have a lovely home and a spare room. It's a house the American Embassy bought with the frozen funds the U.S. had in Ceylon. The Schoellkopfs had two cars, so what with Austin de Silva's car, one at the Schoellkopfs and then Russ's when he was in town, I was pretty well supplied. (I'm not kidding about that lucky star.)

Nothing much unusual happened that last week. I had dinner at the American Ambassador's residence on Sunday, January 15th.

Don Thomas left on Wednesday by air. He works for the *Times of India* and felt he had to get back.

Monday there was another reception at night and then I had dinner with Horton and Eleanor. Tuesday night I had accepted two dinner invitations so stopped briefly at each for a little while, thus pleasing both of my hosts.

On Wednesday we played bridge. Horton and Eleanor like to play and they invited one of the American girls from the Embassy for a fourth. A very nice girl named Sarah Broadbent, but she announced her engagement to an Englishman a couple of days later.

Russ Jepson came home from the hills Wednesday and on Thursday we played golf in the afternoon (twice that day for me) and I had dinner with him that night. Had a good steak at a place called the Hotel Metropole. It's a dive but has the best steaks in town.

Friday evening we played bridge again, this time with one of the Embassy couples coming in.

Saturday I played golf in the morning and again in the afternoon. Russ wanted me to join him that evening, but I called it a day because I was playing golf again in the morning with Mr. Morarji.

Sunday noon I was at the Vlacos' again for drinks and lunch. At five o' clock, Russ and I tore ourselves away and went to the Colombo Zoo for the elephant show. It was just like a circus. Two large elephants and three small ones, dancing to music, playing harmonicas, standing on wooden tubs. Then thrills with the trainer putting his head in the elephant's mouth. But the best part was later when elephants were fed. I was fascinated to see the elephants rip off leaves from the different kinds of grasses fed to them. Also to see them break logs of coconut trees, split them open with their big feet, and then break them into small pieces to eat. Also the zoo had a baby elephant, a tiny morsel, with fuzz all over just like a baby chick. After the show we went back to the house for tea.

Horton and Eleanor had the Italian consul and a couple of Italian tennis players for dinner.

Monday, I played my usual round of golf, had lunch downtown, and in the evening went to drink mint juleps with Lynn and Nita Porter. He works for the Morrison Knudson engineering firm that is building a big dam in Ceylon. We were able to talk about my trip to Afghanistan and my experiences with the company in that country. Also at the Porters were Mr. and Mrs. Olson. He is the project engineer for the dam and in Colombo for a few days. The next time I am in Ceylon I will try to visit the dam. By this time it was raining hard so after a couple of mint juleps (that's enough) we, Russ and I, went back to the house and had dinner with Horton and Eleanor.

Tuesday was a busy day. Customary to my habits, I left most things to the last and was busy seeing newspapers, saying goodbye and shopping all day long. I had lunch with Austin de Silva and then got home to pack. Had dinner with Russ before going aboard the *Stratheden*. Horton and Eleanor didn't feel up to coming on the ship. I got aboard about 8:30 and the ship sailed a little after ten. Russ came on the ship and had a couple of farewell drinks with me.

I became a temporary member of the Colombo Golf Club so that my golfing cost me almost next to nothing. I figured about $40 for almost three weeks, and that included buying two dozen golf balls. (Nice work if you can get it.)

And my golf improved. On the ship, I'm in a double berth cabin with an Englishman who is going on to England. Passage is cheap. I paid only 175 rupees (about forty dollars) for two and a half days with food. Air passage is more than that for the trip between Bombay and Colombo.

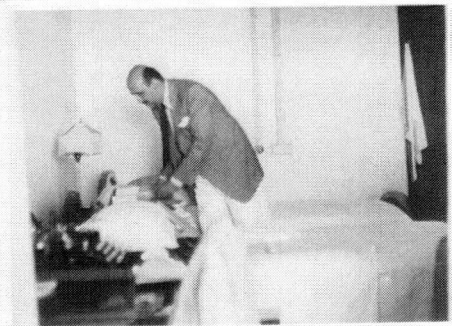

Clockwise from upper left: View from our hotel room; Don Thomas of the Times of India in our hotel room at the G.O.H.; the lady at the left is Indira Gandhi, Nehru's daughter; the foreign ministers at Colombo.

Nations in Commonwealth Split over Red China Nod

By JOHN HLAVACEK

COLOMBO, Ceylon, Jan. 10 — (UP) — Different views on the recognition of Communist China reportedly developed today when the Commonwealth foreign ministers met for the third plenary session of their conference here.

Warning Against Red Inroads Served At Ceylon Conference

By JOHN HLAVACEK

COLOMBO, Ceylon, Jan. 12— (UP)—A top British official in Southeast Asia warned the Commonwealth foreign ministers that they must expect an attempt- Bao Dai in Viet Nam was absolutely necessary to prevent communist influence spreading to (Continued on page 10, Col. 5)

Nehru Calls On US To Withdraw Troops From Japan

By JOHN HLAVACEK
United Press Staff Correspondent
COLOMBO, Ceylon, Jan. 11

Informed sources said Nehru, in the third day of the Commonwealth foreign ministers here, warned that prolonged occupation might drive the Japanese toward communism.

Headlines from articles I wrote about the Conference.

Mao Confuses British Confab

By JOHN HLAVACEK
United Press Staff Correspondent

COLOMBO, Ceylon, Jan. 7 (UP)—Representatives of more than a quarter of the world's peoples meet here Monday to chart the course of the British commonwealth of nations, four members of which, including Britain, have accorded full recognition to communist China.

This recognition of Red China will complicate the discussions of the Japanese peace treaty which tops the agenda of the conference to be attended by the foreign ministers of Britain, Australia, Canada, New Zealand, South Africa, India, Pakistan and Ceylon.

Presided over by Ceylon's prime minister, Don R. Senanayake, the conference will meet in the white, sunlit halls of the government buildings *(Continued on page 16, col. 7)*

India Head Urges Army Withdrawal

Says Occupation Will Force Japs To Become Reds

By JOHN HLAVACEK
COLOMBO, CEYLON, Jan. 11 — (UP) — Indian Premier Jawaharlal Nehru reportedly called today for the United States to withdraw its occupation troops from Japan.

Informed sources said Nehru, in the third day of the Commonwealth foreign ministers here, warned that prolonged occupation might drive the Japanese toward communism.

Nehru, who made similar statements to the Indian parliament and at press conferences, was quoted as saying, "You cannot keep 80,000,000 people under military occupation forever. If the Western powers are worried about communism in East Asia, the sensible thing to do would be not to drive the Japanese to communism by long occupation."

Clippings from articles published in Filipino papers.

19

A SPRING AND SUMMER OF TRAVELS

✦

(1950)

I returned from Ceylon on Friday morning, January 26th, the day that India declared itself a sovereign independent republic. Throughout the city there were celebrations touched off in the evening with brilliant illuminations. I came back to Bombay to our newly acquired flat which, I wrote, "is wonderful, and its swimming pool is out of this world." That night I had dinner with the American vice-consul I was dating, Corey Sanderson, and we had difficulty driving to the Nanking Chinese restaurant as the police were routing traffic in a roundabout pattern because all Bombay was out to see the illuminations.

I had been home only one day when our American Association had a basketball game against an Indian team at the suburb of Matunga. The Indian team beat us 48 to 19 because there were only seven of us and we were in terrible condition. I hadn't played a game since 1943 (seven years earlier) and I was in no shape to run. None of us was. "Soup" Cable (from Firestone), our tallest player at 6'3", had once played semi-professional basketball with the Phillips 66 Team. A big crowd came out to watch the game because the Indians loved to see the Americans get beat. Actually, the sports club at Matunga was very friendly and I was asked several times to award trophies at their sports meetings.

I also wrote that "our flat is now like Grand Central Station on the weekends. One weekend we had 24 golfers in for beer in the morning and then a succession of people all day. Of course with five of us living there, it makes for a lot of guests. The swimming pool at our flat is wonderful and I've been swimming every day. It's pretty cold in the mornings."

My letters home at this time described a mixture of work and play. One weekend, Pat Todd and Gussy Moran came to Bombay for a tennis exhibition. Most people now won't remember Gussy unless they are tennis enthusiasts. Pat and Gussy were in town for two days and one of our American club members had a cocktail party for them. The next day I went to see another Yogi disinterred after spending three and a half days in a cement crypt. It was another good story. Stories of yogis, snake charmers, and Indian holy men always made good copy for European and American newspapers. Usually they got more space than political tomes.

The stories I wrote at the time were varied. The Argentine Polo Team came for a series of games. Later in the week, Col. McCormick, the publisher of the *Chicago Tribune,* came to India with his wife on a sightseeing tour. Because the *Tribune* was a good client of United Press, I had orders to meet him and be available should he want something. I went to the airfield in Bombay when he arrived on his own plane. Actually, Percy Wood, the *Tribune*'s correspondent in India, was on the plane as well, escorting the party throughout India. I delivered some news bulletins to the Colonel so he could see that United Press was on the job.

Of course there was always time for extracurricular activities. Each year the American Women's Club of Bombay put on a dance, and each year one of the acts was billed as a comedy turn. I was usually co-opted and I wrote home telling the folks about my role. "Our act—Rubino, Tucker and myself—is supposed to be the funniest ever. All of us are dressed in long skirts, brassiere and a burqa. (A burqa is a hood worn by Muslim women.) We're billed as the three dancing girls. Over the costume we have saris wound around us, and during the course of the dance we unwind them so it's a version of the Dance of the Seven Veils—only we have four saris apiece. Rubino is about five nine and weighs over 200 with a terrific bay window which, when he gets it in motion, brings down the house. Tucker and I, of course, are not little fellows. We'll see how it goes tomorrow night."

"Dance of the Seven Veils" at the American Women's Club, March 28, 1950. From left: Hlavacek, Rubino, and Tucker.

In one of my letters at this time, I wrote that I went out to the airfield to meet Bob Miller, a United Press roving correspondent who had flown in from Calcutta. We spent the night reminiscing and listening to where he had been and whom he had seen. His last assignment before coming to India was French Indo-China where there is quite a war going on (between the French and the Viet Cong). We talked quite late, mostly about the United Press and its personnel. I had not seen Bob since he had covered the aftermath of the assassination of Mahatma Gandhi.

During the month of April I found myself in Karachi, Pakistan, working a deal to have Radio Pakistan and the newspapers of Karachi take United Press service. Jim Berry and I called on government offices because we wanted to be in operation by May 1st, when the Pakistan Prime Minister, Liaquat Ali Khan, was scheduled to visit the United States. We spent many an hour in conference with government officials.

About this time I told my family that I had no hope of getting home for at least six months. The main reason was that we were negotiating a three-year contract with the radio station in Pakistan. I was almost sure of getting a preliminary four-month contract while details on the three-year contract were worked out. Most of my time was spent visiting newspaper offices, but I noted that I had a couple of "good talks" with the American Ambassador, Avra Warren.

I began my Karachi sojourn by flying up from Bombay on a Tuesday morning. I had lunch with Jim Berry, the Karachi UP correspondent, and then we went to the first of many conferences with Radio Pakistan about the terms of the contract. It wasn't all we wanted, but I advised New York to take it. Of course that was done by cable, and we had to wait another 24 hours before the answer came.

On Wednesday, we did more work on the radio contract and in between times, Jim Berry and I visited all the newspapers advising them that we would have a good service coming into Karachi on May 1st. Most of them were interested, since the Prime Minister was going on tour in May and they wanted good coverage of his visit.

Two days later, on Thursday, we had a setback because New York insisted on a certain wording which the radio people turned down. For a while I thought the whole deal might fall through. So it meant more cables.

On Friday New York still was bucking on a minor technicality and I finally sent a "now or never" cable and then had lunch and went to play golf. I was on the ninth green when the boy from the clubhouse rode up with a message that Stew Hensley wanted me on the telephone from Washington. Luck was with me, since John Hardy of Firestone was just coming to the club and he let me have his car to rush back to the office. We had waited for an hour and a half when Stew's call came through. I told him what he should tell New York, and he promised to get them to agree to my wording and send a cable to that effect. When the call was over, I took Hardy's car back to the golf course and stayed for a beer. Then I had to get back to the office to meet Desmond Sheen, so Hardy gave me the car since he said he could get a ride back with someone else. Desmond and I had lunch at a restaurant called the Shezan: delicious fried shrimps with tartar sauce followed by an ice cream sundae. Then we took Hardy's car back to his hotel and got Desmond's car and went to the Boat Club for a couple of drinks. It being a Friday night (Friday is the Muslim holiday), the bars closed early.

On Saturday we got approval from New York, so we wrote the letters that would be exchanged the following week making it official.

When we got the O.K. cable, I rushed to get a train reservation on the night train for Lahore. I finally got a berth in the afternoon when a cancellation occurred. I was not able to get an air-conditioned first-class coach, so I had to ride ordinary first-class, which got pretty dusty. It was a long ride from Karachi, and the first half was mostly through desert. I slept through most of that and on the last half through the Punjab we passed irrigated fields, although it was the time of year when they were harvesting, so it was dry and dusty.

When we reached the railway station in Lahore, I remembered that the last time I had been in the railway station was in 1940, ten years earlier. I had been in Lahore many times since but never in the railway station.

In Lahore, I met Charley Booth, a vice-consul, whom I had known in Chungking during the war. He was staying at the hotel (Faletti's) while working at the consulate. We had dinner together and then went to a movie, "House of Strangers," the first movie I had seen in quite a few days.

I spent the next two days visiting all the newspapers in Lahore trying to decide whether it would be feasible to send a service. I wrote that I thought we would probably open an office. If we did, it would make the fifth office under my jurisdiction and if we could keep it open permanently we would be in a good position for a couple of years.

I flew back to Karachi on Tuesday, arriving at 9:30 on a DC-4 on Orient Airways. I got back to the office at 10:30 to find a message awaiting me from Barry and Anne Eldridge of Pan American asking me to join them at the Hotel Metropole. I joined them about 11 and stayed at the party until 4 a.m. By that time Barry was too tired to drive me home, so he let me take Annie's MG which I enjoyed driving. (Anne and Barry's earlier Pan American tour had been in Brazil, and Anne had taught me to do the samba.)

The next day, Indian Prime Minister Nehru was scheduled to arrive in Karachi. I went to get the necessary passes because the Pakistan government was insisting on strict security. Then I picked up Annie and took her along to the airport. I was able to get her past the strong police pickets at the gates and she was able to photograph Nehru with her movie camera. I, of course, was able to get up close and take a few pictures. I also spoke with Nehru, but he wouldn't say much to the press. Then back into town for lunch, and Annie let me keep the car. That afternoon, Jim Berry and I worked on the UP file. The MG had a flat and I wasted an hour getting it fixed. Then it was time to watch Nehru place a wreath on the grave of Pakistan's first president, Mohammed Ali Jinnah. I again picked up Annie so she could see the ceremony. After the ceremony we met Barry at the Boat Club and then Annie gave me the MG to take to my office.

Thursday I worked in the morning with Jim and in the afternoon took the MG back to Annie. Then Jim and Gladys and I went to a reception for Nehru at the Pakistan foreign office. On that day, too, I had lunch with the ADC (Aide de Camp) who is going to the U.S. with Liaquat Ali Khan, the Pakistan Prime Minister. Thursday evening I was with the Eldridges again at the Metropole Hotel. Barry had a passenger to entertain, a Miss Gladys Height of the Chicago Dancing School. She was quite a girl: about 60, weighed close to 200 pounds, and talked a mile a minute. All she did, I gathered, was travel, mostly by Pan American.

Then it was back to Bombay the next day and back to my routine of golf and swimming.

In May I wrote to my family in Chicago that the Pakistan Prime Minister and his wife had left London for their tour of the United States. As he did when Nehru took his U.S. tour, Stew Hensley planned to accompany the Prime Minister wherever he went, and he was scheduled to be in Chicago on May 11th. I asked my family to do whatever they could to help Stew.

I added that there were two members of Liaquat's entourage who were friends of mine. One was Colonel Majic Malik, who would be Liaquat's press officer. I said that he had been a good friend of United Press in Karachi. The second person was Captain B. Babar, the Prime Minister's Aide de Camp. I said that I had lunch with him a couple of days before he left and I had given him my family's telephone number in case he had any time away from the tour.

My next letter, dated May 15th, said:

> Now for the week, which has been busy since I've gone almost 2500 miles by plane with a trip to Calcutta and Dacca.
>
> I flew over on the night mail plane. I stayed home until 10:30 when the airline crew picked me up and I rode with the crew to the airport. My Polish pilot friends fly for the airline so when I am to fly they tip off the crew to take care of me. The night mail, so you understand it better, takes off each evening from four cities—Bombay, Delhi, Calcutta and Madras. The planes meet in Nagpur (in the center of the country) where the mail and passengers is exchanged and the planes return to their base. On this flight I saw Stefan Zygnarski (one of the Polish pilots), who was flying the Madras plane, in Nagpur, and we had an enjoyable snack together.
>
> The plane arrived in Calcutta at 7:30 in the morning and it was 8:30 before I reached the Great Eastern Hotel. After a bath and breakfast, I got to the office at ten. My Calcutta bureau manager, Ronnie Rolfe, was in the hospital and he had a friend, Jim Shepherd, filling in. We went to the hospital to make sure he was being taken care of and then Jim and I went on a round of meetings with our newspaper clients. We had to make a new deal with one of our important clients and luckily the newspaper's economy is sound so

there wasn't much trouble. In the afternoon we made reservations for me to fly to Dacca the next day.

I was up at six, the plane took off at eight, and I was in Dacca at nine. I first went to the American Consulate to see Dudley Withers, the Consul, who had been in Bombay. Afterward I saw a prospective client later that morning and I think I sold him. Then I had lunch with Jane and Dudley at the Dacca Club. In the afternoon, I saw another newspaper prospect and then caught the afternoon plane back to Calcutta.

Dacca is a small town, overcrowded as most towns are out here and even more so now because of the trouble between the two countries on the Muslim-Hindu question. There was trouble in East Pakistan in February, but since March, everything has been quiet. But there was a lot of trouble in Calcutta in March and April with the result that there has been a mass migration of Hindus from East Pakistan to India and an equally large migration of Muslims from India to East Pakistan. Calcutta is still restless and there may be more trouble but everyone is hoping for the best. I shall have to go back to Dacca again in a couple of months and stay a bit longer than I did this time.

When I got back to Calcutta, my friends, Charley and Lois MacArthur picked me up for dinner again. Before dinner, I went to see Eddie and Betsy Quin, who live near the MacArthurs.

Friday was another busy day. I concluded my deal with our big client in the morning and then rested in the afternoon after a big lunch at Firpo's with Charley and Jim Shepherd, who is acting as my Calcutta bureau manager. I went back to the hotel to have a bath and cool off under a ceiling fan. At six I met with another round of publishers I had missed. We hired a taxi and dashed about town. Back at the hotel at eight, checked out and got to Eddie and Betsy Quins' for a Chinese dinner at nine. Had a wonderful Chinese meal with the Quins because they had a Chinese amah and of course I had to show off my Chinese. The Quins were nice people. They had Australian passports and Eddie was part Chinese and part Australian. He was a former CNAC (Chinese National Airline Company) pilot who flew the "Hump."

I slept from Calcutta to Nagpur, and Kazik Garstecki was there to meet me as I got off the plane. We had a snack at the airport and then flew on to Bombay. Kazik was flying as pilot in the left seat and Hlavacek was in the right seat as co-pilot, even on takeoff and landing. I had done it many times before, but I still got a kick out of being "up front" when the plane took off and landed. Kazik enjoyed it, too, because he has someone to talk to on the two-and-a-half-hour trip to Bombay. The co-pilot was right there in the jump seat for takeoff and landing, but the rest of the time he slept. I noted that he wasn't needed because the plane flew on auto pilot practically all the way.

I had no sooner got home than I had to plan another trip, this time to Karachi again, and then Lahore, New Delhi, and back to Bombay before the end of the month.

On a Monday morning I flew to Karachi and this time stayed at the Metropole Hotel, since our office had become rather crowded. I called Harry Spielman, my good friend from Bombay days, who was staying at the Sind Club. After seeing how the office was running (well) and checking on a few things, I met Harry later that afternoon and we had dinner at the hotel. Harry had been in Karachi for two weeks, after being transferred from the Consulate in Bombay to the Embassy in Karachi.

On Tuesday I put in a long day working and then later in the afternoon I went golfing with Harry. He had a new set of clubs and I borrowed a set. At the 19th hole we met a couple of my friends and they gave Harry an application blank and he filled it in and he was a member—and could sign for drinks. We stayed late drinking on Harry and then left for John Hardy's (a Firestone representative who had been with me in Afghanistan) room at the hotel. We then went to the Boat Club. It was dance night, and everyone was in dress clothes except us. We got a table next to the dance floor, ordered drinks and danced. Later, Hardy got a reprimand from the club for bringing guests to the club on dance night in golf togs.

After working all day Thursday, I was up at 3:45 on Friday and took the Orient Airways bus to the airfield. The plane took off at 6 and we arrived in Lahore at 10. The Bata Shoe man, a Mr. Dolesal, was on the plane. His wife and baby met him and gave me a ride into town. I stayed again at Faletti's. But in the afternoon I met Charley Booth and went swimming in the Consulate pool which had cool water—a treat because Lahore was like an oven. (At night I again dunked the sheets in the bathtub and slept under the fan. People warned me that I could get pneumonia or rheumatism from it but I did it whenever I was in hot spots like Lahore, and there had been no ill effects.

The next day I flew to New Delhi on Indian National Airways and met with Bob Branson, our New Delhi correspondent, at 2. We went first to the airline office to get a seat on the non-stop flight to Bombay that evening. That evening there was a party at the Afghan Embassy in celebration of Afghanistan Day. I met a number of persons I hadn't seen in a long time. Bob and I later went with Bob Trumbull (*New York Times*) and Kay Wood (wife of Percy Wood of the *Chicago Tribune*) to the Imperial Hotel grill and danced until 11:45 when I had to leave for the airfield.

I had packed in the afternoon and left my bags at the booking office, so I boarded the plane in dress clothes. P.D. Sharma, our New Delhi correspondent, came with me because he was boarding the new Indian cruiser, *The Delhi,* that evening to accompany Prime Minister Nehru on a cruise to Indonesia.

Back in Bombay I had a lot of correspondence from New York. I would be busy for the next couple of weeks because we had to make new plans for Pakistan. We would have to set up a separate corporate organization to do business in Karachi. Jim Berry would be the manager and would report to me.

In mid-June the rains came. The monsoon broke on a Saturday and it rained all weekend. I wrote, "It will be a little cooler, but I must admit I haven't suffered much this year."

I wrote that one night in June I went to the airport to meet Devadas Gandhi, the managing editor of the *Hindustan Times.* He was also the son of the Mahatma. He had been to South America for a UN Conference on the press and then stopped in New York and Washington. His paper was one of our oldest customers. I had a good interview with him at the airport, about the only place I could meet with him since he came in one afternoon and left the same night.

And a few days later I write that the big news was the declaration of war in Korea on June 25th. We put on extra shifts to keep our clients well supplied with the news. Usually on a Sunday we tried to keep to a minimum staff, but when something like a war happened we immediately called out the reserves. I had to put on a radio operator part-time the rest of the week to keep us right on top of the news. Our news from Korea had been excellent, and we had been getting good play in the Indian newspapers with our United Press bylines.

In July, Bob Branson, our correspondent in New Delhi, was ordered to Saigon and so the New Delhi spot was open for an enterprising correspondent.

I wrote to my folks: "No, I won't be home in 1950, but I expect to make it about March of 1951. I've already written suggesting that I be home in the spring when the United Pres has its annual meeting."

During the summer, our American Club's baseball team had a number of games with visiting teams from the Navy and the passenger ships that made stops in Bombay.

Later in the month of July I wrote:

> United Press business continues to be good. Of course, with the Korean War our report becomes more valuable. But I have a new contract with a chain of papers in Madras, Bombay and Delhi which is a good one. And one of the papers that had thought of canceling cancelled the cancellation. So, as far as the news agency is concerned, we're in better shape than at any time since I got the job almost two years ago. As my Calcutta correspondent said: "It's an ill wind that doesn't blow somebody some good. The more startling the news, the more business we get."

Also in July I had two minor car accidents. One evening on the way home from a dinner, I hit a woman who was crossing Marine Drive. She wasn't badly hurt, fortunately, but we struck her a glancing blow and she hit her head on the curb of the middle parkway. I picked her up—she was bleeding pretty badly—and took her to the hospital where the doctor bandaged the wound, then took her home after reporting the accident to the police.

Two days later I had another small brush with a Ford on the way to work. This time it was raining and the car in front of me, a Ford, was away on the left-hand side and decided, without signaling, to turn to the left. I was passing at the time and managed to swerve so that we only brushed but I was mad. That evening I was invited to a party at Bandra, a Bombay suburb. On the way I had a flat just before crossing the causeway that joins Bombay with Bandra. So I changed a tire and arrived at the party minus my shirt and a bit dirty. But we had a great dinner. My hosts, the Lewises of National Carbon, had a great place but it was 12 miles out.

Also that month, Corey Sanderson gave a dinner for Sir Benegal Rama Rau (Governor of the Reserve Bank of India) and Lady Rama Rau. Also at the dinner were the Danish Trade Commissioner and his wife as well as the deputy governor of the Reserve Bank. I had known Sir Benegal and Lady Rama Rau ever since I arrived in Bombay in February of 1945.

My letters are sprinkled with stories about my golf games. I wrote that one day I played with the Chief Justice of India, Sir Hiralal Kania. I wrote that I had heard his name but I hadn't met him. My comment: "a nice old guy".

Also, about this time, I got a summons to appear in court. This time on a charge of parking in a "no parking" area. I wondered how much it was going to cost me. When I got to court, I was fined 20 rupees (about $4 US).

In August the big news for Europeans was that the Bombay High Court upheld Bombay's prohibition law and also ruled that there could be no special cases. This means that all the foreigners permanently living in Bombay could no longer have permits. My comment: "It will probably do me good."

In September I wrote about a trip to Nasik, a city 114 miles north of Bombay. It was the site of an Indian National Congress meeting (similar to a Republican or Democratic convention in the United States). I went for only one day and I took Corey along. We had a good trip with no trouble. We brought a picnic lunch and stopped by the roadside. We arrived at the camp at about 1 p.m. and managed to get in without trouble with our passes even though the cars and people were all over the place. It was a dull session but I wanted to show my face to let the congressmen know that the UP was interested. There were 20,000 delegates inside the pandal (a temporary structure erected for the meeting) and about 500 news reporters. The new President of the Congress Party, Purhatom Das Tandon, made an inaugural speech that took all afternoon.

At these meetings it was always a struggle to keep the people who didn't have passes out of the enclosures, and this day was no exception. I happened to be out front when the Prime Minister (Nehru) came in. He rode in an Olds convertible, sitting up so that everyone could see him. As he came through the main gate, the crowd surged forward and almost crushed him. He got into a temper, and no wonder. He finally made his way to the pandal only to find his way blocked so he had to get back in his convertible. There he sat in the middle of the crowd, his car being the island in a sea of humanity.

We left the Congress camp at five and drove through Nasik city, getting home at about nine.

It wasn't all work. One Saturday I accompanied Corey to have dinner aboard a Panamanian ship that was in port. The Captain was Swedish, and we had all sorts of liquor and good food: smoked oysters from Japan, pickled herrings from Hong Kong, and cold sliced chicken and ham, all topped off with Pabst Blue Ribbon beer.

Another evening Corey invited Dr. Ambedkar, the Indian Law Minister, for dinner. Dr. Ambedkar was a well-known person. He was the leader of the so-called Backward Classes—the untouchables. He was one himself. He was educated in England and had risen to be an eminent lawyer. However, he was still an untouchable to most Indians, who were extremely caste conscious.

And a small paragraph in one of my letters:

> All the foreigners are feeling sorry for themselves because the Bombay government has made new rules on the liquor permits. Now in order to drink one must get a medical certificate and then the person gets only three bottles per month!

I wrote that it didn't concern me because my date was a vice-consul and had diplomatic privileges and could buy all the liquor she wanted because the local laws did not affect the Foreign Service.

In another letter dated October 9th, I noted that I met Senator and Mrs. Claude Pepper of Florida at tea at Corey's home. The Senator had expressed a desire to meet the American press corps of Bombay—me. The senator and his wife were very pleasant, and we talked for over an hour. I told him what I thought about American policy and what we could expect from India in the next few years. He seemed interested.

Later in the week, my housemate, Olaf Hauge, and I went to meet Marquis Childs, at the time a well-known Washington columnist. His column was handled by United Features, and we had been trying to sell it to Indian newspapers. Out to meet him also were Julie Timberlake, the wife of the Consul General, and Les and Eloise Squires of the consulate. When Childs arrived I asked him if he'd like a night's sleep. Both Doyle and Garstecki, my housemates, were out of town and we had empty beds. He was booked to go through on the night mail plane but we changed the reservations and he came home with Olaf and me. We had a good conversation but not for long because he needed sleep. We took him to the plane the next morning for New Delhi.

Interspersed with descriptions of my work for United Press, my letters included many references to baseball (softball) games and golf tournaments. (These activities are partially recorded in the chapters on golf and baseball.)

It was after a baseball game in Calcutta when I called the office to learn that New York and London were wondering why I was in Calcutta playing baseball when there was a revolution going on at the India-Nepal border. I rushed around and found the American Ambassador, Loy Henderson, who was in Calcutta for the American Club's weekend. He gave me a ride to New Delhi in his plane, and the rest, as they say, is history.

20

GOLF

When I arrived in Bombay that spring of 1945, there were few American civilians living in the city. The war in Europe was in its last stages as Allied armies advanced across France and into Germany. The war in the Pacific also looked encouraging, with American forces leapfrogging across the Pacific islands toward the Japanese homeland.

In Bombay, there was a small contingent of American transportation troops involved in moving American supplies from the port of Bombay to the China-Burma-India theatre. Many of these Americans were avid golfers. Thus, for relaxation and exercise, since I did not know cricket or football (soccer) which the Indians and the British played, I gravitated toward golf.

Until I got to India, I had never so much as touched a golf club. When I was growing up in the Midwest in the 1930s, golf was a rich man's sport. My family did not have the status nor the money to join the one private country club in our village. My first overseas assignment was as an English teacher in China and during the five years I spent in that country from 1939 to 1944, golf was literally unknown. The Japanese had occupied the coastal areas and the large cities on the mainland, and the only golf course in the area was in Hong Kong, which the Japanese conquered in 1941 soon after Pearl Harbor.

My first games of golf were with a few American Army troops who were stationed in Bombay to move war supplies from the port to the China-Burma-India theatre of war. At the time the Willingdon Sports Club offered American army officers honorary memberships to the club for the duration of the war. As I was still an accredited war correspondent with a simulated rank of an officer, I was also given an honorary membership so I could use the Club for swimming and golf. The Sports Club had a swimming pool, tennis courts, and an 18-hole, par 65 golf course. I had access to the Army Post Exchange and was thus able to buy golf balls, and my army buddies found me a set of golf clubs, which, in those days, had wooden shafts.

The Willingdon Sports Club was unique, since it was one of the few British/European Clubs in India that was open to Indians. Most of the other golf clubs in the large cities—Calcutta, Madras, and Delhi—had clubs that restricted membership to persons of European stock. The only Indians at most clubs were either caddies or servants in the clubhouse. But Lord Willingdon, a former Viceroy of India, and earlier the Governor of Bombay, was responsible for establishing the Club. He decreed that it would be open to all. Therefore, many of my golfing partners during the years I lived in Bombay were Indians. In 1945, the Club had a long waiting list because there was a maximum number for membership. The entrance fee at the time was one thousand rupees (about 300 dollars) which also limited the number of persons who could join since it was at that time a princely sum.

As the months went by and peace came in the summer, I met two young Scotch bankers who had played golf from childhood. In Indiana it was said that babies were born with a basketball in their hands. In Scotland, the saying was that babies were born with a golf club in their hands. My friends, Bill Rae of the Chartered Bank and Bill Needham of Barclays Bank, were champion amateurs in their homeland. (Rae was a scratch golfer and Needham played to a two handicap.) These two Scotsmen took this American in tow and proceeded to teach him the ancient game of golf. They showed me how to grasp the club with an overlapping grip, and how to stand over the ball and keep my eyes on the ball. The two had their own car—a small MG—and they invited me along as they tooled out early in the morning to the Bombay Presidency Golf Club, at Chembur, fifteen miles north of the city. The course was established in 1827 (that's correct, not a misprint) and it had lush fairways and greens. Its par was 70 and although the fairways were narrow and long, it took a good golfer to make par. I still had my military privileges as a war correspondent—although there wasn't much war in Bombay—and I had access to the Army Post Exchange where I could buy golf balls. Also, the entrance fee for the Presidency Club was minimal and I could afford it even on my United Press salary. Thus, during those first few months I played regularly. And I was bitten by the golf bug. In my letters home at the time, there are many references to early morning tee times.

After peace was declared in Europe and later in the Pacific, American and British forces left India and my honorary membership in the Willingdon Club expired, which meant I could no longer play the Willingdon course. In 1945 the Club had a long waiting list and it was only in 1948 that I was able to join.

In early June of that year, I received a letter from the Willlingdon Club saying that my candidacy would come up during the first half of July. I wrote:

> This means that I can play golf or swim every morning (or evening) since the club is just around the corner from where I live. I've been trying to get into this club for some time but during the war it had a big waiting list. The club only opened the waiting list last October (my friend Velma Ham tipped me off about the change) when the club decided it would have to have some more members to help the exchequer—my belonging will put a hole in my exchequer.
>
> In the first week of July I met the members of the balloting committee. One has to meet the members. Before prohibition, one bought drinks for the members of the committee. Now, one only has to say 'hello.' I will go again next week because I met only half of the required number of members. However, I now have the privileges of the club.

Two weeks later I received my notice that I was elected a member of the club. They asked for an entrance fee of 1,000 rupees. "Rather high," I wrote, "but I expect to be around a while and the club is a lot of fun. At that, it's only about $300 U.S., and what country club can you join in the U.S. for that amount of money?"

The climate in most of the Indian subcontinent was excellent for the sport of golf. In Bombay on the Arabian Sea, golf was played year round. The Willingdon Sports Club, for instance, had beautiful manicured fairways and the greens were as smooth as billiard tables. There were no water holes but the course was liberally sprinkled with sand traps. The Bombay Presidency Club also had grassy fairways and manicured greens. A stream meandered through the course so there were water hazards where I lost many a golf ball.

During those first few years—the last year of the war and then the two years leading up to the partition of India into two countries, India and Pakistan—I continued golfing at the two Bombay courses. Although I was putting in many hours in the United Press office, it was still possible to play 14 holes of golf early in the morning before my shift began. And on those days when I finished my shift late in the afternoon, it was possible to play at least nine holes, and possibly 14, before darkness fell.

In addition to being tutored by my Scottish friends, I was able to take lessons from the Indian golf professional at the Willingdon Club. I found that his tutoring helped my game so that I felt good about hitting the ball. It took many months of practice to bring my handicap down from 20 to a respectable 12. I have a note in one of my letters that I broke 100 for the first time on May 1, 1945—a 97 for 18 holes.

During my first two years in Bombay, I did little travel because the major stories in Delhi and Calcutta were reported by Jim Michaels and P.D. Sharma and I was anchored to Bombay and Hyderabad. After my home leave in 1947, Gerry Rock left India and I was named manager for the area. Thereafter, whenever I traveled the territory in India, Pakistan, and Ceylon, I managed to find the time to play golf. Each of these countries, as a carryover from its days as a British colony, had golf courses.

Whenever I traveled in India, or Pakistan or Ceylon, I could always borrow or rent a set of clubs at the various courses. There were always clubs available, and sometimes there was not even a charge for their use. When traveling abroad, as I did on occasion, I would take my own clubs.

Bill Needham (right) taught me how to play golf.

21

BASEBALL

Baseball—America's game—was unknown in India. A few Indians may have watched American troops during World War II playing pickup games at their billets, but for the most part, it was a game that only a few Indians had ever seen. Indians, under British colonial rule for 150 years, had learned the English game of cricket. Indian international cricket teams hosted British and Australian cricket teams. And the Indians played football—a game we Americans call soccer. So it was a bit presumptuous that arriving Americans were anxious to show the Indians what they were missing.

At the end of World War II, in 1945, there was little time for sport as the political situation in India was fraught with communal struggles leading up to the partition of the country into the dominions of India and Pakistan in 1947. But by 1948, the political climate in the country had improved and American companies such as General Motors, Firestone, Caltex and Standard Vacuum, as well as other smaller companies, had established commercial businesses in the large cities of Bombay and Calcutta. Those two cities had had American Clubs for many years. The American Club of Calcutta was organized in 1942 as a charitable and sociable association. In 1943 an American volunteer fire department was organized and two fire engines were brought from the United States. After the war the engines were donated to the city of Calcutta. In 1948 there were approximately 140 members, of which 100 were active. The main activities were bi-monthly luncheons, golf tournaments, tennis, baseball, swimming, hunting, an annual 4th of July dinner dance, a county fair, and a Boxing Day party.

The American Association of Western India was formed at a General Meeting of American citizens held in Bombay on November 2, 1933. The purposes of the organization were (1) to foster the interest of the United States in India and to promote good feeling between Americans and persons of other nationalities resident in India; (2) to encourage a beneficial acquaintance and association of American residents in India, and (3) to assist worthy Americans in distress. From

56 members in the first enrollment, the Association had grown, in 1948, to more than 250 Americans. Activities included monthly meetings, sports competitions, and periodical social functions.

Thus, when the rains tapered off late in the summer of 1948, it was time for baseball. We began by playing pickup games with other members of the American community, which now numbered in the hundreds. We began a series of games with the married men playing the bachelors. Bombay had many open fields—called *maidans*—so there were many places to play. We received a challenge from the American Club of Calcutta to join them for a weekend of golf, tennis, and baseball to be played in November. To get ready for the trip, we began regular practice to organize a softball team.

I still have the instructions for that first weekend trip. We were all told to gather on Friday, November 12th at one of Bombay's parks at 6:45 a.m., where we would be transported to the airfield courtesy of Firestone vehicles. We were to board a charter for take-off at 8 a.m. with the plane stopping at Nagpur for refueling and scheduled for arrival in Calcutta at 2:30. We were limited to 25 pounds of baggage each, and the members who were to play in the golf matches were instructed to ship their clubs the day before. One paragraph read: "Liquor is not rationed in Calcutta; also it is cheaper there than in Bombay. Therefore it is not necessary to bring any with you."

The instructions also included the following details:

> We are having uniform shirts made with our logo—A.A.W.I.—with a number on the back. The uniforms won't be ready until Thursday so they will have to be distributed on the plane.

> On the trip we would like everyone to wear his uniform sweater, white shorts, and white socks. This will really impress the Calcutta group when they meet us at the airport.

> We are asking each member going on the trip to send a cheque for Rs. 100/ ($30) to A. E. Beaver Jr., Firestone. The maximum expenses per each member, including transportation, will not exceed this amount. In the event there is any surplus after all expenses have been paid, the same will be divided equally among all.

It was quite a weekend. Of course, we partied all the way across India and then, after being met and escorted to our various hosts' residences, there were cocktail parties and dinners on Friday night.

On Saturday morning Calcutta won the golf matches. On Saturday afternoon, we salvaged a little pride by winning the tennis match. But on Saturday evening, the Calcutta baseball players left the party early while their wives were ordered to keep the party going and to encourage the Bombay players to have another drink or two. It worked. The next morning our center fielder couldn't see the ball. And we lost the baseball game, but good. But we had a great time and we challenged the Calcutta club to a return weekend the next year.

In the spring of 1949 the American Association organized a baseball league. We formed three teams. The first team comprised members of Caltex and Standard Vacuum, and it was called the Oilers. The second included men from the American Consulate, Firestone, General Motors, and TWA, and it was called the Ciplomats. The third team included anyone from any other company and was known as the Independents (better known as Hlavacek's Hlollipops). We played every Tuesday and Friday evening and generally had a good time.

When November 1949 arrived, it was time to invite the Calcutta American Club for a return weekend to give Bombay a chance to even the score. During the year I had been elected the Sports Chairman for the Bombay American Association and also the captain of the baseball team. With the help of Bob Lubar, the Time/Life correspondent (later the editor of *Fortune* for many years), I suggested that we play the game as a charity benefit. Once my idea got started, it was widely accepted. The Association appointed Consul General Clare "Tim" Timberlake and me to get it going. "Tim" arranged for the Governor of Bombay, His Excellency Raja Maharaj Singh, to throw out the first ball. Tim's wife, Julie Timberlake, had her picture taken selling the Governor the first ticket for the game. I arranged to get the Cooperage—an outdoor stadium that was usually used for cricket. It had stands that could accommodate up to 5,000 spectators. Other members began arranging to sell hot dogs and hamburgers. One of our members succeeded in getting the Police Band to play between innings and the Royal Indian Navy band to meet the Calcutta team on arrival.

Because we had decided to promote the game as a charity affair for the United India Tuberculosis appeal, both the men's and women's clubs heartily joined in. Members began selling tickets at one rupee apiece (about 30 cents) because we wanted as many Indians as possible to come. We also printed programs that sold for four annas (about five cents). There were to be no reserved seats, except for the Governor and his wife, as it was to be first-come, first-served.

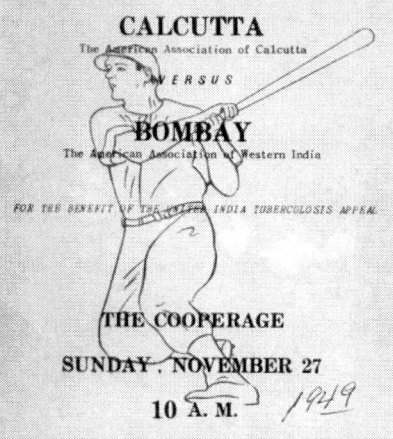

Program for the November 27, 1949 baseball game between the American Association of Calcutta and the American Association of Western India.

A number of American and Indian businesses agreed to become sponsors. Among the sponsors were The American Export Lines, The Bombay Police Force, Caltex (India) Ltd., Chicago Telephone and Radio Co., Firestone (India) Ltd., General Motors (India) Ltd., Mr. D. F. Karaka, The New Zealand Insurance Company, J.R. Lourdes Pereira, the Bombay Provincial Hockey Association, the Royal Indian Navy, and L.A. Stronach & Co.

Lee Kamern, the Metro Goldwyn Mayer film distributor, was our announcer. Lee, an experienced professional, entertained the crowd with his explanation of how the game is played and what was going on at any given moment.

Bob Lubar and I invited the sports reporters from the Bombay newspapers to a meeting to publicize the game. We detailed the plans for the weekend and answered all their questions.

The Calcutta Club, 21 strong, arrived on a Friday afternoon and we had the 40-piece Indian Navy Band to meet them. The Calcutta team, dressed in their red baseball caps and jerseys, looked impressive as they deplaned. They were also surprised at their welcome.

A Bombay weekly newsmagazine, Forum, featured the game on its cover and printed the following story (which, except for the first paragraph, I wrote):

> Bombay recalled before the thirties had arrived how British Test player Earle hit his century in Gilligan's Team touring India before a dazed crowd and how the next day the great C. K. Naidu outstripped the record by another century—almost 161 runs with about fifteen sixers or so. Naidu dazzled the crowd on the Old Cricket Grounds—the Bombay Gymkhana. Something like that happened or even more exciting than that when American Consul General Timberlake, a real all-rounder, hit a magnificent and unforgettable home run on behalf of the American Association of Western India against the Calcutta American Association. Mrs. Julie Timberlake rushed and kissed her lord, the hero of the afternoon. And no cameraman shot that unforgettable sight!
>
> Five thousand shouting American and Indian baseball fans lunged to their feet in the last half of the tenth inning to cheer American Consul General C. H. "Tim" Timberlake as he sped around the bases to score his game-winning home-run which enabled Bombay to beat Calcutta, 5 to 4, in the annual game between the two teams which represent the American Clubs of India's two largest cities.
>
> Timberlake's home run, a hit to right center field, was the climactic blow of a thrilling, drama-packed game which held the crowd on the edge of their

seats in Bombay's Cooperage which, according to the Americans present, looked like any baseball park in the United States on the day of a big game.

The baseball game was the feature attraction of a gala week-end as the American Association of Western India entertained a visiting group of golfers, tennis and baseball players representing the American Club of Calcutta.

The baseball game was to be just another completely American contest but the Bombay Club decided that Bombay citizens, if they wished, should have the chance of joining in the fun. It was therefore decided to charge a nominal admission of Rs. One [about thirty U.S. cents] so that everybody in Bombay who wanted to see the ball game could come. Since all the Calcutta team's expenses were paid by the Calcutta Club, the entire proceeds from the match were donated to the Indian Tuberculosis Appeal.

A feature of the game was that everyone—spectator, player, press reporter, umpire—had to buy his ticket. There were no reserved seats, except for the Governor who threw out the first ball, and all seats were on a first come, first serve basis.

Crowds began to filter into the Cooperage as early as 9 a.m. and by 10 o'clock both stands were complete filled. Shortly thereafter the pre-game ceremonies began.

From the west side of the field marched groups of teen-aged Indian boys carrying the Indian and American flags to the music of the Bombay Police Band. The flags were marched up the east side stand where the Governor of Bombay, Raja Maharaj Singh, and Rani Maharaj Singh, sat in the only reserved seats.

Following the flags came the mascots of the two teams—a small donkey for Calcutta and a bullock for Bombay—to the surprise and amusement of the crowd. The Bombay Police Band then struck up the Indian National Anthem followed by the American National Anthem, the crowd standing to attention.

The Governor then came on the field and was introduced to both teams by John Hlavacek, the captain of the Bombay team who is also the United Press (of America) Manager for India. The Governor, meeting the players, took pleasure in asking after their home towns, remarking that on many occasions he had the pleasure of visiting many of the large cities in the United States.

With introductions finished, the Governor took his place in the stand and then threw out the first ball to begin the game. Throwing out the first ball is an American tradition. It is customary for the President of the United States to open the American baseball season in the spring of each year by throwing out the first ball.

The Bombay Governor, an excellent cricketer and all-round sportsman in his Oxford University days, heaved the ball well out into the field toward the waiting members of both teams. The ball was caught by H. W. "Soup" Cable, the 6 foot 3 inch Personnel and Labor Relations Director at the Firestone Tyre and Rubber Co. of Bombay. "Soup"—the nickname comes from soup-bone which his school mates gave him because of his long, lanky frame during his school days and which was later shortened to "Soup"—leaped high in the air and ran to the Governor's box for the traditional autograph. The autographed ball now reposes in the Cable household and is a prized possession of "Soup's" 12-year-old son, Torkey.

The game, although a nerve-packed one, was made all the more interesting to the Indian spectators by the work of Lee Kamern, the genial Metro Goldwyn Mayer boss in India, who kept up a running commentary on the game. Lee announced the players as they came to bat and explained the intricacies of the game. Thus the spectator knew when to yell at the umpire (an American custom), when to cheer for a good play, and why the players ran, hit and threw as they did.

Also helpful to the crowd were the programs which explained the game and also gave the opening line-ups and numbers of each player. These were sold by members of the American Women's Club of Bombay.

Everyone enjoyed the game and the festivities and most spectators thought that given a little encouragement this American game could catch on in India as it has in Japan and several South American countries.

BASEBALL

In addition to the *Forum* story, we got publicity in all the Bombay English-language newspapers with stories on the game as well as pictures. There were even some comments about the game from the local columnists. The author of a column titled "Leaning on a Lamppost" compared American and Indian diplomats. He wondered if any of the Indian "big shots" would come out on the field and have a snack at hockey—similar to the American consul General being the "hero" of the game.

As the excitement of the Calcutta game ebbed, our next ball games were with the ships of the U.S. Navy. Bombay was a good port for visitors and in December the U.S. Navy Seaplane tender, the *Valcour,* came into port. On their arrival, we went aboard and offered to play the crew in a baseball game.

For Christmas, I had invitations to dinner at Juhu beach but instead I invited the Valcour baseball team to a party at my house. I went aboard and had Christmas dinner with them at noon and then they came to my house for an afternoon party, bringing with them 12 cases of beer. I invited a number of friends and the girls who worked at the American Consulate General. We all had a fine time and they had to get back to the ship so left at 6:30. They were most appreciative. I noted in my letter home that I left the party for a little while to check in at the office. And I recorded we went through 256 cans of beer that afternoon.

The next morning (Boxing Day in Britain/India) we played the men of the *Valcour.* The score was 3 to 0, in favor of the Navy. After the game both teams gathered at "Tim" Timberlake's for beer. Even though there was partial prohibition in Bombay, the fact that Timberlake was the Consul General and had diplomatic privileges eased the procurement of beer. I then had lunch at the home of John Hanlon—a member of our team—and went down to the ship to say goodbye.

A month later, the Navy was back in town. The *Valcour* was on a six-day visit to Bombay. The *Valcour,* launched in Washington State on June 5, 1943, was under the command of Captain R. H. Stroh and had a complement of 13 other officers and 140 enlisted men. The ship was assigned to the Persian Gulf area. Also aboard for the visit was Captain D. M. Eller, USN, Commander of the Middle East Forces.

We had been in contact with the ship and on January 26th, Indian Republic Day, we had another "show" day of baseball at the Cooperage. We again had the Governor of Bombay throw out the first ball, and the naval officers sat with him in a reserved section of the stands. This was the first of three games we played with the Navy while the ship was in port. We won only one of the three games. The Navy won the first, 13 to 5, but we won the second when I pitched and also hit a home run with two on. However, we were able to visit the ship daily. I took a young American, the son of a consular officer, down to the ship's P.X. for ice cream and later my housemate, Olaf Hauge, and I went to see a movie. Even later I stopped at a party for the navy men at the home of Charles Macarthur, a member of our team.

After the Navy left town, I did a little work for the United Press. But our baseball team kept practicing and on a Friday in the middle of March, the *S. S. President Polk,* one of the liners of the President Lines, arrived in Bombay on its regular run to the Far East. As the ship was to be in port for three days, I went aboard with Lee Kamern to meet the captain and the ship's baseball team. We were invited to lunch so that Lee could get the information about the members of the team for his commentary at the game, which we were arranging for Sunday.

After lunch Lee and I took the *Polk's* team to our practice field and they played a practice game for about an hour and a half. We stayed with them and then took them back to the ship. The next day, a Saturday, I went aboard the *Polk* again and had some drinks at the bar with sandwiches. Then I took the ship's doctor and the second steward out to our flat for a swim. On Sunday, we had the big game at the Cooperage. By this time I knew all the sports reporters of the local papers, and the game received good coverage.

In July of 1950, the *President Polk* made its regular stop in Bombay on a Tuesday. The *Polk* baseball team wanted to play us to avenge their loss on their previous visit. But it was monsoon season and it rained almost every day the *Polk* was in port. However, I went aboard to have lunch with Captain McGann. I was pleased because the crew looked forward to playing a game. McGann said: "Hlavacek can have anything on the ship as far as the crew is concerned." And all I did was arrange for them to play baseball and to have a beer party after the game.

But then the rain subsided for a few hours on Friday and the sun came out. When the day stayed dry until three in the afternoon, we had the game. We were pretty ragged since we had not played since April but we still beat the *Polk* team 10 to nothing. They were a sad bunch but still happy that we had the game.

After the baseball game, I took the crew back to the ship and picked up a birthday cake for the son of a consular officer. We sat in the air-conditioned dining room of the *Polk* while the stewards, which we had just beaten on the ball field, plied us with ice cream, Coca Cola, and coffee and spoiled our appetites for dinner.

In mid-June, we received the invitation from the Calcutta club for the rubber match in our friendly annual meetings. This year our Calcutta trip would be a long weekend (four days) because the time coincided with Indian holidays. The dates were Thursday November 9th to Sunday November 12th.

In October, at a meeting of the executive committee of the Bombay club, the committee voted to use Rs. 6,000.00 (about $2,000) from club funds, which gave me, as the sports chairman, enough money to arrange for a charter.

When the time came in November for the team to go, the new uniforms that we had ordered from the United States had not arrived. Although they were shipped by air, they had been off-loaded somewhere between New York and Bombay. So we dressed in our old uniforms. I had 32 persons who wanted to go and only 20 seats on the charter. So I arranged with Himalayan Aviation—the company which flew the night mail service—to fly a second flight on Wednesday night for the 12 persons I could not accommodate on the charter which left on Thursday morning. (Himalayan Aviation was the company for which my Polish friends were pilots.)

Thus on Thursday morning, November 8th, our team of 20 met at a Bombay park and drove out to the airfield in a convoy. We left on time at 8 a.m. On the trip over I played bridge while other team members got into crap games or poker. We stopped at Nagpur for fuel and a lunch and then flew on to Calcutta. We landed at the Barrackpore field and the Calcutta club had a band to meet us. But we surprised them—as we landed we released 96 pigeons that we had carried from Bombay. We had brought them as a surprise because our uniforms had not arrived. As the leader of the visiting squad I was presented with a huge corkscrew which read "The Corkscrew to the City of Calcutta." Then I was presented with a scroll that was read by Ray Cottini, the leader of the Calcutta team.

After the ceremonies on the field, we were taken to one of the clubhouses at Barrackpore for sandwiches and a drink. We were then taken to our respective hosts' homes for the weekend. Bill McComb (General Motors) and I stayed with at Jack Drane's home. That evening there was a cocktail party for all of the visitors and their hosts where we had a great time meeting old friends. Later we went on to a party at the home of Ned Potts, which lasted until all hours.

The next day, Friday, we had the golf matches. I played on the Bombay team with Jack Scott and we lost both our morning and afternoon rounds. Our Bombay team took a trimming, 24½ to 7. That evening there was a reception for the American Ambassador, Loy Henderson, who had been invited to Calcutta especially for the weekend. After the reception I was invited to the 300 Club for a party that ended at 2 a.m. The 300 Club was one of Calcutta's most popular night clubs—one that many American and British servicemen had frequented during the war years. It was organized originally by Boris Lissanovich, a former Russian ballet dancer, with the help of an Indian Prince. (Boris later became a celebrity on his own when he was the Manager of the Royal Hotel in Kathmandu.)

On Saturday we had the tennis matches. Since I was not on the tennis team, I spent the day working at our Calcutta office. I visited one of our important newspaper clients and then went to the Burmese Consulate to get my visa for Burma. (I was to leave the group in Calcutta and fly to Rangoon.) I also spent time at the Himalayan Aviation office to get my party of twelve back to Bombay on another Himalayan night flight. Incidentally, we also lost the tennis match, three to two. With the loss of the tennis and golf, we had already lost the series but we still had a chance to salvage the weekend with the baseball game.

On Saturday night the Calcutta Club hosted a "Shipwreck Party." I went in a couple of towels and managed to keep warm. The party was held in a huge mansion with a large lawn decorated in a South Sea motif called "The Lost Weekend." I had my baseball team leave the party early so we would all be sober for the morning. We remembered our first outing in Calcutta when the Calcutta team had been successful in getting their visitors drunk.

The Calcutta Club, after seeing the arrangement we had made for their visit, went all out to publicize the game. The game was played at the Calcutta Football Club grounds and was sponsored by the Governor of Calcutta, His Excellency Dr. K. N. Katju, and by the American Ambassador to India, Loy Henderson. The Governor's message, which was published in a 44-page program of advertisements that sold for eight annas (15 cents) a copy, read,

> National games of all countries should, as far as practicable, be common possessions of all mankind. That way lies the promotion not only of community welfare but also of international cordial relations. Football (soccer to Americans) is a source of perennial delight in this great cosmopolitan city. The great game of cricket links continents together. We are indebted to American Clubs of Bombay and Calcutta for this exhibition match of baseball. I am sure it will make a great appeal to all sports-loving citizens of Calcutta and become popular thereby strengthening friendly ties between us and the American people. Further the desire of the organizers to devote the gate receipts to local charities will be widely appreciated.

The American Ambassador, Loy Henderson, as co-sponsor of the match, included this message in the program:

> It gives me great pleasure to act with His Excellency the Governor of West Bengal as Co-sponsor of the 1950 annual baseball game between the Ameri-

can clubs of Bombay and Calcutta, the proceeds of which are to be contributed to worthy charitable enterprises in West Bengal. Baseball is frequently called "The National Game" in the United States where it is watched by millions of people annually. For this reason I am happy to see a game played in Calcutta and I hope that all those who attend it will agree that its popularity is well deserved.

That Sunday morning, we borrowed the Calcutta Club's old uniforms from the previous year and looked presentable. There was a good crowd and our own Lee Kamern, the Metro Goldwyn Mayer representative, flew over to do the announcing. Lee was great in explaining the game in good humor. An account of the game in the Statesman newspaper of Calcutta had this to say about Lee:

> An account such as this would not be complete without a word of praise to the skilled commentator, Lee Kamern, whose explanations and opinions put to every situation kept interest alive throughout the match. The only criticism that can be leveled against him concerns his singing, for when the brass band in the green stands struck up "Take Me Out To The Ballgame," his vocal accompaniment was more than a semi-tone off the mark, not to mention that he did not know the words of the song.

We won the game and I as the Captain contributed a couple of hits in the victory. The score was 7 to 3 and after the game, Ambassador Henderson handed me the winning cup.

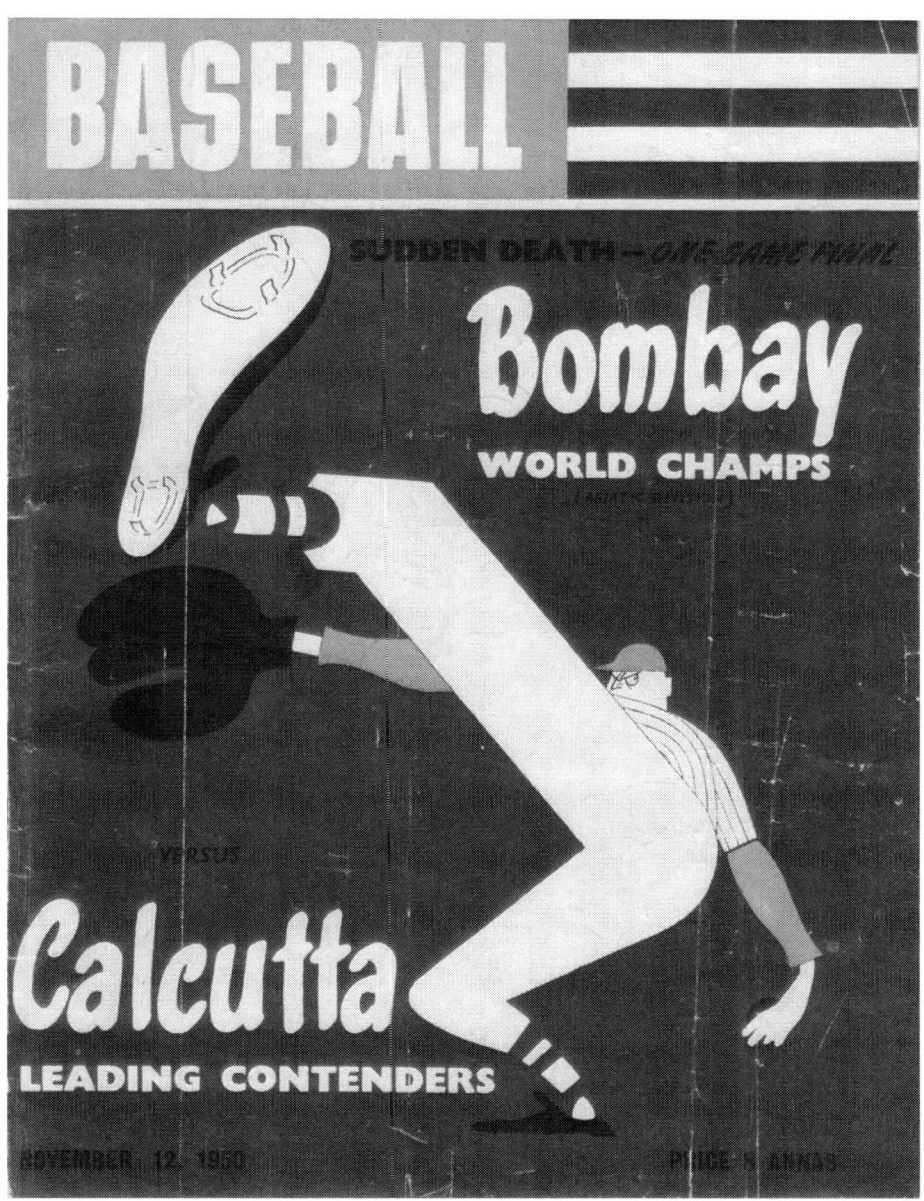

Front cover of the 44-page program published by the American Club of Calcutta.

After the game, I returned to my host's house and called the office. I learned that New York and London wanted to know why I was in Calcutta when there was a war going on at the Indian/Nepal border. They suggested I get to Delhi immediately. I packed, found Ambassador Henderson, asked him if I could get a ride with him to Delhi, and just made it to the airfield in time for take-off. What happened next is described in the chapter titled "Nepal P.O.W."

Our next big intercity sports weekend was with Karachi, Pakistan. My very good friend, Harry Spielman, had been transferred from Bombay to Karachi and organized the Karachi team. We invited the group down and they flew in one Friday afternoon in the last week of March, 1951. They arrived in a C-46 airplane owned by Crescent Airlines. We had the Bombay Police Band out to meet them and we escorted them to their respective Bombay hosts. We had the usual cocktail party and a dinner for the Karachi guests.

On Saturday, Bombay won the golf match which was played at the Willingdon Club. My note said that the Karachi golfers were not very good and we matched them with our highest handicap golfers. Even then, Bombay still managed to win.

That evening we had a dinner dance for the Karachi team. We had the party at the residence of Mr. Kali Mody because Bombay had prohibition at the public restaurants and clubs. At a private residence we were able to have a bar for drinks. It was a late night, and my letter home said I got home at 2 a.m.

On Sunday morning we had a crowd of more than 1,000 spectators at the Cooperage to watch our baseball game. Bombay won easily, 11 to 3, and we again invited the Bombay's sporting governor, H.E. Raja Maharaj Singh, to throw out the first ball. He also was gracious and presented the winning trophy to Bill McComb, the captain of the Bombay Bombers.

We had good newspaper publicity about the game and all the stories remarked about the "very humorous and lucid commentary of Lee Kamern, the announcer who explained each play so that the large crowd could follow the game without difficulty." Lee, who represented Metro Goldwyn Mayer in India, had been the announcer at all of our games.

After the game we had a beer party for all at Bill McComb's residence before the Karachi team left for home that afternoon.

The inscription on the back of this photo says, "Bombay: January 28, 1951."

22

NEPAL P.O.W.

◆

(November 1950)

The cable from United Press in London to me in Calcutta was cryptic: "Indian press reports heavy fighting on India-Nepal border."

I hitched a ride to New Delhi with American Ambassador Loy Henderson on his plane. He had been in Calcutta as co-sponsor with the Governor of West Bengal for the annual baseball game between the American Clubs of Bombay and Calcutta. Arriving on a Sunday night, I spent the next day, a Monday, buying my airline ticket to Lucknow and renting a bedroll from Thomas Cook travel agency for the train journey from Lucknow to the Nepal border.

Early on Tuesday morning, November 14th, I flew to Lucknow, arriving at ten o'clock. I had to wait three hours for my train. While waiting, I called on the Governor of the United Provinces, Sir Homi Mody, for an interview. I also had time to visit the newspaper offices of United Press clients and to buy a couple of bottles of whiskey because I didn't know how cold it was going to be at the border.

After lunch at the railway station, I boarded my train shortly after noon and settled in for the long ride. The railway was the Oudt Tirhut Railway—its nickname was the "Old and Tired Railway." It was a slow train, and the trip took all afternoon and evening. In the morning we arrived at the junction of Muzaffarpur, where I had to change to a train going north. Because my train from Lucknow was running three and a half hours late, I had missed my morning connection and had a few hours before to wait for the afternoon train to Raxaul, the Indian city on the Nepal border. I repaired to the Muzaffurpur Club to shave and have lunch. Because Muzaffurpur is close to the border, I tried to find someone who might know what the situation was. I found Mr. M. Weatherall, who, I learned, was one of the engineers who had built the ropeways in Nepal (more on this topic later) in 1926 and still had a lot of connections there. He gave me some background information on the region, and later that afternoon I caught my train for Raxaul, arriving on Wednesday evening at seven o'clock. The town had no electricity and was pretty dark. But I was lucky. A United Press of India reporter was on my train and he had a man meeting him, so they took me along and got me a room at the Nepal State Guest House, which had been taken over by the so-called insurgent Congress forces.

That evening I met the rest of the press corps, including the *London Observer* correspondent, Rawle Knox, the only other foreign correspondent in the place. We had dinner at the railway station, and while we were there I came up with the brilliant idea to use bicycles to travel over the border and see where the front lines were. Knox had been over that afternoon but was in a jeep with other correspondents and there was no agreement as to how far forward they would go. At dinner that evening a couple of Indian correspondents said they could arrange the bicycles for us and would have them ready at eight o'clock the next morning. We had a couple of drinks from my stash of whiskey and then went off to bed.

Thursday morning I woke up early and had a bath, a cold one but welcome after traveling in a dusty train from Tuesday afternoon to Wednesday night. Then to breakfast with Knox and the UPI man, but the two correspondents who had promised to bring bicycles didn't show up. Knox and I decided to try to borrow bicycles. Knox succeeded in getting one from a prominent businessman, a Mr. Joshi, and I got one from the little tea shop next to the Guest House. I told the owner that we would be back within four hours since we had planned to file a story before one o'clock that afternoon.

At about nine-thirty we started cycling and rode up to the bridge at the border. We encountered a guard on sentry duty on the Indian side, but he made no motion to stop us. He only objected to me trying to take his picture. We rode on into the little town of Birganj on the Nepal side of the border. On the outskirts of the town, about a mile inside the border, we stopped at a compound to watch a group of about a hundred Congress volunteers (the insurgents) getting basic military training—and very basic it was. We weren't learning anything, so we rode on into the main street of Birganj. The pedal on my bike came loose, so we stopped at a shop to fix it. The inevitable crowd gathered around, all in good humor. Evidently the townspeople were not too worried about the administration of the town by the rebels. After fixing the pedal we rode along the narrow-gauge railway that runs north to the town of Amlekganj, about 25 miles from the border. There was a dusty road alongside the tracks, but we found it easier to ride along the path adjacent to the rails. We saw nothing unusual while cycling north for what we guessed was about six or seven miles. We passed one little village, but the people just looked out at us from their houses. Everything seemed calm and peaceful, and it was difficult to believe there was any kind of a war going on.

We took a short rest and then went on further, still following the railway until we came to the little town of Parwanipur, which is eight miles inside the border. Here we met our first sentry, a man carrying a rifle, wearing a white cap and a dhoti. (A *dhoti* is a sarong-like cloth wrapped around the waist.) He took us over to a little group of men guarding the bridge over a small stream. This, it seems, was the front line. Knox spoke to the group in Hindustani and learned that the Nepal State troops had been up the bridge that morning and had fired a shot but after return fire had retreated. It was probably a patrol. Knox asked them if they had any objections to us riding on. The leader said, "No, but I'm not going with you."

We crossed the bridge and rode on slowly, single file, keeping our eyes peeled for Nepal State troops. I was in the lead, wearing a white shirt, white cotton trousers, and a red baseball cap. All of a sudden I saw a little brown figure go running back along a ditch beside the tracks, but before we could turn around we found a company of state troops had risen up and had their rifles trained on us. (When we saw that first figure Knox said to me, "I think, old man, we may have come a little too far.")

We didn't even wait for a command. We put down our cycles and raised our hands, and they came up and took us prisoner. I don't know who was more surprised, they or we, but they followed the correct prisoner-of-war procedure and took our cycles, all our money, pens, passports, my camera and watch. Knox, speaking Hindustani, explained who we were and what we were doing. (Knox had spent time in a prisoner-of-war camp in Singapore during World War II and spoke good Hindustani.) Knox and I thought we could stay with this company and go with them as they fought their way across the river and back into Birganj. But they had other ideas. They said they would have to send us back to their battalion headquarters. This they did by walking us back about a half-mile to where a truck was waiting. They sent a solider with us and put both of us and the bicycles in the back of the truck and drove us about four miles back to battalion headquarters at the town of Jitpur. It was a rough road, only ruts along the railway, and we crossed over the tracks whenever there was a gully. We met only one truck coming forward with more troops.

At Jitpur we got off the truck and were led through a thicket (just like in the movies) down a ravine and finally out onto an open field where we were taken to the battalion commander (a big, fat man who had trouble getting up by himself), his chief of staff, and an army doctor who acted as interpreter. This time the conversation was in English, and again we explained who we were. They made us write our names and evidently telephoned through to higher headquarter to see what was to be done with us. We must have waited about two hours before they came back and said they would have to send us back to general headquarters. By this time we knew we wouldn't get back to Raxaul that night and immediately began thinking of ways to get them to send us to Kathmandu. We waited for another hour. By this time they had given us back all our belongings except my camera. They finally came up and led us to a bus. The bus was a typical Indian-style model with a long seat parallel to the driver's seat across the width of the bus, behind which were the lower-class accommodations with seats placed lengthwise. They put the cycles in the back part of the bus. But before we boarded the bus, we were blindfolded, and they sent a guard along to make sure that we wouldn't peek. We felt like real prisoners of war.

It was a long, bumpy ride. We found that we had been driven between 45 and 50 miles straight into Nepal. It was already dusk when the bus finally stopped and we were permitted to get out, still blindfolded, and were led into a compound with high walls. Here we were greeted by four high-ranking army officers, including the general commanding the area. They apologized for detaining us and sat down with us to tea and biscuits (cookies), the first food we had eaten since breakfast. After several cups of tea because it was getting cold and we were not dressed for cold weather, the officers finally pointed to a building on the hill behind us and told us we would spend the first night there and go on to Kathmandu in the morning.

At about seven o'clock, accompanied by three policemen, we began climbing the first pass. It was two and a half miles straight up. Since it was cold we walked as fast as we could and worked up quite a sweat, so much so that we worried about catching a serious cold. But we made the climb and arrived about 8:30. At the fort—its name was Chisa Pani Ghari (sometimes spelled Sisapanighari) which means "Cold Water Fort"—we were shown to a guest room with two beds with blankets. We both took off our sweaty clothes and wrapped ourselves with the cold but dry blankets. I asked for extra blankets and they brought them to us. They brought dinner—chicken curry and rice—and we stayed under the blankets as we ate. I stayed in bed to keep warm. And we slept.

We were up early the next morning because we thought we would be going on to Kathmandu. All through the night we had guards pacing through the front and rear of our room. Every time I woke during the night I could hear them. (I wondered where they thought we two could escape to.) The sun rose early, and we walked around the fort wrapped in blankets until tea came at seven o'clock and then breakfast at eight. We couldn't leave until the civil governor of the fort had his orders for us to go on. We met him and asked if we could leave for Kathmandu. He told us he had no orders but would telephone. A half-hour later we met him, and he said that the telephone line was out and we would have to wait, which we did, playing a type of Indian checkers. We sat in the sunlight on the stone steps of our room. At about eleven, he came to us, all smiles, and said we could go back to Raxaul. We protested that we didn't want to go to Raxaul, that we were only 16 miles from Kathmandu and that we wanted to go on. We waited another half-hour. Then Knox began talking to the military governor as well as the civil governor explaining that it would be wise to let us go on, and that the army men at Bhimpedi (the town where we had got off the bus the night before) had told us that we were to go on to Kathmandu. Finally, after we had beaten down their arguments that it was too difficult a journey without horses, they said we could go to Kathmandu but that we should have lunch first. We gulped down our lunch and, with one pony for the two of us, we started for Kathmandu. Then we started climbing. We thought we had reached the top of the pass the night before. Not so. We still had quite a climb, but when we reached the top of the pass we saw the white snow on the Himalayas gleaming in the sunlight. And I had no camera. Despite all my pleadings they had refused to give it back to me but said it would be sent on to Kathmandu on the ropeways.

At the top of the pass we could see the ropeways, a wonderful system for transporting goods in the mountains. The principle is the same as a ski lift. The moving cables run from mountain top to mountain top carrying platforms which can support up to 600 pounds of freight going in either direction. When the moving platforms reach the towers they are automatically transferred to another series of cables. (I understand that similar ropeways have been used in Europe in many places where the mountains make land journeys difficult. In 1950, there were no roads from the Indian border to the Nepalese capital of Kathmandu.)

From the top of the Chisa Pani Ghari pass we began the long trek down into the valley. It was a beautiful walk once we reached the valley floor and could follow the winding river through to the second and last pass which leads to the Kathmandu Valley. We walked rather quickly because we wanted to reach Kathmandu in daylight if possible and we had many hours to go. On the way we met further reinforcements of Nepal Government troops moving south to the plains below to ensure that the "rebels" would be removed from the border towns.

We walked all afternoon and stopped at the base of the Changra Ghiri Pass for tea. Then we began the climb up the second pass protecting the Kathmandu valley. It was another long, sweaty climb, but we reached the top of the pass at dusk and could just make out the valley and the mountains beyond. Then we began the descent and luckily we had a full moon, so we came down to the valley in moonlight. We reached the village of Thankot, from which a motor road leads into Kathmandu. We had been told a car would meet us here, but no car was waiting. So we sat in a little teahouse on the side of the road and drank tea and ate peanuts until a telephone call to Kathmandu brought us a car. I well remember Knox, eating peanuts at the teahouse, declaring, "I am not going to walk another step." The car that appeared was a 1924 Dodge which had been carried over the path we had just completed by porters, about a hundred of them, because at the time there was no road into Nepal and there were only about sixteen miles of roadways in the valley of Kathmandu. Into the Dodge piled the two of us and our three escorts who had walked all the way with us from Chisa Pani Ghari. It had taken us six hours to make the trip.

When we arrived in the city, we were taken to one of the Nepal Government guest houses and given blankets and a good dinner. I tried to send a message immediately and gave it to the guest house superintendent so that our correspondent friends at the border would know we were safe. However, the message was not sent until the next morning.

We woke early and discovered that our legs were stiff and sore and the soles of our feet hurt. I had worn a comfortable pair of shoes—ones I used for playing golf—so I had no blisters, but my feet were sore. We were filthy. I had worn white when I left the Indian border and 48 hours of knocking about had gotten my clothes quite dirty. After early morning tea at seven and breakfast about eight, I went next door to another State Guest House to visit four Swiss. I introduced myself, explained briefly our predicament, and asked for the loan of some clothes. "Sure," they said, "Come on upstairs." They laid out their wardrobe and even though none of the four were the same size as Knox or me, we found enough to keep us warm. We shed our dirty clothes, sent them to a dhobi (laundryman), and settled down to try and find out how we could send our messages.

A young man appeared at our door. He said that he was the son of the Prime Minister, Narindramani Dikshit, and that we were now guests of the government. The young man had previously written to me asking to be a "stringer" correspondent for United Press. I had been very courteous in my reply even though I had not hired him, and he was grateful.

Before I had borrowed the clothes from the Swiss, the superintendent of the guest house, a man who came around three times a day to see if we were comfortable, had looked at us in horror when we said we wanted to interview the Nepalese Prime Minister. He said that he would call a tailor and have suits made so that we could call on people. The tailor was called but he didn't come until that evening. Naturally the suits would be paid for by the government, and we would be the guests of the government for our stay in Kathmandu.

Perhaps I should explain about Nepal and its attitude toward visitors. Nepal doesn't like foreigners of any kind. It has always been very difficult to get into Kathmandu, taking several weeks to get the required permits. Usually one had to be invited by one of the Nepalese government officials or by the British Embassy, the one foreign embassy in Nepal. But once you were accepted, you were the guest of the Maharajah (Prime Minister). And that is what we were once we got over our status as war prisoners. When we wanted to go somewhere, a car appeared. When we wanted some beer, beer appeared. The only trouble we had was trying to get information for a story.

To give you some idea of the remoteness of Nepal, only 230 foreigners visited Kathmandu between 1880 and 1925. Since that time the visits became more frequent but the number remained small. During the previous year only about 65 foreigners, including 15 Americans, had visited the city. As far as we could find out, Knox and I were the only two foreigners ever to get to Kathmandu without a permit or prior invitation. (Shows what comes of learning to ride a bicycle.) One additional fact: Nepal doesn't allow Christian missionaries. The last missionaries, the Capuchins, were kicked out before 1800 and the Nepalese have not allowed any missionaries into the country since. The country is mainly Hindu with a small number of Buddhists, and Nepal doesn't want any westerners trying to proselytize its people. In addition there are some towns in Nepal that have never been visited by a foreigner. So one can see how lucky we were, especially when practically every press man in Delhi would have paid a lot to get to Kathmandu. I told Knox that I might not be the best correspondent but I sure was the luckiest.

We spent the rest of the morning writing our stories and trying to get them sent to our offices. The Indian press had published stories reporting that we had been captured; some said we were injured, and some reports had us killed. So it was important to let our offices know were alive and able to tell our stories.

That morning we received an invitation, by messenger, from the British Ambassador to come and have drinks that afternoon. After lunch at the guest house, we visited with our newfound Swiss friends. The four made up a scientific team that had been invited by the Nepal Government in cooperation with the

Swiss Federal Institute, to make a survey of the country. The leader of the expedition, Walter Custer, an architect from Zurich, was most kind and sent over a bottle of whiskey the day after we arrived. The others, equally friendly, were Emil Rauch, an agronomist, Dr. Toni Hagen, a geologist, and Alf de Spindler, a civil and hydro-electric engineer. They were the only foreigners in the county visiting except for a Swiss lady, a Mrs. Hefflinger, who had come as a tourist. The only other westerners in Nepal were the staff of the British Embassy (seven people) and a British engineer and his wife who worked for the Nepal Government and who had lived in Kathmandu for 25 years.

(Dr. Toni Hagen later surveyed the whole of the country under the auspices of the United Nations. He was the author of *Nepal,* a book about his geological surveys of the country.)

That afternoon a car came for us, and we had a sightseeing ride about the city. Kathmandu reminded me a little of a Chinese town although the country was a curious mixture of Indian and Tibetan-Chinese cultures.

That evening we went for drinks at the British Ambassador's residence. Sir George and Lady Falconer (pronounced Faulkner) were very gracious. At the embassy they were waiting, dressed in formal clothes, at the top of the long stairway leading to their quarters. (Both Knox and I were six-footers. When we borrowed the clothes from the Swiss, we found that none of the four was our size. Some were tall and thin, others squat and bulky. My trousers came up to my shins. Knox's jacket hung loosely. But we did have scarves about our necks. And here were the Ambassador and his wife in formal clothes as Knox and I walked up the stairs looking like Laurel and Hardy.)

Over drinks, the Ambassador asked about our "adventure." He told us that when we were captured, he was contacted by the Nepalese because one of the "prisoners" was a British subject (Knox). He had told the Nepalese to let us come to Kathmandu. So we were in his debt because his intervention probably was the reason the Nepalese at the fort allowed us to leave.

The ambassador also briefed us on the political situation in Kathmandu and the diplomatic impasse between the Nepalese and Indian governments. He believed that the Indian government was behind the Nepalese insurgents at the border.

That evening we had dinner at the guest house and retired early. There was not much to do in Kathmandu in the evening. There was a general curfew for all Nepalis at 9:20 p.m. that had been in effect for 80 years. The curfew was a general precaution against theft and also against any kind of a popular movement to overthrow the Rana regime. Also, there was very little social life because so few foreigners were allowed into the country and the Nepalese were strict Hindus. We were told that there were very few banquets because of the different eating habits of the citizens, but there were parties at which soft drinks were served. Nepal had strict prohibition and a local resident found imbibing or drunk would spend a month in jail for the first offense.

The weather in the Kathmandu Valley in November was very pleasant. It was warm enough in the daytime that a regular suit could be worn. Evenings, when the sun goes down, were cold but not freezing. Most mornings there was a mist hanging over the valley that cleared as the sun came up over the Himalayas.

On Sunday morning, Knox and I worked on the story about the flight of King Tribuvan and the coronation of the new King, his five-year-old grandson. Nepal had for many years been ruled by the Ranas—the actual maharajahs of the country. A Hindu King, Tribuvan, was, for all intents and purposes, a prisoner. On a drive into the country, the King, with the help of the Indian Government, took asylum in the Indian Embassy. When the story was sent out we found that the Indian press never published it. (The King was duly re-installed a year later after the Indian Government had succeeded in driving the Ranas from power.)

Later that morning, we were invited, along with the Swiss engineer, Alf de Spindler, for drinks at the Kilburnes. Roy and Mrs. Kilburne had lived in Nepal for 25 years. He was the engineer to the Nepalese government and the only foreigner employed by Nepal. He ran everything—electric plants, telephones, ropeways—and was treated as a member of the government family. We were with the Kilburnes less than an hour but enough to talk a bit and get invited back later. The Kilburnes had a beautiful compound with lots of space and a very comfortable home. They, too, wanted us to tell our story of how we got to Kathmandu.

At lunch we were the guests of the British Ambassador and Lady Falconer. It was an excellent lunch but very formal—so different from our rangy talks of the previous evening. (I wrote, "Maybe whiskey makes one talk more freely.") After lunch we spent a few minutes on the lawn of the beautiful, spacious Embassy grounds.

Afterward we went to the Indian Embassy to pay a call and to ask for an interview with the ambassador. We didn't see him but we sent in our cards. (We never did get an answer from him.) We surmised that he might not want to see us because there were many rumors both in India and Nepal that he, the Indian ambassador, was behind the revolt against the Nepalese Government as it was into his embassy that the King of Nepal had taken asylum before being flown to India.

Later that afternoon, Knox and I had our interview with the Foreign Minister. His name was a jaw breaker (as all Nepali names are): Major General Bijaya Sham Sher Jang Bahadur Rana. Besides being the Foreign Minister he was also the son of the Prime Minister. With him was the Foreign Secretary, Sardar N. M. Dikshit (also spelled Dixit). The latter, by a coincidence, was the father of the young man with whom I had corresponded three years previously. We met the foreign minister in the Durbar Hall of the palace, a huge hall decorated with full-length portraits of Nepal's kings and prime ministers. Hanging from the ceiling were crystal chandeliers. (I learned later that most of them had come from London and were bought during the days of the Crystal Palace in Brighton at the turn of the century. All of them were carried over the two mountain passes on our route on the backs of porters, since the ropeways were not built until 1926.) Also in the hallway leading to the Durbar Hall were mounted wild game—lions, tigers, panthers, and even a polar bear—shot by former Maharajahs of Nepal. The Foreign Minister was a young man of about 35, and we had a very frank talk about the political situation, especially the machinations of the Indian ambassador. No one said it was "off the record," but later we learned it was—and since the only way to send it was by Nepal Government cables, the story was kept "off the record." After our interview, there was a slight stir, and we were told that the Prime Minister, His Highness Moham Sham Sher Jang Bahadur Rana, wanted to meet us. (We were quite the celebrities and found that a number of people wanted to meet us.) We all stood as he came in, a man about 65 or 70 wearing a military hat and sporting a mustache. He spoke perfect English. After sitting down and motioning us to take seats beside him, he asked after our welfare and wanted to know that we were being treated well. We assured him we were and tried to get him to make a startling statement that would look good in our stories. But he was very reticent about saying anything because the "war" was not yet over and Nepal's relations with India were (and still are) very delicate.

After the interview we returned to the guest house and were measured for our "famous" suits. We had already had our interview wearing our "Laurel and Hardy" costumes but we were to be fitted with our suits nevertheless. The tailor brought us bolts of British woolens and I picked out a grey pinstripe. We also were measured for white cotton shirts.

That evening we had dinner at the guest house and for entertainment, listened to news on the radio.

Monday morning (November 20th) I wrote the story of our interview with the Foreign Minister. (It was never transmitted but I did not know it until the next day.) I spent some time sightseeing in the city. I still didn't have my camera but I managed to borrow one from Alf de Spindler and I was able to buy film in Kathmandu. I complained bitterly to the superintendent of the guest house, Mr. Mani Ram Bhandari. He promised to try and get the army to send it over the ropeways. (It never did get to Kathmandu.)

We had lunch at the guest house, mostly curry and rice and either chicken or mutton. But it was good food and we had plenty of fresh vegetables—raw onions, tomatoes—and cooked cauliflower and spinach. All very tasty. Daily, too, we had gallons of tea and a generous supply of bread and butter. We didn't think to ask for coffee, though we did ask for beer and whiskey and soda.

After lunch we had our driver take us to the British Embassy to see Colonel R. R. Proud, the First Secretary, to ask about the geography of Nepal. He was busy so we had only a few minutes with him, but he invited us for drinks at his home that evening. Since we had the car, we drove to Patan, one of the old capitals of Nepal. It was a holiday and few shops were open, but we wandered around looking at the temples and the town in general. Nepal has Kathmandu as its capital now, but back a few hundred years it had two other capitals, Patan, about two miles from Kathmandu, and Bhatgoan, about six miles away. (We visited Bhatgoan another day.)

That evening we returned to Colonel Proud's for drinks. We met his wife and the other members of the British Embassy, a Mr. and Mrs. Killick and Mr. Swayn, the radio operator. The embassy as its own wireless communications with New Delhi. The American Ambassador in Delhi, Mr. Loy Henderson, had inquired about us on Saturday and the British Ambassador had sent a message that we were safe. Our disappearance from Raxaul had caused some concern in Bombay and Delhi.

Tuesday (November 21st) after breakfast, Mr. Dikshit came by with the dispatch I had tried to send out the day before. He explained that he wasn't censoring it but that the talks on Sunday evening had been "off the record" and that if I sent out the dispatch it would only worsen relations between India and Nepal. There was nothing I could do about it. However, we had more conversation and he gave the two of us more information that we could not use at the time and probably would only be able to use as background information in the future.

In the afternoon, Knox and I went sightseeing: first to the Kathmandu Museum where we wandered the halls viewing exhibits of arms that had been used for the past century. Nepal has always been a center of intrigue and scheming, and I had read some of its history. It was about 1850 before a prime minister died a natural death. Before that time, they were all murdered by assassins so that another family member could assume power. A hundred years later, Nepal was fairly peaceful. After visiting the museum we drove to the temple at Shaambunath, a few miles from the city.

That evening we called on some fellow guests in another guest house. They were Indian businessmen from Calcutta who had been there for a few weeks and were waiting until the road was re-opened so they could return to India.

I should explain that the government had several guest houses of different sizes. Knox and I had a small one with just one bedroom and a large bath and a dining room. The Swiss, being a group of four, had a large guest house: a large living room, a dining room, and a study downstairs, with four large bedrooms upstairs. The superintendent of the guest house kept apologizing to us because he couldn't give us more spacious accommodations. We insisted we were quite comfortable sharing a room.

On Wednesday (November 22nd) I spent the morning writing dispatches and then took a walk through town window shopping. We were invited to the Kilburnes' for lunch. Our conversation was all about living in Kathmandu and their experiences over the past 25 years. After lunch, we asked for a car and drove to Bhatoan, the ancient capital, about six miles from the city. It was a beautiful day, and we were out most of the afternoon. The farmers were preparing their land for planting, plowing the ground behind plodding water buffalo. The women were breaking up the big clumps with long sticks. That part of the valley is a rising plateau, and all the fields are terraced.

We were at the guest house for dinner and the evening. In Kathmandu there was no nightlife.

Thursday (November 23rd) I went shopping in the morning and bought a few souvenirs. After lunch at the guest house, we had a short meeting with the Nepalese Commander-in-Chief, General Baber Sham Sher Jang Bahadur Rana. He really was not the C-in-C, but he was next in line for the Prime Ministership. He was a brother of the Prime Minister. In Nepal, the prime ministers were the ruling class and the succession went from one brother to the next for all of one generation. Then the eldest son of that line became Prime Minister and all his brothers for that generation followed. The King of Nepal was a figurehead with no real power. After visiting the C-in-C, we went shopping and then later went to see the Foreign Minister for a farewell visit. We were presented with kukris (a ceremonial curved knife)—a high honor. On leaving the palace, we saw the five-year-old king, newly installed after his grandfather had escaped into the Indian Embassy, romping on the palace lawn. An attendant followed him with a large umbrella wherever he wandered. The Nepalese wouldn't let me near him to take a picture. (If I had stayed a few more days it might have been arranged but then it would have been a posed picture, which I already had obtained.)

Then, back at the guest house, the tailor and our suits had finally arrived. We wore them for our last night in Katrhmandu. It was a big joke to us for we now we each had a suit as a present from the Nepal Government. In our new suits we made a round of farewell calls because we were leaving for India in the morning. First, to the British Ambassador and Mrs. Falconer who were very friendly and wished us well. Then to the Prouds and Killicks where we had a couple of drinks and said our goodbyes. Then to the Kilburnes, and many, many drinks later to the guest house for our final meal.

Also, that afternoon I got a cable from London suggesting that I go to Kalimpong or Gangtok, a trip of about six weeks. I vetoed the idea, not because I didn't want to go there, but because there was other business that had to be attended to in Bombay and I didn't want to be out of my office for that long.

I also got a message from Corey, my girlfriend in Bombay, that made me chuckle. It said, "You have been a hero long enough, come on back here." The Government of Nepal also must have been amused since it went through government facilities and was given to me by Mr. Dikshit.

Friday (November 24th), we were up early, 5:30, because we had a long way to go. The Nepal Government was good about arranging everything because we needed their help to make the trip back to India. A car was ready for us at six o'clock and we were driven to the end of the road at the bottom of the first pass at Thankot. Here two ponies were waiting and we set off immediately climbing the first pass. Both Knox and I were determined that we were not going to walk a step up the hill, so the horses had a good workout. At the top of the pass, we looked back and took a last glimpse of the valley and the snow on the Himalayas jutting up above the mist that hung over the valley. Then the long walk down to the valley floor. It was easier walking down than riding a pony, but one's legs became very sore. We made good time down to the valley floor and began walking quickly to the second mountain pass. We had to wait for the horses to catch up and then we rode up the second pass and reached the Chisapani Ghari Fort. The civil governor met us with smiles and told us our lunch was ready and that we would have to hurry to catch our train. We hurried down the hill to Bhimpedi and as we came off the pass a truck was waiting to take us to the head of the ropeways to get our bicycles and my camera. We then took off for Amlekgang, the terminus of the little narrow-gauge railway to the Indian border. We had a little Nepalese jockey behind the wheel who loved to gun the truck up to great speed and then throw out the clutch and coast, riding the brake when he needed to slow down. Both of us wished we were blindfolded as we had been on the way up. It was pretty country, though, and between Bhimpedi and Amlekgang was another range of hills. We arrived at Amlekgang about four o'clock to find that the train had been held two hours waiting for us. Messages had been sent all the way down the line that we were coming and people were waiting for us at every stop. The train started as soon as we were aboard and it took two hours to reach the last town on the Nepal side, Birganj, which we had left a week before. At the station the doctor interpreter who had questioned us after capture and the chief of staff of the battalion shook our hands warmly and laughed about the whole show. Then the train pushed on to Raxaul and we were met by the owners of the bicycles. I had borrowed mine for four hours and returned it nine days later. The teahouse owner just grabbed the cycle and rode away before I could thank him. Our belongings were safe in the Nepal State Guest House. We packed and went to the railway station for dinner. We found canned spaghetti and canned soup in the station. We also had a few drinks to celebrate our return. I had left a bottle and a half of whiskey in my belongings and it was safe when I returned. A United Press of India correspondent and a Press Trust of India correspondent joined us. Then we caught the night train for Patna at ten o'clock and went right to sleep. So far we had made all connections.

Saturday (November 25th), I awoke early to find that the train was running almost two hours late. It would be impossible to make plane connections in Patna, so we were facing a 24-hour delay. Knox and I got off at Muzaffarpur about 8:15 hoping that we could find a way to fly to Patna. We reasoned that, in any case, it would be good to get off the train, have a bath and breakfast at the Muzaffarpur Club and then catch a later train to Patna. At the club, I tried to reach M. Weatherall because I knew he had his own plane. But he was away and expected back later that morning. At the club we telephoned the Bihar Flying Club at Patna to try and get a small plane to fly us to Patna. By the Hlavacek Hluck, Weatherall was in the Flying Club office and he said, "Hello, Hlavacek, I'm flying to Muzaffarpur and I will be there at 10:30 and if you are at the field you can take the plane back." That was perfect, because Patna was only a half-hour flight from Muzaffarpur, and the Bharat Airways plane didn't leave for Calcutta until 11:50. So we had a shave and a leisurely breakfast with a goatskin buyer from Calcutta. The Muzaffarpur region has goats that make an extremely good grade of leather.

Knox and I got out to the airfield in bicycle rickshaws and were there at 10:30 but Weatherall was missing. We waited and waited and Weatherall finally arrived about 11:30. I thought there was no chance of catching my plane, but he said that though it was a little late I would make it. So I left Knox (he couldn't have made a connection to Delhi anyway), climbed into the little two-seater with my baggage, and took off. We flew at over 100 mph (cruising would have been at 85) and settled down at the airport just as the Bharat Airways plane finished refueling. My little plane taxied right up to the larger plane. I jumped out, got a ticket, and boarded the plane for Calcutta. Hlucky Hlavacek had 40 minutes before a plane left for Bombay. I managed to borrow 20 rupees from a fellow passenger so I could buy my ticket. My Airways India plane took off at 2:30, stopped at Nagpur for refueling and a meal at 6:30, and flew on to Bombay, arriving at 9:30. My flat mate, Olaf, and my girl friend, Corey, met me at the airfield. (I had called my office from Calcutta saying that I would be on the plane.) I think I must have set a record traveling from Kathmandu to Bombay in 39 and a half hours and by every conceivable means of transportation—walking, horseback riding, bus, train, rickshaw, private plane, and commercial planes.

Press reaction to our "adventure" was limited to a few printed stories. However, a United Press critic from Buenos Aires, in reporting how United Press stories compared to AFP, Reuters, and Associated Press, sent the following missive to all UP bureaus: "John Hlavacek's bicycle ride to Kathmandu punctured all the AFP, Reuter, and Associated Press' 'bloody battles' by telepathy and put the Nepal story in its true perspective. We were not wholly guiltless but John sure showed the old Richard Harding Davis tradition still springs within the Unipresser's breast."

VOL. XV: NO. 464
Eight-Page Colour Supplement Free
BOMBAY: SUNDAY, NOVEMBER 19, 1950.

BIRGANJ RECAPTURE CLAIMED BY GOVT.

Rising Quelled, Says Katmandu

INSURGENTS ADMIT CRITICAL PHASE

KATMANDU, NOVEMBER 18.

A GOVERNMENT SPOKESMAN SAID TODAY GOVERNMENT TROOPS HAD CAPTURED BIRGANJ AND QUELLED THE INVASION BY NEPALI CONGRESS FORCES, WHO SOUGHT TO OVERTHROW THE RANA REGIME REPORTS JOHN M. HLAVACEK.

The spokesman said Nepal, full on Friday troops who struck int

Government sour here had been litt during the weekend

The State troops in t in the Birganj sector ir everthing but only recovered night's advance, and r moved to within a thirte the matter mud-jacked the River Shanka, near

A second light for the at hours was reported to

The insurgents today progress either in the w the western sector. In the strong Nepali State army rushed down for .... wards the towns of Baratu kata on

Nepal Congress circle were, at their that that of the troops, would hit insurgent smash m involve throughout the in the occupied areas.

In the west, the pe cated by a ..... the key of Bhairwai headquarters district .... still out t though they gained th a fierce action around of soldiers and have pinnamed road

MR. KOIRALA'S V

Katmanu Showdown J Rana ..... of Commander sergeants and Mr. H. P about of the Nepali Con the premises this evening the delegates and said co the ....

The State troops in this hera after three took m ehige can and other n. insurgent military spokesman today

CORRESPONDENTS MISSING

RAXAUL:- It is reported that Mr. Knox of London 'Observer' and Mr. Cheberlech of the U.P.A. who had cycled beyond the Nepali Congress force position north of Birganj on Thursday morning, were awaited at Raxaul last night.

Nepalese arriving at Birganj from areas controlled by State troops said that they had seen two white men wounded and taken into custody by State troops.

No further information about the two foreign correspondents was available. They two correspondents had arrived at Raxaul on Wednesday to report developments on this front.—PTI

KALIMPONG: Dr. Rammanohar Lohia, Socialist leader, told pressmen here today that the Government of India should withdraw the recognition of the "Rana regime in Nepal on constitutional grounds."

NO DISAFFECTION IN NEPAL ARMY

Katmandu Peaceful, Says Pressman

KATMANDU, Nov. 18.

"I arrived at this capital on Friday night after being captured by Nepali army troops, nine miles inside Nepal territory, Thursday morning, while trying to find the front line" writes Mr. John M. Hlavacek one of the foreign press correspondents reported missing.

Mr. Hlavacek adds: "At the Indian border town of Raxaul on Wednesday, there had been reports for several days of successes by Congress forces which, at one time, were reported north of Amlekhganj, 20 miles inside Nepal.

"On Thursday morning, Mr. Rawle Knox of the London Observer and I borrowed bicycles at Raxaul and decided to .... we found the fr........ tereening where Nepa.... government forces were.

.... newspaper, eight miles ...th of the ...... order, the first s .... a group of ...rd- ...ry .... can....... half mile... we ......de into .... and tro....... An offi....... and ... sear.hed us. He took away our .... money and passports. We ...... set us in trucks with our cycles to a ...batta.. headquarters three miles to

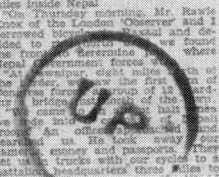

2 Newsmen Seized By Nepali, Released

John Hlavacek, United Press correspondent, arrived at Khaimandu, the capital city of Nepal, Nov. 17 after being captured by Nepali army troops nine miles inside Nepal territory while trying to find the front line, U.P. reported.

On Nov. 16, Rawle Knox, of the London Observer, and Mr. Hlavacek borrowed bicycles in Raxaul and decided to ride north until they found the front to determine just where the Nepal government forces were.

They rode into Birganj, the Nepal border town, then in the hands of invading Congress forces. At Pawnipur, eight miles north of the border, they saw the first sign of Congress forces, a group of 12 guarding a bridge just north of the

Captured UPA Manager reports from Khatmandu—

No unrest in Nepal: State troops disciplined: officials puzzled at Bharat's unfriendly attitude

Note: UPA Manager for Bharat, John M. Hlavacek, arrived at the Nepali capital of Khatmandu after being captured on Thursday by the Nepali State Forces. Hlavacek was captured with a British correspondent when he entered Nepal to report on the fighting near Birganj between Government and Nepali Congress forces fighting to depose Nepal's hereditary Prime Minister Maharaja Chandra Rana. Hlavacek was the first American newspaper reporter to reach Khatmandu. His despatch, delayed in receipt, follows:

By JOHN M. HLAVACEK
UPA Staff Correspondent

KHATMANDU, Nov 18: I arrived at this capital on Friday night after being captured by Nepali army troops nine miles inside Nepal territory on Thursday morning, while trying to find the front line.

At the Bharati border town of

23

HOME LEAVE AROUND THE WORLD

✦

(July to November 1951)

It was standard practice for Americans—and other westerners—to go on home leave after two or sometimes three years living in faraway places such as India, China, Japan, and other Asian countries.

Most large corporations such as Firestone, General Motors, Ford, and the motion picture companies had rules for their employees as to when they could leave and how many months they could spend at home. Usually, after three years, a person could expect to be away for six months with his travel expenses paid and his salary continuing during the time away.

For United Press employees, there was *no* established practice. In some cases, if you wanted to get away for a month or two, the company made you pay your own way. During the World War II era when correspondents were accredited to the military, getting home for short periods was possible since the military provided the transportation. But in peacetime it was another story. It then depended upon how important a person was to the organization. If, as sometimes happened, the correspondent was in an area where there was important news, he or she had a good chance of New York authorizing a trip home. Or, as in my case, if our business was good—that is, Indian newspapers were buying our service—I had some leeway. When I first joined United Press, in China, during the last two years of the war, I was able to go home for four months in the autumn of 1944. And then, in India, in 1947, I was allowed to go home for four months. I had the advantage of being a bachelor. It did not cost the company much money to pay for *one* airplane ticket. And in 1947, I was lucky that my boss in India was sympathetic because he, too, was expecting to have home leave at some time in the future.

In July of 1951, I decided that it was time for me to go home again and also to reflect on what I wanted to do for the rest of my life. So I left India by air, making brief stops in Rome, where my Bombay friends, the Timberlakes, had been transferred, on to Belgium to sightsee in Brussels and Bruges, and then on to England. I had business with the London office of United Press. We discussed how London could help our news service. Harold Guard was now in the London office, and he had primed me to see if he could get more time to follow up on stories about India which would interest our Indian newspaper clients. There were large Indian communities in many British cities, and there was always a market for those stories.

I had some free time, so I traveled to Scotland. I went to St. Andrews to play the old course at the famous links. I played three rounds and, believe it or not, was joined by friends from India and Ceylon. After St. Andrews, I traveled to Dollar, a city in the highlands midway between Edinburgh and Glasgow. Here I stayed with the Pender family, who had been host to my brother on a leave from the war in Europe. He had stayed with the family for a week before he had to return to his unit fighting the "Battle of the Bulge."

Dollar was so far north that one could play golf morning, afternoon, and evening—playing until ten or eleven o'clock at night. I enjoyed hitting the golf ball among the herd of sheep that grazed on the fairways. Also, Colin Pender took me to the local pub. Here I learned that one paid for his drinks as soon as he received them. I had been conditioned in India (and China) to "run a tab" and to pay for my bill when leaving. In a British or Scottish pub, one pays for the drink when he gets it. I learned fast.

After a few days with my Scottish hosts, I took the train down to London and spent several days with Harold Guard, both in the office and sightseeing in London. Then it was on to New York and several meetings with my head office bosses. I was welcomed because my reporting of a few stories had been well received, many of my pictures had been printed by Acme News Photos, which was owned by United Press, and the Indian, Pakistani, and Ceylonese operations were all productive and making money.

I had time to interview with Trans World Airlines. Gordon Gilmore, the Vice President for Public Relations for TWA, offered me a position with the airline. If I decided to accept the position, I would be the Public Relations manager for the Middle East, with my headquarters in Cairo, Egypt. I took all the information home and promised I would give him an answer within two weeks, as I was then headed for my home outside Chicago to visit my parents who were anxiously waiting to see me after three years away.

I thought about the TWA invitation: it had all the perks that United Press did not provide: a guaranteed salary, travel benefits, medical insurance, and pensions. United Press had none of these. But I had an exciting profession. I was, for all practical purposes, my own boss. I did have a Far Eastern Manager based in Tokyo as an overall boss, but as long as I worked well in India, I had no interference. And I thought about the kinds of stories I covered: mountain climbers in Nepal, political leaders of two emerging countries, travels in the region from Afghanistan to Ceylon and Burma, country club privileges and a comfortable home in Bombay. I was a bachelor and thus had no responsibilities to anyone except myself. So I said "No" to TWA. However, I kept my friendly ties with the airline, which proved to be valuable later when TWA aided me in my travels.

During my time at home, I dated several young ladies whom my mother encouraged me to see. She did not want me to marry a Chinese or Indian bride, but was determined to see me married to an American Midwestern girl. I was already 33, and Mother did not want me to become like my two uncles, both of whom were bachelors.

Now it was back to work. First I traveled with M. Stewart Hensley, who was then the State Department correspondent for United Press and had been my earlier boss in India, to San Francisco to cover the birth of the United Nations. I listened to, and reported on, several days of speeches. Stew said I had done a good job, but I wasn't so sure. After the meeting, Stew and I flew to San Diego to visit my sister and my new niece. Stew had known Marie and her husband, Marshall Holbrooke, when he stayed with us at the "Shack" in Bombay when I became acting manager. (Marie and Marshall were married in November of 1949.)

After I had spent a few days relaxing in the San Diego climate, my sister and her husband, Marshall, drove me to Los Angeles to catch a Pan American plane for Honolulu to begin my long way back to India and Bombay. My plane took off at midnight and arrived in Honolulu the next morning at 9:30. My friends from college days, Kay and Jack Briscoe, met me and invited me to stay with them at their home in Wahiawa, some 20 miles from the city. It was my first time back in Hawaii since my arrival there in 1939 on my way to China. I went out to dinner with Jack and Kay in Honolulu and then we wandered about Waikiki Beach.

The next day I reported in to the Honolulu Bureau, had lunch with Jack Burby, the bureau manager, and spent the rest of the afternoon downtown. That evening I had dinner with Jack and Lois Burby and Fred Sparks, the correspondent for the *Chicago Daily News*. Later we met with Jim Butler of radio station KAHU (United Press client) and that night, the Butlers invited me to stay with them in the city. As is usual when newspeople get together, we talked about news.

I filled them in on the news of India, Pakistan, Ceylon, and Nepal. The next day I relaxed by spending the whole day at the beach with Pete Gruening, another United Press correspondent. In the evening I went to dinner with the Briscoes, the Burbys, and Pete Gruening. Saturday afternoon, my last day in Hawaii, we took a trip around the island of Oahu. That evening I had another dinner with the Burbys in Honlulu and spent the night as a guest of the Butlers. On Sunday I said my goodbyes to the Briscoes and at 2:30 that afternoon took off on Pan Am for the long flight to Tokyo.

Our plane was a Boeing Stratacruiser, which had a small lounge in the belly of the fuselage where I spent most of the flight in the company of an attractive blonde Pan American public relations girl, Diane Mecham. We spent most of the trip together as the plane made refueling stops at Johnson Island, Wake Island, Guam, and finally, Tokyo. At Johnson Island, the air strip was right along the ocean and we spent an hour walking on the beach at two in the morning.

I arrived in Tokyo on Tuesday morning—there was no Monday as we had lost a day crossing the International Date Line. No one met me at the airport, as the cable I had sent from Honolulu arrived after I did. I went immediately to the Correspondents' Club of Tokyo where I got a room. At the club, I met Joe Fromm, the president of the club and an old friend. I had coffee with Joe and then Ernest Hoberecht, the United Press Manager for the Far East, arrived and we had breakfast together. Immediately after breakfast we went to the UP office and began the process of getting accredited to the military. I was fingerprinted and photographed. Then we had lunch at the club, where Diane joined us. That afternoon Ernie gave me his car and driver and Diane and I went on a sightseeing tour of Tokyo. It was a gray, overcast day but we were able to see much of the city. Ernie's driver knew the area, and we saw the Emperor's palace grounds, the shopping areas, and the large department stores, as well as the military's post exchange, which was a smaller version of an American department store. That evening Diane and I had a Chinese dinner followed by a dance at the Occupation Club. In 1951, Japan was still occupied by American troops.

On Wednesday, my boss, Ernie Hoberecht, took me to meet the editor of the Japanese newspaper, Mainichi. The newspaper was United Press's largest news client in Japan. Then in the evening, with Diane and three other United Press correspondents—Bill Chapman, Warren Franklin, and Gene Symonds, we sampled Japanese night life. We bar hopped until four in the morning. I was told that there were six tough spots in Tokyo and we managed to hit four of them.

On Friday, I took the office jeep and Diane and I rode to Fujia, a little town just below Mount Fuji. The American army had a beautiful hotel there. We had lunch and then wandered over to the golf course where one can see the snow-covered Mount Fuji as he tees off. On the way back into Tokyo we stopped to see the Great Buddha and then got lost on our way into the city. We almost ran out of gas but I managed to get a gallon of gas in Yokohama and we arrived in Tokyo safely.

On Saturday night the Correspondents' Club had a dance. It was a great party as Diane had to leave the next day. The Correspondents' Club was one of the more popular places in Tokyo because it served drinks after 11 p.m. Therefore a goodly number of people—army officers and others—found their way to the club after other drinking places had closed. We closed the place down at 4 a.m.

On Sunday I drove Diane out to the airport to catch her plane to Hong Kong. We managed to get lost on the way out, but we finally found the right road and she made it to her plane on time.

On Monday morning I joined a press party that left for the military airfield at Tachikawa. We were flown in a C-47 (DC-3) to Ashiya in southern Japan, just opposite Pusan in Korea. It was a long flight in bucket seats that were not very comfortable. On arrival we were briefed on the activities we would see the next day—a large paratroop maneuver—and then we were finally able to get some dinner. After dinner, Bob Otay, an Associated Press photographer, and Ed Dougherty, an army public relations officer, and I stayed up talking and drinking at the Officers' Club bar until it closed. Then to our billets for a couple of hours' sleep.

On Tuesday morning we were up at five, breakfasted on coffee, and then hied ourselves aboard a C-46 to watch the drop. Our plane left ahead of the formation and flew over the drop zone so that our press cameramen could get their pictures. It was quite a story as it was the biggest drop in Korea in many months; 3700 men were dropped that morning, 2700 in the first two saves and another 1,000 about two hours after the first ones landed. It was quite a sight to see five thousand parachutes floating down to the drop zone which was along the Naktong River, 17 miles southwest of the city of Taegu. After the drop we landed at Taegu, where we had lunch. The rest of the press party flew back to Tokyo. I remained behind and caught a plane for Seoul at about five o'clock and arrived at Seoul's Kimpo Airfield at 7 p.m. I made a call into the city and Roy Hansen, the UP man in Seoul, drove out to get me. Roy took me to the United Press rooms in the press billets where I met Dick Applegate, a UP reporter I had been writing to for several years but had never met. After dinner we sat and talked over a couple of drinks. I brought the men a case of scotch that I had carried in my bedroll, and so I proved to be a popular visitor.

The next day, a Wednesday, I listened to an 8th Army press briefing with Dick and then took a ride around Seoul to see the damage the war had caused. It was pretty well beat up with rubble still on the street corners. After lunch I took the United Press jeep and drove north to Munsan and the Press Train where the correspondents lived while they covered the peace talks at Pan Mun Jom. The train was quite luxurious by Korean standards. It had a string of seven cars, including three cars fitted with triple bunkbeds, a work car, a dining car, and a car for the servants. The food was very good. An army cook was teaching the Koreans how to cook for the American mess. Archie, the American chef in charge, was a favorite of all the reporters. There was also a bar with good, cold beer, but the reporters had to work long hours. They would get a briefing from the United Nations spokesman each evening and then write their stories, which were telephoned to Seoul and relayed from there to Tokyo and around the world.

Left: Watching the paratroop maneuver in Korea; right: meeting with the Indian Ambulance Unit of the British Commonwealth Division.

Thursday morning I rode with the correspondents up to Panmunjom. It was an hour's ride over Korean roads and on this morning it was raining. Panmunjom was called a village, but it had only three thatched-roof huts and a tent where the negotiators from both sides met. There were two other tents, one for the UN correspondents, one for the military policemen guarding the area. The two sides sat across a long table, with the UN negotiators—Americans, British, and South Koreans—on one side, and opposite them, the North Korean and Chinese negotiators. It rained the entire day I was there. We had lunch at the mess tent, which was at the southern end of the neutral area. The day I was there, the meeting broke up early and we were able to get back to the train at Munson about three o'clock. [At a later date, in 1968, Pegge and I had another trip to Panmunjom during the Vietnam War. Then there was a regular glass-walled building and the correspondents could walk around and watch the proceedings. At the time, Pegge looked over the shoulder of a Chinese negotiator taking notes in shorthand. Pegge exclaimed, "I can read what he is writing. It's Gregg Shorthand."]

My stories on the Indian Ambulance Unit were well received by Indian newspapers.

Back at the train, I got a jeep and drove to the headquarters of the British Commonwealth Division and arrived there after dark. I had wired ahead, so a cot and a meal awaited me. On the drive to the HQ, I got lost once but the whole trip from Munson took only about two hours. The roads were wet and slippery but the jeep went through fine.

Friday morning I drove with Lt. Col. Chowdry in my jeep to visit the Indian Ambulance Unit that was attached to the British Commonwealth Division. I particularly wanted to see the unit in action because it was good copy for our United Press service to my Indian newspaper clients. We arrived at the unit's advance station about 11:30. We stopped for lunch and then that afternoon we drove up to the front with one of the officers of the unit to their casualty clearing posts. The front was quiet this day and aside from long-range booming in the distance, there wasn't any activity. I had visited with the doctors on duty at both posts, and, being from India, I was treated like a long-lost relative. I returned to the advance base that evening and Lt. Col. Chowdry and I had dinner with the unit. After dinner, we played a couple of hands of bridge and then I drove back to Division headquarters and from there I left again for Seoul, arriving at the city at about two a.m.

On Saturday morning, the army had arranged a press plane to take correspondents to Tokyo for the sixth anniversary party of the Tokyo Correspondents' Club. We took off from Kimpo Airfield at nine a.m and arrived in Tokyo about five hours later. The Air Force provided a bus into the city and I got a bed at the Press Club, checked into the office and wrote my story. After making sure my story was sent I joined the big party at the Press Club, which lasted until the early morning hours. Danny Kaye dropped in for dinner and he brought with him actress Monica Lewis. Joe Louis, who was in Tokyo on an Army tour, was invited but he didn't show.

On Sunday, I went to the office to collect my passport, and I learned that my plane for Hong Kong would be delayed by a day. I then had lunch with Dr. Jar Solhaug, the brother of a friend from La Grange. We went shopping, and upon learning that my plane would be delayed, we went to the 361st Station Hospital for dinner and a reception. Jar was assigned to that hospital.

Monday was a long day. I spent most of the time in the office and at the Press Club, and I spent a couple of hours on my airline ticket. Finally at 11 p.m. I drove to the airport and took off on Northwest Airlines at 1 a.m. The plane stopped at Okinawa and then flew on to Taipei (Formosa). At Taipei, I telephoned Colonel David Barrett, the American Military Attaché. He came to the airfield and we reminisced until the plane took off. Colonel Barrett had been my boss when I worked at the military attaché's office in Chungking during the war. He filled me in on the whereabouts of the staff who had worked for him in 1943 and 1944.

I arrived in Hong Kong in mid-afternoon and was met by three United Press correspondents: Jack James, Vic Kendrick, and Chang Kuo-sen. Jack was the UP correspondent who had the scoop on the beginning of the Korean War. Chang Kuo-sen was the United Press correspondent in Nanking when the Japanese invaded in 1937. Everything was fine except for one thing: I had no luggage. Northwest Airlines, by mistake, had offloaded it in Taipei so that I had no clothes except what I was wearing. But this was Hong Kong, and I was able to buy Arrow shirts, underwear, and even got two suits made, all within 24 hours. I had dinner that night with the United Press correspondents.

I checked in at the UP office in the morning, then had lunch at the Hong Kong Foreign Correspondents Press Club where I met a number of old friends: Bob Neville of Time, formerly in New Delhi; Graham Barrow of Reuters, from Chungking, and Stan Rich of the Associated Press. One of the Chinese waiters recognized me. He had been in the Press Hostel in Chungking. That afternoon I went to Bob Neville's home to say hello to his wife and then returned to have a Chinese dinner with a fellow passenger from the plane. He worked for an airline flying from Seattle to Alaska and he was looking for surplus airlines that he could buy.

Thursday morning I got my new suits and caught a BOAC flight to Bangkok. Charlie and Lois MacArthur, friends from Bombay who were then based in Bangkok, came to the airport to meet me. We had a beer or two at the bar while the plane was being refueled. Then on to Rangoon, Burma. Russ Hadley, the Paramount Pictures representative, joined the flight. At Rangoon, we stayed at the Strand Hotel where I met my correspondent, Ed Law Yone. While having dinner, I met Vic Jurgens and his wife. Vic was the March of Time correspondent in Chungking during the war. (March of Time was a newsreel series.) He no longer worked for March of Time but he was doing a film for the Burmese Government.

On Friday, we flew on to Calcutta. My Calcutta correspondent, Ronnie Rolfe, met me and I stayed for a day at the Great Eastern Hotel. I spent the afternoon checking up on the office and visiting a couple of Indian newspapers. In the evening, Russ Hadley and I had dinner together and then we went to the Prince's night club, where we met Lee Kamern, the Metro Goldwyn Mayer representative. I remarked it was like a small town: wherever we landed there were always friends we had known from other times.

Saturday I flew in the Air India Constellation to Bombay with my office staff at the airport to complete my home leave. Then it was back to work.

24

BACK TO WORK AFTER HOME LEAVE

◆

(December 1951 to January 1952)

It didn't take too long to get back into harness. My Bombay editorial staff handled the news operation to our clients and I now had the task of trying to promote new business. I came back with no permanent place to live and spent the first few days at the Taj Mahal Hotel and later moved into the Ambassador Hotel. For recreation I began playing a few rounds of golf and swimming at the Willingdon Sports Club pool. And I began practicing baseball—it was really softball, but we called it baseball. In one letter I wrote that I was recuperating from a baseball game.

One day I had lunch with Al Beaver, the Sales Manager of Firestone, with whom I had made the trip to Afghanistan three years earlier. We talked about Firestone, and he told me that if the job at United Press didn't turn out the way I thought it would, there would still be a job for me at Firestone. It was very tempting, but I had just thrashed out a contract (verbal) with United Press.

Also I had a date with the Indian tax man. I had all the relevant papers for him, but he wanted a few more. I felt that we had most everything in order and was not too worried. We weren't making enough money to cause any catastrophe.

Also I met during that week with Phil Brown who was interested in starting a radio program in Colombo on Radio Ceylon. We were discussing the technicalities. The plan was that we would make the recordings in Bombay, at St. Xavier College, and airmail them to Colombo for broadcast. The Jesuit Fathers at the college would record the disks.

During the second week of December, I took the Frontier Mail, the night train, to Delhi. My friend George Small helped me pack my things and took me to the train, which left at 6:30. I was able to get an air-conditioned compartment. While riding the train I wrote letters and prepared my proposals for All India Radio. I was trying to get the government radio station to buy United Press.

My correspondent, P.D. Sharma, met me at the railway station and took me to the Ambassador Hotel, a new hotel in the city and very comfortable. That afternoon I went with P.D. to the Delhi Gymkhana club where a friend of his was giving a cocktail party. While there I met several persons whom I had met before. At dinner at the hotel I met Margaret Brown, a girl I had met several years earlier in Bombay at the home of Santha Rama Rau. After dinner Maggie and I went to the Imperial Hotel Tavern, New Delhi's version of a nightclub. At the bar we found Stephan Zygnarski, one of my Polish pilot friends from Hyderabad. Ziggy was in fine form, sported a goatee, and insisted we have a couple of drinks on him. Ziggy also offered me his car for the next day (but it never materialized).

The next morning, P.D. Sharma and I went to the Indian government offices to begin negotiations with All India Radio. I had hoped that we might be able to negotiate a contract this time. However, we still had three months before the new fiscal year began so anything could happen. P.D. and I had lunch at the hotel and then had another two-hour meeting with the editors of All India Radio.

The next day, a Wednesday, was a holiday in New Delhi, it being the birthday of the Prophet. On a holiday not much work could be done. I stopped in at the Imperial Hotel to see Bob Trumbull, the *New York Times* correspondent in New Delhi. He was not in, but in the lobby I met Pat Mohan, the Movietone cameraman who sometimes did work for United Press. Then I had lunch with Felix Naggar, the Agency France Press correspondent. For lunch we had chicken, Muslim style, roasted over a fire after being dipped in various spices, followed with a chaser of cold beer.

At 2:30 I went golfing with Maggie Brown. (Most embarrassing, because she beat me.) The New Delhi golf club was improving because it had become a private club. For many years the New Delhi municipality had operated it and, as a result, it had deteriorated badly. Now the clubhouse has been renovated, and on a chilly day in New Delhi a roaring fireplace helped the atmosphere as we sipped whiskey and sodas. That evening we went to a cocktail party given by our correspondent, P.D. Sharma, at the Gymkhana. P.D., one of the better reporters in the capital, was trying to get re-elected to the governing committee of the club, and he had invited men whom he thought would vote for him. After the party, at which Tim and Julie Timberlake of the American Embassy were also present,

Maggie and I went for dinner at the Imperial Hotel Tavern. Later we met another correspondent who suggested we ride out to the airfield, it being a beautiful moonlit night. And there we met two of India's most notorious communists: Russie Karanja of the weekly *Blitz* of Bombay, and A.S.R. Chari, one of the Communists' leading lawyers. Both had been friends of mine of many years in Bombay, and we had an interesting evening arguing our points of view. Neither of them had any truck with my ideas nor I with theirs, but I enjoyed badgering them and sometimes using their points of view in political stories. Karanja, in his magazine, *Blitz*, regularly criticized United Press for its "lousy" reporting.

After the holiday, I worked all morning preparing letters and proposals for All India Radio. At noon, I traveled to Old Delhi to have lunch with Harold and Evelyn Milks of the Associated Press.

Harold was a hunter, and we had venison steaks which were very good. Harold, though a competitor, was a good friend. (Much later he found himself in Havana, Cuba and he was also a good friend of Pegge, my future wife, when she was at the Consulate in Lahore.)

In the afternoon, with P.D., I delivered my proposals to All India Radio, and my work in New Delhi was complete. That evening P.D. and I called on the Nepalese Ambassador to check on a story from Kathmandu. The Ambassador had been the Foreign Minister when I made my trip to Nepal, and he remembered me. We had to wait for an hour for him, during which P.D. and I liberally imbibed of the Ambassador's supply of scotch. Later I went to dinner with Jean Lyon, a freelance newspaperwoman who had been in the Far East for many years. I had first met Jean in Chungking during the war. She was also a good friend of Jim Burke of Time-Life, an old friend from China and New York.

On Friday, I finished up odds and ends. I met a number of journalist friends in the government offices. After lunch I went to see Claude Scott, an English journalist who had taken over the management of a new English-language newspaper, *The Delhi Express*. He had been there only a few weeks but already had cleaned it up. I was working with Claude on a deal to install teleprinter lines into Delhi. That night, my last night on this trip, I had dinner with P.D. at the Gymkhana and met a number of my newspaper friends, including Mr. and Mrs. J. Natarajan from Ambala, whom I had not seen for some time.

Saturday morning I went to the airport and flew to Lahore, Pakistan. There was a time change that I didn't know about. I thought I was arriving at noon, but it was only eleven o'clock. Thus I wasted an hour when I could have been calling on potential clients. It made little difference because the Pakistan Newspaper

Society was meeting in Lahore and many of the editors were happy to see me. They said they wanted me to begin my United Press service in Lahore. They were dissatisfied with the local news agency and wanted me to begin a competitive service. I stayed at Faletti's Hotel, one of the well-known hostelries in Pakistan.

Sunday morning I went golfing with Ian Ritchie, the Manager of the Allahabad Bank in Lahore. Ian had been a golfing partner in Bombay before he was transferred to Lahore. The Lahore golf course was flat and has sand "browns" instead of greens. It had some grass on the fairways, but it was good fun. Lahore was quite cool in the morning at that time of the year, but the sun soon warmed the city. While in Lahore I inquired after Kurshid, Mohammed Ali Jinnah's former secretary, and learned that he had not returned from London. The paper he was working for had folded and his friends said he might decide to stay in London to study. Sunday afternoon I went to a tea party given by the Pakistan newspaper editors. I sat with an old friend, S. H. Mahmud, and with G. H. Thaver of the newspaper *Dawn*. Mahmud was the editor of a newspaper called *Nawa I Waqt*, and I had known him for several years. Thaver was the general manager of *Dawn*. Before the partition, he had beem the editor of a newspaper in Bombay. At the meeting I met Mrs. Pegge Mackiernan, the information officer of the American Consulate in Lahore. She was the widow of Douglas Mackiernan, the State Department officer who had been killed at the border of Tibet after escaping from Northwest China before the Communists took over that territory. That evening I had dinner with Ian Ritchie and later went to a movie, "King Solomon's Mines," a not very good film. But in Lahore, a movie was a movie. It was a dull town in those days. When it was in India, it was known as the Paris of India but that was before partition and prohibition. Muslims were not supposed to drink and therefore there were no public bars. A foreigner could get a permit to buy liquor and could drink in the privacy of his hotel room or in a private home.

Monday I went about town visiting old clients and trying to collect overdue bills. I saw the clients but I didn't do too well collecting the money. Later in the afternoon I had coffee with Pegge Mackiernan and in the evening I had dinner with all the Pakistan editors at Mahmud's home. It was good Muslim food and I had my share, perhaps more than my share. Most of the talk was about the investigation in Rawalpindi into the assassination of Prime Minister Liaquat Ali Khan last October. Much of the conversation was in Urdu, so I only got bits and pieces, but my friends filled me in on the details.

Tuesday morning I called on more prospective clients. Then I had lunch with Pegge Mackiernan at her small flat. In a letter, I described her as "a good-looking girl with wanderlust." We talked mostly about a proposed trip to Kathmandu that she was to make over Christmas. She wanted suggestions on the best way to get to Nepal. In the afternoon I wrote letters and telegrams and visited with two Karachi newspapermen who were leaving Lahore that evening. That night I took Pegge Mackiernan to dinner. I wrote that it was not a very good dinner, but it was dinner.

Wednesday morning I flew back to New Delhi. I met with P.D. Sharma and made arrangements to send our United Press news to Lahore. I visited with the airlines and with the Customs, and P. D. said he would do the rest. That evening I had dinner with Maggie Brown at the Gymkhana Club and we went to the Imperial Tavern later for dancing.

I was on my way to Karachi and it was easier at the time to go via New Delhi. The Orient Airways service had only three flights a week, on Sundays, Mondays, and Thursdays. The only other transportation was a 27-hour train ride from Lahore to Karachi. Flying was easier and not much more expensive.

Thursday morning I took the Indian National Airlines Dakota (DC-3) from New Delhi which made stops at Jaipur and Jodpur and finally Karachi, arriving about one o'clock. I had lunch with Jim Berry, my Karachi manager, at the United Press office where we discussed our service to the Karachi newspapers. Late in the afternoon, Harry Spielman, who was now the Agricultural Attaché at the American Embassy, came to get me. I stayed with Harry at his flat at Clifton, a suburb of Karachi. I stayed with Harry the few days I spent in Karachi. Harry had a new dog, a smooth-haired fox terrier that the American Ambassador, Avra Warren, had given him. In the evening, we had dinner at the home of Jan Rendel, Harry's then-girlfriend (later his wife). Also at the dinner were Hugh and Dorothy Crumpler. Hugh was a former United Press correspondent in Calcutta and now worked for the United States Information Agency attached to the Embassy.

Friday morning I worked with Jim Berry at the office, and then he and I called on our clients. All seemed to be quite satisfied with the service they were getting. On Friday it was a half-holiday in Pakistan because Friday is the Muslim day for prayer. After lunch at Harry's, we played golf on the Karachi golf course. The course was completely sand—no green fairways—and the greens were "browns." But it was enjoyable to hit a golf ball in the desert. After the golf game we had drinks with Dudley and Jane Withers, who had been at the American Consulate in Bombay, then in the Embassy at Dacca in what was then East Pakistan. They were now assigned to the Embassy in Karachi. Then we had dinner with a number of old friends at Harry's.

On Saturday I was in the office making last-minute preparations for leaving that evening. The service was progressing smoothly. And with everything completed by lunchtime, I had lunch with Harry and Jan. Then Harry and I left for a game of golf, joining two others for a foursome. After the match, Harry rushed me out to the airport in time for me to catch my Air Ceylon plane for Bombay. The Air Ceylon service was being run by the Australian National Airways and the pilots and air hostesses were Australian. I had dinner aboard the plane and arrived in Bombay at midnight.

Arriving back in Bombay on the weekend, I checked into the office and then spent the next week getting ready for Christmas and the New Year. The weather in Bombay in December was perfect, and I found myself spending a lot of time on the golf course. At Christmas, I made the rounds, visiting friends. The day after Christmas in India was Boxing Day, and a holiday. Although India was now independent, many of the British holidays had been retained.

I spent one evening at the home of Nat and Sophie Natarajan. The two had been in the United States on a USIS-sponsored (United States Information Service) trip. Nat was the editor of the *Free Press Journal*, and both he and Sophie had become very good friends. We spent the evening talking. They had been able to visit my parents in La Grange, Illinois, and so they brought back personal stories of my family.

On December 30th, a Sunday, the American Association held its golf tournament at the Willingdon Sports Club. It was an annual event for the American community. I didn't win any cups, but I enjoyed playing golf in December on a beautiful course.

The American Women's Club of Bombay held a New Year's Eve dance at Washington House, the American Consulate's new residential building for its American employees. The residence was in the Cumballa Hill section of Bombay—the high-rent district and an excellent location for a party. After the dance, I went to another party and finally got back to my hotel room at 3 a.m.

On New Year's Day, The American Association held its annual eggnog party. The party this year was held at the large apartment of Don Wenzel, the boss of Firestone in Bombay. All of the Americans attended and wished each other a happy new year.

The first week of January 1952, we had elections in Bombay, the first in the history of free India. The elections throughout the country had begun in November in one of the states near the Himalayan border and had been continuing ever since. The task was so great that India spread out the election over several months instead of having one polling day for everyone.

For the past few weeks we had been inundated with electioneering. A couple of my friends were running for seats in Parliament. Sharouk Sabavala, a Parsi friend, was running, as was Raja Hutheesing, who was married to Prime Minister Nehru's younger sister, Krishna Hutheesing. Both Sophie Natarajan and Roshan Sabavala were out canvassing for them. The result of the elections in Bombay was a big victory for the party in power, the Indian National Congress. The Socialists—the party of my friends Sabavala and Hutheesing—won only two seats of the twenty-two in the city of Bombay, and both my friends lost their races.

My notes at the time record dinners out, golf games, bridge games, and even a trip to the "Shack" to visit Bill and Rene Kollmeyer, who had succeeded Ray and Mary Helen Crews of Western Electric.

After the holidays, in the second week of January, I sailed to Colombo, Ceylon, on the *City of Calcutta*. It was a two-day sail. I left on a Tuesday morning and arrived in the harbor at Colombo on a Thursday evening, although I didn't leave the ship until the next morning. On this trip I was staying at the Grand Oriental Hotel—everyone called it the G.O.H. It was close to the Harbor and in the center of the city, and a popular meeting place for business meetings. That morning I had a meeting with the station director of Radio Ceylon about providing news programs for his station. I was encouraged by the prospect of having a new client. After lunch, I met with the editor of the Lake House Newspaper group, where my correspondent also worked.

That evening I joined Howard Imbrey, a friend from Bombay now stationed at the American Embassy in Colomgo, and his friends to watch a Perahera. This was a procession complete with elephants, dancers, and drummers to celebrate the 1500th anniversary of the Buddha's first visit to Ceylon. The procession took an hour to pass by the spot on which we were standing and we enjoyed every minute of it. Afterward we all went to a Chinese dinner.

On Saturday, I met Doris Jepson, the wife of the Firestone manager for Ceylon, on the street and I was invited for drinks before lunch, which I was to have with Walter Hecht of Peabody Associates, a public relations firm in New York. I never got to lunch because the Jepson gimlets did not stop until about 3:30 and then I rushed to the golf club to play with George Koch, the Colombo amateur champion. George was Russ Jepson's No. 2 in Firestone. We had a good match and afterward met with some old friends in the clubhouse. Colombo was not dry, so the 19th hole lasted until nine o'clock. One of the friends was George Brown of the National Bank, a fellow I had played with in Bombay some years earlier. Another was Whitey Lorenze, whom I had met several years previously in India and also, believe it or not, at the old course at St. Andrews in Scotland the preceding year. It's a small world.

On Sunday, I tried to find a ship to take me back to Bombay, without success. So I made arrangements to fly the next morning. In the evening I met the Jepsons for a drink and then Russ Jepson, Walter Hecht, and I went our for a steak.

Monday morning I was up early and flew Air India to Madras. The plane stopped at Trichinopoly, where all the passengers went through Customs and Immigration. Then on to Madras and I stayed at the Connemara Hotel. It was a holiday so I didn't get much work done. At lunch I met young Jimmy Carmichael and we looked up Jack and Kay Scott, friends who were previously stationed in Bombay. Jack told us to go to the Gymkhana for a swim, which we did all afternoon. In the evening I was at the Scotts' for dinner. While there, early in the evening, a couple came in for drinks and before the evening was over I had been offered a dachshund puppy, which I accepted.

Tuesday was only a partial holiday so I got some work done. First to the English-language newspaper, *The Hindu,* to speak with Mr. K. Srinavasan, the editor, and then to several of his staff. Then lunch with Mrs. Fred Lawrence and her son who were on their way to the American school in Kodai Kanal, the hill station which I had visited briefly on my auto trip to South India and Ceylon. In the afternoon I visited the other English-language newspaper, *The Indian Express,* and its owner/editor, Mr. Ramnath Goenka. I always got along well with both Srinivasan and Goenka and both were good customers of United Press. In the evening I was with the Scotts at another party at the Gymkhana. Also in the party were a couple from Caltex and a Parsi couple with their daughter. We danced until eleven and then went to the Scotts' for a hamburger dinner.

Wednesday morning I picked up my dachshund, then checked in at Air India to buy my ticket and a ticket for the puppy. The ticket for the dachshund read, "Live Dog." He weighed eleven pounds and cost me twelve rupees ($3.50) in air freight. He rode on the seat next to me and slept all but the last 15 minutes of the four-hour ride to Bombay. Then I put newspapers under him and he did his business without disgracing himself. I didn't have a name for him immediately. In Bombay, I was staying with Art Doyle at a flat on Carmichael Road so the puppy had a place to stay. I was to be with Art, who represented a movie company, for a month.

At lunch the next day, John and Irene Vincent, friends from my China days with the International Red Cross, came for lunch. The had been in India for a month and were starting on a tour of South India.

One of my friends, Lee Kamern, who represented Metro Goldwyn Mayer, was being transferred to Rome and Art Doyle and I were trying to get his flat. We met with him and his lawyer. Changing the lease is a complicated matter in Bombay, but we hoped we would be able to swing it. (As it turned out, we were unsuccessful.) Also I was negotiating to buy Lee's Buick. The price was 2500 dollars but by selling my Chevrolet, the difference will be about 700 dollars and I would have a much better car. I thought I could sell my Chevrolet for 9000 rupees and I had only paid 8400 for it four years earlier.

I noted in a letter home that early one morning I played golf with Ali Mecklai, whose family is a follower of the Aga Kahn. (Through Ali, I was able to rent a top-floor apartment in the Mecklai residence on Warden Road after I married in October of 1952.)

As far as news, India was hosting an international table tennis championship in Bombay and there were players from all over the Far East: Japanese, Chinese, Koreans, Thais, and players from Malaya and Singapore. My staff covered most of the play and I only had to oversee the results and make sure the stories were sent to their country's newspapers. The Japanese proved to be the wonder team and had the crowd with them all of the time.

As the days went by I continued to play golf but one Sunday the American Club's basketball team, of which I was the captain, was invited to play against a Bombay club. There were only seven of us, and none of us was in any condition to play. One of our players, H. "Soup" Cable, had been a semi-pro player in Oklahoma on the Phillips 66 team. "Soup" was 6 foot 3 but he, like I, could only run for a few minutes. We substituted liberally but still lost the game. However we had fun and the Indian crowd loved to see us come out and play. Two of the young men from the club asked me to come to their club to give away the prizes at the finals of the tournament. I had to refuse because I was to be out of town, so I got Lloyd Britton of General Motors to do the honors.

I had been planning on another trip to Ceylon, but New York said they wanted the story of the American ambassador Chester Bowles presenting his credentials in Kathmandu. So I was off to Nepal.

25

BOWLES IN KATHMANDU

◆

(February 1952)

Early in February, two stories were on the horizon, and I could cover only one of them. Either I would travel to Colombo, Ceylon, to cover the visit of Princess Elizabeth and her husband, the Duke of Edinburgh, or I would make another visit to Kathmandu, Nepal, to cover the presentation of credentials by Ambassador Chester Bowles. New York chose Nepal.

After telephoning New Delhi to check on when the Ambassador would be leaving, I caught a night plane to New Delhi on a Friday evening. The plane was a Viking and not too comfortable, but I made the trip without trouble.

Arriving on Saturday morning I got a room at the Ambassador Hotel and slept for a couple of hours. Then, accompanied by P.D. Sharma, my Delhi correspondent, I went to the Nepalese Embassy to get my visa for the trip and then to the American Embassy to check on the Ambassador's plans.

Offices closed in the afternoon and I played a round of golf with Maggie Brown and a Tata Industries director. After golf we had drinks at the Tata man's home and I went back to the hotel for dinner and an early bed. It had been a long day and with practically no sleep on the night flight from Bombay.

Sunday morning I slept late, checked in at the office with P.D. Sharma, and lunched at the hotel. In the afternoon I visited with Tim and Julie Timberlake, the American Consul, who were to be leaving shortly for a new post in Hamburg, Germany. I had dinner with Gladys and Vinnie Ryan. They were friends from Bombay, and Vin was one of the ballplayers on the American team.

Monday was a busy day, as I was buying my train tickets, getting film, and planning to leave that night. I had lunch at the hotel and then went to have my first meeting with the new Ambassador, Chester Bowles, who told me that I could not go with his official party. He said that he had made an agreement with the Delhi press corps and no one would go except a USIS (United States Information Service) staff girl to take pictures. I said that I wished someone had informed me in Bombay when I had called for information on the trip. I said that I had already made private arrangements. He said he couldn't stop me but that I couldn't go with his party. After dinner, I took the night train to Lucknow. It was cold at that time of year, but I was warm in my bedroll and had a sound sleep. It was dusty in the compartment. Arriving at Lucknow in the morning, I had breakfast at the railway station and bought my ticket to Raxaul. This journey was similar to the one I made in 1950, so I knew the way. I had time before the afternoon train so I met some of my newspaper friends: S.N. Ghosh, the editor of the *Pioneer,* and Mahesh Chandra, the *Statesman* (of Calcutta) correspondent. We went together to a press conference given by Bowles. The Ambassador's party of 12 weren't too happy to see me there and treated me like an untouchable. The official party left on the same train that afternoon. I was in a first-class compartment, and the Bowles party had two special cars. It was a long ride from Lucknow to Raxaul on the "Old and Tired Railway," and one had to change trains at Muzaffurpur and again at a little town near Raxaul. I was in a compartment with two other men, one a Goodyear Tire Company manager for the area, and the other, a National Tobacco manager. We arrived at Muzaffurpur at 5:30, changed trains, changed again about 10 o'clock and finally arrived at Razaul, the border town, at noon. I went immediately to see Mr. Joshi, the Nepalese businessman who had loaned his cycle to Rawle Knox in 1950. I asked him about getting further transportation. I found that I would have to leave the Ambassador's party here because the Nepalese had arranged a special train—two cars and an engine—for the Bowles party and there was no room for anyone else. The Ambassador's party had lunch at the railway station and then walked across the border to be met by Nepalese officials and an honor guard of Nepali soldiers (Ghurkas). In view of the Ambassador's attitude, I decided to let them go and not to tag along any further.

When the party left, I said goodbye to Mr. Joshi and caught the afternoon train back to Muzaffurpur. At the junction where I changed trains, I met George Freeman of Caltex, and we both left the train at Muzaffurpur and went to the Club, another old haunt of mine. We had a couple of drinks, dinner and then went to bed at the Club. We had mosquito nets, but the mosquitoes came right through the netting so I had a fitful night's sleep.

In the morning I was up early and caught an Indian National Airways plane that arrived from Calcutta and flew to Patna. Then, on the same plane, I flew into Kathmandu, arriving in the city at 10:30. By the time I got through Customs and into the city it was noon. I calculated that the Ambassador and his party would still be trekking. I went immediately to the guest house where the superintendent, Mr. Maniram Bhandari, remembered me and gave me a room. There I met Paul Rose, a Point Four representative in Nepal, and we had lunch together. Rose and I decided to go and meet the Ambassador, so we went to Thankot by car (that's the end of the road) and then lugging my cameras, climbed to the top of Chandra Chri pass. We were in plenty of time and we waited for good couple of hours and I took pictures as his party appeared. Bowles, then broke down, smiled, and said, "How did you do it? The last we saw of you was at Raxaul when you waved goodbye." I then told him, although I later thought I should have said that I had passed him in the dead of night. He said that as long as I was there I was now invited to join his party and accompany him on his round of visits. We, Rose and I, walked down the pass to Thankot where the Ambassador had to review an honor guard. It was dark by this time and later by the time we arrived in the city.

Earlier in the day, on arrival, I had written notes to the Kilburnes and the Prouds and I found a note waiting for me from Mrs. Proud inviting me to dinner. But I could not find a taxi so had to miss.

The Ambassador went sightseeing the next day, and I went into town to meet Mr. Joshi's brother. He arranged a car for me to go to the British Embassy as I wanted to apologize to the Prouds for not showing up the previous evening. I walked in on a British Embassy service for King George VI who had died on February 6th, whereupon Princess Elizabeth had become Queen. I had completely forgotten about it, but it all worked out all right. After the memorial service I had a beer with the Prouds at their home and we discussed the situation in Nepal. Colonel Proud was the First Secretary of the Embassy and had worked with Ghurka troops most of his life and thus knew a great deal about the country. I returned to the guest house for lunch and in the afternoon met P. C. Tandon, the Press Trust of India correspondent who stayed in the guest house next to mine. Together we went into town and rented cycles—so I was back on a bicycle again. Taxis were very expensive, and on the cycle I could get around the city. I rode through the bazaar looking for Peter Aufschneiter, an Australian mountain climber whom Colonel Proud had told me about. I finally found him and made a date to see him the next morning. He was an amazing man, a mountain climber who was caught in India during the war. He escaped from an internment camp in Dehra Dun in Northern India in 1944, made his way to Tibet, and had been there ever since. He had come out of Tibet in January (the previous month), leaving only when the Chinese communists entered Lhasa. He went westward and mapped the western regions of Tibet before entering Nepal. (Aufschneiter was in Lhasa with Heinrich Harrer, author of *Seven Years in Tibet*.) In the evening I bicycled over to the Kilburnes' for drinks and then back to the guest house for dinner. Ambassador Bowles had invited me to come to the big guest house where his party was staying. I was there for only a little while because they were all so exhausted that they had to retire early. They were feeling the effects of their twenty miles on horseback.

I took this picture of Ambassador Chester Bowles for United Press. The accompanying caption in the February 27, 1952 issue of the Washington Times-Herald said, "Chester Bowles (on horseback), first U.S. ambassador to Nepal, makes a 20-mile trek over mountainous roads to present his credentials to King Tribuvan at Katmandu. Walking at left is his daughter Sally. At right, wearing hat, is Paul Rose, American technical administration advisor in Nepal."

On Saturday morning I met with Ausfchneiter, and he gave me a good story that was widely played in papers using United Press. That afternoon the Ambassador presented his credentials and I got the story and pictures. The presentation ceremony was quite impressive, with the Ambassador and his aides riding in open coaches to the Durbar Hall and the King sitting on a large red velvet throne. I took pictures for United Press and also sent out a story for the wires. That evening I had dinner at the guest house. I had a great cook who did an excellent job. My dinners were usually chicken or mutton with potatoes or rice. Tea, beer and whiskey were always available.

Sunday, I was up early again, this time to ship my films off to London. Then I stayed around the guest houses. I wrote, "It is beautiful in Kathmandu as I have told you before. Each day the sun shines and to the northeast one sees the snow peaks of the Himalayas. While flying into the valley on this trip, I sat in the cockpit of the plane and saw Mount Everest and Mount Kanchenjunga, the two highest peaks in the world. In the evening the Ambassador had a party for the King of Nepal and other high officers of the government. It was a regular American dinner: tomato soup, pâté de fois gras, shrimp Newburg, roast turkey with all the trimmings, and peach shortcake with all the required wines. There was even a place for me."

The next day, Monday, I had an interview with the Defense Minister. In the evening Ambassador Bowles had a reception at his guest house for a large number of Nepali dignitaries and also the few foreigners resident in Kathmandu. (The Nepal government had a number of guest houses, and the large one that housed the Ambassador was designated the American Embassy for his visit. There was a large American flag flying over the building.)

On Tuesday morning, I was up early and traveled by car to Godavare, about 14 miles from Kathmandu, to visit the four Jesuit Fathers and their grammar school. This was the first missionary school and the first missionaries to be allowed in Nepal since 1768 when one of the kings from Ghorka captured the valley and kicked out the Capuchins. The present school was founded by Father Marshall Moran, a Jesuit priest from Erie, Pennsylvania. The fathers, three of them Americans, greeted me at breakfast. The school, with about one hundred students aged 8 to 12, reminded me of the school in Chintang, China, where I had taught in 1940. After visiting the classrooms, I returned to Kathmandu in time to see the parade celebrating the first-year anniversary of the new Government of Nepal. It was quite impressive, with the marching army followed by a column of elephants.

After lunch I went to the airfield to watch the Ambassador and his party leave for Delhi. By this time we were pretty good friends, as I had been invited to all of his dinners and receptions. From the airport I traveled to Bodinath, the site of the Buddhist colony. I interviewed the "China Lama" and his 15-year-old daughter. We had a long chat about Buddhism in the valley while we drank Tibetan tea. The daughter was most attractive, and although her father was a Buddhist, she attended a Catholic Convent school in Kalimpong, India and was quite westernized. She read Hollywood magazines, was the apple of her father's eye, and was terribly spoiled. But she was very pretty, four feet 10 ½ inches tall and weighed about 99 pounds—on the plump side. She said her schoolmates kidded her that she was fat.

That evening I went to the Kilburnes and then to Sardar Shum Sher's for dinner. Sardar was the Minister of Education and a minister in the old government of the Ranas. He was one of two ministers from the old government in the present cabinet. I was at his home at 8:15 and he had left word that he had been called away to the King's residence. I waited until eleven when he and his wife returned. They apologized for their late arrival but it was unavoidable. We had drinks and then had a Nepalese meal at midnight. After dinner the minister sent me home in his car, which was a good thing to do. Katmandu had a curfew from 11 p.m. to 4 a.m. and one could not be on the streets without a pass. Since there were few roads, checkpoints were frequent and one halted at the shout of a sentry who had his rifle with fixed bayonet pointed at the car. After examination of the pass, one was allowed to go on. There were three checkpoints between Sardar Shum Sher's house and my guest house, so it took some time to get home.

Wednesday morning I had an appointment with the Home Minister and we talked for a good hour about the situation in Nepal, which, at the time, was quiet and hopeful. There were plans for a motor road from India and another from Kathmandu to the Tibetan border. In time one would be able to travel by road from Lhasa to Kathmandu and on to India.

After lunch I went on a brief shopping tour and then Peter Aufschneiter came to the guest house. We had a long conversation about mountain climbing and Tibet. Mountain climbers, no matter what their nationality might be, are interesting people. Aufschneiter had no desire to return to Europe. He said the people there put too much importance on things that in the long run really don't matter. I wrote, "I think I agree with him."

Late in the afternoon I was at the Indian Embassy for drinks. I spoke with the Ambassador, his first secretary, a Mr. Gupta, and with the Nepal Transport Minister, a Mr. Mehra. It was very friendly. Of course the new Nepal government had very friendly relations with India because the Indian Government was largely responsible for the overthrow of the previous Rana Government.

That evening I had dinner with the Kilburnes. Roy and Bobbie had been in Nepal for 25 years. They were a bit discouraged but planned to stay for another year. They were part of the past Rana Government and did not know how they would fit in with the new government. Bobbie gave me three large eggs, fresh from her English chickens, for my breakfast the next morning. I had them soft-boiled so the cook couldn't spoil them.

In Kathmandu I usually rode a rented bicycle, and got around that way most of the time. For the long trips I took a taxi, but taxis were expensive in the valley. You paid so much per day and also pay for the gasoline. Taxis cost me about $15 per day when I used them—an expensive rate for that part of the world.

Thursday, my last day in Kathmandu, I made a farewell call on the Prime Minister, thanking him for his courtesy while I had been a guest of his government. Then I had a final lunch at the guest house with the Indian correspondent, P. C. Tandon, who had been very helpful during the week I was there. He worked for the Press Trust of India, which was not a competitor to United Press.

Then I went to the airport to get my plane to Calcutta, which made stops at Patna and Muzaffarpur. I stayed at the Great Eastern Hotel, where I had a good hot bath and then dinner. I was tired, as it had been a long and busy week.

I spent the next day at the United Press office. Our Calcutta correspondent, Ronnie Rolfe, had tuberculosis. I discussed with him his entrance into a sanitarium and also hiring someone to staff the office while he was away. We managed to hire a very good man, Mr. Ajit K. Das, who was able to run the office for a number of years. After lunch I made my plane reservations for the night flight to Bombay. Before the plane took off I visited my newspaper clients and then had drinks with some old Bombay friends, Eddie and Betsy Quin. Then I took the long flight back to Bombay.

Large Areas Of Tibet Not Taken Over By Chinese Communists As Yet

By John M. Hlavacek, United Press Staff Correspondent

KATMANDU. — There are still large tracts in Tibet which have not yet been taken over by the Chinese Communists while practically the whole of the Tibetan-Nepalese border continues unoccupied by Chinese soldiers, according to Peter Aufschnaiter, an Austrian who left Tibet on January 23 of this year through the Kuti Pass, some 60 miles north of Katmandu.

Aufschnaiter, who has lived in Tibet since 1944 when he escaped from a British intern- along the border of Kashmir to the Uttar Pradesh border of India. The second attack came from West China, on Chamdo, toward Lhasa. However, after the Chinese took Chamdo, they stayed in that city for almost a year and did not enter Lhasa until December 13, 1951.

He said the Dalai Lama's departure from Lhasa in October 1950 was not a flight because of the imminent approach of the Chinese but a protest against the Chinese attack.

The latest reports which Aufschnaiter gave said that the Chinese have now moved troops into the Shigatse-Gyantse-Lhasa triangle

26

MRS. ROOSEVELT'S VISIT

◆

(1952)

Arriving back in Bombay on a Saturday morning, I learned that the American vice-consul I was dating was in the hospital. Art Doyle went with me to see her, and we were told the doctors didn't say anything except general debilitation. She was to be in the hospital until Monday when the doctors said she could go home. In the afternoon I went to the office to read the accumulated mail and to check on the messages from New York and London. Later in the afternoon I went to the Willingdon Club for an hour of hitting golf balls.

Ambassador Chester Bowles came to Bombay that week. It was his first visit to the city since he had assumed his ambassadorial post. There were two receptions for him. The one at the Willingdon Club was given by the Governor of Bombay and city officials. Because Bombay was a prohibition city, only soft drinks were served. The other reception, at which alcoholic drinks were served, was given by the American Association of Bombay and was held at the residence of the American Consul-General. I got along fine with the Ambassador now that we had made the trip to Kathmandu, but I thought he looked tired. He gave two speeches on the Monday he arrived and two more on Tuesday sandwiched among his official calls.

At this time I sent a letter to my parents warning them that they might be receiving some money from United Press. When I was in New York on my last leave, I had negotiated to be paid a commission on profits made in India and Pakistan. By my figures, I was expecting to make an additional 600 to 800 dollars a month. United Press had a limit on how much I could make—no more than $10,000 per year. I also wrote that I was expecting to open new offices in New Delhi and in Madras during the year. I reported that we were building slowly but surely.

On the next Sunday afternoon, Mrs. Eleanor Roosevelt arrived in Bombay on a special Indian Air Force plane. I accompanied my vice-consul friend to the airport to meet her. The plane was late, and Mrs. Roosevelt had to rush to a big reception that was being held for her at the Taj Mahal Hotel. Afterward she held a press conference, and I was able to talk to her briefly because she wrote a column "My Day" that was published by United Features Syndicate. I was to get her latest column to send to New York.

The next day I had work at the office, but after lunch I met Mrs. Roosevelt to pick up her column. She asked me to read it, and she wanted to know how her column was being received. She asked if I had any suggestions for changing it. I said, "Mrs. Roosevelt, I would not dare to change anything you have written." On the following day, Mrs. Roosevelt was busy going from one meeting to another and I did not speak to her. She was scheduled to fly to South India after Bombay and I tried to get permission to fly with her. Because she was flying on an Indian Air Force plane, I could not get permission. However, I met with her secretary and gave her instructions on how to send the daily column to me so I could forward it to New York.

On Wednesday morning I went to the airport early to see Mrs. Roosevelt and her party off for Trivandrum and to pick up her daily column. I was late getting to the office, and after checking my mail and seeing that the work was going well without me, I took off to play a round of golf.

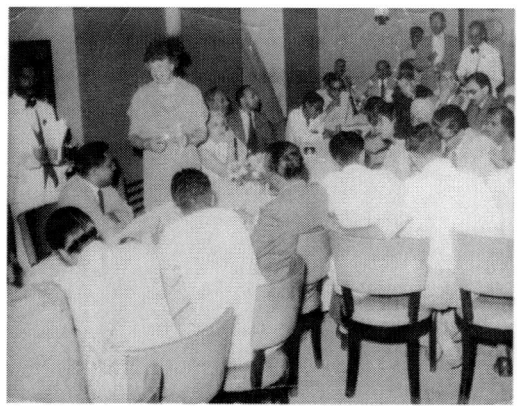 

Left: Mrs. Roosevelt gives a press conference at the Taj Mahal Hotel (I'm at the upper right in the photo); right: farewell talk over All India Radio.

After Mrs. Roosevelt's visit, I got back to the normal routine of office, lunch, and golf in the late afternoon. I noted in my letters that Art Doyle, with whom I was living, was a good cook and his specialty was spaghetti. He taught our cook to make spaghetti sauce, and we invited people over to enjoy this special dish at luncheon parties. Our cook was also good at making pies and was an all-around excellent cook.

Although the office was working well, there were always some problems to solve. One was our income tax problem, and I was closeted with our lawyers and the Indian tax man for several days. The tax man wanted more information and, I wrote, it would probably be settled but it would take a few more months. (In a later letter I noted that my personal income tax for India was $1,250.00 per year. I had asked for receipts of the insurance I had paid because the insurance payments were the only reductions for Indian income tax.)

On March 13th, my birthday, I invited John and Irene Vincent, my friends from China days, to my place for lunch. Then I took the afternoon off to play golf. And in the evening I picked up my Buick—a 1948 model, black with only 29,000 miles. It was my birthday present to myself. In the new Buick, I took my vice-consul date to Juhu to have dinner with John and Irene, who were staying at the beach.

During that spring, in addition to playing golf several times a week, I also spent many an afternoon practicing baseball. Actually, with most of our players, like me, being in their late twenties through early forties, we played a type of softball. The bases were only sixty feet apart and the pitcher threw underhanded. It was good exercise, and since Indians had never played baseball (their game was cricket) we always had a crowd watching us. One Sunday we played a game against a British team at the Gymkhana Club. I wrote, "We won easily during the regular game but everyone was having so much fun that we gave the British our pitcher and catcher and took theirs and played another five innings. Then we went out to the Kollmeyers' for lunch at Juhu at the shack. The Kollmeyers were hosting Miles Goldrick, the CEO of Western Electric, who was on a round-the-world inspection tour. After lunch I stopped at the Willingdon Club for a few holes of golf before dinner at home."

The next day, a Monday, I joined a press party for a one-day special train tour to the city of Bulsar to report on the opening of the Atul Products Ltd. factory, a joint Indian-American enterprise. There were 120 special guests including Prime Minister Nehru, and I went mainly to get pictures of Nehru and a story about the enterprise. We arrived at Bulsar at 2:30 and then drove over dusty roads to the factory site. At the factory we had tea and then attended a huge meeting which

Nehru addressed. Several thousand people showed up to see their Prime Minister. After the meeting, we had dinner and then boarded the special train back to Bombay. I took a number of pictures of the Prime Minister which I developed and radioed as soon as we arrived back in Bombay.

Each year the Bombay American Women's Club held a dance and floor show. I was usually drafted to be part of an amusing skit. All through the spring I would go to the rehearsals. After the rehearsal, I would sometimes be invited out for a Chinese dinner at the Nanking Restaurant. It was one of the better Chinese restaurants and as I still had a little of my Chinese language I was able to order the meal in Chinese.

Bob Trumbull, the *New York Times* correspondent, dropped into my office on his way to Goa, the Portugese colony on India's west coast. I had been in Goa and gave him some names of people to interview. He was leaving on a ship that afternoon, so I invited him back to our house for lunch. My housemate at the time, Arthur Doyle, who represented Fox Movietone pictures, had invited some of his exhibitors as well as a few other Bombay residents so it turned into a big farewell luncheon for Bob. In the afternoon I took Bob to his ship. It was a one-day trip, and he would be back in a day or two.

Over the weekend, the American Association had a golf match with the Willingdon Club. I played on the Association team with Al Beaver, my friend from Firestone, and we won our match. It was the first time since 1949 that the Americans had won. We usually played the Club twice a year, and we usually got beat. After the match, there was the usual luncheon with plenty of beer.

After a few more rehearsals, we finally performed our skit at the American Women's Club dance at the Taj Mahal Hotel. The dance was a huge success, and our floor show was said to be good. At least we looked pretty funny as we dressed up as charwomen and sang and danced to the tune "Rag Mop."

The "Rag Mop" crew at the American Women's Club: Jack Tucker, Bill McComb, and me.

In the last week of March, early on a Friday morning, nineteen members of the American Association of Bombay flew in a chartered plane to Karachi, Pakistan, to play the Karachi American Club at golf, tennis, and baseball. The time passed quickly as most of the members played bridge or poker while the stewardesses handed out Bloody Marys. On arrival we were met by Karachi American Club members and were taken to our respective hosts for the weekend. Art Doyle and I stayed with Harry Spielman, the Agricultural Secretary at the American

Embassy and our friend from the time he was in Bombay. (Harry had also made the automobile trip through South India with me.) That night there was a cocktail party for the Bombay guests and their hosts and later we went to a party at the home of Al Galpin, another of our friends who had worked in Bombay. It was a late party; we finally got to bed about 2 a.m.

On Saturday morning I worked at the United Press office with Jim Berry, my Karachi office manager. With Jim, I made several calls on our various newspaper clients and then went back to Harry's for lunch. In the afternoon we had the golf matches on Karachi's desert-like course where there was little grass on the fairways and the greens were "browns." Karachi won the golf matches, but it wasn't very serious because most of their players had high, high handicaps and we had to give them strokes on every hole. But it was a lot of fun. That evening Harry hosted a large dinner and then we all went to a dance to which all the Americans in Karachi had been invited.

On Sunday morning we had the ball game, and the Bombay Bombers beat the Karachi Camels by a score of 13 to 1. After the game there was beer and hamburgers for everyone and the presentation of the trophies. Bombay won the baseball and tennis trophies and Karachi the golf trophy. I got a special award, a big Mad Hatter's hat for supposedly the most valuable (or maybe the most voluble) player on the visiting team. But it was fun.

After the game we went to Harry's for an engagement lunch. Harry announced his engagement to Miss Jan Rendel of Los Angeles. Harry had met her at the American Embassy where she was a secretary. Of course we had champagne to toast the engagement. Then we departed for the airfield, and a good crowd of Karachi people came to wave us off. On our flight back, like the one to Karachi, we played bridge and poker all the way home. It was a great weekend, as the Karachi Club showed us a fine time. Harry had not set the date for the wedding but had said it would be within the next month or two. I planned to go back to Karachi for the ceremony, as Harry had asked me to be the best man.

Back at the office I got the good news that the Indian Government had approved my United Press proposal for selling news to All India Radio. This, for us, was a big contract amounting to more than $1,000 per month—a big step for United Press. There were still some minor negotiations to be finalized and I planned to return to New Delhi for them.

In Bombay, the local news was the crowning of Miss India. I had met all of the contestants at the Taj Mahal Hotel during the preliminaries. The winner was a girl from Calcutta who had competed against ten other contestants. It was the first pageant since India had become a free country, so the interest was great within India although it was not a big story for the world.

I also got back to playing golf almost every day. I played in a golf tournament at the Chembur Presidency Club and lost a single match to Jimmy Marr.

My vice-consul date left for home that week and many of the days and nights were spent attending farewell cocktail and dinner parties. She sailed on the Italian liner *Oceana* for Genoa and since she was going home by ship I had given her a number of presents to take to my family. She knew many of my Indian friends as well as her contacts at the Consulate, so she had a large number of well-wishers at the docks.

Also during the week, I was asked by the Matunga Gymkhana (Matunga is a suburb of Bombay) to preside and give away the prizes at their annual athletic meeting. We had played against the Matunga Club in a game of basketball and lost. I wrote home that I was getting to be quite a celebrity.

As a working photographer, in addition to my other responsibilities, I was anxious to see my pictures in print. I asked my parents to watch for any pictures from India and Nepal that appeared in Chicago newspapers and in the news magazines. I told my parents that I knew that *Time* magazine had printed my pictures of Nepal in the issue with John Wayne on the cover.

That April, with the weather getting warmer in Bombay, I found myself doing more swimming in addition to the golf and baseball. I became a "volunteer" swimming instructor and I soon had a bevy of Indian children waiting for me to enter the pool. I encouraged them to learn to swim and to dive off the lower diving boards, and in general I ended up having a better time than they did. I called them my little tadpoles.

Also, I wrote home that even though India was primarily Hindu, Good Friday was still a holiday in Bombay. It had been that way when the British were here and many of the same holidays were carryovers. On this Good Friday, after playing golf in the morning, Art Doyle and I went down to the docks to visit the *Steel Executive*—an American freighter—to see if the crew would like to play a game of baseball on Sunday morning. They agreed, and on Sunday morning we played the ship's team. It wasn't much of a contest—we won 14 to 2—but it was great fun. I managed to hit a home run over the right field bleachers. It was hot, though, so after the game we went down on the ship for lunch and then to the swimming pool to cool off. And in late afternoon, Art Doyle and I went out to play another 18 holes of golf and in the evening we had dinner with the Marines at Washington House. (The American Consulate had a Marine Guard, as did all diplomatic offices. The Marines were billeted in the "Washington House," a five-story residence with apartments for consulate personnel.)

After a week of my usual golf, swimming, cocktail parties and dinners, my negotiations with All India Radio came due and I flew up to New Delhi one Sunday night on the night plane. Long before FedEx's Frederick Smith devised the pattern of planes taking off from several cities to one center, the Indian airlines had begun their night service with planes from four cities—Bombay, New Delhi, Calcutta and Madras—taking off each evening and landing in Nagpur, the city in the center of India. In Nagpur mail, freight and passengers were shuttled to the planes from the four cities. Therefore, when I flew from Bombay in the evening, I flew first to Nagpur, then caught the plane to New Delhi, arriving in the morning.

On arriving in New Delhi I spent the morning in talks with All India Radio and also with the Post and Telegraph people. The Indian Posts and Telegraphs controlled all the landlines, and we had to get their permission to run a teletype line from Bombay to New Delhi to serve All India Radio. With the talks completed for the day, I was able to have lunch and then play a round of golf with my friend in Delhi, Maggie Brown.

The next day, a Tuesday, I had more talks and negotiations with the government. I also was able to see many correspondent friends. I had lunch with Bob Trumbull of the *New York Times* and in the evening I had dinner with Vin and Gladys Ryan, friends who had once lived in Bombay. Vin Ryan was with Caltex and was one of my sources for news. Whenever I went into a region of India, Pakistan, or Ceylon, I would ask my friends in the oil industry for introductions to their agents in the area I was visiting. These agents knew the local people, industry, and politics, and were also a wealth of information for me.

On Wednesday I worked in the morning, swam at the Gymkhana Club during the lunch hour and then worked the rest of the afternoon. Bill Kollmeyer of Western Electric flew up that day and we both met with the telegraphy people about leased lines for our teletype line. That evening I had dinner with Maggie Brown after drinks at the Gymkhana Club.

On Thursday I flew in the early morning to Lahore in Pakistan on business. I did not accomplish much but I renewed acquaintances with the newspaper people in the city. I met an old friend, Dick Deverall of the American Federation of Labor, over several beers. It was very hot in Lahore and I was not able to go swimming at Faletti's Hotel because the pump used to fill the pool was broken.

The next day I flew back to New Delhi and after lunch, I had more negotiations with All India Radio. I tried to telephone New York to apprise the office of our negotiations and to get their okay, but the telephone call never went through. I had dinner with Bill Kollmeyer and then flew back to Bombay on the night mail, arriving home on Saturday morning.

There was lots of work waiting for me at the office just catching up on the mail that had accumulated during the week I was away. Also, I arranged to ship teletype equipment to New Delhi and sent two of my office staff and a messenger boy along with the shipment. After the train left, I relaxed, went for a swim at the Willingdon Club and then home for dinner.

Sunday, I played golf at the Chembur course in the morning, then I went for a swim and played another 14 holes of golf at the Willingdon Club in the afternoon. In the evening Art Doyle and I went to a private showing of a movie, "The Marx Brothers at the Circus."

It was the end of April and I was excited because I was about to set up the first teletype line to Delhi and I also hoped to have an internal circuit working before the end of May. I wrote home that it was a big step forward and I just hoped I wouldn't stub my toe. I had telephoned New York for approval, and I was awaiting a cabled confirmation of my call.

During the first week of May, I put in the first United Press teletype line in India and I also signed the All India Radio contract to provide the station with United Press news. I flew to Delhi on a Thursday night with Ken Parrish, one of the Marine Guards, taking me to the airport. On Friday I went to All India Radio to negotiate the final terms of the contract. The rest of the day we were working on the lines, with the Western Electric engineer doing all the work and the rest of us kibitzing. That weekend the President of the Mainichi Newspapers of Tokyo came to Delhi and P.D. Sharma, our New Delhi correspondent, arranged a cocktail party and dinner for him to meet the New Delhi press corps. Mainichi was a big client of United Press in Japan.

On Monday I was in the office at 5 a.m. to open the teletype line. It was a relief when the clicking started and the news came through for delivery to All India Radio. It was great day for United Press and, of course, for me. And that night the Japanese hosted a party for us at the Imperial Hotel tavern for dinner.

Tuesday, we were monitoring the teletype lines to see that they were working. In the evening I had a date with a young American divorcee who was in India to write a book. My comment: "Not very exciting, but perhaps the poor girl was tired as she had been flying all night. She wanted information about Nepal and I, from my several trips to Kathmandu, am the resident expert on Nepal."

On Wednesday morning I flew to Lucknow to visit the newspapers there. I had lunch with Roy and Barbara Bisbee of the American Consulate. In the evening I had a date with the only American girl in Lucknow, one Cheryl Kirby. It was a very hot night. She had a car and we went riding to see the sights of Lucknow by moonlight. We saw the area where the movie "Kim" was filmed, particularly the school where, in the film, Kim studied.

Next day another flight to Calcutta, arriving in mid-afternoon. I worked in the office and in the evening I had dinner with Bill and Yvonne Needham. Bill Needham was one of the two Scottish golfers who had taught me the game when I first arrived in Bombay seven years earlier.

Friday I went to visit my Calcutta correspondent, Ronnie Rolfe, at the sanitarium where he was being treated for T.B. If one had to be in a hospital, the sanitarium in Calcutta was an oasis in the heat of that city. I had lunch with John and Janet Hanlon who were back in Calcutta after ten months on home leave in the United States. John and Janet once lived in Bombay and John was a regular on the Bombay Bombers baseball team. I remembered how he would walk, and he and I agreed that we could tell a good athlete by the way he walked.

That afternoon I bought two teletype machines from army surplus as well as teletype paper. And with that, my business in Calcutta was finished. I had dinner at the Great Eastern Hotel and in the morning I took the non-stop Air India Constellation back to Bombay.

I went straight to the office to relieve my staff who had been working day and night for the past week. I left early for a game of golf and a swim and then had dinner with Al and Katherine Beaver at their flat.

A note in my journal: "Bombay is really hot at the moment (mid-May). It's sticky, but so far I have not got any prickly heat, which is fine. It's an excuse, if I need it, to swim every day. Latest news is that Harry will get married about May 20th or 21st."

In a letter dated May 22, 1952, I wrote:

> The bachelor dinner for Harry was held at the Metropole Hotel, complete with dancing girls. Lots of fun. I got Harry home in good shape although some of the others didn't do so well.

> Tuesday I went to my Karachi office for a little while. Then spent the rest of the morning with Harry and Jan looking for a wedding ring. She finally decided to wear her grandmother's. Also we were at the Ambassador's where the reception was to be held and Mrs. Avra Warren was making arrangements for flowers. One of the Marines in Karachi baked the wedding cake, a huge thing that rivaled anything one could get at home.

Harry, Dudley Withers, Bill Parsons, and I had lunch together—Harry's last lunch as a bachelor—and then we had a short nap. At four thirty we left, picked up Jan and her witness, Fern Burch, and then went to the court house where the civil marriage was performed. Very simple ceremony, Fern and I signing our names to the papers necessary. Then a rush to get Jan back to her place to change into her dress for the reception and Harry and I to get back to his house to change into our dress suits. Picked up Jan again and went to the reception which was given by Ambassador and Mrs. Avra Warren. About 200 people were there. After the cutting of the cake, the Marines kidnapped Harry, tying him up in a strait jacket and taking him out to his house. Jan had been tipped off, and she had to untie him with everyone looking on. The Ambassador had sent food and drink there and the party finally broke up. Bill Parsons and I were the last to leave, and we shared a bottle of champagne with Harry and Jan.

They couldn't go anywhere on a honeymoon because there is no place to go from Karachi. They will take some time on their way home in June when they go on leave.

Wednesday morning I took Harry's car back to him and then went to the office. Made a round of calls and found out I couldn't get out to Bombay that day. In the evening I watched a ball game between the Karachi team and the Monroe and then went out to the ship with Lynn and Betty Lou Clarke. They were meeting friends, and I saw the Keelers and the Landsbergs again. Had dinner with them and stayed aboard ship. Lots of visitors in Karachi because the ship is not dry and everyone visited the bar. In Bombay because of prohibition, the ship is not allowed to open the bar.

I spent Thursday morning in the office, and then Harry and Jan and Mrs. Crumpler drove me to the airport where I caught the Air India plane for Ahmedabad. Arrived there at five in the afternoon and spent a couple of hours calling on the editors of the newspapers there. We don't have any clients in that city so I am making a preliminary survey. Then I caught the air-conditioned train to Bombay at nine thirty at night and arrived in Bombay in the morning. I'll be here for a while yet, though there is urgent work in Delhi and also I should go back to Karachi to relieve Jim Berry, who needs a vacation.

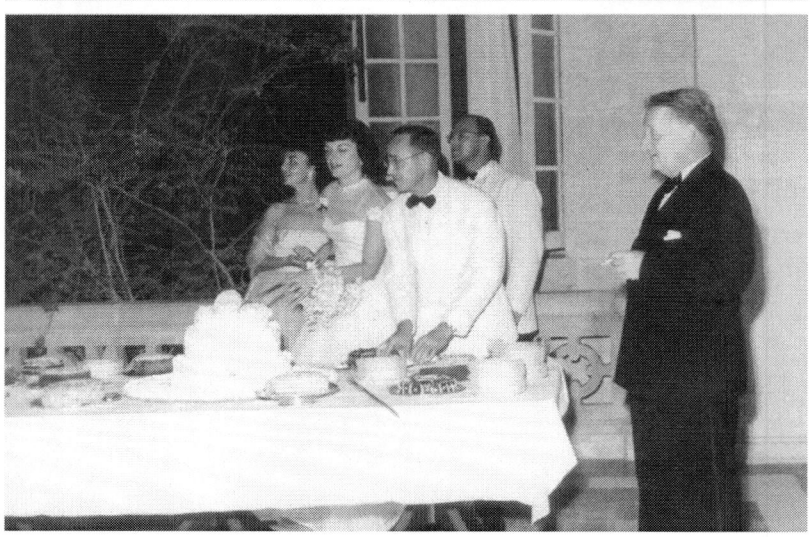

Top photo: Harry Spielman and Jan Rendel's engagement; bottom: at Harry and Jan's wedding reception (left to right), Fern Burch (bridesmaid), Jan, Harry, me, Ambassador Warren.

27

THE COURTSHIP OF PEGGE

◆

(December 1951 to October 1952)

Originally, I had planned to title this memoir *India B.P.* (India Before Pegge) because I had lived in India for more than six years before I met Mrs. Douglas Mackiernan in Lahore, Pakistan, in December of 1951.

I was in Lahore attending a meeting of the Pakistan Newspaper Editors. Also attending the meeting was Mrs. Douglas Mackiernan, the Press Officer of the American Consulate in Lahore. She had the rank of a vice-consul. She was there on official business—the Consulate wanted to find out what the Pakistan editors were saying.

There were only two women at the conference, Mrs. Mackiernan and another woman who was covered head-to-toe in a burka. I was introduced to Mrs. Mackiernan by the editor of the newspaper *Nawa I Waqt,* Mr. S. H. Mahmud, a friend of mine who previously had a newspaper in Bombay.

Mrs. Mackiernan later invited me to tea at her residence. It was there that I learned that she was a widow with two-year-old twins. There was a picture of the twins on her coffee table. I then discovered that her husband, Douglas S. Mackiernan, had been a vice-consul at the American Consulate in Tihwah, China. He had been shot at the border of Tibet while escaping ahead of the arrival of the Communist Chinese into the area. His vice-consul title was a cover for his work for the CIA.

I invited Mrs. Mackiernan to dinner, where we talked of her job and her background.

She had earned her press credentials. At 19, she had begun her career as an advice columnist for teens, an early version of Ann Landers. Shortly after, she took her clippings to Washington where she became the women's editor for the *Washington Times-Herald.* It was wartime, and she reported on the training of

American servicemen—riding with the tank men, flying with the paratroopers, and slogging with the infantrymen.

In 1943, she left Washington to become a reporter for the *Fairbanks Daily News Miner* where in her spare time, she wrote a story for the *Reader's Digest*. She made so much money from the story that she quit her job and sailed, after the war, to Shanghai where she took a job with the American Graves Registration Unit. Her adventurous spirit took her on stories as far south as French Indo-China and as far north as Manchuria. On one trip to China's Northwest Frontier, she met her husband, fell in love, and subsequently married him.

At the time I met her, she was planning a trip to Nepal and I, since I had been there the year before, gave her information on how to travel to Kathmandu.

I then returned to my headquarters in Bombay, and we had no further contact until the spring of 1952. In the ensuing months, Mrs. Mackiernan had been transferred from Lahore to Karachi where she became the Press Officer for the American Embassy.

Karachi was part of my territory for United Press and I traveled there frequently to check on my office. I was there in May and June of 1952 to fill in for my vacationing Karachi manager and also to attend the wedding of my good friend, Harry Spielman. It was at the wedding reception that I met Mrs. Mackiernan again.

Shortly afterward, she (now being called Pegge) made a trip to Goa, a Portuguese Colony on India's west coast south of Bombay. She had alerted me that she was to make the trip and I met her and her companion, Miss Joy Hutsell, and saw them off on their train. When they returned from Goa, I again met them, and as their reservations to fly back had been cancelled, we had a few days to get to get better acquainted. I took her to dinner and also to Juhu Beach to show her the Shack and to walk on the sand.

We met again in Karachi in July when I visited my Karachi office. We had the chance to get to know one another, and our budding romance began to flower. However, there were obstacles. Pegge had been corresponding with the editors of the *Ladies Home Journal,* and she had live with her twins in Philadelphia. (The twins were cared for by her in-laws while Pegge was overseas.)

Our romance continued by mail and telephone calls. I finally persuaded Pegge to come to Bombay at the beginning of September for a long weekend. It was then that we decided to be married in October. Our wedding took place in the Chapel of St. Xavier's College and was performed by a Spanish Jesuit priest, Father R. Conesa (a friend of mine), on October 20, 1952.

(The above is only a brief outline. Pegge, an accomplished writer, recorded her innermost feelings in letters to her mother. Those letters will be the basis of another book for our immediate family.)

When we were married, the betting among my friends in Bombay was that the marriage wouldn't last a year. I'm writing this chapter on January 28, 2006—more than fifty years later!

For those who are interested in "the rest of the story": Pegge's book, *Diapers on a Dateline,* provides vivid (and entertaining) descriptions of Hlavacek family life in Bombay. *Alias Pegge Parker* describes her life before and during our time together.

318   United Press Invades India

Top left photo: Pegge arrives in Bombay for our wedding, October 1952; at right and bottom: clippings from Indian newspapers.

TRAVEL THE WORLD
WITH TITLES FROM HLUCKY BOOKS

www.HluckyBooks.com